Using QuickBooks Payroll 2009

... With High Speed

College Edition-Revised

Using QuickBooks Payroll 2009

... With High Speed

College Edition-Revised

Emmanuel Ike, MBA
SOW Publishing

QuickBooks Payroll with High Speed *College Edition*

© 2008 by SOW Publishing
PO Box 702063
Dallas, TX 75370
Website: www.sowpublishing.com
E-mail: publisher@sowpublishing.com

TRADEMARKS

ISBN 0-9770693-1-1
Library of Congress Control Number 2008907772
Printed in the United States of America.

Using QuickBooks Payroll with High Speed College Edition
SOW Publishing
Dallas, TX 75370

10 9 8 7 6 5 4 3 2 1

SOW Publishing

PO Box 702063, Dallas, TX 75370, USA. www.sowpublishing.com

ABOUT THE AUTHOR

Emmanuel Ike is an expert in accounting software, database management, and spreadsheet programming. He has been an accountant for more than 12 years, specializing in the areas of cash flow, asset management, and financial reporting. He teaches individuals and small businesses about credit and credit reporting. As a hobby, he enjoys aggressive legal research. Mr. Ike has a Bachelor of Science degree in accounting and a master's degree in finance with honors. He also has a certificate in private investigation and holds a diploma in the legal assistant program, specializing in medical and legal research, from a prestigious law school. Mr. Ike is an author, publisher, and entrepreneur.

ACKNOWLEDGEMENTS

My un-ending whole-hearted gratitude goes to God for the incredible passion, energy, and determination to publish this book. I wish to extend a special thank-you and profound gratitude to the people at Intuit, especially the technical staff at QuickBooks for their hard work and cooperation in being market-driven and customer-focused. Over the years, QuickBooks has dominated the personal finance software market because of its unwavering determination to respond to ever-changing and ongoing customer demands for product improvements. I wish Intuit and QuickBooks strong and fruitful years ahead.

Also, a special thank-you goes to the staff, associates and consultants at SOW Publishing, including designers and editors, for the tremendous task of putting this project together. I also extend my sincere gratitude to all the professors, assistant professors, teachers, and tutors of various schools, colleges, and universities who participated in testing and fine-tuning this book.

NOTICE

Dedication

This book is dedicated to my family, especially my father who taught me wisdom, understanding, power, and concentration are the keys to success. And to my mother who taught me love, beauty, kindness, peace, and integrity are the keys to life.

After all, genius is simple!
Emmanuel Ike

Mastery is the ability to perform a task with confidence and precision acquired by training and practice. I will provide the training, you will provide the practice— and the rest is history!   *Emmanuel Ike*

TABLE OF CONTENTS

PREFACE

As you may know, QuickBooks is one of the best, if not the best, accounting software in the market today. Therefore, it is no accident that we chose to write this textbook on QuickBooks software. *Using QuickBooks Payroll with High Speed 2009 College Edition* is the answer to a large number of students and teachers who prefer a hands-on approach to teaching and learning QuickBooks. We condensed this material to provide a step-by-step approach, rather than create 735 pages of unnecessarily laborious and detailed textbook. The book was written on QuickBooks Pro 2009 software; however, it may be used on the QuickBooks 2008 software version with no adverse effects on the financial results generated.

ORGANIZATIONAL FEATURES

The payroll department is not an isolated island; the mission of this textbook is to therefore, introduce other accounting functions to produce a well-rounded accounting student. The textbook is also arranged in sequential order, starting with a review of the software menu. There are 13 menus in QuickBooks software with numerous submenus. The purpose of the review section is to explain the action and reaction of these submenus. Also, by explaining the functions of these submenus, one is able to remember where and why a submenu is placed under a particular menu. The intention of this approach is to increase comprehension and recall of the subject matter.

Following the review sections are the instructional activities, the heart of this textbook. The activities are direct and their results are predictably accurate. Financial statement reports are also presented for students to instantaneously compare their results with the textbooks. By matching their results, students build extraordinary self confidence in their performance.

Next is the summary of accomplishments, which is a snapshot of financial activities that took place within the chapter.

Lastly, at the end of each chapter are financial reports which students should print and examine for accuracy. These reports are turned in for grading to see how students' achievements are progressively increasing.

UNIQUE FEATURES

The textbook chapter materials are arranged according to the QuickBooks software menus to make the book very user-friendly. By arranging the chapters in sequential order according to the software, the textbook focuses on implementing as many submenus as possible.

Each chapter starts with a review of all the submenus under each menu, and under each title page there is an explanation of why certain tasks react the way they do. This is followed by instructions on how to perform the task, and, lastly, there are financial statements that test students on what happened. Additionally, this text uses real numbers and names to which students can relate. So in the future, an individual is able to re-create accounting data and information presented in the book. The pinnacle of every chapter is the end-of-chapter exercises, included in the teachers manual, which focus on the financial results of their respective chapters.

INSTRUCTOR'S SUPPORT

This textbook is provided with accurate financial results and instructors are supported to ensure positive classroom achievements. The instructor's manual is comprehensive material composed of financial results, exercises, questions—true and false and multiple choices—and examinations, all with answer keys.

Using QuickBooks Payroll with High Speed College Edition is an integrated hands-on manual that is geared toward attaining accurate results; therefore, an instructor's support is of utmost importance.

CREDIT COURSES

Using QuickBooks Payroll with High Speed College Edition is a featured textbook in payroll by computer, computerized payroll accounting, microcomputer payroll, and practical payroll courses and labs. The textbook is used for one to three credit-hour courses and can be completed within one semester or split between two semesters, introductory and intermediate levels. If a student can point and click, he or she can use the textbook with speed and accuracy.

Please Note!
You do not have to read the entire book before practicing with it, just open page 19 and you're ready, but first read the helpful hints.

INTRODUCTION

The subject of payroll accounting is important to almost everyone. Sometime, in your lifetime, you will either be an employer or an employee; therefore, correct and accurate understanding of the employment compensation language is beneficial to everyone, especially to students entering the job market. It has been said time and again that many prospective applicants short change themselves because they don't understand employment negotiation strategies. If 200% represents the total employment compensation package, applicants concentrate on the first 100% which is wages and forget about the second 100% which is other compensation, thereby leaving a lot of money on the table due to ignorance of the payroll language.

Applicants forget to talk about other compensation such as:

- Other wages: bonus, commission, annual wage increase percentage
- Pre-tax employer-sponsored health benefits: health insurance, dental insurance, vision insurance, flexible spending account, health savings account, group term life, medical care FSA, and dependent care FSA
- Pre-tax employer-sponsored retirement benefits: 401(k) company match, 403(b) company match, 408(k)(6) SEP company match, simple IRA company match, and pension benefits as applicable to each individual candidate
- Employee reimbursements: mileage reimbursement, car allowance, housing allowance, travel allowance, and interest-free cash advancement
- Paid time off: paid and unpaid sick leave, paid and unpaid vacation leave, sick hours, and vacation hours

We hope that by the end of this course, a student will have a complete grasp of these payroll items and be able to apply them to any employment situation, either as an employer or an employee. Due to the personal nature of the payroll items listed above, every payroll accounting student must understand the importance of keeping confidential matters and not divulge an employee's compensation information to anyone except the immediate superior, and only on a need to know basis.

Most textbooks come with CDs, and students are asked to edit or update the CDs; however, our textbooks allow students to create those CDs from scratch by themselves. The textbook gives students practical steps on how to run a complete payroll cycle. It takes a different approach from other books by showing students step-by-step how to create a company, set up preferences, create employees, pay employees, pay taxes, and run reports from beginning to end with complete real-life numbers. Since the book provides all the information a student needs, all he or she does is open the book and starting running the payroll process. Within minutes, a student will be processing and printing financial reports. This hands-on approach is profoundly preferred by students, teachers and business professionals. This is a results-driven textbook, an experiential learning tool that leads students to predictable accurate results. The goal of the textbook is to prepare students to independently run the payroll accounting office and be able to service the human resources department with a high degree of efficiency.

The two driving forces of this book are speed and accuracy. Students don't have time to flip through accounting manuals that are too complex to understand, or that leaves them empty not knowing where to start or what to do next after they are employed. We've provided the answer by arranging the textbook according to the Menus and Submenus in the QuickBooks software to increase your speed of mastery.

In no time, a student will be creating files, accounts, employees, payroll items, customers, vendors, and writing checks—all with real numbers. Not only that, you will be reconciling bank statements, doing journal entries, and printing reports easily and effortlessly, guaranteed. When you can accomplish these tasks with ease and confidence, I have succeeded.

— Emmanuel Ike

Free Trial QuickBooks Software

If you want QuickBooks Pro, it is better to buy the full version from the store or from the Internet by going to www.quickbooks.com. However, if you are in a hurry and want to practice at home immediately by using the Simple Start trial version, you can do so at the same website. When you open the download window, under the Simple Start image, click the Learn More… link to read what features the Simple Start version can or cannot do. You need enough computer space to download the software. It's faster to use a high speed internet (DSL) for this process.

Activities:

- ❖ Open the Internet
- ❖ Address: Type **www.quickbooks.com**. Press **Enter**
- ❖ In the **Select** box (left of the window): Type **trial version**. Press **Enter**
- ❖ Click **QuickBooks Trial Products**
- ❖ Click **Download** under **Simple Start** image
- ❖ Email: Type your email address
- ❖ Click **Start Download**
- ❖ Click **Save** on File Download window
- ❖ Click **Save** on Save As window
- ❖ As soon as the Save As window disappears, go to the desktop
- ❖ Double click **Setup QuickBooks** Icon on your desktop
- ❖ QuickBooks Simple Start Direct.exe will start to download
- ❖ When download is completed
- ❖ Click **Finish**

Helpful Hints

- It is easier to run your left finger through the practice activities (if you're right-handed) while you click in the QuickBooks window, to make sure you don't skip a line.

- When you see a phrase followed by a colon, you have to look for that phrase in the window currently in front of you. The colon will be followed by activities of what you're required to do such as type, click, select, accept, or checkmark.

- When an instruction says to checkmark a box, click an option or select a word or phrase. If the box is already checkmarked, or the option is already clicked, or the word or phrase is already selected, just skip the activity and go to the next instruction, and not remove the checkmark, the click or the selection in the window.

- When an instruction says to type a word or phrase in a text box, if the word is already typed, just skip the activity and go to the next instruction. Just make sure the word or phrase is entirely what is required. For example, if the instruction says, "Type Quick Payroll 2009." If you see only "Quick Payroll," make sure you add the "2009" to complete the instruction.

- For best results, the year on this book and the year of the QuickBooks software you're using must be the same. You must use the names, numbers, and dates in this book.

- From time to time you will see "Very Important" at the end of an instruction. It's absolutely necessary that you perform that instruction and not skip it to receive the intended results.

- Only essential and relevant activities you need are included. Hence, do not worry about empty boxes or defaulted statements not in the activities.

- Be sure to complete all the activities in each section, irrespective of screen shots, charts, and other inserts in the middle of the activities. Relax and enjoy the ride, before you know it, you will be cruising through the pages with ease and confidence.

Navigation Tips

I urge you to read this entire section before using this book. The section is included to enable you navigate through your QuickBooks software with ease. Every effort has been made to ensure your journey with QuickBooks is exciting and rewarding. Some helpful hints are repeated in this section for a purpose. Like a new automobile, you'll need to get used to the features and know where they are located. As soon as this is taken care of, the rest is history! Relax and enjoy the ride!

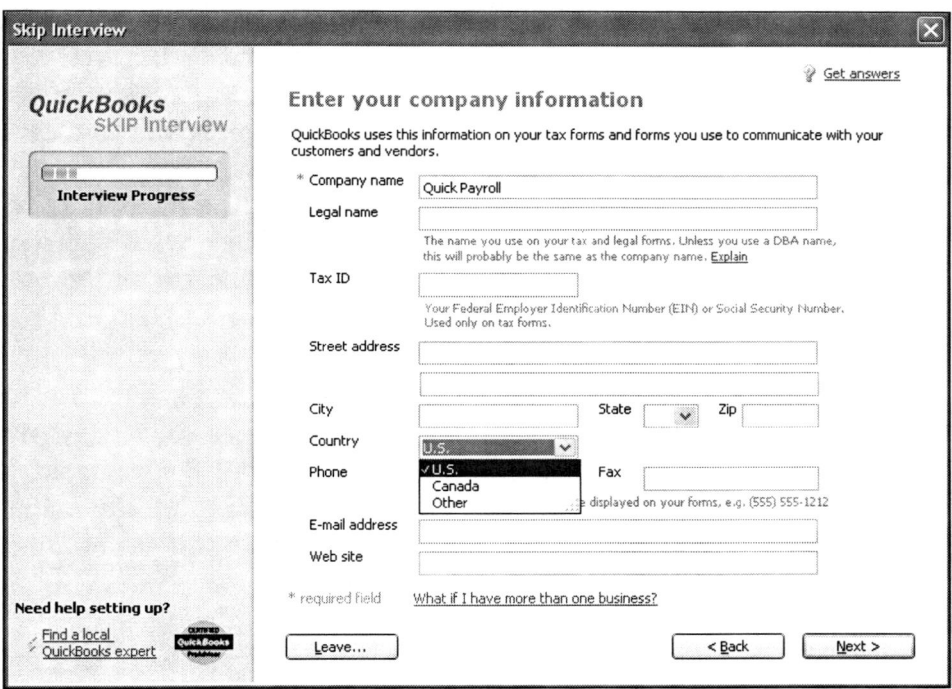

- **Common Sense:** As you go through these windows, you will see a lot of default information. When in doubt, accept the default QuickBooks is suggesting. You can override it only if you know a better option. The more you practice, the more your speed, comprehension, and expertise will increase. Remember: Practice makes perfect!

- **Colon:** You will see many phrases that are followed by a colon (:). The statement before the colon is found in the window you've just opened, whether a small or big window! The statement after the colon is the activity you have to perform such as: Type, Select, Read, or Accept. For example, as in the image above, you will see, "Company name: Type Quick Payroll" Look for "Company name" in the window, and then type "Quick Payroll."

- **Accept:** Sometimes, QuickBooks will default words or information in a box or a field for you, and the instruction will be to accept what is given. In that case, I will include the word "Accept." For example, as in the image above, "Country: Accept U.S." For Country, the instruction is asking you to accept U.S. All you need to do is make sure the information in the box or field is U.S. If QuickBooks defaults another word other than U.S., you must change it to U.S. before you leave the area. I have included only the activities you need, and have ignored irrelevant empty boxes and defaulted statements. Hence, do not worry about empty boxes or defaulted statements not in the activities.

- **Checkmark:** When the instruction is to checkmark an option, a box, or phrase, be sure there is a checkmark in the option or box before you leave that window. If you see a checkmark already in the option or box, go to the next instruction, and do not remove the checkmark already on the option, box, or the phrase. Sometimes, there will be an option or a check box beside a phrase and if you're told to click the option of the phrase, checkmark the box, not just the phrase itself.

- **Type:** An instruction may require you to type information in a field or box. If the information is already in that box or field, just make sure it says exactly what you're told to type, then go the next instruction. For example, if the instruction is to "Type Quick Payroll," if Quick Payroll is already in the field or box, confirm that it says "Quick Payroll." As soon as you've confirmed the information is correct, go on to the next instruction.

- **Select:** Sometimes, the instruction will tell you to select a word or a number from a drop-down window, if you know the first letter of the first word, it is recommended that you press it on the keyboard to pull up the entire word. For example, as in the image above, you can press "T" twice to select Texas. Also, if the word you are told to select is already in the box or window, just make sure it's the right word or number, then keep going.

- **Click:** When the instruction is to click a word or phrase in a drop-down window, if that word or phrase has a checkmark already on it, do not click it again for that will remove the checkmark and as a result, nullifies the instruction. When you see the checkmark, just press the Esc key on your keyboard or click on a blank space on the window to make the drop-down window disappear. Keep an eye on Save & Close and Save & New. Do not click Save & Close when you want to click Save & New.

- **Menus and Submenus**: This book is arranged according to the QuickBooks menus. There are 13 menus located at the top of your computer, and every time I refer to these menus, I'll use the word "Menu." If you did not see "Menu" after a word, then I'm not referring to one of 13 menus. The word I'm referring to is located in the window or subwindow you've just opened. Titles within this book are also arranged according to the QuickBooks' submenus for easy reading and location.

- **Window Directions:** I have used phrases such as: top right, top left, bottom right, and bottom left, to give you directions on where to find information on the window, thereby increasing your speed. Every instruction is directed to the current window you've just opened. If, for instance, you opened a small or subwindow, any instruction given at that moment is for that small or subwindow. Do not look at the big window.

- **Tab and Enter key:** Use the Tab key, especially in a window where you have to provide information for several boxes or fields. Sometimes, you have to press Enter on your keyboard for QuickBooks to accept your action. You can choose between pressing the Enter key on your keyboard and clicking Enter in the window, but it's a good idea to stay consistent to increase your speed. The resolution or the size of your monitor will determine how much information is displayed on the screen. If you have a small monitor, you may have to scroll down to find information. However, rest assured, the information is there; you just have to look for it. It is important to repeat this: When an instruction says click Print or click Report, it is talking about the report or print in the smaller window and not the Report or Print menus located at the top of the window; otherwise, it would be followed by the word "Menu." When you are in a text box or a field, you may press the Home key to go the beginning of the text box or field, and you may press the End key to go the end of the text box or field.

- **Review:** Most of the time, an instruction will ask you to review a window, report, register, etc. All you have to do is read or browse through the information on the report or the window. The purpose is to allow you to gain a visual experience of the information, which helps you to gain in-depth knowledge of the subject matter as you work through the software.

- **Exit:** Some instructions will require you to click X to exit or close the window. The X is referring to the submenu not the QuickBooks' main window X located at the top right corner of the window. The submenu X is located below the main window X. You will not be asked to click the QuickBooks' main window X. QuickBooks has many "doors" to different windows, and the purpose of this book is to show you as many doors as possible. Later on, as you continue to use the software, you will choose where to go and which doors to open.

QuickBooks Window Parts

If you have a working knowledge of Microsoft Windows, you might find this section redundant. That's OK; I recommend you scan through it anyway. If you are not experienced in using Microsoft Windows, that's alright. I have taken nothing for granted. You will notice QuickBooks has many parts when you open its window. In all Microsoft Windows, the top part is called the "TMT," which stands for Title, Menus, and Tools. Following the TMT is the Workspace. Any instruction without the words "Menus" or "Tool" (such as "Report Menu and "Print Tool") is talking about the information in the Workspace. Navigation tips are arranged according to the QuickBooks image below.

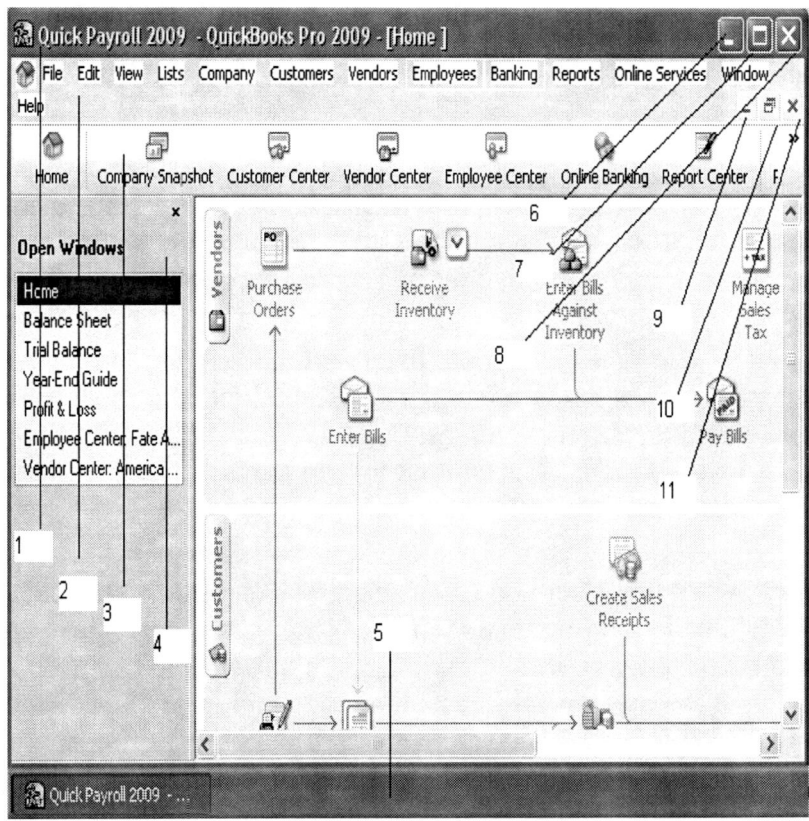

1. Title bar
2. Menu bar
3. Tool bar (or Icon bar)
4. Open window
5. Taskbar
6. Minimize (Main window)
7. Maximize (Main window)
8. Exit (Main window)
9. Minimize (Sub window)
10. Maximize (Sub window)
11. Exit (Sub window

- **Title bar:** Every time you open a QuickBooks window, you should immediately look at the title bar to make sure you're in the right Company or File window. It is imperative to be in the right file, because if you spent hours working on the wrong file, it will take more time to fix the problems.

- **Menu bar:** Below the Title bar is the menu bar. QuickBooks has 13 menus, and they are arranged in this book according to how they are arranged when you open the QuickBooks window. It is important to recognize the 13 QuickBooks menus. In your free time, click on these menus and submenus to see where they are located. As you build your confidence using QuickBooks with this book, you will remember where most of the submenus are located.

- **Tool bar or Icon Bar:** Below the menu bar is the Icon bar. It's recommended to display your most-used Icons on the Icon bar. Reports and check registers should be placed on the Icon bar for easy access. It is professional to access the windows by going through the Icon bar rather than going through the menus. However, most instructions will take you through the menus for consistency's sake during your training period.

- **Open Window List:** If you want to have instant access to the most-used windows, always see if they have already been open and are now on the Open Window List. To display the Open Window List, click the View menu and Open Windows List. Then, you should be able to see all open windows and access them instead of going through the menus and submenus.

- **Taskbar:** From time to time, you would like to minimize windows for easy access at a later time. When you minimize a window it goes to the taskbar, where you can click it again to maximize it. And if you click minimize on the QuickBooks main window, it takes QuickBooks to the taskbar where you can click it again to maximize it.

- **Minimize main window:** After you have launched QuickBooks, the default main window will be in the Maximum mode. If you want to see other programs on the desktop, you should minimize QuickBooks to the Task Master. From time to time, you will be instructed to minimize QuickBooks to review information that has been saved to the desktop, or to minimize QuickBooks to open other programs such as Excel or Word.

- **Maximize main window:** This is the square button located at the top right of the computer. You will maximize a window when it is too small to view all the window data or after it was minimized to the Task Master. Subwindow's Exit, Maximize, and Minimize buttons will be under those of the main windows. From time to time, you will be required to minimize, maximize, or exit a subwindow to perform certain activities.

- **Exit main window:** Most Exit or X instructions will be referring to the subwindows. The subwindow X is located below the main window X. While you're still working with QuickBooks, you will only be clicking the smaller X for the subwindow. Any time you click the big X or the main window exit, be sure you really want to shut down your QuickBooks program.

- **Minimize sub window:** At other times when you click a menu and a submenu, the window that opens will cover the workspace and will not allow you to drag it around. The best action is to minimize it, so you are able to move it around from one side of the window to another. If you click the View menu and One Window, you will not see the Minimize button, only the Exit.

- **Maximize sub window:** After you've opened the main window, other windows are subwindows. Most of the time, when you click a menu and submenu, the subwindow that opens will be too small to see all the content of that subwindow. The next thing to do is maximize the subwindow. If you click Multiple Windows from the View menu, you can minimize and move the subwindows around; otherwise, you will not see the Maximize button.

- **Exit sub window:** This button is important when you want to exit a subwindow. Many times, I've seen clients who exit the main window and shut down QuickBooks, when in fact they wanted to exit the subwindow. Every time I say exit a window, I'm referring to the subwindow, not the main window.

Installation Tips: Window Appears

If you order the QuickBooks software through the mail, you will receive a CD. When you put the CD into the drive, the welcome window will appear after a few seconds. Read each window carefully to determine exactly what you should do. Your QuickBooks software will default options it thinks you need. Unless you know exactly the result of another option, you should accept the suggested defaults. The instructions below might be different if this is the first time you're installing QuickBooks on your computer. However, the instructions will get you started. You should note the location of your QuickBooks folder during the installation process.

Activities:

- ❖ Load **CD in the drive**
- ❖ In seconds installation window will open.
- ❖ **Welcome to QuickBooks Installations wizard!** Click **Next**
- ❖ Read **Software License Agreement?**
- ❖ Click **Accept.** Click **Next**
- ❖ Click **One user** or **More than one user**. Click **Next**
- ❖ License Number: Type number from yellow sticker
- ❖ Product Number: Type product number from yellow sticker
- ❖ Click **Next**
- ❖ Accept the click on **Install QuickBooks Pro 2009.**   Click **Next**
- ❖ In Copy previous QuickBooks settings window
- ❖ Please select...Click **down arrow**
- ❖ Select **QuickBooks Pro 2008**. Click **Next**
- ❖ Ready to Install QuickBooks window
- ❖ Click **Install**
- ❖ When Installation is completed
- ❖ Click **Finish**

Installation Tips: No Window Appears

When you put the CD into the drive and wait for few minutes, if nothing happens, click Start, Settings, and Control Panel. If you have Windows XP, you might not see Settings, so click Control Panel and proceed as shown below. QuickBooks is user-friendly. Here are a few instructions to get you started.

Activities:

- ❖ Load **CD in the drive**
- ❖ If after a few seconds Welcome does not appear
- ❖ Click **Start. (**Click **Setting** if available**)**
- ❖ Click **Control Panel**
- ❖ Double click **Add/Remove Programs**
- ❖ Click **Add New Programs** (left)
- ❖ Click **CD or Floppy.** Click **Next**
- ❖ Click **Finish**
- ❖ Welcome to QuickBooks Installation Wizard. Click **Next**
- ❖ Continue as in the previous page
- ❖ When Installation is completed
- ❖ Click **Finish**

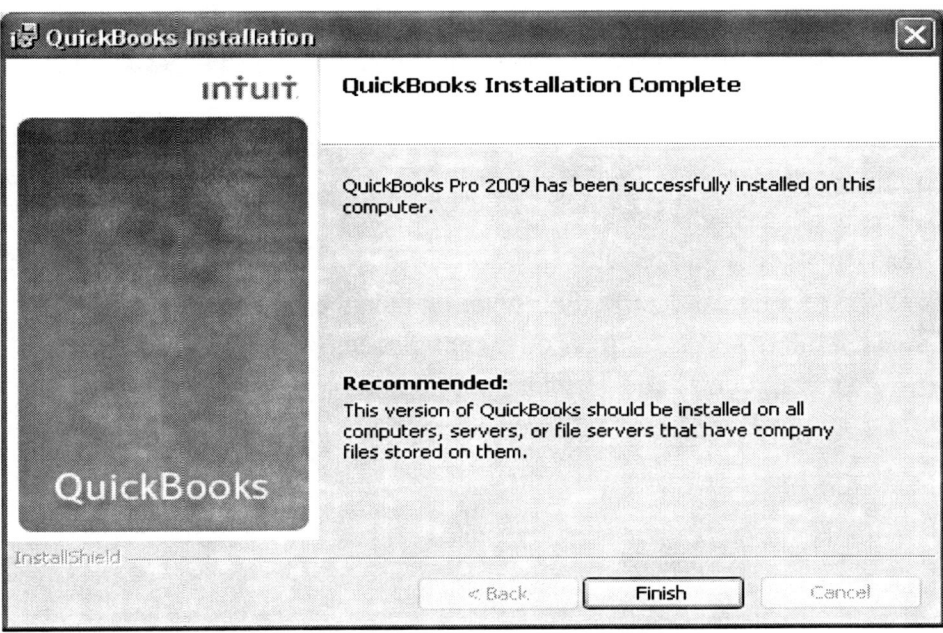

$

Chapter 1

File Menu

Objectives: After you've completed this chapter, you will be able to:

- ✓ Explain the File submenus
- ✓ Create a new company
- ✓ Create bank accounts
- ✓ Create liability accounts
- ✓ Create customers and enter their opening balances
- ✓ Create vendors and enter their opening balances
- ✓ Run financial reports and compare your results

Review File Submenus

When you start practicing with this book, you should skip all pages with the word "Review" in their titles. After you have finished practicing the activities, you may come back and read the "Review" pages; they are theory and will not prevent you from successfully completing this book. The File menu is one of the key menus in QuickBooks, and understanding its submenus is essential for using QuickBooks. The File menu has activities that are not specific to a QuickBooks window, but are global in nature. For example, when you are using the backup, restore, or password windows, it is for the entire company not just for one window. When logging off, click File menu and then Exit, the last item in the File menu drop-down window or click the red X at the top right corner of your computer.

- Click **File menu**

The following submenus are found under the File menu:

- **New Company:** The New Company function will help you create a complete set of files that are needed to operate a company. You may choose to skip the detailed process by clicking the Skip Interview button. If you choose to skip the interview, you must select your form of business window. QuickBooks will use your company information to provide you with a set of accounts appropriate for your company. The name you give your company is what is reflected on the window title. If you copy a file, your title will reflect the name of the original company. To change the title of the new file, you must click the Company menu and then Company Information; only then will the window title be changed.

- **Open or Restore Company:** By clicking on this submenu, you will be taken to a window that lists all the files you've just created and other default QuickBooks files that are associated with your work. You must come to this window anytime you want to see all the files available to you. Restore allows you to load your backup or your portable files.

- **Open Previous Company:** This is one of the most used handy tools in your QuickBooks financials. Anytime you want to open a previous window, it is quicker to use the Open Previous Company. Do this instead of clicking the File menu and then Open Company submenu, because you're not looking for all the files you have created. Rather, you are looking for the file you've recently closed. QuickBooks will keep only 10 files you've previously closed in the drop-down window. You may increase that number by clicking the "Set number of previous companies…" located at the end of the drop-down list. A small window will open to allow you to change the number to a maximum of 20.

- **Save Copy or Backup:** You should save or back up your files at the end of every month. This way, you can re-create a month of activities if you happen to lose your computer to a virus or fire. Don't forget to store your backed-up files somewhere outside your current QuickBooks work location.

- **Close Company:** As the name implies, when you choose this submenu, QuickBooks will close the current window and open the "Select a Company" window. Do not click Close Company when you mean to logoff from the QuickBooks program, in which the best action is to click the File menu and then Exit. Another option you may use to close a company is to click the X button located at the top right corner.

- **Switch to Multi-user Mode:** If your QuickBooks database is accessible to more than one person, click this submenu. Every time you keep getting the message window, "Create New User immediately," you should know you are in the Multi-user mode, unless you disable the message window. You have previously clicked the Switch to Multi-user mode.

- **Utilities:** This is one submenu you want to pay much attention to. To start with, you must remember QuickBooks activities that are hidden under this submenu. They include the following: Import, Export, Synchronize Contacts, Convert, Verify Data, Rebuild Data, Clean Up Company Data. When you back up, it is for the entire company file, not just an account such as the bank account. If you've had a computer problem like a virus attack and your files are corrupt, this is the time to run the Verify Data function. If QuickBooks find any damaged files, it will go ahead and rebuild it. If you started with Quicken Home and Business, and with rapid business growth, you may have decided to change to QuickBooks. The Convert tool allows you to move your files from Quicken to QuickBooks.

- **Accountant's Copy:** This is one of the most complex submenus in the entire QuickBooks program. If you have an accountant and you want him or her to review your files for mistakes, one way is to send your files to your accountant. When you use the Accountant's Copy tools, QuickBooks restricts the accountant from changing certain files such as the Chart of Accounts.

- **Print:** Different Print functions will be activated depending on which window you are in. For example, if you are in the Chart of Accounts or Item List windows, and you click the File menu you can only see Print List, and if you go to a report window, Print Report will only come up or be activated.

- **Save as PDF:** With the information age, document security is becoming absolutely necessary. If you send your financial files on programs like Excel, someone can change that file and make it seem like the original. To restrict someone from tampering with a file, it is becoming a universal practice to send financial information as a PDF. This way, originality of data is assured, and tampering is made difficult.

- **Print Forms:** QuickBooks has several reports you can print or preview, including paycheck stubs, checks, credit memos, invoices, labels, purchase orders, sales receipts, timeshares, and 1099s/1096. An important use of these forms is to preview for availability of data, before you go to other windows. For example, if you want to find out if you have checks to be printed, the quickest way is to click File menu, Print Forms, and then click Checks. Any checks you have to be printed will be listed in this window.

- **Print Setup:** When it comes to the layout of reports, people have different tastes. One person might like to have a report in Portrait while another person may like to see the same report in Landscape format. It is important to come to the Print Setup submenu and choose the options you like. When you have reports displayed in a way you don't like, remember to come to Print Setup window for changes.

- **Send Forms:** If you communicate with your customers and vendors via Internet, this is one submenu you will want to know how to use. After you've completed an invoice, click the "To be e-mailed" box located at the bottom left of the invoice window. Then when you are ready to send your invoice by e-mail, come to this submenu. Select the invoice and click the Send button. I prefer to send a batch of invoices at one time instead of individual invoices.

- **Shipping:** This submenu allows you to send packages by FedEx or UPS. It allows you to find a drop off location, schedule a pickup, track or cancel shipments, and print Ground End-of-Day manifest.

- **Exit:** Generally, you will have two X buttons, one for the main window and the other for the subwindow. Both are located at the top right corner of subwindow and main window. If you want to exit the subwindow, use the small X, but if you want to log off and shut down QuickBooks, you will need to click the big X at the top right corner. Another way of logging off from QuickBooks without clicking the big X is to click File menu and then Exit.

Create New Company

Important note: You do not need to read this theory to practice the instructions below. The same goes with all other pages. You will be creating a new company called Quick Payroll. It is recommended that you use the year of creation on the company name for identification purposes. The name you give your company here is reflected as the window title. You can only change the window title here.

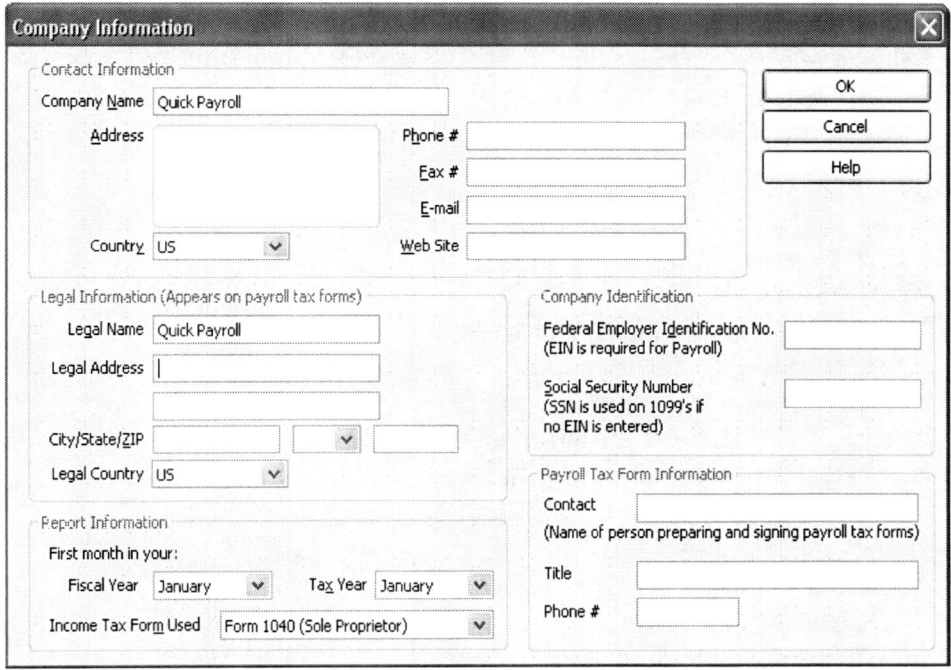

Activities:

- ❖ Double click **QuickBooks 2009** shortcut on desktop
- ❖ Click **File menu**
- ❖ Click **New Company…**
- ❖ Click **Skip Interview** (bottom right of the window)
- ❖ Company name: Type **Quick Payroll**. Click **Next**
- ❖ Click **Sole Proprietorship.** Click **Next**
- ❖ My fiscal year start in: Accept **January**. Click **Next**
- ❖ In the left window. Scroll to the bottom
- ❖ Click General Service-based business. Click **Next**
- ❖ Create your company file. Click **Next.** Click **Save**
- ❖ You're almost done. Click **Next**
- ❖ Launch Web Browser? Click **Cancel**

After you double clicked QuickBooks 2009, if you don't see the File menu

1. Click Create New Company
2. Click Skip Interview

Then continue with the rest of the activities.

❖ Click **Edit menu.** Click **Preferences**
❖ Click **Desktop View.** Uncheck **Show Live Community.** Click **OK**
❖ Click **X** to close Live Community (top right of the window)

Create Bank Accounts

You will be creating new accounts in the Chart of Accounts window. The bank option allows you to create accounts such as checking, savings, payroll, petty cash and other accounts that are banking-related. You will be allowed to enter the opening balance and the account date in the "Enter Opening Balance" window. To correct the opening balance, click List menu and Chart of Accounts, double click USA Checking, change the amount and click save and close.

Activities:

❖ Click **Edit menu**
❖ Click **Preferences…**
❖ Click **Accounting** (left of the window)
❖ Click **Company Preferences** tab
❖ Uncheck **Warn if transactions are 90 day(s) in the past**
❖ Uncheck **Warn if transactions are 30 day(s) in the future**
❖ Click **OK** to close Preferences window
❖ Click **View menu**
❖ Click **Open Window List**
❖ Click **Lists menu**
❖ Click **Chart of Accounts**

> Maximize your Chart of Accounts window or any other windows that are not fully opened.

❖ Right click in the window. Click **New**
❖ Click **Bank**
❖ Click **Continue**
❖ Account Name: Type **USA Checking**
❖ Click **Enter Opening Balance…**
❖ Statement Ending Balance: Type **800,000**
❖ Statement Ending Date: Type **1/1/09.** Click **OK**
❖ Click **Save & New**
❖ Account Name: Type **USA Payroll**
❖ Click **Enter Opening Balance…**
❖ Statement Ending Balance: Type **250,000**
❖ Statement Ending Date: Type **1/1/09.** Click **OK**
❖ Click **Save & Close**
❖ Click **No** to "Set up online services…"

Create Liability Accounts

Chart of Accounts window is also used to create a liability account. After you right click in the Chart of Accounts window, and click new, the next window is where you create the liability account. You must click the "Other Account Types" option and the down arrow to see the Long Term liability accounts. To correct the opening balance, click List menu and Chart of Accounts to open the window. Double click Office Building Loan, change the amount and click save and close.

Activities:

- ❖ Right click in the Chart of Accounts window
- ❖ Click **New**
- ❖ Click **Other Account Types** (bottom of the window)
- ❖ Click **Long Term Liability**
- ❖ Click **Continue**
- ❖ Account Name: Type **Office Building Loan**
- ❖ Click **Enter Opening Balance...**
- ❖ Opening Balance: Type **50,000** as of: Type **1/1/09.** Click **OK**
- ❖ Click **Save & Close**

Create Customers

You must create customers if you plan to sell goods or services. A customer can be created "on the fly" by typing the name only without completing the entire costumer's window. The opening balance is the amount you currently have on your books for that customer. You can use the detailed method by re-creating the entire customer's invoice to show the content of the invoice, instead of just entering the total amount. To correct the opening balance, click List menu, click Chart of Accounts to open the window. Double click Accounts Receivable, change the amount and click save and close.

Activities:

- ❖ Click **Customers menu**
- ❖ Click **Customer Center**
- ❖ Right click in the left window
- ❖ Click **New Customer**
- ❖ Customer Name: Type **John Allen**
- ❖ Opening Balance: Type **550,000** as of: Type **1/1/09**
- ❖ Click **Next** (right of the window)
- ❖ Customer Name: Type **Tommy Brown**

❖ Opening Balance: Type **455,000** as of: Type **1/1/09.** Click **OK**
❖ **Look! You have Customers and balances left of the window**

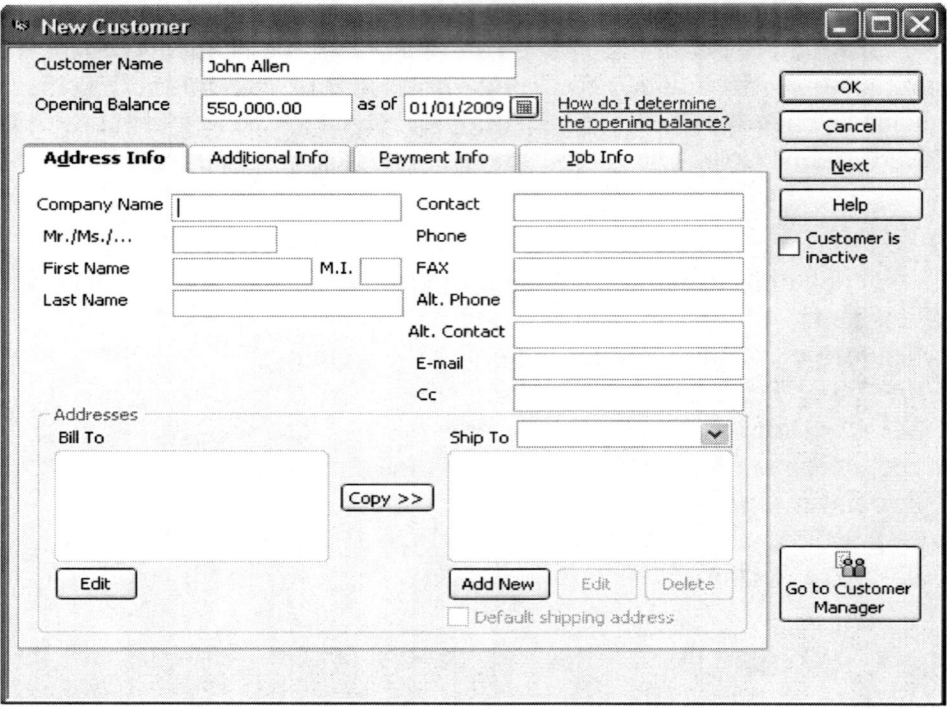

Create Vendors

Like customers, you must create vendors before you can receive merchandise and supplies. QuickBooks will not allow you to delete vendors, if it has been linked to other accounts. The opening balance is the closing balance you have on your books as of the date you create the new vendor. To correct the opening balance, click List menu, click Chart of Accounts to open the window. Double click Account Payable, change the amount and click save and close.

❖ Click **Vendors menu**
❖ Click **Vendor Center**
❖ Right click in the left window
❖ Click **New Vendor**
❖ Vendor Name: Type **Telephone America**
❖ Opening Balance: Type **3,500** as of: Type **1/1/09**
❖ Click **Next** (right of the window)
❖ Vendor Name: Type **Electric America**

❖ Opening Balance: Type **1,500** as of: Type **1/1/09.** Click **OK**
❖ **Look! You have Vendors and balances left of the window**

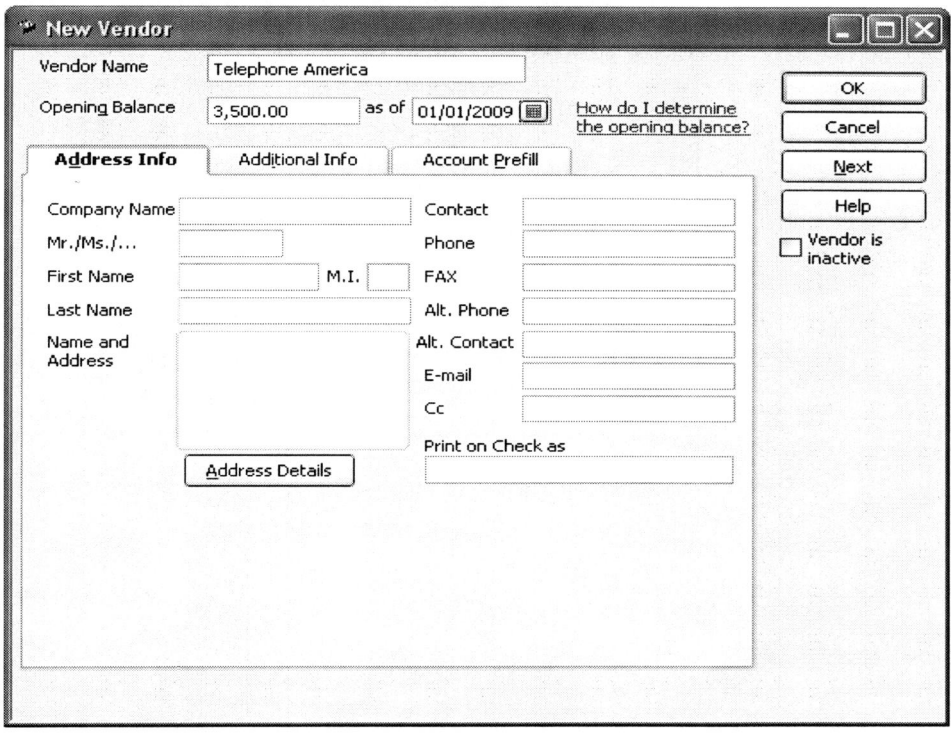

Financial Results: Profit & Loss

I expect you to get the end-of-chapter report numbers to the penny. However, if you do not get the exact figures, that's OK! The intention is to make sure you are following accordingly and to help you figure out where you made an error. Mistakes are inevitable in accounting, and it happens to everyone. As you continue to practice, you will build an extraordinary confidence with numbers. The first report is Profit & Loss statement, which includes income and expenses. Net income is 1,000,000.

Activities:
❖ Click **Reports menu**
❖ Click **Company & Financial**
❖ Click **Profit & Loss Standard**
❖ Dates (top left): Click **Down arrow**
❖ Select **This Fiscal Year**
❖ From: Accept **1/1/2009** To: **12/31/2009**

- ❖ **Look! Net Income is 1,000,000**
- ❖ Click the small **X** under the red X (top right of the window)
- ❖ Checkmark **Do not display this message in the future**
- ❖ Click **No** to close the Memorize Report window

Quick Payroll
Profit & Loss
January through December 2009

	◇ Jan - Dec 09 ◇
Ordinary Income/Expense	
Income	
Uncategorized Income	▶ 1,005,000.00 ◀
Total Income	1,005,000.00
Expense	
Uncategorized Expenses	5,000.00
Total Expense	5,000.00
Net Ordinary Income	1,000,000.00
Net Income	**1,000,000.00**

Financial Results: Balance Sheet

After you process the Profit & Loss statement, your next financial report is the Balance Sheet. Unlike the Profit & Loss statement, the Balance Sheet report is made up of Assets, Liabilities, and Owner's Equity. Make sure you select the right date from the top left side of the window; otherwise, your results will be different from the book. After the date, make sure you are in the right company. Hence, the company and the date are two vital pieces of information on your financial reports.

Activities:

- ❖ Click **Reports menu**
- ❖ Click **Company & Financial**
- ❖ Click **Balance Sheet Standard**
- ❖ Dates (top left): Click **Down arrow**
- ❖ Select **This Fiscal Year**
- ❖ As of: Accept **12/31/09**

- ❖ **Look! Total Assets is 2,055,000**
- ❖ Click **X** to close Balance Sheet Standard
- ❖ Congratulations on your first financial reports!

Quick Payroll
Balance Sheet
As of December 31, 2009

	◇ **Dec 31, 09** ◇
ASSETS	
Current Assets	
Checking/Savings	
USA Checking	▶ 800,000.00 ◀
USA Payroll	250,000.00
Total Checking/Savings	1,050,000.00
Accounts Receivable	
Accounts Receivable	1,005,000.00
Total Accounts Receivable	1,005,000.00
Total Current Assets	2,055,000.00
TOTAL ASSETS	**2,055,000.00**

Chapter Summary

The main objective in this chapter is to give you an overview of how quickly you use QuickBooks to create financial information. We created a new company called Quick Payroll and ran some transactions. There are several submenus under the File menu, and their actions and reactions affect an entire QuickBooks Payroll. We will skip some submenus that are not directly useful in running the payroll cycle. From time to time, we will come back to the File menu to practice some submenus.

What we accomplished:
- Reviewed the File submenus
- Created a new company called Quick Payroll
- Opened a bank account with opening balance
- Opened a payroll account with opening balance
- Created new customers with opening balance
- Created new vendors with opening balance
- Processed financial statements

Additional financial activities:
- Created USA Checking account for 800,000
- Created USA Payroll account for 250,000
- Created Office Building Loan account for 50,000
- Opened John Allen's account opening balance at 550,000
- Opened Tommy Brown's account opening balance at 455,000
- Created Telephone America's account opening balance at 3,500
- Created Electric America's account opening balance at 1,500

Optional Test 1

Questions: True/False

Answer the following questions by placing the T for True or F for False in the space provided before the question number.

_____ 1. When setting up a new company you must use the EasyStep Interview and you must complete every window available.

_____ 2. QuickBooks allows you to back up only one account at a time not the entire company files.

_____ 3. You can only import Excel spreadsheet into QuickBooks not the other way around.

_____ 4. The Send Form submenu allows you to send Purchase Order, Estimates, and Invoices by e-mail.

_____ 5. When setting up a new company you must select a form of business which QuickBooks uses to default a set of Chart of Accounts.

_____ 6. QuickBooks allows you to convert Quicken, Peachtree or Microsoft Small Accounting into QuickBooks files.

_____ 7. The only time you can change the name of a company is during set up, after that time, it is impossible to do so.

_____ 8. You can set up only a Sole Proprietorship form of business in QuickBooks and not any other form of business.

_____ 9. It is impossible to delete a company once it has been created because QuickBooks uses it to create other companies.

_____ 10. You can only convert Invoices and Estimates into PDF file not reports with QuickBooks.

Questions: Multiple Choices

Answer the following questions by placing letter A, B, C, or D in the space provided before the question number.

_____ 1. When setting up a new company which of the following forms of business is available for selection?
A. Sole Proprietorship
B. Partnership
C. Corporation
D. All of the above

_____ 2. During the Export processes which of the following can you be able to? export between two QuickBooks files?
A. Chart of Accounts
B. Item Lists
C. Both A and B
D. None of the above

_____ 3. Under the File menu the Utilities submenu allows you to perform which of the activities?
A. Import
B. Export
C. Verify Data
D. All of the above

_____ 4. When you want to make a duplicate copy of your QuickBooks file and store it away for security reasons, you use which of the following functions?
A. Safety Copy
B. Priority Copy
C. Backup Copy
D. Accountants Copy

_____ 5. If you want your QuickBooks database to be accessible to more than one individual, you use which of the following File submenus?
A. Multi-user Mode
B. All Users
C. Multiple Staff
D. More user Form

_____ 6. During the Import process which of the following is NOT one of the files QuickBooks is capable of importing?
   A. Excel file
   B. Word file
   C. IIF file
   D. Web Connect file

_____ 7. During the Export processes, QuickBooks can allow you to export which of the following activities?
   A. Lists from IIF Files
   B. Addresses from Text File
   C. Lists from Text File
   D. Timer Lists

_____ 8. Using the Open Previous Company submenu, what maximum number of windows can QuickBooks display?
   A. 10
   B. 15
   C. 20
   D. 25

_____ 9. If you had a virus attack that may affect your QuickBooks file you must first run which of the following tool to check the integrity of your data?
   E. Integrity Data
   F. Verify Data
   G. Troubleshoot Data
   H. Compile Data

_____ 10. QuickBooks allows you to set up your printer to print your document by portrait, landscape or smart orientation, which of the following forms would you be able to set up?
   A. Timesheet
   B. Credit Memo
   C. Notes
   D. All of the Above

Chapter 2

Edit Menu

Objectives: After you've completed this chapter you will be able to:
✓ Explain the Edit submenus
✓ Back up files
✓ Restore files
✓ Make an entry in the check register
✓ Use the calculator
✓ Use the simple and advanced find functions
✓ Setup QuickBooks preferences windows
✓ Run financial reports and compare your results

Review Edit Submenus

You have more submenus under the Edit menu than under any other menu. Always remember that if you open the Home page, you will not activate a lot of Edit submenus. If you don't see many submenus, it could be because you have not opened the right windows that could force the submenus to be activated. For example, if you open the Chart of Accounts window, you will see more submenus. Preferences are vital submenus under the Edit menu—easy to set up, learn, and use. Edit menu works best when a check register or a report window is open, since more submenus are activated.

- Click **Lists menu**
- Click **Chart of Accounts**
- Double click **USA Checking**
- Click on a **Check Number** with **CHK** under the number
- Click **Edit menu**

The following submenus are found under the Edit menu when you click in the check register:

- **Undo Typing:** When you highlight an amount and press the Delete key, the amount will disappear. If you want the amount you've just deleted to re-appear because it is the right amount, just click the Edit menu, and choose Undo. The deleted amount will return in the amount field. You must delete the amount and not do anything else for the Undo function to come up. If you press the Tab or Enter key, Undo will not be activated.

- **Revert:** This tool works much like the Undo function. After typing an amount you may decide to change back to the original amount you had earlier, all you have to do before you press Tab is to click Edit and then Revert.

- **Cut:** Cut will allow you to cut a field or an entry to another location, most probably, the last blank line. Cut will not come up unless that field is highlighted. If you cut a field by mistake, remember to restore it by using Revert or Paste or by clicking Restore located at the bottom right of the register.

- **Copy:** Like the Cut function, the Copy works best when the Check Register is opened and a field is highlighted. You can copy any part of the entry as long as it is highlighted.

- **Paste:** When you cut or copy a field, Paste will allow you to paste that field to another location. Make sure you're pasting the right information in the right field. If you're pasting an entry, remember to change the basic information of that entry; otherwise, you will have two identical entries. At the least, you should be changing the number of the new entry.

- **Edit Check:** After writing a check, you may find out there is a problem with it. For example, you may find out that you typed 456 Adam Lane instead of 465 Adam Lane. Edit Check will allow you to make changes to the check. Be sure to click the Save & Close button; otherwise, a message window will come up and ask if you want to accept the changes you've just made.

- **New Check:** The window allows you to go to the check window. You must click an entry in the check register with the letters CHK, then click Edit menu and the New Check submenu will be activated.

- **Delete Check:** It is highly recommended that you void a check rather than delete it. If a check has been reconciled, QuickBooks still allows you to delete that check though it has been used behind the scenes to debit and credit different accounts and the check also has hit several reports. Before you delete a check, make sure you really want to. You can also delete the amount of the check and preserve the information about the check for future reference.

- **Memorize Check:** This is one of the best features in QuickBooks. If you have a need to write the same check to the same vendor for the same amount every month many times in the future, it's best to go ahead and memorize it. This way next month, your check register will automatically be populated with the check's information. Automating or memorizing a check is more efficient than manually writing the same check month after month.

- **Void Check:** It is better to void a check than delete it, unless it's the last check you've just written and, therefore, not yet reconciled. If you want to avoid wasting checks and keep your work clean, it is recommended that you rewrite a voided check to another vendor. There is nothing like having all your check numbers all lined up. Be sure when you are rewriting a check to another vendor that you rewrite every field or box. It will be a bad check if you left the old address that belonged to the previous vendor.

- **Copy Check:** If you want to type a transaction that is already in the register, there is no need re-typing it when you can just click on the line, click edit menu and copy check. It saves you even more time when you have to repeat the process two or three times.

- **Go To Transfer:** To use this feature, you must transfer some money to another account and the account field must be other accounts, except Income and Expense accounts such as a Savings Account or a Payroll Account. The Go To Transfer lets you jump over to the other register account where the amount was transferred to, so you can see the account balance after the transfer.

- **Transaction History:** This submenu does not come up unless you are in a check register and a transaction is clicked. If you click a transaction in the check register and click QuickReport located at the top of the window, Transaction History will also be activated.

- **Notepad:** This feature will not come up unless you click on an entry in the check register. You must open a check register and click on an entry, and then the Edit menu before Notepad is listed.

- **Change Account Color:** If you don't like the color of the check register, QuickBooks has given you an option to change it. Just click on this submenu and a window opens where you can select your favorite color.

- **Use Register:** This submenu will allow you to select the exact bank account you want to open. It's pertinent to choose the right account from this window; otherwise, you could be entering data in an incorrect account. It will cost you time and effort to correct an error because you chose a wrong account.

- **Use Calculator:** From time to time, you will want to do some additions and subtractions in the check register. Always remember that there is a calculator handy in your QuickBooks software. I've seen many people reaching for their calculators when they can easily switch to their QuickBooks calculator.

- **Search:** If you're working on a project and you want to search for some information online, this is the submenu to come to. It will take you to the Internet where you can conduct your online search. Be sure to read how your financial information is protected from being transmitted through the Internet.

- **Find:** You cannot truly enjoy using your QuickBooks software until you know how to use the Find window. Any time you want to find information about a vendor, the Find is your best ally.

- **Preferences:** This is one of the most important submenus under the Edit menu, because it helps you to set up the following areas: Accounting, Checking, Desktop View, Finance Charge, General Information, Integrated Application, Job & Estimate, Payroll & Employees, Purchase & Vendors, Reminders, Reports & Graphs, Sales & Customers, Sales Tax, Send Forms, Service Connections, Spelling, Tax: 1099, and Time Tracking. Selecting your preferences is paramount to using QuickBooks correctly. Most windows and submenus will not be activated if the right preferences are not selected. In fact, if you did not see any windows described in this book, it may be because you have not selected the right preferences to activate that window or the window is not a part of your QuickBooks software due to version differences.

Back Up

You are going to backup the Quick Payroll file to the desktop. From time to time you should backup your files and store them away for security reasons. **If you are practicing backup the second time with the same file, after you click "Local backup" and Next, QuickBooks will skip to "Save it now" because it memorized what you did the last time.** Therefore, if you have to backup the same file before, be ready to skip to "Save right now" after you've clicked the "Local backup" and the Next button.

Activities:
- ❖ Open the Quick Payroll file
- ❖ Click **File menu**
- ❖ Click **Save Copy or Backup**
- ❖ Click **Backup copy**. Click **Next**
- ❖ Click **Local backup**. Click **Next**
- ❖ Tell us where to save your backup copies
- ❖ Click **Browse...**
- ❖ Scroll up. Click **Desktop.** Click **OK**
- ❖ Tell us where to save your backup copies
- ❖ Accept **C:\...Desktop.** Click **OK**
- ❖ Click **Use this Location**
- ❖ Click **Save it now**. Click **Next**

> The "Use this Location" button will not appear if you've backed up to the desktop before or you're using Floppy, CD, USB, or any other external destinations.

❖ Save in: Select **Desktop**
❖ File name (bottom left): Type **Quick Payroll**
❖ Click **Save**
❖ Click **OK** to "QuickBooks has saved this…"

Restore

There are two ways of restoring your file. You can restore a file to create another file or restore a file to replace the original file. Your objective here is to create a second file not to replace the old file. You should back up each chapter to a CD for security reason, should anything happen to the computer. If you lost the Quick Payroll file for instance, you will restore it from your CD and still call it Quick Payroll or whatever file name you lost.

Activities:

❖ You're still in Quick Payroll window
❖ Click **File**
❖ Click **Open or Restore…**
❖ Click **Restore a backup copy.** Click **Next**
❖ Click **Local backup**. Click **Next**
❖ Look in: Select **Desktop**
❖ Click **Quick Payroll**
❖ Click **Open**
❖ Where do you want to restore the file? Click **Next**
❖ Save in: Accept **Company File**
❖ File name: Type **Quick Payroll 2009.** Click **Save**
❖ Click **OK** to "Your data has been restored successfully."
❖ Click **Company menu**
❖ Click **Company Information…**
❖ Company Name: Type **Quick Payroll 2009**
❖ **Students add your first name initial and your last name after 2009**
❖ Click **X** to close Overview & Setup window
❖ Click **OK**
❖ Congratulations! You have created the 2009 file.

Make an Entry

Creating a transaction is very easy with QuickBooks, but you have to assemble your information by having the actual bill in front of you. The name of the payee must be exactly as it is shown on the bill. Make the habit of entering customers and vendors names exactly as you see it on the invoice or bill. The check in the amount of 150.00 to Telephone America does not mean we reduced any amount we already owe them directly. If you want to reduce the amount you owe Telephone America directly, you should open the pay bill window and select the bill to reduce the account payable balance.

Activities:

❖ Click **View menu**

❖ Click **Open Window List**

❖ Click **Edit menu**

❖ Click **Use Register**

❖ Select Account: Select **USA Checking.** Click **OK**

❖ On the highlighted Date: Type **1/1/09**. Press **Tab.**

❖ Number: Type **1001**

❖ Payee: Select **Telephone America**. Press **Tab**

❖ Payment: Type **150.00** Press **Tab**

❖ Account: Select **Telephone Expense**. Press **Tab**

❖ Click **Record** (bottom right of the window)

> An easier way to select an account from a drop down window if you know the name, is to press the first letter on your keyboard and QuickBooks will display all the accounts with the same first letter for your selection.

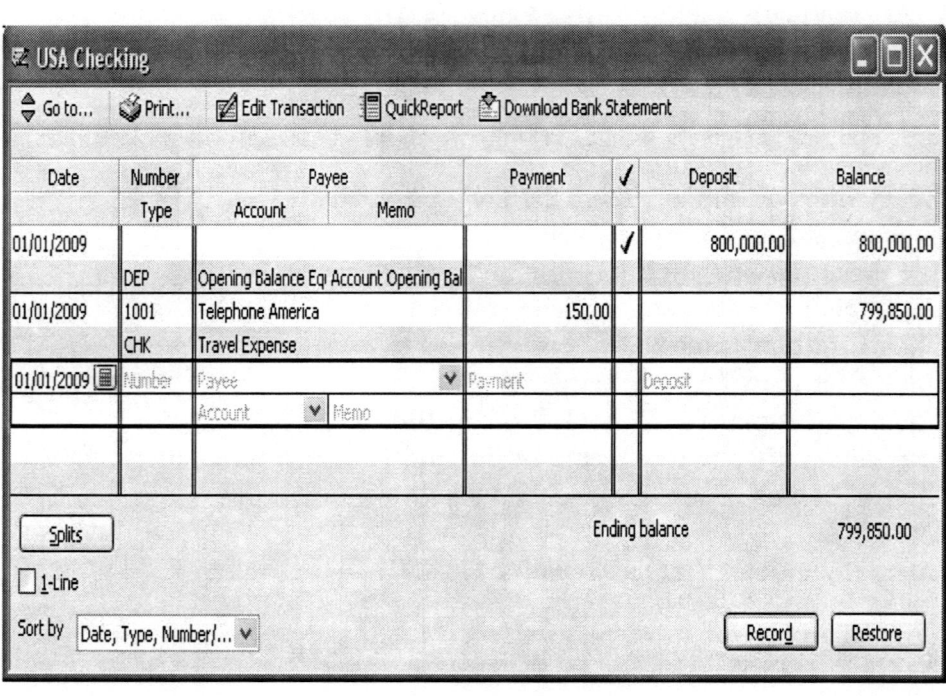

Use Calculator

QuickBooks calculator will increase your speed and prevent you from looking for a calculator in your desk. As long as your keyboard Num Lock is on, you can use the keyboard numbers and functions instead of clicking the calculator itself with your mouse. Letter C clears the calculator and letters CE clears the last entry. Do not click the plus sign (+) followed by the equal sign (=); you'll get a wrong result. QuickMath is activated when you press the Equal to or Plus sign in most amount boxes.

Activities:

* Click **Edit menu**
* Click **Use Calculator**
* On your keyboard perform the following:
* Type **1234**
* Press **Backspace** on keyboard **to delete 4**
* Type **+ 1000. Press Enter**
* Answer is 1123
* Press **Delete** on keyboard to clear calculator
* Type **251 + 863 + 741 + 145. Press Enter**
* Answer is 2000
* Press **Delete** on keyboard to clear calculator
* Type **100,000 * .25 (25%). Press Enter**
* Answer is 25000
* Click **View** (top of Calculator)
* Click **Scientific**
* Click **View**
* Click **Standard**
* **Minimize Calculator** to the Taskbar for later use

> Always minimize the calculator to the taskbar for future use.

Simple Find

Using the Find function is worth every penny you spent on this software. You can find information in your database using a lot of criteria including invoices, estimates, sales receipts, credit memos, bills, checks, credit cards, purchase orders, sales orders, and journals. What if a company calls or you receive a mail that says you have not paid your old bill? All you need to do is open the Find window and search for the name of the company with check as the Transaction Type. Then click the Find button and voila!

Activities:

- ❖ Click **Edit menu**
- ❖ Click **Find...**
- ❖ Accept **Simple** tab (top left)
- ❖ Transaction Type: Click **Down arrow**
- ❖ Select **Check**
- ❖ Payee: Click **Down arrow**
- ❖ Select **Telephone America**
- ❖ Click **Find** (top right of the window)
- ❖ Look! You have one entry
- ❖ Click **Reset** (right of the window)

In the Simple Find:

When the transaction is an invoice you search for a customer
When the transaction is a bill you search for a vendor

When the transaction is a check you search for a payee.

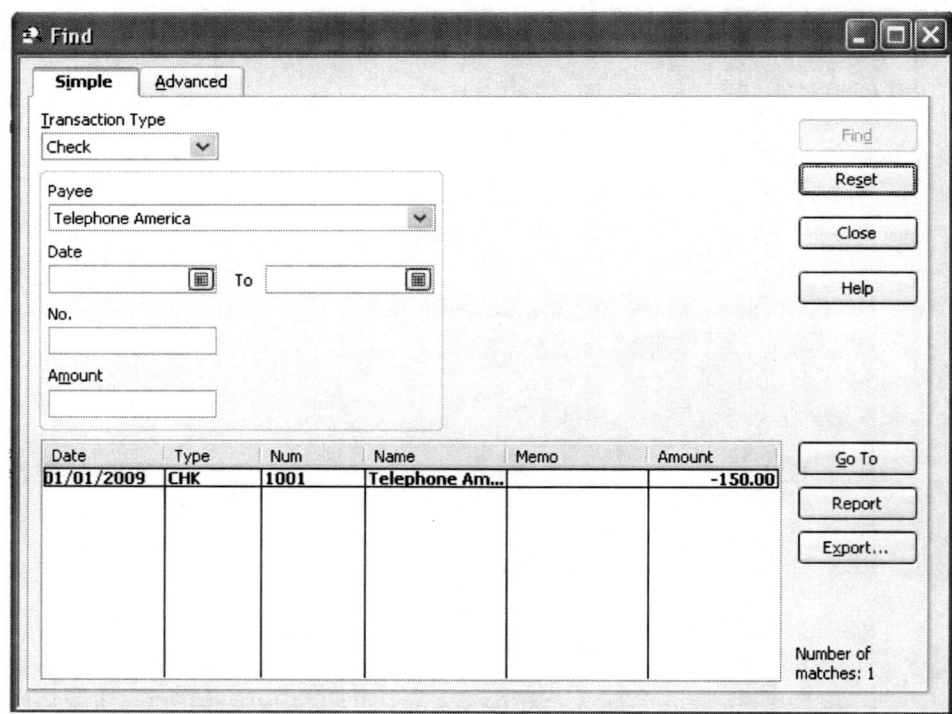

Advanced Find

We've talked about the Simple Find tab. Wait until you see what you can do with the Advanced Find. You have more options to zero in on the financial information you're looking for. I call this speed! If this is the only reason you want to switch from Quicken to QuickBooks, it's worth it. In Quicken, when you find a list of information, you will not have the total at the bottom of the list. This is not a problem in QuickBooks. The Find Report will have total at the bottom of the list.

Activities:

- ❖ Click **Advanced** tab
- ❖ In Choose Filter box. Click **Account**
- ❖ Account (right of Filter): Click **Down arrow**
- ❖ Select **All assets**
- ❖ Click **Find**. (right of the window)
- ❖ Five entries are displayed
- ❖ Account (right of Filter): Click **Down arrow**
- ❖ **Scroll down.** Select **USA Checking**
- ❖ Click **Find**. Look! Two entries are displayed
- ❖ Click **X** to close Find window

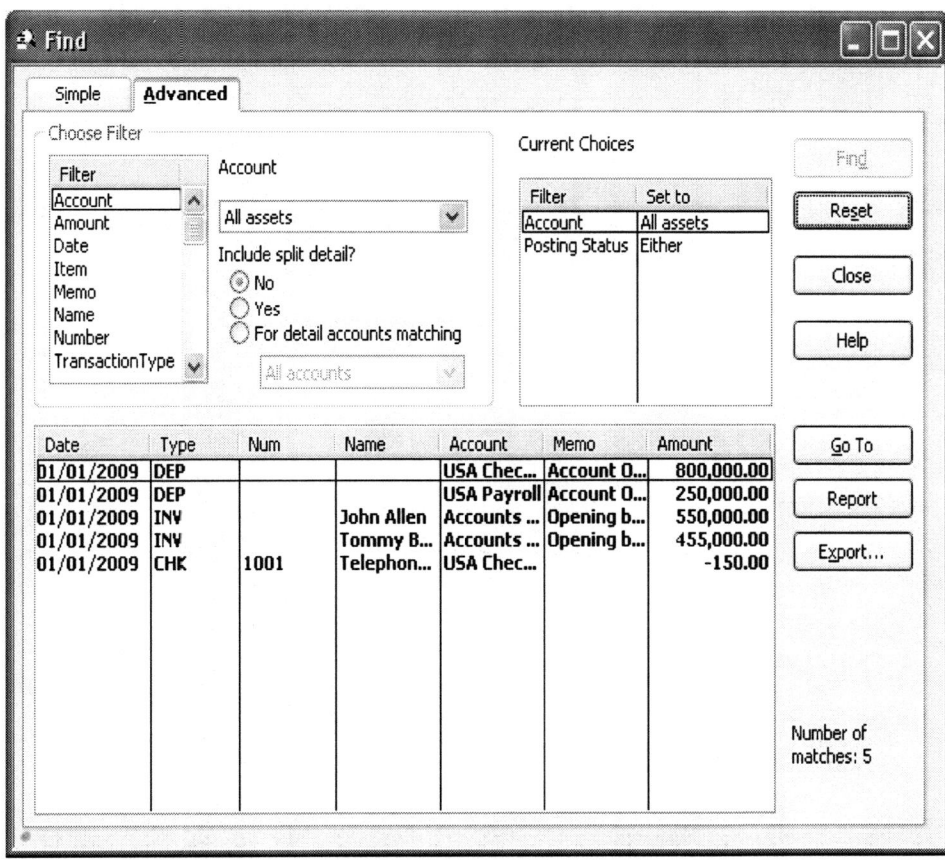

Accounting Preferences

If you plan on using account numbers, class tracking, or setting a password, you need to pay particular attention to this section. Many account numbers will be defaulted for you, but you'll need to provide account numbers to the new accounts you have created yourself. QuickBooks will allow you to set a password to edit transactions, on or before the closing date. The reason is that you don't want an intruder to change your financial information for last year; with a closing date and password, all is safe!

Activities:

- ❖ Click **Edit menu**
- ❖ Click **Preferences**
- ❖ Click **Accounting** (First item left column of the window)
- ❖ Click **Company Preferences** tab
- ❖ Click **Use class tracking**
- ❖ Uncheck **Prompt to assign classes**
- ❖ Uncheck **Warn if Transactions are 90 days in the past**
- ❖ Uncheck **Warn if Transactions are 30 days in the future**
- ❖ Click **OK**

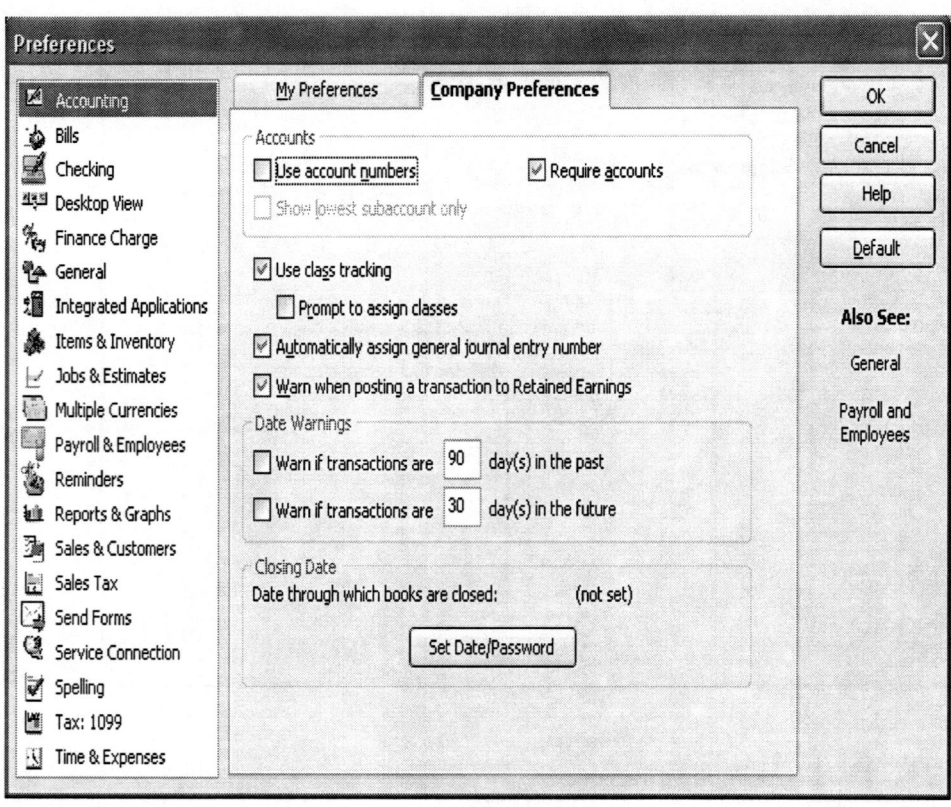

Bills, Items & Inventory

You should double check your work after completing the Inventory windows. I cannot tell you the number of times I have seen clients pay duplicate purchase orders and bills. For some companies, it is an honest mistake. But for others, it's just a game of testing your accounting systems. You must key in Vendor Purchase and Bill numbers on your checks and other documents. This allows QuickBooks to track duplicates for you. If you skip this process, you're doing so at your own risk. If you purchased goods and received a discount, it becomes a reduction of the cost of purchasing the goods, not an income. And if you sale goods and give a discount, it becomes a reduction of income of selling the goods, not an expense.

Activities:

- ❖ Click **Edit menu**
- ❖ Click **Preferences**
- ❖ Click **Bills** (left of the window)
- ❖ Click **Company Preferences** tab
- ❖ Bills are due: Accept **10** days after receipt
- ❖ Checkmark **Warn about duplicate bill numbers…**
- ❖ Checkmark **Automatically use discounts and credits**
- ❖ Default Discount Account: Click **Down arrow**
- ❖ **Scroll up.** Click **Add New**
- ❖ Account Type: Select **Cost of Goods Sold**
- ❖ Account Name: Type **Discount Received**
- ❖ Click **Save & Close**
- ❖ Click **Items & Inventory.** (left of the window)
- ❖ Click **Yes** to "You made changes…"
- ❖ Click **Company Preferences** tab
- ❖ Checkmark **Inventory and Purchases orders are active**
- ❖ Accept **Warn about duplicate purchase order numbers**
- ❖ Accept **Warn if not enough inventory quantity on hand(QOH) to sell**
- ❖ Click **OK**
- ❖ Click **OK** to "QuickBooks must close all…"
- ❖ Click **Company menu**
- ❖ Click **Home Page**

Checking Preferences

By now, you know that your QuickBooks will act and react in a certain way due to the ways you set your preferences and hence, it's pertinent to set your preferences correctly. One of the most essential preferences you will be setting is the Payroll default account. In the payroll liabilities box, you want to select the payroll account. Anytime you want to write a payroll-related check, you want that check to come from the payroll account not the regular checking account.

Activities:
- ❖ Click **Edit menu**
- ❖ Click **Preferences**
- ❖ Click **Checking** (left column of the window)
- ❖ Click **My Preferences** tab
- ❖ Checkmark **Open the Write Checks** form with: Select **USA Checking**
- ❖ Checkmark **Open the Pay Bills** form with: Select **USA Checking**
- ❖ Checkmark **Open the Pay Sales Tax** form with: Select **USA Checking**
- ❖ Checkmark **Open the Make Deposits** form with: Select **USA Checking**
- ❖ Click **Company Preferences** tab
- ❖ Checkmark **Warn about duplicate check numbers**
- ❖ Checkmark **Open the Create Paychecks** form with: Select **USA Payroll**
- ❖ Checkmark **Open the Payroll Liabilities** form with: Select **USA Payroll**
- ❖ Click **OK** to enter changes

Finance Charge Preferences

Finance charges can be a legal issue and therefore, must be set with the help of a tax professional or an accountant. You have to find out the industry standard in the business you are operating in, and what Finance Charges customers are suppose to pay. Annual interest rate and the grace period must be provided. You may also set a minimum Finance Charge, and when a customer does not pay a bill by a certain date, your QuickBooks software will enter the charges as you run the process.

Activities:
- ❖ Click **Edit menu**
- ❖ Click **Preferences**
- ❖ Click **Finance Charges** (left column of the window)
- ❖ Click **Company Preferences** tab
- ❖ Annual Interest Rate (%): Type **12**. Press **Tab**
- ❖ Minimum Finance Charge: Type **5**. Press **Tab**
- ❖ Grace Period (days): Type **30**. Press **Tab**
- ❖ Finance Charge Amount: Click **Down arrow**. Click **Add New**
- ❖ Account Name: Type **Misc Income**
- ❖ Click **Save & Close**
- ❖ Click **OK**

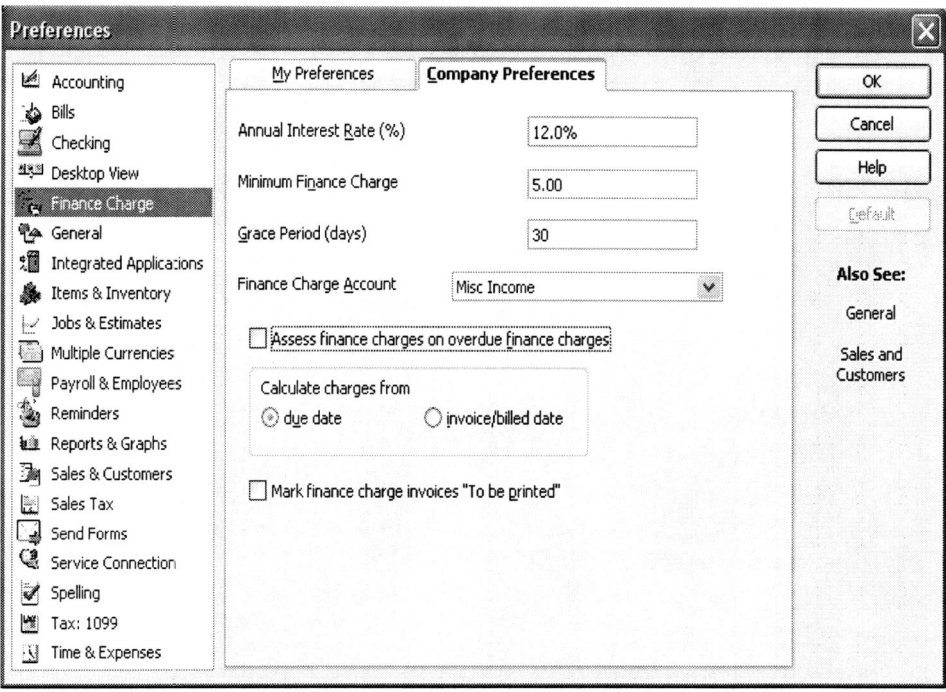

General Preferences

There are many preferences you can set up on your QuickBooks software. You have the more specific ones that relate to a particular window or task, and the general preferences available every time you perform certain tasks in all the windows. A general preference is for QuickBooks to beep every time you record an entry. You must understand where this preference is located. I've seen customers who allow the beep to go on, just because they don't know how to turn it off.

- ❖ Click **Edit menu**
- ❖ Click **Preferences**
- ❖ Click **General** (left column of the window)
- ❖ Click **My Preferences** tab
- ❖ Checkmark **Automatically open drop-down lists...**
- ❖ Uncheck **Beep when recording a transaction**
- ❖ Click **OK** to close window

Integrated Applications & Service Connection

For security reasons, you have to pay particular attention to this exercise. Because QuickBooks respects your privacy, it gives you the option to accept or reject other applications' access to your database. If you don't want other applications to access your QuickBooks files behind your back, you must checkmark the "Don't allow any application to access this company" box. Also, QuickBooks gives you the option of entering your password before connecting to the Internet.

Activities:

- ❖ Click **Edit menu**
- ❖ Click **Preferences**
- ❖ Click **Integrated Applications (left)**
- ❖ Click **Company Preferences** tab
- ❖ Checkmark **Don't allow any application to access this company**
- ❖ Click **Service Connection** (left of the window)
- ❖ Click **Yes** to "You have made changes to Interpreted Application…"
- ❖ Click **My Preferences** tab
- ❖ Checkmark **Give me the option of saving a file whenever…**
- ❖ Checkmark **If QuickBooks is run by my browser**
- ❖ Click **Company Preferences** tab
- ❖ Click **Always ask for a password before connecting**
- ❖ Uncheck **Allow background downloading of service messages**. Click **OK**

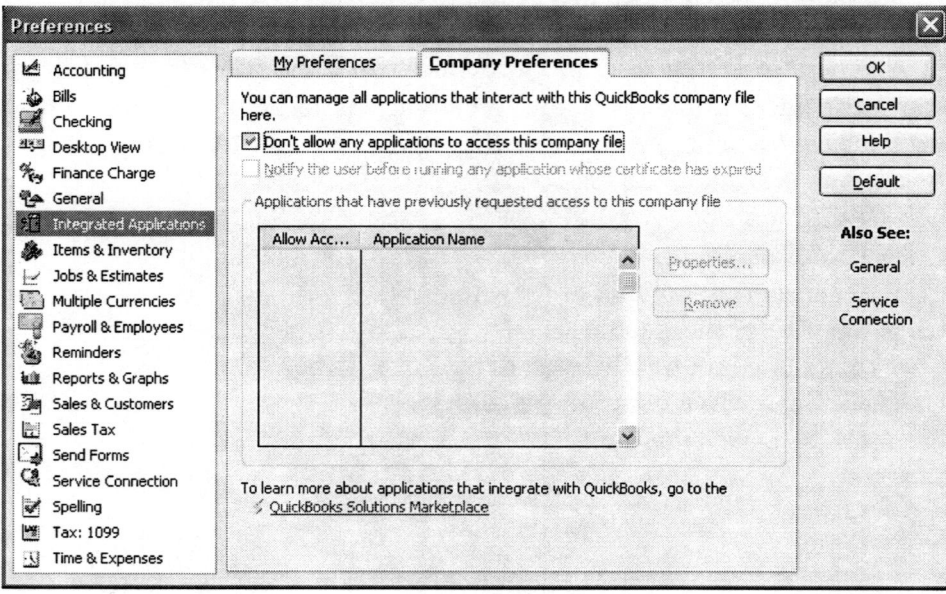

Jobs & Estimates, Sales & Customers

In the Jobs & Estimate preferences windows, there is one check box that is of utmost importance to every QuickBooks user: "Warn about duplicate estimate numbers." You should checkmark this box; it's for your protection. You don't want to accept two estimates; most likely the same company will send you two invoices. So, the earlier you deal with duplicate estimates, the better. In the Sales & Customer Preferences windows, you should check "Warn about duplicate invoice numbers."

Activities:
- ❖ Click **Edit menu**
- ❖ Click **Preferences**
- ❖ Click **Job & Estimates** (left
- ❖ Click **Company Preferences** tab
- ❖ Click **Yes** on Do You Create Estimates?
- ❖ Click **Yes** on Do You Do Progress Invoice?
- ❖ Checkmark **Warn about duplicate estimate numbers**
- ❖ Checkmark **Don't print items that have zero amount**
- ❖ Click **Sales & Customers** (left of the window)
- ❖ Click **Yes** to "You have made changes to Job & Estimates…"
- ❖ Click **OK** to "QuickBooks must close…"
- ❖ Click **Company Preferences** tab
- ❖ Checkmark **Warn about duplicate…**
- ❖ Click **OK**
- ❖ Click **Company menu.** Click **Home Page**

Payroll & Employee Preference

As always, it is advisable to set up your Preferences windows before you embark on practicing with the rest of the payroll and employee windows. It is much more important to set up the Payroll & Employee Preferences first before attempting to work with the submenus. This way, the necessary submenus are activated after the Preferences are set up. More submenus are displayed after you've completed the payroll setup, without which fewer Payroll & Employees submenus are available.

Activities:
- ❖ Click **Edit menu**
- ❖ Click **Preferences**
- ❖ Click **Payroll & Employees** (left of the window)
- ❖ Click **Company Preferences** tab
- ❖ Click **Full Payroll**

❖ Uncheck **Copy earnings details from previous paycheck**
❖ Click **OK** again to close

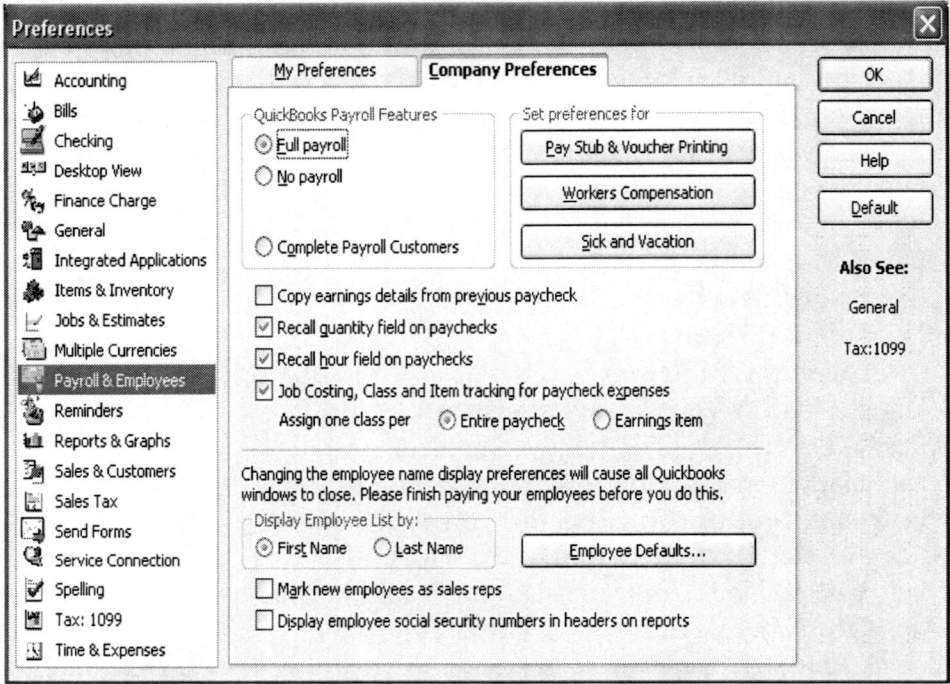

Reminders

Whatever you do, be sure to set up your Reminder Preferences. I will not tell you the cost of missing payments to vendors, including government regulators—you already know! Do not forget to checkmark "Always check spelling before printing." With this preference, your financial reports will have little or no spelling errors. You will uncheck "Show Reminder List," but in actual business settings, you check this box for Reminder to appear each time you open QuickBooks.

Activities:
❖ Click **Edit menu**
❖ Click **Preferences**
❖ Click **Reminders** (left of the window)
❖ Accept **My Preferences** tab
❖ Uncheck **Show Reminders List when opening a Company file**
❖ (Using QuickBooks for your business, checkmark Show Reminder List…)
❖ Click **Company Preferences** tab

❖ Click **all middle options under Show List column**
❖ **See image below**
❖ Click **OK**

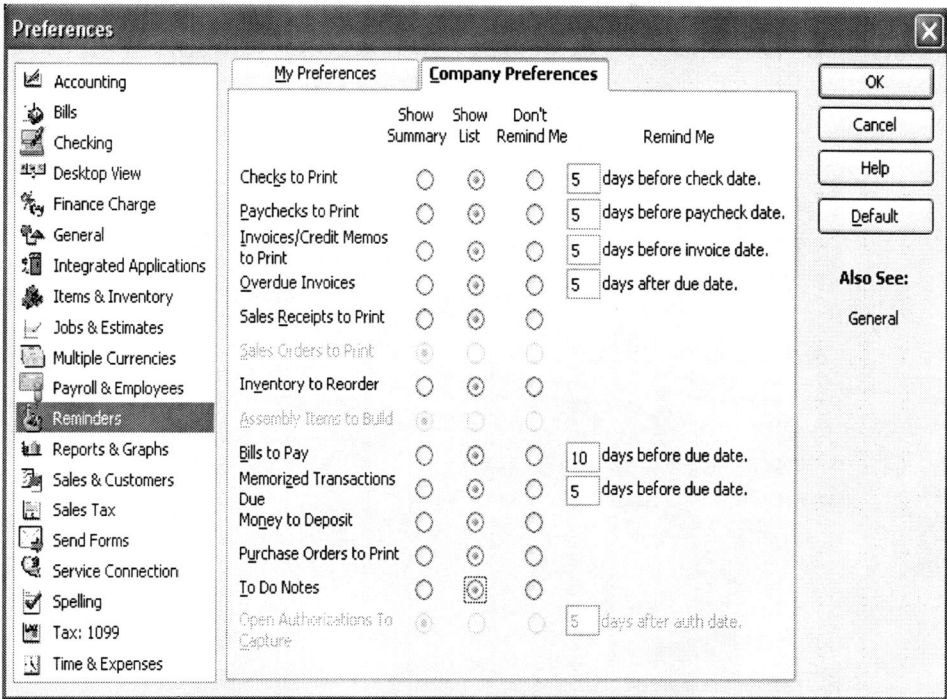

Reports & Graphs

How the report appears when you run the Reports menu will depend on how you set up your Report & Graph Preferences window. You should click the "Refresh automatically" so you don't have to confront the message window that asks you if you want to refresh your Report window. Also, make sure the "Draw Graph in 2D" box is unchecked. Most companies use the Accrual basis of accounting, but if for any reason you're using the Cash basis, you must click the Cash option.

Activities:

❖ Click **Edit menu**
❖ Click **Preferences**
❖ Click **Reports & Graphs** (left of the window)
❖ Click **My Preferences** tab
❖ Click **Refresh automatically…"**
❖ Click **OK**

Sales Tax Preferences

You must understand which items on the Item List window are taxable and which ones are nontaxable. You don't want to be collecting taxes from the public and not remitting them to the government. If you don't know which items are taxable or nontaxable, you should consult with your local tax agency or a tax accountant. You should also set up the Tax Preferences if you want to pay your Sales Tax monthly or quarterly.

Activities:

- ❖ Click **Edit menu**
- ❖ Click **Preferences**
- ❖ Click **Sales Tax**
- ❖ Click **Company Preferences** tab
- ❖ Do you charge sales tax? Click **Yes**
- ❖ Your most common sales tax item:
- ❖ Click **Down arrow.** Click **Add New**
- ❖ Type: Accept **Sales Tax Item**. Press **Tab**
- ❖ Sales Tax Name: Type **TX Sales Tax**
- ❖ Description: Type **Taxable Sales**
- ❖ Tax Rate (%): Type **7.5.** Press **Tab**
- ❖ Tax Agency: Click **Down arrow**
- ❖ Click **Add New**
- ❖ Vendor Name: Type **Texas Comptroller.** Click **OK**
- ❖ Click **OK** again to close new item window
- ❖ Taxable item code: Accept **Tax**
- ❖ Non-Taxable item code: Accept **Non**
- ❖ Click **OK** to close Preference window
- ❖ Click **OK** to Updating Sales Tax
- ❖ Click **OK** to "QuickBooks must close..."
- ❖ Click **Company menu.** Click **Home Page**

Tax: 1099, Time & Expenses

If you have vendors, some of them may qualify for the Form 1099, especially your subcontractors. When setting up the New Vendor windows, click the Additional Info tab and click the "Vendor eligible for 1099" box. Before you create a New Vendor, you must come to the Preference window and click Yes to "Do you file 1099_MISC forms?" If you don't click yes, most Form 1099–related windows will not be activated. You may also set up the Time Tracking preferences here.

Activities:

- ❖ Click **Edit menu**
- ❖ Click **Preferences**
- ❖ Click **Tax: 1099** (bottom left of the window)
- ❖ Click **Company Preferences** tab
- ❖ Click **Yes on "Do you file 1099-MISC forms?"**
- ❖ Click **Time & Expenses** (bottom left of the window
- ❖ Click **Company Preferences** tab
- ❖ Click **Yes** on "Do You Track Time?"
- ❖ First Day of Work Week: Accept **Monday**. Click **OK**

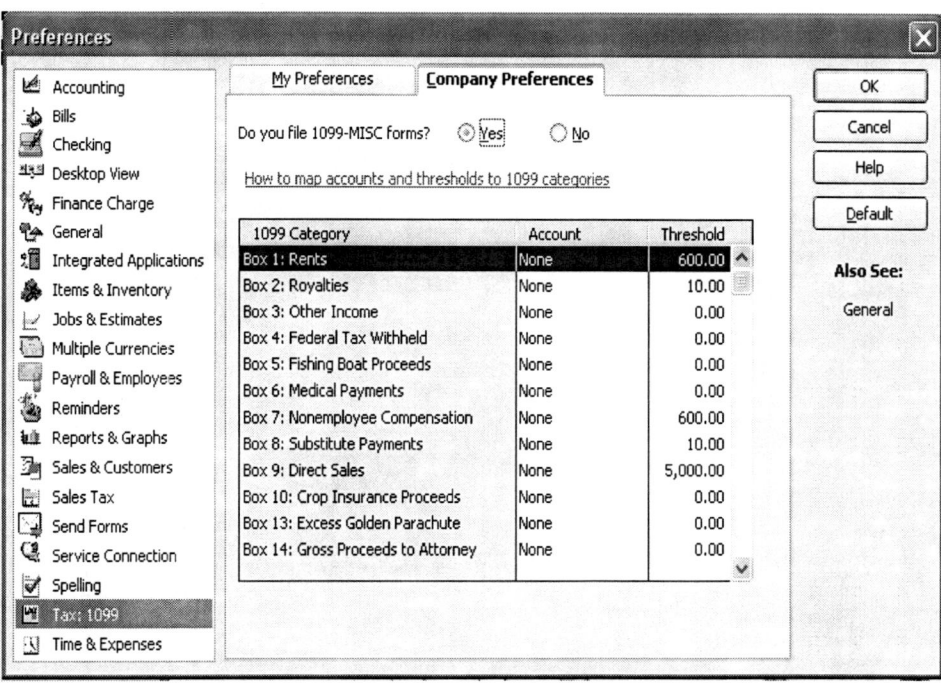

Financial Results: Profit & Loss

In this chapter, we made a transaction in the check register for Telephone America for 150.00, which is reflected on the Profit & Loss statement. **It is extremely important that after you open a financial report, you change the date.** In most of the reports, you will be asked to select "This Fiscal Year"; otherwise, your results will not match the results in this book. You must look at the "From" and "To" text boxes to make sure you have the right dates.

Activities:

- ❖ Click **Reports menu**
- ❖ Click **Company & Financial**
- ❖ Click **Profit & Loss Standard**
- ❖ Date: Select **This Fiscal Year**
- ❖ From: Accept **1/1/09**
- ❖ To: Accept **12/31/09**
- ❖ **Net Income 999,850.00**
- ❖ Click **X** to close window
- ❖ Checkmark **Do not display this message….** Click **No**

Quick Payroll 2009

Profit & Loss

January through December 2009

	⋄ **Jan - Dec 09** ⋄
Ordinary Income/Expense	
Income	
Uncategorized Income	▶ 1,005,000.00 ◀
Total Income	1,005,000.00
Gross Profit	1,005,000.00
Expense	
Travel Expense	150.00
Uncategorized Expenses	5,000.00
Total Expense	5,150.00
Net Ordinary Income	999,850.00
Net Income	**999,850.00**

Financial Results: Balance Sheet

Because we wrote a check for 150.00 to Telephone America, the USA Checking account balance is reduced by that amount. Let me reiterate once again that you must click the Date down arrow any time you open a financial report and select This Fiscal Year; otherwise, your figures will not match the book's result. The date on a Profit & Loss statement is between two periods; however, the date on a Balance Sheet report is "as of" a given date. This is a major difference between the two reports.

Activities:

- ❖ Click **Reports menu**
- ❖ Click **Company & Financial**
- ❖ Click **Balance Sheet Standard**
- ❖ Date (top left): Select **This Fiscal Year**
- ❖ As of: Accept **12/31/09**
- ❖ **Total Asset 2,054,850.00**
- ❖ Click **X** to close window

```
                    Quick Payroll 2009
                    Balance Sheet
                  As of December 31, 2009

                                    ◇  Dec 31, 09  ◇
        ASSETS
          Current Assets
            Checking/Savings
              USA Checking          ▶   799,850.00 ◀
              USA Payroll               250,000.00
            Total Checking/Savings    1,049,850.00

            Accounts Receivable
              Accounts Receivable     1,005,000.00
            Total Accounts Receivable 1,005,000.00

          Total Current Assets        2,054,850.00

        TOTAL ASSETS                  2,054,850.00
```

Chapter Summary

If you want great results from your QuickBooks software, setting up preferences is very essential and in this section, we accomplished just that. We covered all the set up preferences that are necessary to integrate all the windows and provide a smooth ride throughout your journey with QuickBooks. You should pay particular attention to the set ups we covered and what options we selected during the process, because preferences affect the entire QuickBooks output, not just the Employees and Payroll section.

What we accomplished:
- Reviewed the Edit submenus
- Backed up Quick Payroll
- Restored backup and called it Quick Payroll 2009
- Made an entry in the check register
- Practiced using the calculator
- Practiced using the find functions
- Set up preferences
- Processed financial statements

Financial activities:
- Made a entry Telephone America for 150.00

Optional Test 2

Questions: True/False

Answer the following questions by placing letter the T or F in the space provided before the question number.

_____ 1. If you want to get more submenus activated under the Edit menu, you can do so by just opening the QuickBooks Home Page, instead of a Check Register.

_____ 2. Notepad will be activated if you click on a check-related entry in the Check Register.

_____ 3. Though it is not advisable to do so, QuickBooks allows you to delete a check even if it was written last year.

_____ 4. If you click an amount in a Check Register and press the equation sign (=) or the plus sign (+), QuickMath is activated.

_____ 5. In using the Calculator, QuickBooks will not allow you to use the keyboard to key the numbers, you must always use the mouse to click the numbers.

_____ 6. You can delete a check as long as you are in the Check Register, you will not be allowed to do so if you are in the write check window.

_____ 7. Once you make an account inactive it is permanent, QuickBooks will not allow you to change the inactivity.

_____ 8. The Find function allows you to find information relating to a customer, but not allow you to find information relating to a vendor.

_____ 9. If you want to hear a beeping sound or not when entering a transaction you can set it up by going to the General window under the Preferences submenu.

_____ 10. If you want Reminders window to pop up every time you open a company you can set it up by going to the Alert Manager window under the Preferences submenu.

Questions: Multiple Choices

Answer the following questions by placing letter A, B, C, or D in the space provided before the question number.

_____ 1. From time to time, you may have a need to write a check to the same vendor for the same amount, which of the following actions is recommended about the check?
A. Create a new check
B. Modify the check
C. Memorize the check
D. Document the check

_____ 2. In using the Find tool which of the following is NOT a Transaction Type information you can locate in the window?
A. Invoice
B. Bill
C. Check
D. Accounts Payable

_____ 3. In a Check Register you cannot run the Go To Transfer tool on an entry if it has which of the following accounts?
A. Asset
B. Expense
C. Liability
D. Equity

_____ 4. To create a note you must launch the Notepad and click a payment related entry in which of the following windows?
A. Receipt
B. Invoice
C. Bill
D. Register

_____ 5. If you want QuickBooks to display the Reminders List window every time you open a company you set it up in which of the following windows?
A. Alert Manager
B. Reminders
C. Account List
D. Notepad

_____ 6. If a check has not been cashed by a vendor within six months, which of
     the following is the best way to handle the check?
     A. Delete the date
     B. Delete the Name
     C. Delete the Memo line
     D. Delete the amount

_____ 7. You can write a check from different windows, which of the following is
     the best QuickBooks window for writing a check?
     A. Report check
     B. Print check
     C. Write check
     D. Deposit check

_____ 8. There are different ways of opening a Check Register, but through the Edit
     Menu, you must click which of the following submenu?
     A. Use Banking
     B. Use Register
     C. Use Account
     D. Use Checkbook

_____ 9. The submenus that defaults under the Edit menu depends on the windows
     you open, which of the following is NOT an Edit submenu?
     A. Notepad
     B. Preferences
     C. Chart of Accounts
     D. Calculator

_____10. If you don't want QuickBooks to connect to the internet automatically but
     always ask you for a password before connecting, you set it up in which of
     the following Preferences windows?
     A. Service Connections
     B. Reminders
     C. Integrated Applications
     D. Alert Manager

$

Chapter 3

View Menu

Objectives: After you've completed this chapter you will be able to:
- ✓ Explain the View submenus
- ✓ Customize the icon bar
- ✓ Implement the "add window to icon bar" process
- ✓ Run financial reports and compare your results
- ✓ Review the payroll tax guidelines

Review View Submenus

When you think about the View menu, you think about what you can see on your Desktop. Most icons on your desktop are defaults. In other words, they have been preset by QuickBooks. For example, if you want to change what you see on the Tool or Icon Bar, click the Customize Icon Bar to add or subtract the Icons. The easy access to these Icons is worth every second you spend in setting them up.

- Click **View menu**

The following submenus are located under the View menu:

- **Open Window List:** Most of the time, you want to have the Open Window List displayed on the left side of the window and, other times, you want the list to go away so you can have enough space to display the main window. When you click View menu and uncheck the Open Window List, the list will disappear. But it's vital to display the Open Window List so you can always reach for it instead of first clicking the menus and then the submenus.

- **Icon bar:** Tool bar or the Icon bar, as QuickBooks calls it, is where you will place the most frequently used tools. Check Registers, Customers, Vendors, and Reports should be placed on the Icon bar for easy access.

- **Customize Icon bar:** Not only are you able to place tools on the Tool bar, you can also customize the Tool bar the way you see fit. Customization, for example, allows you to rearrange the position of the tools and allows you to add, edit and delete tools.

- **Add "USA Checking" to Icon bar:** After you've opened a favorite window, such as the USA Checking register window, you can decide whether to place the window on the Tool bar for easy access. This is one of the most popular functions under the View menu.

- **One/Multiple Windows:** These two functions work in reverse to one another; that is, if your window is on the One Window default, you can switch to the Multiple Windows by clicking on the function. When you click Multiple Windows function, you will be able to move multiple windows you've opened to the left or to the right, up or down the screen as you see fit.

Customize Icon Bar

You can customize your Icon bar by adding, removing, or editing icons. Reordering the Icon bar is also one of the easiest tasks in QuickBooks. It is recommended that you place the most frequently used windows on the Icon bar for easy access, instead of going through the menus each time. Be sure you have enough room on the Icon bar to place your icon; otherwise, it will be hidden where you cannot see it immediately. You may have to delete some icons to make room.

Activities:

❖ Click **View menu**
❖ Click **Customize Icon Bar**
❖ Click **Add…**
❖ Scroll down to the bottom (left of the window)
❖ Click **Use Register**. Click **OK**
❖ Click **Reg**
❖ Click **Edit…**
❖ Label: Type **Register**
❖ Description: Accept **Use Register**. Click **OK**
❖ Click **Add…**
❖ Click **Adjust Sales Tax**.(left window) Click **OK**
❖ Click **Adjust Tax**.
❖ Click **Delete**
❖ Click **OK** (bottom) to close Customize Icon bar window

Add Window to Icon Bar

Adding windows to the Icon bar, I think, is one of the best features on your QuickBooks software. Can you imagine adding your favorite windows like reports to the Icon bar list? It is now possible. All you have to do is open that hard-to-reach window, click the View menu, and then Add Window to the Icon Bar. In less than a second, you now have your favorite window listed with other icons. Bank accounts and financial statements reports are the best candidates for the Icon bar.

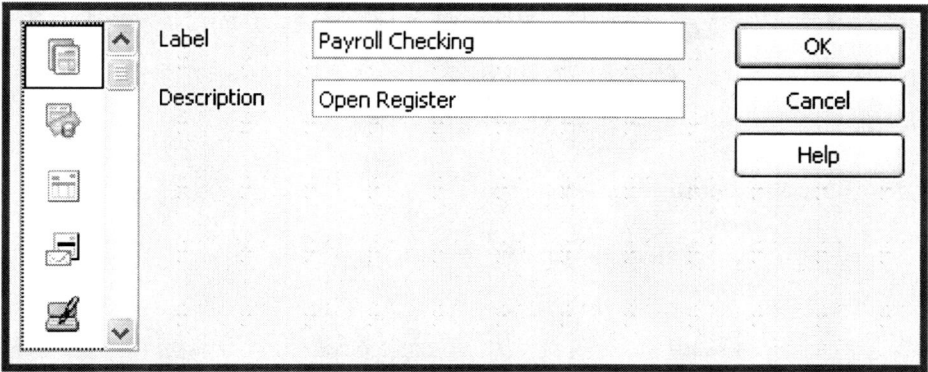

Activities:

- ❖ Click **Edit menu**
- ❖ Click **Use Register**
- ❖ Select Account: Select **USA Payroll**. Click **OK**
- ❖ Click **View menu**
- ❖ Click **Add "USA Payroll" to Icon Bar**
- ❖ Label: Accept **USA Payroll**
- ❖ Description: Accept **Open Register**. Click **OK**
- ❖ Click the **double arrow** at the end of the toolbar
- ❖ Click **USA Payroll** to open
- ❖ Click **X** to close USA Payroll check register

Financial Results: Profit & Loss

In the View menu chapter, we concentrated on navigating through QuickBooks. We used One Window and Multiple Windows functions. We did not perform any entries that increased or decreased any account in the Profit & Loss statements. You may customize your financial report by clicking Modify Report located at the top left of the report window, then Header/Footer tab. This window allows you to make changes to the way you want your reports to look.

Activities:

- ❖ Click **Reports menu**
- ❖ Click **Company & Financial**
- ❖ Click **Profit & Loss Standard**
- ❖ Date (top left): Select **This Fiscal Year**
- ❖ From: Accept **1/1/09.** To: Accept **12/31/09**
- ❖ **Net Income 999,850.00**
- ❖ Click **X** to close window

```
                        Quick Payroll 2009
                        Profit & Loss
                  January through December 2009

                                        ◇ Jan - Dec 09 ◇
        Ordinary Income/Expense
          Income
            Uncategorized Income      ▶ 1,005,000.00 ◀
            Total Income                1,005,000.00

          Gross Profit                  1,005,000.00

          Expense
            Travel Expense                    150.00
            Uncategorized Expenses          5,000.00
            Total Expense                   5,150.00

          Net Ordinary Income             999,850.00

        Net Income                        999,850.00
```

Financial: Balance Sheet

Like the Profit & Loss statement above, the Balance Sheet result is unchanged. We started Total Assets with 2,054,850.00, and we ended with the same amount. Note that the report below did not include the Total Liabilities & Equity, the bottom half of this report, because of space. However, the Total Assets and Total Liabilities & Equity will always be the same number. If your result is different from the book's result, it may be that you have not selected the right date range—"This Fiscal Year."

```
                    Quick Payroll 2009
                    Balance Sheet
                 As of December 31, 2009
                                        ◇  Dec 31, 09  ◇
            ASSETS
              Current Assets
                Checking/Savings
                  USA Checking          ▶   799,850.00  ◀
                  USA Payroll               250,000.00
                  Total Checking/Savings  1,049,850.00

                Accounts Receivable
                  Accounts Receivable      1,005,000.00
                  Total Accounts Receivable  1,005,000.00

                Total Current Assets      2,054,850.00

            TOTAL ASSETS                  2,054,850.00
```

Activities:

- ❖ Click **Reports menu**
- ❖ Click **Company & Financial**
- ❖ Click **Balance Sheet Standard**
- ❖ Date (top left): Select **This Fiscal Year**
- ❖ As of: Accept **12/31/09**
- ❖ Click **Collapse**
- ❖ **Total Assets 2,054,850.00**
- ❖ Click **X** to close window

> Remember to always select "This Fiscal Year" to view the financial report for this year. Your total assets must be equal to your total Liabilities & Equity.

Tax Guidelines

The rest of this chapter is devoted to the IRS guidelines relating to business and payroll taxes. In addition to consulting a tax professional, the IRS would like you to have a basic understanding of these tax rules. You need to login to their website www.irs.gov to review the guidelines. Let's look at a few of theses from the IRS website:

Major tax guidelines relating to payroll are:

Starting a business
Business structures
Employer identification number
Business taxes
Record keeping
Employment tax record keeping

Starting a business

When you're conducting a business you need to know if what you're doing is considered a business for tax purposes. If your activity is not considered a business, it is a called a hobby. Your activity is considered a business if you make profit in at least three of the last five tax years including the current year. If your business consists primarily of breeding, showing, training or racing horses, you are required to show profit in at least two of the last seven years. Other considerations are:

- Does the time and effort put into the activity indicate an intention to make a profit?
- Does the taxpayer depend on the income from the activity?
- If there are losses, are they due to circumstances beyond the taxpayer's control or did they occur in the start-up phase of the business?
- Has the taxpayer changed methods of operation to improve profitability?
- Does the taxpayer or his/her advisors have the knowledge needed to carry on the activity as a successful business?
- Has the taxpayer made a profit in similar activities in the past?
- Does the activity make a profit in some years?
- Can the taxpayer expect to make a profit in the future from the appreciation of assets used in the activity?

Business Structures

QuickBooks gives you options to choose which business structure you are setting up. The name of the structure you chose determines the chart of accounts QuickBooks defaults in the new company. And according to the IRS, there are five major business structures namely:

- Sole Proprietorship
- Partnership
- Corporation
- S Corporation
- Limited Liability Company (LLC)

Employer Identification Number (EIN)

Generally, businesses need the EIN, otherwise know as the Employer Identification Number. You can apply for this number through the IRS and it is a free service. You will need an EIN, if you answer yes to any of the following:

- Do you have employees?
- Do you operate your business as a corporation or a partnership?
- Do you file any of these tax returns: Employment, Excise, or Alcohol, Tobacco and Firearms?
- Do you withhold taxes on income other than wages paid to a non-resident alien?
- Do you have a Keogh plan?
- Are you involved with any of the following types of organizations?
    - ✓ Trusts except certain grantor-owned revocable trusts, IRAs Exempt Organization Business Income Tax Return
    - ✓ Estates
    - ✓ Real estate mortgage investment conduits
    - ✓ Non-profit organization
    - ✓ Farmers cooperatives
    - ✓ Plan administrators

In general, you need a new EIN when you change ownership or business structure. For sole proprietors, you need a new EIN if any of the following are true:

- You are subject to a bankruptcy proceeding
- You incorporate
- You take in partners and operate as a partnership
- You purchase or inherit an existing business that you operate as a sole proprietorship.

You will not be required to obtain a new EIN if any of the following statements are true:
- You change the name of your business
- You change your location and/or add other locations
- You operate multiple businesses

Business Taxes

The form of business you operate determines what taxes you pay. There are four general types of business taxes:
- Income Tax
- Self-Employment Tax
- Employment Taxes
- Excise Tax

Self-employment tax or the SE tax is a Social Security and Medicare tax primarily for individuals who work for themselves. Your Social Security coverage provides you with retirement benefits, disability benefits, survivor benefits, and hospital insurance (Medicare) benefits. You must pay SE tax and file Schedule SE (Form 1040) if either of the following applies:

- If your net earnings from self-employment were $400 or more
- If you work for a church or a qualified church-controlled organization (other than as a minister or member of a religious order) that elected an exemption from social security and Medicare taxes, you are subject to SE tax if you receive $108.28 or more in wages from the church or organization.

Employment taxes are required when you have employees and you must file the related forms. The following are the employment taxes:
- Social Security and Medicare taxes
- Federal income tax withholding
- Federal unemployment (FUTA) tax

Record Keeping

Businesses must keep accurate records if they plan to be profitable. You may not keep your records forever and therefore should follow certain guidelines in keeping or destroying records. The length of the time you keep your records depends on the action, expense, or event the document records. These are the general guidelines on how long to keep your records:

- Keep for 3 years: if you owe additional tax and you reported all your income in the previous years and you did not file a fraudulent returns and you filed a return.
- Keep for 6 years: if you did not report all income that you should have been reported and it is more than 25% of the gross income shown on your return
- Keep indefinitely: if you file a fraudulent return.
- Keep indefinitely: if you did not file a return.
- Keep for 3 years from the date you filed your original return: if you file a claim for credit or refund after you file your return or keep for 2 years from the date you paid the tax whichever is later.
- Keep for 7 years: if you file a claim for a loss from worthless securities or bad debt deduction.
- Keep for at least 4 years: for all employment tax records after the tax due date or tax is paid whichever is later.

Employment Tax Record Keeping

Extra care must be given to employment documents especially payroll and tax related documents. You are required to keep employment taxes for at least four years after filing the 4th quarter of the year. The following records should be available for IRS review:

- Your employer identification number
- Amounts and dates of all wages, annuity, and pension payments
- Amounts of tips reported
- The fair market value of in-kind wages paid
- Names, addresses, social security numbers, and occupations of employees and recipients
- Any employee copies of Form W-2 that were returned to you as undeliverable
- Date of employment
- Periods for which employees and recipients were paid while absent due to sickness or injury and the amount and weekly rate of payments you or third-party payers made to them.
- Copies of employees and recipients income tax withholding allowance certificates (Form W-4, W-4P, W-4S, and W-4V)
- Dates and amounts of tax deposits you made
- Copies of returns filed
- Records of allocated tips
- Records of fringe benefits provided including substantiation

Chapter Summary

There is not much to the View menu except the Icon bar and the Open Window List. With practice, you can understand how to manipulate other functions under the View menu, such as the One and Multiple Windows functions. Both functions allow you to either view one window at a time or view multiple windows by dragging the windows around. The Open Window List is handy because it allows you an instant access to Open Window rather than going through the menus each time you want to open a window.

What we accomplished:
- Reviewed the View submenus
- Learned how to customize icons
- Learned how to attach windows to the icon bar
- Processed financial statements
- Reviewed starting a business
- Reviewed business structures
- Reviewed employer identification number
- Reviewed business taxes
- Reviewed record keeping
- Reviewed employment tax record keeping

Additional Financial activities:
- No financial activities

Optional Test 3

Questions: True/False
Answer the following questions by placing letter the T or F in the space provided before the question number.

_____ 1. In the Customize Icon Bar window you can be able to add and edit icons but not be able to delete icons.

_____ 2. If you want to have a quick access to windows you have already opened you would click the Navigation Bar.

_____ 3. You can be able to move windows around by grabbing the subtitle bar of the window if you click the One Window submenu.

_____ 4. By un-checking the Navigation Bar submenu under the View menu, you will remove the major menu centers from the icon bar.

_____ 5. By un-checking Icon Bar submenu under the View menu, you will be able to see some minor submenus on the Icon Bar.

Questions: Multiple Choices
Answer the following questions by placing letter A, B, C, or D in the space provided before the question number.

_____ 1. By un-checking the Navigation Bar submenu under the View menu, which of the following Icons will you be able to see?
   A. Customer
   B. Vendor
   C. Employee
   D. Reminders

_____ 2. You are trying to open a submenu, which of the following will NOT be able to display in the Open Window List?
   A. Chart of Accounts
   B. Check Register
   C. Reports
   D. Exit

_____ 3. You are trying to customize a window, before you can do that you must checkmark which of the following submenus?
   A. Open Window List
   B. Navigation Bar
   C. Icon Bar
   D. All of the above

_____ 4. You have already opened some windows, which of the following view submenus would allow you to move the opened windows around?
   A. One Window
   B. Multiple Windows
   C. Double Window
   D. Linked Window

_____ 5. You want to have easy access to a window on the Icon Bar, which of the following windows can you be able to add to the Icon Bar?
   A. Check register
   B. Reports
   C. Chart of Accounts
   D. All of the above

$

Chapter 4

Lists Menu

Objectives: After you've completed this chapter you will be able to:

- ✓ Identify the Lists submenus
- ✓ Identify chart of accounts listing
- ✓ Create accounts in the chart of accounts
- ✓ Merge main and sub accounts
- ✓ Design financial reports
- ✓ Create items and sub items in the item list
- ✓ Create price level items in the price level list
- ✓ Create sales tax items in the sales tax code list
- ✓ Create class items in the class list
- ✓ Complete the customer & vendor profile lists
- ✓ Complete the memorized transactions list
- ✓ Run financial reports and compare your results

Review Lists Submenus

The Lists menu is one of the most useful menus in QuickBooks, in terms of setting up accounts and items, because this is where the foundation of your ivory tower is laid. If the concrete is not strong and the steel is not properly laid and connected, sooner or later the entire building will come crashing down. I have seen customers spend thousands of dollars trying to correct mistakes that should have never happened in the first place, if they knew how to use QuickBooks. This is where an "I can do it" attitude can get you into trouble if you did not set up your Chart of Accounts and Item List window correctly.

- Click **Lists menu**

The following submenus are located under the Lists menu:

- **Chart of Accounts:** Any time you think about accounts, you should think Chart of Accounts. Whether you are creating a new account or editing an old one, you can't do it without the Chart of Accounts window. It lets you write checks and make deposits. You can access the windows in the Chart of Accounts by right clicking anywhere in the window. If an account is associated with another account or an item, it cannot be deleted. Some functions cannot be accessed by right clicking in the window, but rather by clicking the account button.

- **Item List:** By implication, if you are using the Chart of Accounts to create accounts, you will be using the Item List to create items. Items can be what you sell to your customers or what you buy from vendors. The purpose of the Item List is to keep records of all items, sort of a warehouse where every item that pulls into QuickBooks windows is stored.

- **Fixed Asset Item List:** Fixed items are long-lived assets used in the operation of a business. If you are going to pull certain Fixed Assets information into QuickBooks windows, you have to set them up in the Item List window. Major assets such as Trucks, Building, Equipments, and Computer are recorded in the Fixed Asset windows. Remember Fixed Assets are also recorded in the Chart of Accounts first. The difference between the Fixed Asset window and the Chart of Accounts windows is that Fixed Asset has full details of each asset, while Chart of Accounts has limited information of the assets, such as amount. Like other accounts in the Chart of Accounts window, you can change the opening balance when you know the original amount is incorrect.

- **Price Level List:** Whether you are in a product or services business, sometimes, you have different price levels for different types of customers. If you have price levels in your pricing policy, you should let QuickBooks know by completing this window, because sooner or later in one of the windows, you will be required to pull the price level.

- **Sales Tax Code List:** You have to let QuickBooks know whether or not you collect taxes or not from your customers. If you do, you will have to choose the sales tax code to be included anytime you sell merchandise with tax. You are also able to pay and Adjust Sales Tax from this window.

- **Payroll Item List:** If you have employees and plan to use QuickPayroll, it is imperative to list your Payroll Items. QuickBooks will preload most of the Payroll Items for you. However, you must double check to see if you need additional Payroll Items, which you can create by right clicking in the Payroll Item List window and clicking New to complete the window. You may not see this submenu until you complete the Employees menu.

- **Class List:** If you have more than one type of business line, it is recommended that you use the Class List. It will help you monitor income and expenses by Class or line of business. When one class is identified as making more money than others, you want to know why. As you find out what you're doing right in that business, you can leverage that experience to other lines of businesses.

- **Other Names List:** You might have other names that are not a good fit with other list windows. The Other Names List window is the place to come anytime you have a name that is not related to other names, for example, Transfer to Checking, Transfer to Saving, Transfer from Checking, and Transfer from Savings. These are names that belong to the Other Names List window.

- **Customer & Vendor Profile Lists:** This is a unique submenu that keeps other lists not included above. The Profile List has many lists including Sales Rep, Customer Type, Vendor Type, Job Type, Term, Customer Message, Payment Method, Ship Via, and Vehicle List.

- **Templates:** It is to your benefit to preview what's available in the Template window. You do not need to waste time duplicating effort by creating forms that are already provided for you. The following are available in the template: Invoice, Credit Memo, Sales Receipt, Purchase Order, and Sales Order.

- **Memorized Transaction List:** If you have recurring transactions, it is efficient to memorize that transaction, rather than manually processing the same information on a daily, weekly, or monthly basis. You don't want to process the same transaction every week to a customer or vendor when you can just memorize it. It is also highly recommended that you group your transactions according to time—daily, weekly, monthly, quarterly or annually.

Review Chart of Accounts

The Chart of Accounts is where you create and manage all your accounts. You open accounts mainly by going through the Chart of Accounts window. Depending on the type of business you selected at the time you created the Company and how you set your Preferences, QuickBooks will create certain accounts for you. The five major account types are Assets, Liabilities, Equity, Income, and Expenses.

The following are sample accounts for Assets, Liabilities and Equities:

Account	Category
Payroll Checking	Bank
USA Checking	Bank
USA Saving	Bank
Money Market Account	Bank
Prepaid Insurance	Other Current Assets
Accounts Receivable	Account Receivable
Inventory Asset	Other Current Asset
Furniture and Equipment	Fixed Asset
Cars & Trucks	Fixed Asset
Accum Depreciation	Fixed Asset
Original Cost	Fixed Asset
Accounts Payable	Liability
Payroll Liability	Other Current Liability
Sales Tax Liability	Other Current Liability
Mortgage Loan	Long Term Liability
Office Building Loan	Long Term Liability
Opening Bal Equity	Equity
Owner's Equity	Equity
Owner's Contribution	Equity
Owner's Distribution	Equity
Owner's Retained Earning	Equity

The following are sample accounts for Income and Expenses:

Landscaping Services	Income
Equipment Rental	Income
Job Materials	Income
Labor	Income
Supplies	Income
Subcontractors	Income
Markup	Income
Discount Received	Income
Cost of Goods Sold	Cost of Good Sold
Materials	Cost of Good Sold
Supplies	Cost of Good Sold
Misc	Cost of Good Sold
Automobile	Expense
Insurance	Expense
Fuel	Expense
Repairs & Maintenance	Expense
License & Registration	Expense
Bank Charges	Expense
Delivery Charges	Expense
Job Expenses-Subcontractors	Expense
Insurance	Expense
Disability	Expense
Liability Insurance	Expense
Worker Compensation	Expense
Office Expenses	Expense
Office Rental	Expense
Professional Fees	Expense
Accounting	Expense
Legal	Expense
Repairs	Expense
Computer	Expense
Faxes	Expense
Other Equipments	Expense
Federal	Expense

QuickBooks will not allow you to delete an account if it has a balance. Right click on the account and click QuickReport at the bottom of the list to see the account details. Then you can move the balance to other accounts before you try to delete.

Bank Account: Money Market

When you think about managing accounts such as creating, editing, or deleting, you think Chart of Accounts window. QuickBooks will default some of the accounts based on the type of business you selected when you created the company. When creating a new account, remember to enter the opening balance and the date of the new account. If you have multiple bank accounts, use the Next button to enter the next account instead of leaving and entering the Chart of Accounts window.

Activities:

- ❖ Click **Lists menu**
- ❖ Click **Chart of Accounts. Maximize window**
- ❖ Right click in the window
- ❖ Click **New**
- ❖ Click **Bank**. Click **Continue**
- ❖ Account Name: Type **Money Market Account**
- ❖ Click **Enter Opening Balance…**
- ❖ Opening Balance: Type **100,000** as of: Type **1/1/09.** Click **OK**
- ❖ Click **Save & Close** to close window
- ❖ Click **No** to Set up online services

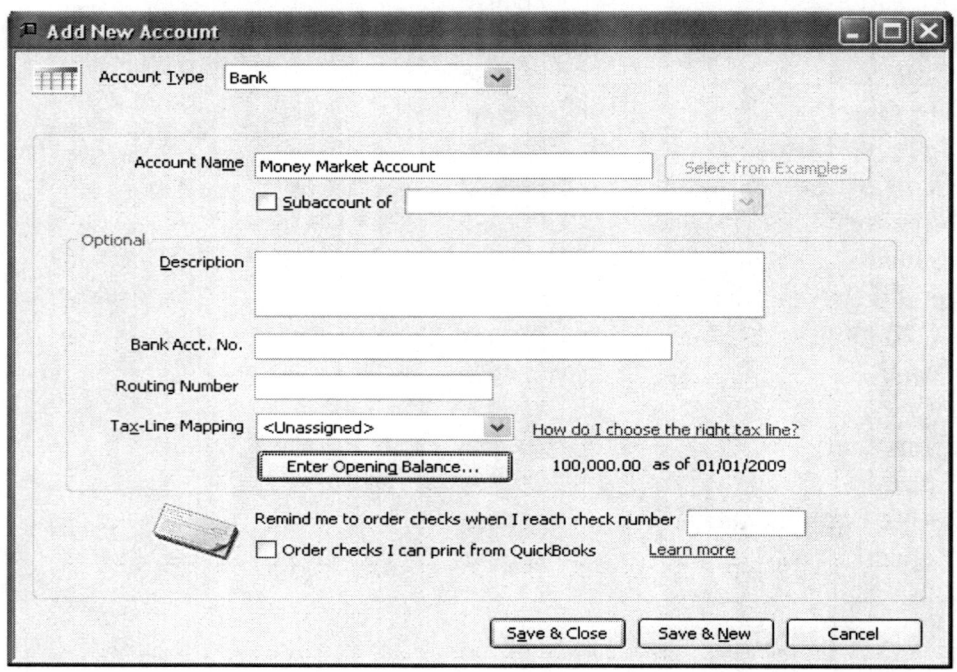

Fixed Asset: Truck

After creating bank accounts, sometimes you may have assets you need to bring into the Company. Bear in mind that most assets depreciate over time and, therefore, a corresponding Depreciation Expense and an Accumulated Depreciation accounts should be created. As usual, you need to complete the opening balance amount and the opening date you're employing the asset into your business. The opening balance and date are the closing balance and ending date from your old books.

Activities:

- ❖ Right click in the Chart of Accounts window
- ❖ Click **New**
- ❖ Click **Fixed Asset (major purchases)**
- ❖ Click **Continue**
- ❖ Account Name: Type **Truck**
- ❖ Click **Enter Opening Balance…**
- ❖ Opening Balance: Type **0.00** as of: Type **1/1/09.** Click **OK**
- ❖ Click **Save & New**
- ❖ Account Name: Type **Truck at Cost**
- ❖ Click **Sub-account of**: Select **Truck**
- ❖ Click **Enter Opening Balance**
- ❖ Opening Balance: Type **40,000** as of: Type **1/1/09.** Click **OK**
- ❖ Click **Save & Close** to close window
- ❖ Right click **Accumulated Depreciation** (towards the top left of the window)
- ❖ Click **Edit Account**
- ❖ Account Name: Accept **Accumulated Depreciation**
- ❖ Click **Sub-account of**: Select **Truck**
- ❖ Click **Save & Close**

Credit Card: Visa Credit Card

Credit Card may be one of the new accounts you would like to create for your business. It's vital to remember that you should select Credit Card as the Account Type. There may be different credit cards for different purposes. It is essential to complete the description box, so anybody can see for what purpose an account was created. The tax line for credit card is Unassigned because QuickBooks has pre-assigned the right tax line for your business.

Activities:

- ❖ Right click in the Chart of Accounts window
- ❖ Click **New**
- ❖ Click **Credit Card**
- ❖ Click **Continue**
- ❖ Account Name: Type **Visa Credit Card**
- ❖ Click **Enter Opening Balance**
- ❖ Statement Ending Balance: Type **500**
- ❖ Statement Ending Date Type **1/2/09**
- ❖ Click **OK** to close window.
- ❖ Click **Save & Close.** Click **No** to Set up online service.

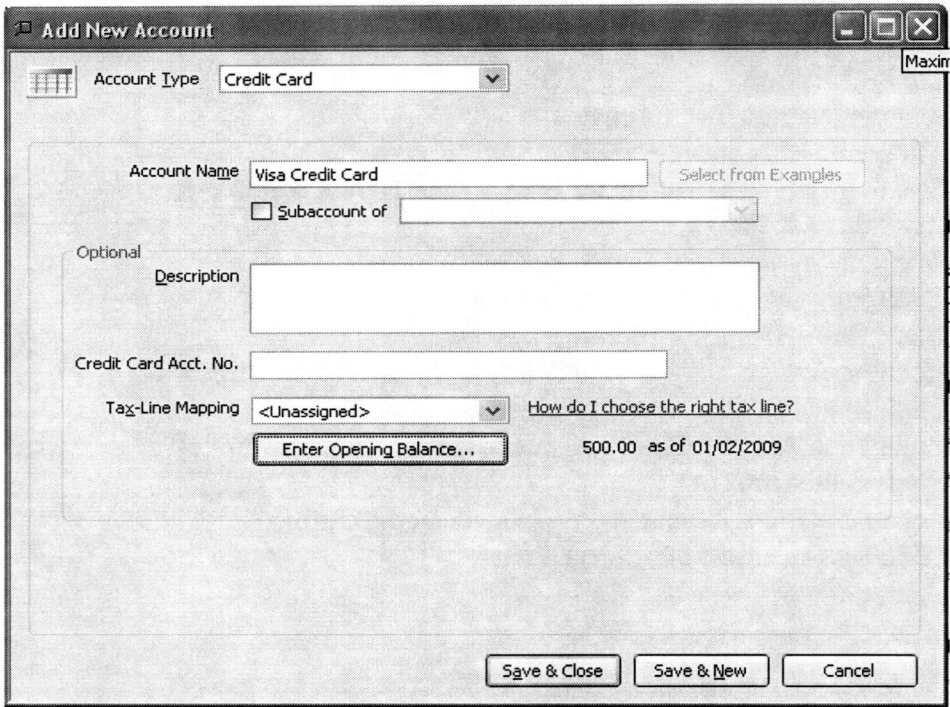

Equities: Owners Account

Before you start your business, you have assets in the form of cash, furniture or equipment you want bring into your business. When you first record these assets, they represent Equities to you. Hence, creating equity accounts is a requirement before you start operating your business. QuickBooks will default few equity accounts; however, your job is to create additional equity accounts and organize them the way you want to see them on the financial reports.

Activities:

- ❖ In the Chart of Accounts window
- ❖ Right click **Owners Equity**
- ❖ Click **Edit Account**
- ❖ Account Name: Type **Owners Retained Earnings**
- ❖ Click **Save & Close**
- ❖ Right click in the window
- ❖ Click **New**
- ❖ Click **Equity**
- ❖ Click **Continue**
- ❖ Account Name: Type **Owners Equity**
- ❖ Click **Save & New**
- ❖ Account Name: Type **Owners Contribution**
- ❖ Click **Sub-account** of: Select **Owners Equity**
- ❖ Click **Save & Close**
- ❖ Right click **Owners Draw**
- ❖ Click **Edit Account**
- ❖ Account Name: Type **Owners Distribution**
- ❖ Click **Sub-account of:** Select **Owners Equity**
- ❖ Click **Save & Close**

Income: Main Accounts

After you've created the equity accounts, the next step is to create the income accounts. Unless you have money already in the bank, before you can write checks and spend money, you must sell something. In this section, you are going to create the income accounts that are related to the product you will sell or the services you will render to your customers. Opening sales balances are regarded as uncategorized income by QuickBooks.

Activities:

- ❖ Click **Lists menu**
- ❖ Click **Chart of Accounts. Maximize**
- ❖ Right click **Sales**
- ❖ Click **Edit Account**
- ❖ Account Name: Type **Landscaping Services**
- ❖ Click **Save & Close**
- ❖ Right click **Misc Income** (towards the bottom of the window)
- ❖ Click **Edit Account**

- ❖ Account Type: Select **Income** (Very Important)
- ❖ Account Name: Accept **Misc Income** (bottom of the list)
- ❖ Click **Sub-account of**: Select **Landscaping Services**
- ❖ Click **Save & Close**
- ❖ Right click in the window. Click **New**
- ❖ Click **Income**. Click **Continue**
- ❖ Name: Type **Markup Income**
- ❖ Click **Sub-account of**: Select **Landscaping Services**
- ❖ Click **Save & Close**
- ❖ Right click **Uncategorized Income**
- ❖ Click **Edit Account**
- ❖ Account Name: Type **Opening Balance Income**
- ❖ Click **Save & Close**
- ❖ Right click **Uncategorized Expense** (bottom of the list)
- ❖ Click **Edit Account**
- ❖ Account Name: Type **Opening Balance Expense**
- ❖ Click **Save & Close**

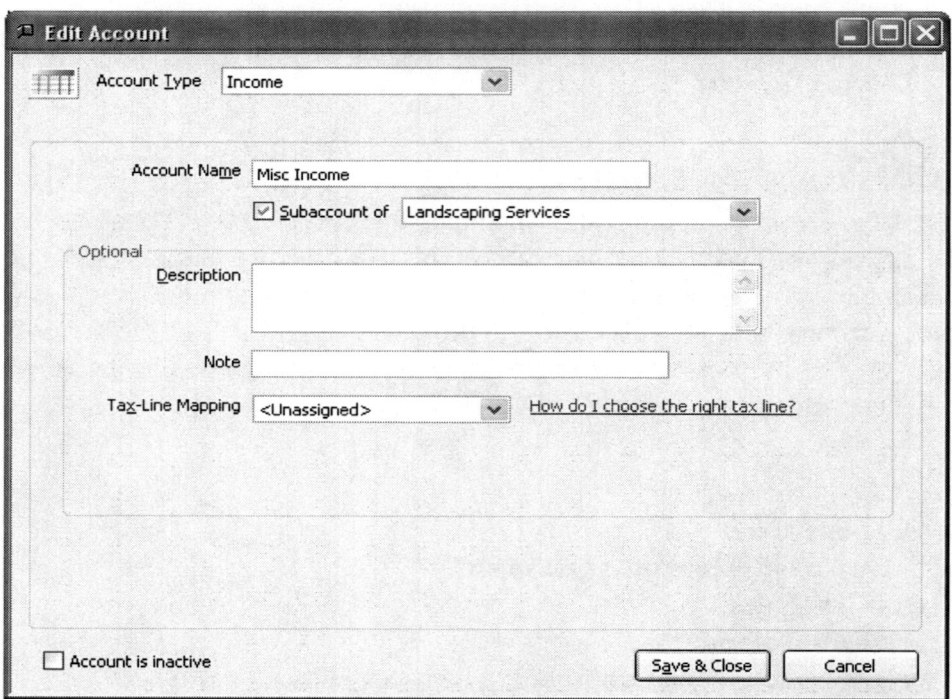

Income: Sub Accounts

This time you will be creating sub-accounts for the main Income account. You have three options on how to create income sub-accounts. You may use the account names, product names or a combination of accounts and products. Here, we are going to use the account names. If you choose the product method, you will be listing the names of the product you will be selling. Don't forget to click the Save & New to stay in the window; otherwise, you will exit the window with Save & Close.

Activities:

- ❖ Right click in the Chart of Account window
- ❖ Click **New**
- ❖ Click **Income**
- ❖ Click **Continue**
- ❖ Account Name: Type **Design Services**
- ❖ Click **Sub-account of**: Select **Landscaping Services**
- ❖ Click **Save & New**
- ❖ Account Name: Type **Equipment Rental**
- ❖ Click **Sub-account of**: Select **Landscaping Services**
- ❖ Click **Save & New**
- ❖ Account Name: Type **Materials**
- ❖ Click **Sub-account of:** Select **Landscaping Services**
- ❖ Click **Save & New**
- ❖ Account Name: Type **Labor**
- ❖ Click **Sub-account of:** Select **Landscaping Services**
- ❖ Click **Save & New**
- ❖ Account Name: Type **Supplies**
- ❖ Click **Sub-account of:** Select **Landscaping Services**
- ❖ Click **Save & New**
- ❖ Account Name: Type **Subcontractors**
- ❖ Click **Sub-account of:** Select **Landscaping Services**
- ❖ Click **Save & Close**

Inventory Accounts

If you have items in your warehouse you purchased and are keeping track of, you use the Inventory type of items and pull in Cost of Goods Sold as an account link. And after you've created the income account, the next account in the order of importance is the Cost of Goods Sold. The only accounts you have here are the materials, supplies and discount given. You do not have labor or subcontractor in this section. If you count labor expense from employees as cost of good sold it will be double counting if you pay the same employees in the payroll expense

Activities:

- ❖ Click **Lists menu**
- ❖ Click **Item List**
- ❖ Right click in the window. Click **New**
- ❖ Type: Click **Inventory Part**
- ❖ Click **Cancel**
- ❖ Click **Lists menu**
- ❖ Click **Chart of Accounts**
- ❖ Right click in the window. Click **New**
- ❖ Click **Other Account Types**
- ❖ Click **Cost of Goods Sold.** Click **Continue**
- ❖ Account Name: Type **Materials**
- ❖ Description: Type **Inventory cost of goods items**
- ❖ Click **Save & New**
- ❖ Account Name: Type **Supplies**
- ❖ Description: Type **Inventory cost of goods items**
- ❖ Click **Save & Close**

> You clicked Inventory Part to make sure it is on the list and to activate Cost of Goods Sold in the Chart of Accounts list.

Cost of Goods Sold Accounts

This section is for non inventory accounts that are used in producing the goods. In other words, these are account such as material, supplies, subcontractors, and others that are used to produce the goods but you do not keep count or inventory of these account. You use this account to link to non inventory items from your vendor. When you receive a bill from a vendor you use the bill to book the items and link those items to the miscellaneous account in the Chart of Accounts.

Activities:

- ❖ Right click in the Chart of Account window
- ❖ Click **New**
- ❖ Click **Other Account Types**
- ❖ Click **Cost of Goods Sold**
- ❖ Click **Continue**
- ❖ Account Name: Type **Miscellaneous**
- ❖ Description: Type **Non inventory cost of goods sold items**
- ❖ Click **Save & Close**

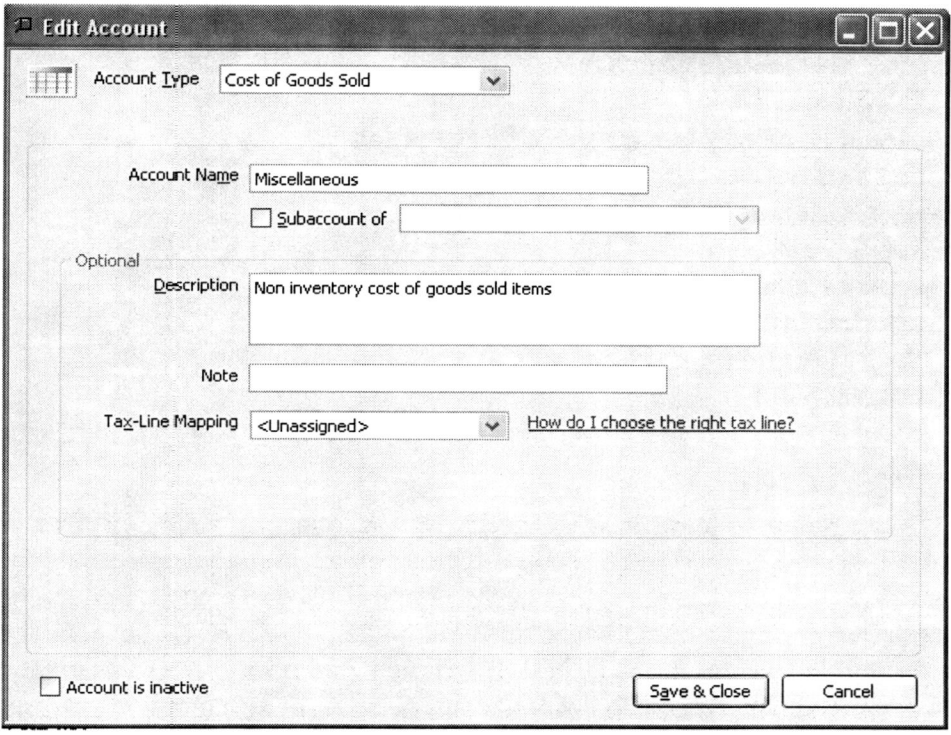

Operating Expenses Account

In this section, you will be treating the administrative or operational expenses. These are expenses not directly used to make the products or provide the services the company invoice to its customers. For example, the use of company automobile to carry office equipment to the office is not directly related to planting flowers for landscaping services. The best method is to lump the automobile expense directly into an administrative expense account and not under a particular product or service.

Activities:

- ❖ Right click in the Chart of Account window
- ❖ Click **New**
- ❖ Click **Expense**
- ❖ Click **Continue**
- ❖ Account Name: Type **Fuel**
- ❖ Click **Sub-account of**:
- ❖ Select **Automobile Expense**
- ❖ Click **Save & New**
- ❖ Account Name: Type **Insurance**

- ❖ Click **Sub-account of:**
- ❖ Select **Automobile Expense**
- ❖ Click **Save & New**
- ❖ Account Name: Type **License & Registration**
- ❖ Click **Sub-account of**:
- ❖ Select **Automobile Expense**
- ❖ Click **Save & New**
- ❖ Account Name: Type **Repairs & Maint**
- ❖ Click **Sub- account of**:
- ❖ Select **Automobile Expense**
- ❖ Click **Save & Close**

Merging Accounts

We are going to learn how to merge two accounts into one. Before we do that, we will create a second main account with a sub-account that acts as a duplicate to the one already in the Chart of Accounts. Merge is used to clean up your Chart of Accounts or merge any unwanted account into another. We already have an account called Automobile Expense on the Chart of Account, and now you will be creating an account called Auto Expense with a sub-account, Gas.

Activities:

- ❖ Right click in the Chart of Accounts window
- ❖ Click **New**
- ❖ Click **Expense**
- ❖ Click **Continue**
- ❖ Account Name: Type **Auto Expense** (not Automobile Expense)
- ❖ Click **Save & New**
- ❖ Account Name: Type **Gas**
- ❖ Click **Sub-account of**: Select **Auto Expense**
- ❖ Click **Save & Close**
- ❖ **Look! You have created Auto Expense with sub-account Gas**

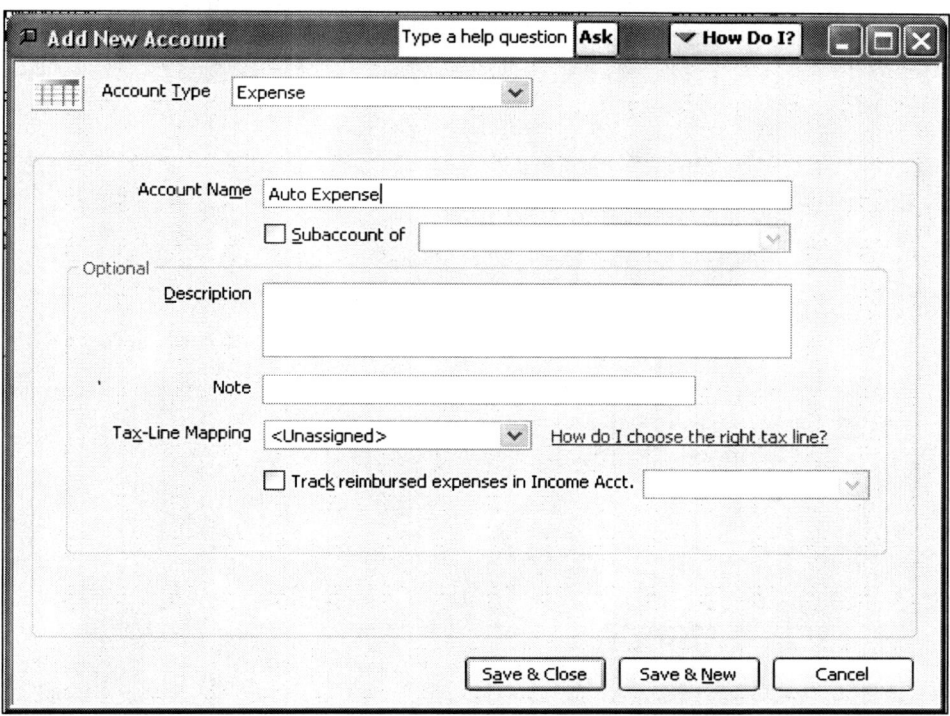

Merging Sub accounts

We have created the second main account, and its sub-account, Gas. The "Good" subaccount is Fuel under Automobile Expenses and the "Bad" sub-account is Gas under Auto Expenses. First, you change name Gas to Fuel and second, you merge the new Fuel to the old Fuel in Automobile Expenses. To know you're on the right track you must receive a message that says, "This name is already being used. Would you want to merge them?" Click Yes and the "Bad" account disappears.

Activities:

- ❖ In the Chart of Accounts window
- ❖ Right click **Gas** under **Auto Expense** (not **Automobile Expense)**
- ❖ Click **Edit Account**
- ❖ Account Name: Type **Fuel**
- ❖ Checkmark **Sub-account of**: Select **Automobile Expense**. (Very Important)
- ❖ Click **Save & Close**
- ❖ Click **Yes** to "This name is already…merge them?" (Very Important)
- ❖ **Look! Gas under Auto Expense is gone**
- ❖ Gas in Auto Expense is now merged with Fuel under Automobile Expense

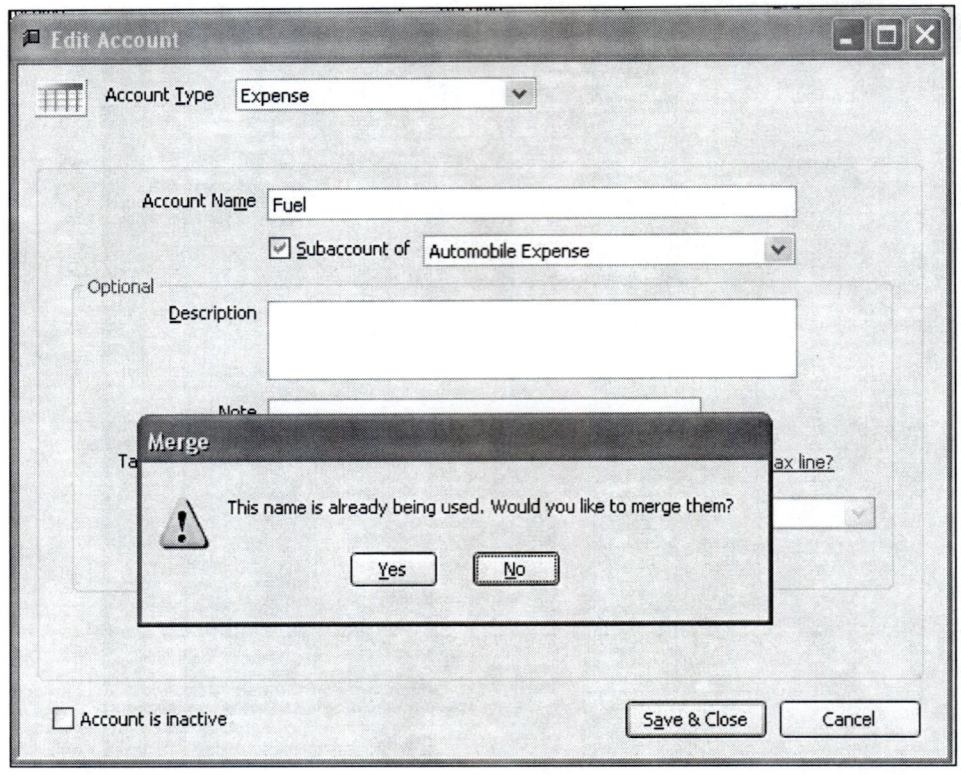

Merging Main Accounts

We've merged the two sub-accounts; the next step is to merge two main accounts. The "Good" account is Automobile Expense and the "Bad" account is Auto Expense. After the merging process, the "Bad" account will be merged into the "Good" account. Be sure to click Yes to the message, "This name is already being used. Would you want to merge them?" You can also use the same process to merge items in the Item List, but note you cannot merge income and expense accounts.

Activities:

❖ In the Chart of Accounts window
❖ Right click on **Auto Expense**
❖ Click **Edit Account**
❖ Account Name: Type **Automobile Expense**
❖ Click **Save & Close**
❖ Click **Yes** to "The name is already…merge them?" (Very Important)
❖ **Look! Auto Expense has been merged with Automobile Expense**

> You must see the Merge message window and you must click Yes for the process to work, otherwise it will fail the process and the merge.

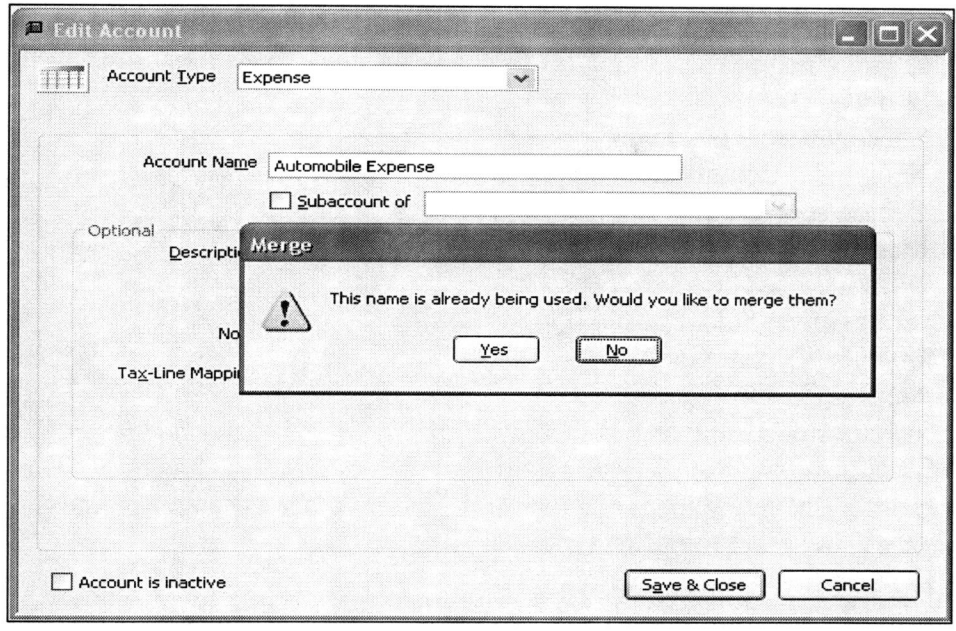

Designing Financial Report

How your financial statements look depend on the way you place the accounts in the Chart of Accounts window. Materials, Labor, Supplies and Subcontractors are placed in that order and Misc is always the last. Discounts and numbers with minus signs are placed below the main account they are subtracting from. Opening balances are always on top in each section. You can move a single or a group of accounts. Your report will look very professional by designing the Chart of Account.

* ❖ In the Chart of Accounts window
* ❖ Click **Materials** under **Landscaping Services** (Very Important)
* ❖ **Place the cursor left of Materials.** You will see 4-way cross
* ❖ **Click and drag Materials** up to under Landscaping Services

> You will see long dash line as you drag up or down. You can use the same process to move a single account or main and subaccount.

* ❖ **Move the following accounts and place them in the following order:**
* ❖ Opening Balance Income (Income. 1st before other income accounts)
* ❖ Landscaping Services (Income)

❖   Materials (Income)
❖   Labor (Income)
❖   Supplies (Income)
❖   Subcontractors (Income)
❖   Equipment Rental (Income)
❖   Design Services (Income)
❖   Markup Income (Income)
❖   Misc Income (Income)
❖ Cost of Goods Sold (Cost of Goods Sold)
❖ Materials (Cost of Goods Sold)
❖ Supplies (Cost of Goods Sold)
❖ Discount Received (Cost of Goods Sold)
❖ Miscellaneous (Cost of Goods Sold)
❖ Opening Balance Expense (Expense. 1st before other expense accounts)
❖ Advertising and Promotion (Expense)

Inventory Type Item: Material

We have finished creating accounts in the Chart of Accounts window. We are going to create Items in the Items List window. The first is Inventory Items. These are items in the warehouse you keep as inventory. As a product or service company, you will pull in two accounts when creating the Inventory Items. Pull in Cost of Goods Sold for the cost side and Landscaping Services account for the income side. Your re-order point should be equal to or lower than your beginning quantity.

Activities:

❖ Click **Lists menu**
❖ Click **Item List**
❖ Right click in the window. Click **New**
❖ Type: Select **Inventory Part**
❖ Item Name/Number: Type **Flowers**
❖ Description: Type **Materials**
❖ Cost: Type **50**
❖ COGS Account: Select **Materials under Cost of Goods Sold**
❖ Sales Price: Type **75**
❖ Tax Code: Accept **Tax**
❖ Income Account: Select **Materials under Landscape Services**
❖ Asset Account: Accept **Inventory Asset**
❖ Reorder Point: Type **1000**
❖ On Hand: Type **1000**

> Like the Chart of Accounts, it's important to right click on an item and click QuickReport at the bottom of the list to see the details. If an item has a balance QuickBooks will not allow you to delete it until you move the balance to another item.

❖ Total Value: Accept **50,000** as of: Type **1/1/09**.
❖ Click **OK** (right of the window)

Service Type Item: Labor

There are two kinds of service labor. One is internal or work done by the employees and the other is external or work done by subcontractors. When a job is done by employees, in general you do not track the cost associated with that job unless you want to; but you may track the cost of using subcontractors. You pull in only the rate and the income account associated with that job. It's vital to complete the description box to identify whether an employee or subcontractor did the job.

Activities:

❖ Right click in the Item List window.
❖ Click **New**
❖ Type: Select **Service**
❖ Item Name/Number: Type: **Trimming**
❖ Description: Type **Employee work**
❖ Rate: Type **100**
❖ Tax Code: Select **Non**
❖ Income Account: Select **Labor under Landscape Services**
❖ Click **Next** (right of the window)
❖ Item Name/Number: Type: **Gardening**
❖ Description: Type **Employee work**
❖ Rate: Type **110**
❖ Tax Code: Accept **Non**
❖ Income Account: Accept **Landscape Service: Labor**
❖ Click **Next** (right of the window)
❖ Item Name/Number: Type: **Tree Removal**
❖ Description: Type **Employee work**
❖ Rate: Type **120**
❖ Tax Code: Accept **Non**
❖ Income Account: Accept **Landscape Service: Labor**
❖ Click **Next** (right of the window)
❖ Item Name/Number: Type: **Delivery**
❖ Description: Type **Employee work**
❖ Rate: Type **150**
❖ Tax Code: Accept **Non**
❖ Income Account: Accept **Landscape Service: Labor**
❖ Click **OK** (right of the window)

Price Level List

There are two types of Price Levels. One is profit and the other is nonprofit. Both Price Levels can be set up in the Edit menu under Sales & Customer of the Preferences tab. For the Profit Level, you are not going to reduce the price you charge your customers. In other words, you are going to charge them full price for the merchandise, and they are not tax exempt. For your nonprofit customers, their prices are reduced by 50% because they are tax-exempt customers.

Activities:

- ❖ Click **Lists menu**
- ❖ Click **Price Level List**
- ❖ Right click in the window
- ❖ Click **New**. Price Level Name: Type **Profit**
- ❖ Click **OK** to close window
- ❖ Right click in the window. Click **New**
- ❖ Price Level Name: Type **Non Profit Tax Exempt**
- ❖ This price level will: Accept **decrease**
- ❖ Item prices by: Type **50**
- ❖ Click **OK** to close window

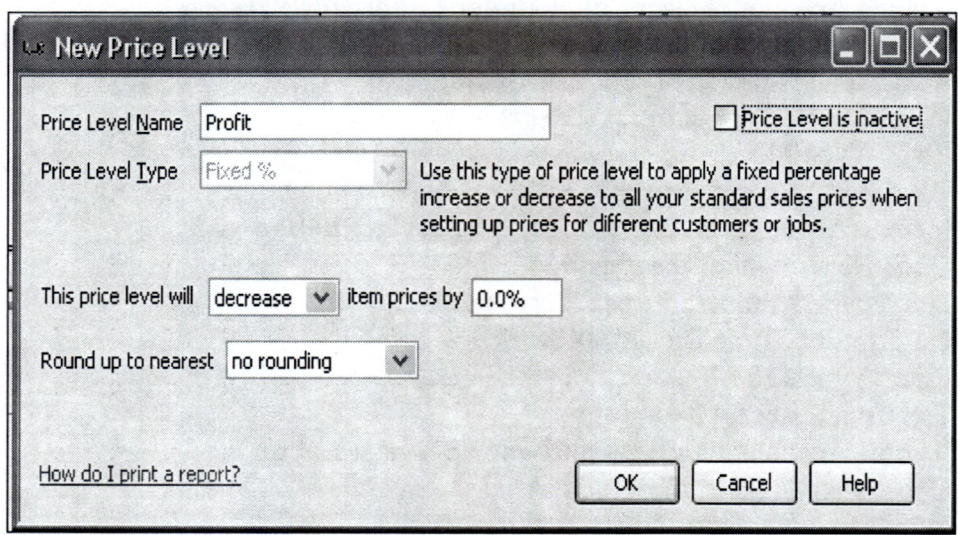

Sales Tax Code List

Customers pay taxes on products you manufacture when you sell the goods. Items such as services that come with personal abilities, skills, effort and knowledge are not taxable to the customer. Most items you purchase for resale will be taxed because you paid taxes on them and, in turn, passed the taxes to the customer. Before you create a taxable and nontaxable item, you must inform QuickBooks if it is taxable or not. To set it up, go to Edit menu, Preferences and the Sales Tax window.

Activities:

- ❖ Click **Lists menu**
- ❖ Click **Sales Tax Code List**
- ❖ Right click in the window
- ❖ Click **New**
- ❖ Sales Tax Code: Type **LBR**
- ❖ Description: Type **Non-Taxable Labor**
- ❖ Accept Click on **Non-Taxable**. Click **OK**

Class List

If you have different types of businesses, you should track them by classes. When you track businesses by classes, you zero in on which ones are making the most money and why and which ones are making the least money and why. By studying your businesses by class, you are able to make adjustments in pricing, advertising and sales. When you want to cut costs by shutting down unproductive lines of business, running your reports by class will show you which products to eliminate.

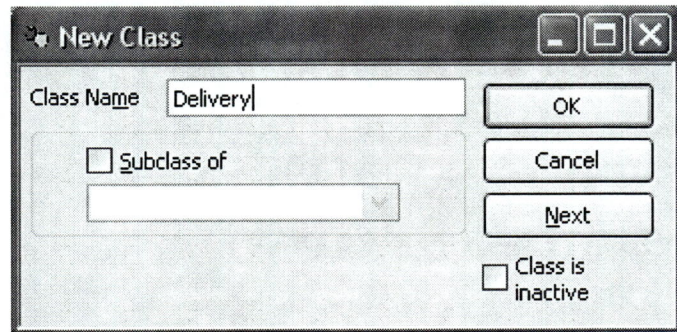

Activities:
- ❖ Click **Lists menu**
- ❖ Click **Class List**
- ❖ Right click in the window
- ❖ Click **New**
- ❖ Class Name: Type **Delivery**. Click **Next**
- ❖ Class Name: Type **Landscaping.** Click **Next**
- ❖ Class Name: Type **Maintenance**. Click **Next**
- ❖ Class Name: Type **Overhead.** Click **Next**
- ❖ Class Name: Type **Administrative**
- ❖ Click **OK**

Other Names List

Use the Other Names List to add names not related to Chart of Accounts or Item List windows like Transfer to/from Checking and Transfer to/from Payroll. Remember that QuickBooks will not allow you to delete any name if it has been used in creating an invoice or bill or has been linked to other accounts, especially when it involves an amount. The best way to treat such name is to make it inactive and, therefore, not show it in the Other Names list window.

Activities:
- ❖ Click **Lists menu**
- ❖ Click **Other Names List**
- ❖ Right click in window
- ❖ Click **New**
- ❖ Name: Type **ATM Withdrawal**. Click **Next**
- ❖ Name: Type **Deposits.** Click **Next**
- ❖ Name: Type **Transfer to Payroll**. Click **Next**
- ❖ Name: Type **Transfer from Payroll**. Click **Next**
- ❖ Name: Type **Transfer to Checking**. Click **Next**
- ❖ Name: Type **Transfer from Checking.** Click **Next**
- ❖ Name: Type **Transfer to Petty Cash**. Click **Next**
- ❖ Name: Type **Transfer from Petty Cash**. Click **OK**

Sales Rep List

What if you divide your business into geographic territories and have to assign sales representatives to different territories? Come to this window to make a list of these individuals. The representatives will be pulled into the invoice window while you're completing your estimates or invoices. Most commission reports are linked to the representative in charge of the territory. You should complete this window with care to make sure the right commission is paid to the right representative.

Activities:

- ❖ Click **Lists menu**
- ❖ Click **Customer & Vendor Profile Lists**
- ❖ Click **Sale Rep List**
- ❖ Right click in the window. Click **New**
- ❖ Sales Rep Name: Select **Add New**
- ❖ Click **Employee.** Click **OK**
- ❖ First Name: Type **Fate**
- ❖ Last Name: Type **Acres.** Press **Tab**
- ❖ SS No: Type **999-45-6789**
- ❖ Gender: Select **Female**
- ❖ Date of Birth: Type **1/1/1977**
- ❖ Click **OK**
- ❖ Click **Leave As Is**
- ❖ Click **OK** to close New Sales Rep window

Customer Type List

Sometimes, for market planning purposes, customers are divided into types and treated differently. Some businesses may divide their customers into individual, corporate, schools and universities and nonprofit. By dividing your customers, you may be able to target a group with a special kind of pricing or advertising strategy. After the planning session is over, you should update your QuickBooks with this information by going to the customer windows.

Activities:

- ❖ Click **Lists menu**
- ❖ Click **Customer & Vendor Profile Lists**
- ❖ Click **Customer Type List**
- ❖ Right click in the window. Click **New**
- ❖ Customer Type: Type **Commercial**. Click **Next**
- ❖ Customer Type: Type **Residential**. Click **Next**
- ❖ Customer Type: Type **Schools & Universities**. Click **Next**
- ❖ Customer Type: Type **Non-Profit.** Click **Next**
- ❖ Customer Type: Type **Parks & Recreation**
- ❖ Click **OK**

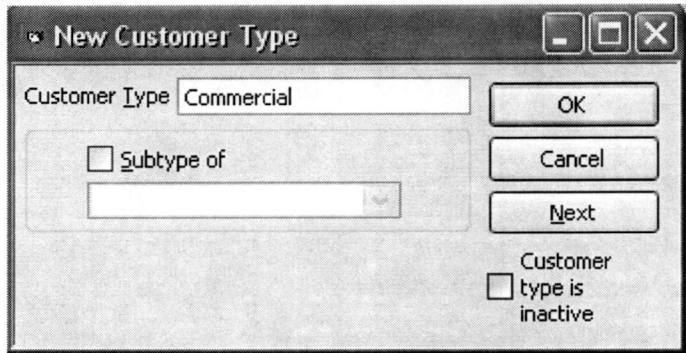

Vendor Type List

Before you start making payments on your bills, you should complete the Vendor Type List window. The purpose is to list your vendors so they can easily be pulled into the Bill Payment windows. Your vendors may be divided into different types like subcontractor, utilities, insurance, repairs and maintenance. You should be able to go to the List menu, click Customer & Vendor Profile Lists to get to the Vendor Type List window. One of the most important Vendor Type List names is the Tax agency, because payroll taxes must be paid on time to the right agency.

Activities:

- ❖ Click **Lists menu**
- ❖ Click **Customer & Vendor Profile Lists**
- ❖ Click **Vendor Type List**
- ❖ Right click in the window. Click **New**
- ❖ Vendor Type: Type **Subcontractors**. Click **Next**
- ❖ Vendor Type: Type **Utilities**. Click **Next**

- ❖ Vendor Type: Type **Insurance**. Click **Next**
- ❖ Vendor Type: Type **Repairs & Maint.** Click **Next**
- ❖ Vendor Type: Type **Construction.** Click **Next**
- ❖ Vendor Type: Type **Financial Services**
- ❖ Click **OK**

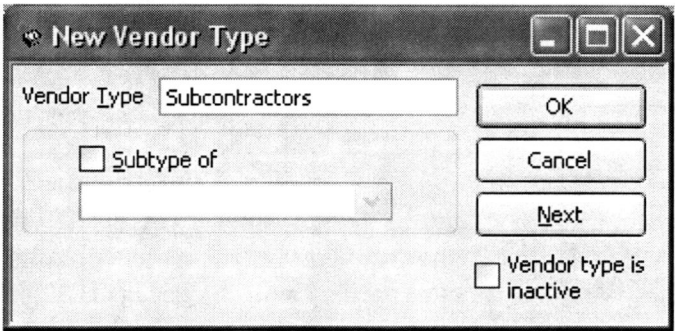

Job Type List

If you are in the services business, you might want to break down your Job into Types. One reason is that QuickBooks will want to know; another reason is that breaking your job into parts will help you to zero in on which type is getting the most or least requests. This way, you can target your cost cutting, marketing and advertising strategies differently to get the most benefit. For example, Job Types can be broken down into Contracts, Installation, New Construction, etc.

Activities:

- ❖ Click **Lists menu**
- ❖ Click **Customer & Vendor Profile Lists**
- ❖ Click **Job Type List**
- ❖ Right click in the window
- ❖ Click **New**
- ❖ Job Type Name: Type **Contract**. Click **Next**
- ❖ Job Type Name: Type **Installation**. Click **Next**
- ❖ Job Type Name: Type **New Construction**
- ❖ Click **OK**

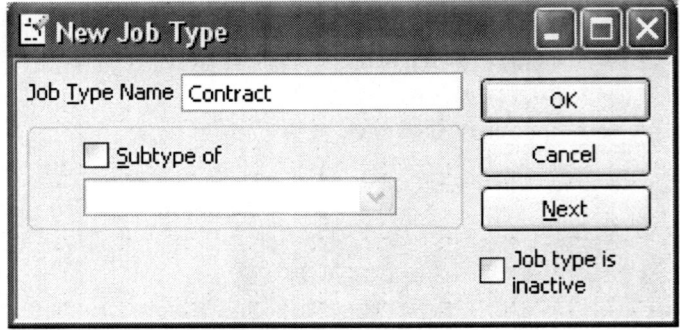

Payment Method List

If you plan on accepting payment in forms other than cash, you should complete the Payment Method List window. You have many options already preloaded for you in the window. For example, you have cash, check, Visa, MasterCard, American Express and Discover. You may create Bank Debit Card and Electronic Fund Transfer (EFT). When you're completing the Enter Sales Receipt window, you'll be required to select the Payment Method your customer prefers.

Activities:

❖ Click **Lists menu**
❖ Click **Customer & Vendor Profile Lists**
❖ Click **Payment Method List**
❖ Right click in the window
❖ Click **New**
❖ Payment Method: Type **Bank Debit Card**
❖ Payment Type: Select **Visa**. Click **Next**
❖ Payment Method: Type **EFT Electronic Fund Transfer**
❖ Payment Type: Select **Other**
❖ Click **OK**

Vehicle List

Recording your assets, especially cars and trucks in the Vehicle List, is of utmost importance. The information in this report is pulled over to the Enter Vehicle Mileage and Fixed Item List windows. To get to the Vehicle List window, you remember to click the Lists menu, Customer & Vendor Profile Lists and then Vehicle List. Most users cannot find this window because they think it should be listed under the Lists menu.

Activities:

- ❖ Click **Lists menu**
- ❖ Click **Customer & Vendor Profile Lists**
- ❖ Click **Vehicle List**
- ❖ Right click in the window. Click **New**
- ❖ Vehicle: Type **Lexus Truck**
- ❖ Description: Type **Board of Directors Truck.** Click **Next**
- ❖ Vehicle: Type **Jeep Grand Cherokee Truck**
- ❖ Description: Type **Sales Reps Truck**. Click **Next**
- ❖ Vehicle: Type **Mercedes Trailer**
- ❖ Description: Type **Distribution Trailer**
- ❖ Click **OK**

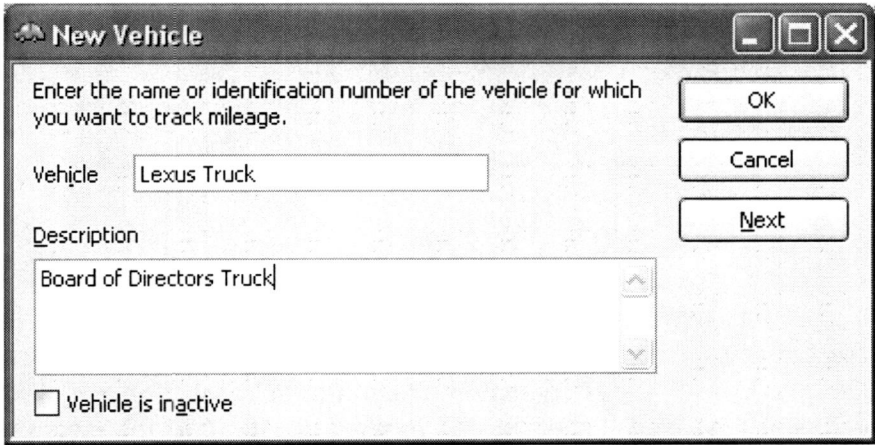

Memorized Transaction List

If you want to make sure you're on top of every task and nothing falls through the cracks, you should consider memorizing your transactions. After you've created identical groups of transactions, you should lump them into a group. Monthly recurring bills such as electric, cell phone, Internet, water, gas and other related bills are grouped together under Recurring Monthly Bills. Normally, you select "Monthly" instead of "Never" in the "How Often" box.

Activities:

- ❖ Click **Lists menu**
- ❖ Click **Memorized Transaction List**
- ❖ Right click in the window. Click **New Group**

❖ Name: Type **Recurring Monthly Bills**
❖ Click **Automatically Enter** option
❖ How Often: Accept **Never**
❖ Next Date: Type **2/1/09.** Click **OK**
❖ Click **Window menu.** Click **Close All**
❖ Click **Company menu.** Click **Home Page**

When using QuickBooks for your business, you should select monthly instead of "Never."

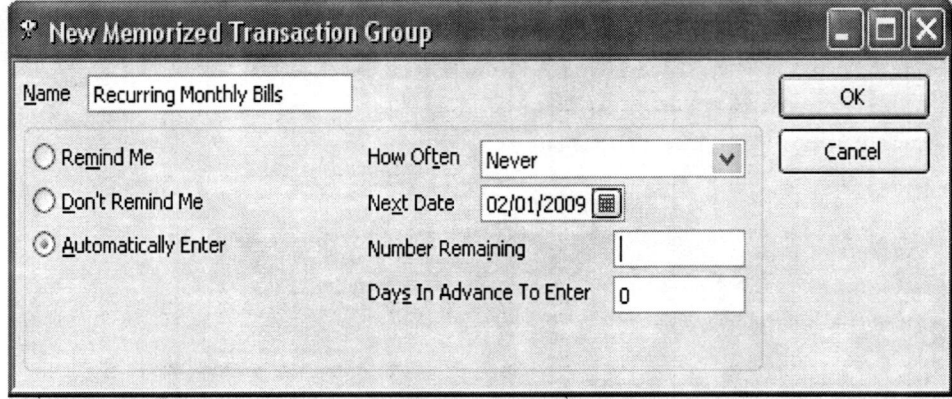

Financial Results: Profit & Loss

This is one the key chapters in terms of creating accounts and items. The Chart of Accounts and Item List windows are the backbone of accounting and finance. You created several income main and sub-accounts such as the Landscaping and Design accounts. You also created some items in the Item List window. Nothing you did in this chapter affected the Profit & Loss statements until the next chapter where you will be making a general journal entry.

Activities:

❖ Click **Reports menu**
❖ Click **Company & Financial**
❖ Click **Profit & Loss Standard**
❖ Date (top left): Select **This Fiscal Year**
❖ From: Accept **1/1/09**
❖ To: Accept **12/31/09**
❖ **Net Income 999,850.00**
❖ Click **X** to close window

```
                    Quick Payroll 2009
                    Profit & Loss
                January through December 2009
                                      ◇ Jan - Dec 09 ◇
        Ordinary Income/Expense
          Income
            Opening Balance Income  ▶ 1,005,000.00 ◀
            Total Income               1,005,000.00

          Gross Profit                 1,005,000.00

          Expense
            Opening Balance Expense       5,000.00
            Travel Expense                  150.00
            Total Expense                 5,150.00

        Net Ordinary Income             999,850.00

        Net Income                      999,850.00
```

Financial: Balance Sheet

You created several Balance Sheet accounts in this chapter. The Credit Card account with a balance of 500.00 is an example of current account and the Truck account with a balance of 40,000.00 is an example of a fixed account. Because fixed accounts need to be depreciated, we set the Accumulated Depreciation account with a 0.00 balance. The purpose of the Accumulated Depreciation account is to collect the monthly expenses from the Truck account.

Activities:

- ❖ Click **Reports menu**
- ❖ Click **Company & Financial**
- ❖ Click **Balance Sheet Standard**
- ❖ Date (top left): Select **This Fiscal Year**
- ❖ As of: Accept **12/31/09**
- ❖ Click **Collapse**
- ❖ **Total Assets 2,244,850.00**
- ❖ Click **X** to close window

```
                    Quick Payroll 2009
                    Balance Sheet
                  As of December 31, 2009
                              ◇  Dec 31, 09  ◇
        ASSETS
          Current Assets
            Checking/Savings
              Money Market Account   ▶   100,000.00 ◀
              USA Checking                799,850.00
              USA Payroll                 250,000.00
            Total Checking/Savings      1,149,850.00

            Accounts Receivable
              Accounts Receivable       1,005,000.00
            Total Accounts Receivable   1,005,000.00

            Other Current Assets
              Inventory Asset              50,000.00
            Total Other Current Assets     50,000.00

          Total Current Assets         2,204,850.00

          Fixed Assets
            Truck                          40,000.00
          Total Fixed Assets              40,000.00

        TOTAL ASSETS                    2,244,850.00
```

Chapter Summary

The Lists menu is all about creating, editing and deleting accounts and lists; and that was the main objective of this chapter: to learn how to create new accounts and lists in the Chart of Accounts and Item windows, respectively. A vital part of creating a new account is entering the opening balance and date. When you think about creating accounts or lists, you think about the Lists menu.

What we accomplished:

- Reviewed the Lists submenus
- Reviewed chart of accounts
- Created the money market account
- Created the truck account
- Created the credit card account
- Created the equity accounts

- Created income main and sub accounts
- Merged main and sub accounts
- Created inventory and service items
- Created the office expense accounts
- Practiced the price level list
- Practiced the sales tax list
- Practiced the class and other names list
- Practiced the sales rep list
- Practiced the customer, vendor and job type lists
- Practiced the payment method and vehicle lists
- Created and memorized a transaction
- Processed financial statements

Additional Financial activities:

- Created Money Market account for 100,000
- Created Truck account for 40,000
- Created Credit Card account 500
- Created Inventory Asset account for a total of 50,000

Optional Test 4

Questions: True/False

Answer the following questions by placing letter the T or F in the space provided before the question number.

_____ 1. After you have created an account you can delete it as long as it has a balance or it is used in at least one other transaction.

_____ 2. When you right click in the Chart of Account window you will not see the Delete function until you click the Edit menu or account button.

_____ 3. You can right click in the Chart of Account window to make an account inactive but you cannot right click to show inactive accounts until you click the Edit menu or account button.

_____ 4. When creating a Service Item in the Item List window, you must click "This service is used in assembly or is performed by a subcontractor or partner" before you can pull in the sales price.

_____ 5. In other to pull in an Inventory Type item in the Item List window, you must first set it up in the Preferences window.

_____ 6. Fixed Assets are short-lived assets used in the operation of the business such as land, building, furniture, equipment, and vehicle.

_____ 7. Once an account has been made inactive, it has to stay that way because QuickBooks doesn't like to change the account any longer.

_____ 8. In the Chart of Account window, you can create, edit, and delete accounts but not be able to make deposits.

_____ 9. When merging two accounts, Merge did not work if you did not see QuickBooks' merge message box.

_____ 10. When completing the Fixed Assets window, it is not necessary to enter the asset account associated with the Fixed Assets.

Questions: Multiple Choices

Answer the following questions by placing letter A, B, C, or D in the space provided before the question number.

_____ 1. If you are pulling in cost and sales price for an item in the Item List window, you must also pull in which of the following accounts?
   A. Expense or Cost of Goods Sold
   B. Income
   C. All of the above
   D. None of the above

_____ 2. When creating a new account in the Chart of Account window, Checking account is an example of what account type?
   A. Income
   B. Bank
   C. Loan
   D. Equity

_____ 3. When merging two accounts, which two accounts will QuickBooks not allow you to merge together?
   A. Income and expense
   B. Two Incomes
   C. Two Expenses
   D. None of the above

_____ 4. If you are looking for a submenu, which of the following submenus will you not be able to find under the Lists menu?
   A. Report List
   B. Templates
   C. Price Level List
   D. Item Lists

_____ 5. Under the Lists menu, the Customer & Vendor Profile Lists submenu allows you to complete the following windows except…
   A. Ship Via List
   B. Vehicle List
   C. Term List
   D. Company List

_____ 6. If you want to use account numbers in your Chart of Accounts window, you must set it up first in which of the following windows?
   A. Accounting under Preferences
   B. Accounting under Lists
   C. Accounting under View
   D. Accounting under Edit

_____ 7. In creating a new account it is advisable to select a Tax Line for the tax mapping box for which of following accounts?
   A. Bank
   B. Income and Expenses
   C. Fixed Assets
   D. Equity

_____ 8. In creating an Inventory Item in the Item List window, you must pull in which of the following accounts?
   A. Cost of Goods Sold
   B. Income
   C. All of the above
   D. None of the above

_____ 9. Which of the following Item Types is used to record goods you are not tracking like office supplies or materials for specific job?
   A. Service
   B. Inventory
   C. Non Inventory
   D. Other Charge

_____ 10. Which of the following Item Types is used to record goods you purchased, track as inventory, and for resale?
   A. Service
   B. Inventory
   C. Non Inventory
   D. Other Charge

Chapter 5

Company Menu

Objectives: After you've completed this chapter you will be able to:

- ✓ Explain Company submenus
- ✓ Identify the home page contents
- ✓ Identify the company snapshot
- ✓ Edit company information
- ✓ Set up administrator and user passwords
- ✓ Edit and delete users passwords
- ✓ Edit admin's password
- ✓ Set up and remove closing date
- ✓ Set up payroll budget
- ✓ Complete To-Do list window
- ✓ Complete reminders & alert manager window
- ✓ Make general journal entry
- ✓ Enter vehicle mileage window
- ✓ Run financial reports and compare your results
- ✓ Explain the principles of journal entries
- ✓ Explain month-end journal entries

Review Company Menu

When you're thinking about updating Company Information such as the address, phone number, income tax form used or Federal Employment Identification Number (FEIN), remember the Company menu. In the Company Information window, selecting the right "Income Tax Form Used" will enable QuickBooks to default vital tax-related forms specifically designed for your business and industry. You can access the Chart of Accounts from the Company or Lists menus. Consistency is the key to speed. Therefore, I encourage you to access Chart of Accounts through the Lists menu.

- Click **Company menu**

The following submenus are located under the Company menu:

- **Home Page:** This is the "central nervous system" of the QuickBooks windows. The Home Page is the gateway that gives you access to most of the other windows. It has more icons than any other window. It has the following icon groups: Vendors, Customers, Employees, Company and Banking group of icons. You can always access the home page by clicking directly it on the tool bar instead of going through the Company menu.

- **Company Snapshot:** The snapshot is the summary of the financial activities of the company. It prominently displays the income and expense graph. Other financial summaries include the following: account balances, customers who owe money, vendors to pay, and reminders.

- **Advanced Reports:** You have to login to the internet to use the advanced reports.

- **Company Information:** After you've created a new company through the File menu, this is where you update the company information. Be sure any information on the company window is complete and accurate, because QuickBooks uses it to populate various forms and reports.

- **Advanced Services Administration:** These are services that QuickBooks provide to its customers online and, therefore, you should be connected to the Internet to review these services and see if they are good for you.

- **Set Up Users & Passwords:** If more than one person will be accessing your QuickBooks file, you are encouraged to set up passwords to allow limited access to only authorized persons. The Set Up Users window enables you to set up, edit and delete passwords. After you've set up your own password or other employees' passwords, you should also remember to change the passwords from time to time, monthly or semiannually. Don't keep the same password for more than one year. The QuickBooks administrator has the right to change passwords and should encourage everyone to change their passwords.

- **Customer Credit Card Protection:** If you accept credit cards from your customers, you must check out this window and see how you can protect your customers' credit cards. Unless you have other protection devices, this is a service you need to look into.

- **Set Closing Date:** At the end of the accounting year, generally December or any other time approved by management, accounting books are closed, and the closing date is set. The date will prevent anyone from making entries to the previous closed year by mistake. A password should be assigned to the closing date, so that only authorized personnel can make prior year entries or adjustments.

- **Planning & Budgeting:** No business is successful without planning and budgeting. You will be able to set up a budget, project your cash flow and analyze your business using the tools under this submenu. I strongly encourage you to review your business using the Decision Tools submenu, which has the following sections: Measure Profitability, Analyze Financial Strength, Compare Debt and Ownership, Depreciate Your Assets, Manage Your Receivables, Employees, Contractors or Temp, Improve Cash Flow and Periodic Tasks.

- **To Do List:** If you don't want anything to fall through the cracks, this is the tool you will use to control your daily tasks. Periodic tasks sometimes get overlooked, but with the To Do List, all is covered. For example, you can make a note to yourself about "calling the bank to refund you the 100 they overpaid on your bank statement last month or a note to check next month's statement for 100 deposited from the bank."

- **Reminders:** Like the To Do List, Reminders will make sure the main tasks are documented to be completed at a certain time. You can use Reminders not only for yourself, but for other workers who use QuickBooks. Reminders are generated by QuickBooks based on the information on your database like invoice due date.

- **Alerts Manager:** QuickBooks has a calendar list of tax and business-related dates your company needs to meet in order to be in compliance with local and state governments' filings. You'll need to browse through this window to see these dates. QuickBooks will automatically drop an item from the list when the scheduled date has passed; you can also checkmark an item when you have completed the task before the scheduled date.

- **Chart of Accounts:** You can access Chart of Accounts from several windows, and this is one of them. It allows you to create, edit or delete accounts and account reports.

- **Make General Journal Entries:** Journal entries are the backbone of accounting and bookkeeping. However, when you are in the Company menu window, it is advisable to complete your company-related journal entries and at the end of the month when you receive your bank statements, you can then complete the bank-related journal entries.

- **Manage Currency:** This submenu allows you to turn on or turn off the currency feature. If you're dealing with international transactions, this is a submenu you should study very well.

- **Enter Vehicle Mileage:** If you have a vehicle for your business, you should practice and understand the Vehicle Mileage window. You should first create your vehicle accounts in the Chart of Accounts, so the vehicle name is pulled into the Vehicle Mileage window. You must manually record your beginning and ending mileage on paper and then transfer it to this window.

- **Prepare Letters with Envelopes:** To make your financial life easy, QuickBooks has prepared some letters for you ahead of time. All you have to do is open the windows and select and complete the required options and boxes. Take a test drive on some of these letters and see how easy it is to write a business letter, and in less time than you think. Check to see if your computer has the required Microsoft Word before you start using letters and envelopes.

Review Home Page

The Home Page is the central hub that holds major icons and windows. Therefore, it is imperative to make the Home Page your default page when QuickBooks initially opens. It has the five major menus with their icons prominently displayed for easy access. They include the Vendor, Customer, Employees,

Company, and Banking menus. With the Home page, you don't have to access a window through the usual main menu. All you have to do is find the window you want to open on the Home Page and click on it. Let's review the contents of the Home Page.

- Click **Company menu**
- Click **Home Page**

Vendors: Vendors section has the following Icons

- Purchase Orders
- Enter Bills
- Receive Inventory
- Enter Bills Against Inventory
- Pay Bills
- Manage Sales Tax

Customers: Customers section has the following Icons

- Estimates
- Invoices
- Statement Charges
- Finance Charges
- Statements
- Receive Payments
- Create Sales Receipts
- Refunds & Credits

Employees: Employees section has the following Icons

- Enter Time
- Learn about Payroll Options

Company: Company section has the following Icons

- Chart of Accounts
- Items & Services
- Adjust Quantity On Hand
- Marketing Tools

Banking: Banking section has the following Icons:

- Record Deposits
- Reconcile
- Write Checks
- Check Register
- Print Checks
- Enter Credit Card Charges

Browse Company Snapshot

If setup correctly in the preferences window, QuickBooks will default you to the home page every time you logon. To get the summary of your financial activities, you click the company snapshot button on the toolbar next to the home page button. This takes you to the snapshot window, where you can view the account balances including who owes you—accounts receivable and who you owe—accounts payable. In the snapshot window you can easily see the alerts on urgent tasks.

Activities:

- ❖ Click **Company menu**
- ❖ Click **Company Snapshot**
- ❖ Under Account Balances (bottom left). Click **Select Accounts**
- ❖ Scroll down. Checkmark **Automobile Expenses**. Click **Update**
- ❖ Under Account Balances (bottom left). Click **Go to Chart of Accounts**
- ❖ Click **X** to close the Chart of Accounts window
- ❖ Under Customers Who Owe Money. Click **Receive Payments**
- ❖ Click **X** to close Integrated Payment Processing window
- ❖ Click **X** to Customer Payment window
- ❖ Under Vendors to Pay. Click **Pay Bills**
- ❖ Click **X** to close Pay Bill window
- ❖ Under Reminders. Click **Set Preferences.** Click **X** to close Preferences

Edit Company Information

It is highly recommended that you complete as much information in your company window as possible. Information from this window is pulled to other windows and used to populate vital financial reports. One of the most vital pieces of information is the type of tax form your company uses. QuickBooks defaults the correct tax information based on the form of business you selected. Also, your FEIN is essential for processing tax-related reports.

Activities:

- ❖ Click **Company menu**
- ❖ Click **Company Information**...
- ❖ Company Name: Accept **Quick Payroll 2009**
- ❖ Address: Type **123 Adam Lane**. Press **Enter**
- ❖ Type: **Dallas, TX 75000**
- ❖ Country: Accept **US**
- ❖ Legal Name: Type **Quick Payroll 2009**
- ❖ Legal Address: Type **123 Adam Lane**
- ❖ City: Type **Dallas**
- ❖ State: Press **T** twice for **TX**
- ❖ Zip: Type **75000**
- ❖ Phone: Type **214-100-1000**
- ❖ Fax: Type **214-200-2000**
- ❖ E-mail: Type **accountant@quickpayroll.com**
- ❖ Website: Type **www.quickpayroll.com**
- ❖ Federal Employer Identification no.: Type **99-1234567** (Very Important)
- ❖ Contact: Type **Kelly Johnson**
- ❖ Title: Type **Director of Finance**
- ❖ Phone #: Type **214-444-3000**
- ❖ Click **OK**

> Your Federal Identification number (EIN) is very important for paying your quarterly federal taxes.

Set Up Administrator & Users Passwords

Set Up Users allows you to set up passwords for both the administrator and users. It also allows you to add, edit, delete, and view user. You will not be able to delete an administrator, but only edit it. In this exercise, you are going to create an administrator and user named Kelly. In creating Kelly's password, QuickBooks will want to know what level of rights you want to grant her. You may grant Kelly full rights to read and write every window or limited rights for a few windows.

Activities:

- ❖ Click **Company menu**
- ❖ Click **Set Up Users and Passwords**
- ❖ Click **Set Up Users...**
- ❖ With Admin(logged on) highlighted in the window
- ❖ Click **Edit User**
- ❖ User Name: Accept **Admin**
- ❖ Password: Type **admin**
- ❖ Confirm Password: Type **admin**
- ❖ Challenge Question: Select **Name of oldest nephew**
- ❖ Challenge Answer: Type **admin**
- ❖ Click **Next.** Click **Finish**
- ❖ Click **Add User...**
- ❖ User Name: Type **Kelly**
- ❖ Password: Type **kelly**
- ❖ Confirm Password: Type **kelly.** Click **Next**
- ❖ Click **All areas of QuickBooks.** Click **Next**
- ❖ Click **Yes** to "Are you sure..."
- ❖ Review Kelly's access rights window
- ❖ Click **Finish**
- ❖ Click **Close** to User List window

> If you don't want to assign the "All areas of QuickBooks", you can allow access only to selected windows.

Edit and Delete Users Passwords

As an administrator, you have full rights to read and write every window and therefore can add, edit, and delete passwords. You can change Kelly's password, or she can do so if she has been assigned a password to enter the database. For Kelly to change her password, all she has to do is logon and click on the Kelly and Edit User button. The administrator is the only one who can delete admin's password. To remove admin's password, type the current password and leave New and Confirm New Password boxes blank. You must select <Select> for the challenge question.

Activities:

- ❖ Click **Company menu**
- ❖ Click **Set Up Users and Password**
- ❖ Click **Set Up Users…**
- ❖ Password: Type **admin**. Click **OK**
- ❖ Click **Kelly.** Click **Edit User…**
- ❖ User Name: Accept **Kelly**. Press **Tab**
- ❖ Password: Type **test**. Press **Tab**
- ❖ Confirm Password: Type **test**. Click **Next**
- ❖ Click **All areas of QuickBooks**. Click **Next**
- ❖ Click **Yes** to "Are you sure you want to give…?".
- ❖ Click **Finish**
- ❖ In the User List box. Click **Kelly.** Click **Delete User**
- ❖ Click **Yes** to "Are you sure you want to delete "kelly"?"
- ❖ Click **Close** to User List window

Edit Admin's Password

The administrator is the one who can add, edit or delete admin's password. To edit or remove admin's password, click the Set Up Users and Passwords and then the Change Your Password submenu, not the Set Up Users submenu. Most administrators think you can remove or delete admin password by going to the Set Up Users submenu, only to find out it is not the right way. You must select "<Select>" for the challenge question for the process to be completed.

Activities:

- ❖ Click **Company menu**
- ❖ Click **Set Up Users and Passwords**
- ❖ Click **Change Your Password**
- ❖ User Name: Accept **Admin**
- ❖ Current Password: Type **admin**
- ❖ New Password: **(leave blank)**
- ❖ Confirm New Password **(leave blank)**
- ❖ Challenge Question: Select **<Select>** (Very Important)
- ❖ Challenge Answer: **(leave blank)**
- ❖ Click **OK**
- ❖ Click **OK** to "Your QuickBooks password…"
- ❖ That's how you remove Admin's Password

Set Closing Date

You need to know how to set up the closing date to prevent you or anyone else from erroneously keying data for the previous year. If you set up the closing date correctly, any time you key transaction with the previous year, QuickBooks will prompt you to enter your password. Be sure to click Cancel and change your entry to 2009 when the message window appears. If you set the closing date/password, you must open it to enter any account opening balances.

Activities:

- ❖ Click **Company menu**
- ❖ Click **Set Closing Date…**
- ❖ Click **Set Date/Password** (bottom of the window)
- ❖ Closing Date: Type **12/31/08** (End of last year)
- ❖ Closing Date Password: Type **admin**
- ❖ Confirm Password: Type **admin**. Click **OK**
- ❖ Click **No** to "This company file does not…"
- ❖ Click **X** to close Preferences window
- ❖ Click **Lists menu.** Click **Chart of Accounts**
- ❖ Double click **USA Checking**
- ❖ **Highlight 1/1/2009 for Check # 1001**:
- ❖ Type **10/10/2008** (Last Year-Very Important). Press **Enter**
- ❖ Click **Yes** to "You have changed…"
- ❖ **Look! QuickBooks will not allow last year's entry without password**
- ❖ Click **Cancel** to "This modification…"
- ❖ **Highlight date again:** Type **1/1/09.** Press **Enter**
- ❖ Click **X** to close Register window.

Remove Closing Date

Setting the closing date and password depends on the number of people accessing the database. If you have more than three people, it is necessary to set the closing date password. Also, it is pertinent to limit the rights of everyone but the accountant and director finance to some windows, including creating paychecks or paystubs, printing payroll tax forms, paying or e-paying payroll taxes, accessing employees and payroll centers, and running or viewing payroll reports.

- ❖ Click **Company menu**
- ❖ Click **Set Closing Date…**
- ❖ Click **Set Date/Password** (bottom)

❖ Closing Date: **Highlight date**
❖ Press **Delete key**
❖ Closing Date Password: **Highlight password**
❖ Press **Delete key**
❖ Confirm Password: **Highlight password**
❖ Press **Delete key.** Click **OK**
❖ Click **No** to **"This company file does not…"**
❖ Click **X** to close Preferences window

Set Up Payroll Budget

Most companies operate their businesses on budgets. Few companies can survive long without a budget. Planning and budgeting set up is the first step in the budgeting process. You go through the Company menu to set up your budget; then you choose if you want to create a budget from the previous year's data or from scratch. In this exercise, you will create a budget from scratch. You may look at the image below for sample entries.

Activities:

❖ Click **Company menu**
❖ Click **Planning & Budgeting**
❖ Click **Set Up Budgets**. Select **2009**
❖ Click **Profit and Loss...** Click **Next**
❖ Click **No additional criteria**. Click **Next**
❖ Click **Create budget from scratch**
❖ Click **Finish**
❖ Under **Jan09** Click **Landscaping Services** line (1st item)
❖ Type **100,000**. Click **Copy Across** (bottom left)
❖ Scroll down to the bottom
❖ Under **Jan09.** Click **Payroll Services** (Expense ?)
❖ Type **20,000**. Click **Copy Across**
❖ Click **Save**
❖ Click **OK** to close window

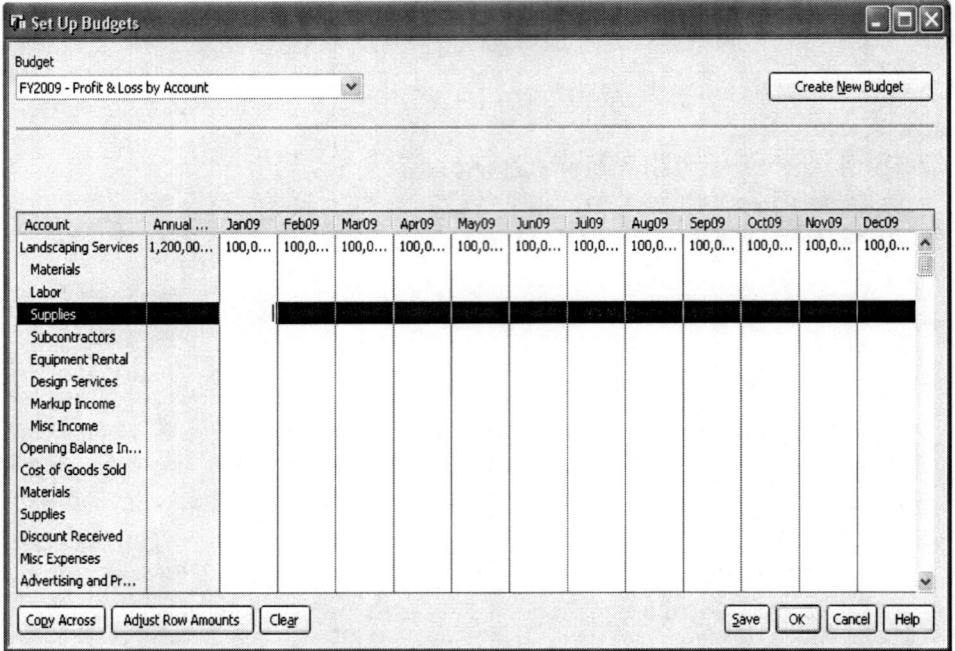

Complete To Do List

This is one function most businesses cannot do without. The To Do List has the advantage that your employees or associates can work from the same list and get you caught up on key financial tasks. It is easy to set up, but the hardest part is completing the tasks you set out to do, and not procrastinate until the next day or week. Most businesses have gone out of business because they did not meet important financial deadlines. Don't let this happen to you!

Activities:

- ❖ Click **Company menu**
- ❖ Click **To Do List**
- ❖ Right click in the window. Click **New**
- ❖ Note: Type **Transfer funds to brokerage account.** Press **Tab**
- ❖ Remind me on: Type **1/10/09**. Click **Next**
- ❖ Note: Type **Backup QuickBooks**. Press **Tab**
- ❖ Remind me on: Type **1/31/09**. Click **OK**
- ❖ Right click on **1/10/09 for Transfer funds to...**
- ❖ Click **Edit To Do Note**
- ❖ Click **Done** (bottom right). Click **OK**
- ❖ **Look! The Transfer funds note has a checkmark**

Complete Reminders & Alert Manager

Apart from the To Do List, you have the Reminders and the Alert Manager. QuickBooks is doing everything possible to make sure you're on top of your financial tasks—that you get the job done—on time! One advantage of the Reminders is that it will be staring you in the face every time you open your QuickBooks file, if the Preferences are set up correctly. For this reason, you must set up your Reminder in the Preferences window, and you should review your Reminder window daily.

Activities:

- ❖ Click **Company menu**
- ❖ Click **Reminders**
- ❖ Click **Collapse All** (bottom of the window)
- ❖ Click **Expand All**
- ❖ Click **X** to close window
- ❖ Click **Company menu**
- ❖ Click **Alert Manager**
- ❖ Review window
- ❖ Click **X** to close window

> When reviewing the Alert window if an item is completed and the date has passed, click a checkmark in the box left of the Alert.

Make General Journal Entries

When a fixed asset loses its market value due to wear and tear, it is said to be depreciating. You can make entries by clicking Company menu and then Make

General Journal Entries. Company-related journal entries are depreciation expense, prepaid insurance, use of supplies, and accrual of wages liabilities. Additional entries are bank reconciliation process-related, such as interest expense, interest income, overpayment, underpayment, bank fees and entry on the statement not on the books.

Activities:

- ❖ Click **Company menu**
- ❖ Click **Make General Journal Entries**
- ❖ Click **OK** to "QuickBooks now automatically assign numbers..."
- ❖ Date: Type **1/31/09**
- ❖ Entry No.: Accept **3**
- ❖ Click under **Account.** (left of the window)
- ❖ **Scroll down to the bottom.** Click **Depreciation Expense**
- ❖ Click under **Debit:** Type **666.67**
- ❖ Click under **Memo:** Type **Jan Depreciation on truck**
- ❖ Click **under Depreciation Expense**
- ❖ Select **Accumulated Depreciation** under Truck.
- ❖ Click under **Credit:** Type **666.67**
- ❖ Click under **Memo:** Type **Jan Depreciation on truck**
- ❖ Click **Save & Close.** Click **OK**

> Instead of re-typing the memo, you can highlight the previous memo, and apply the copy and paste to the new memo.

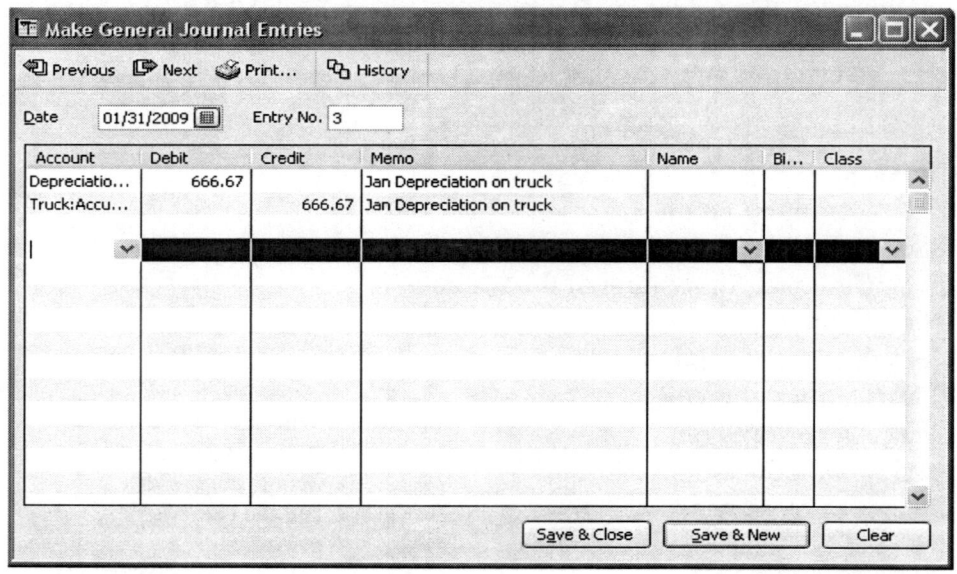

Enter Vehicle Mileage

For tax and financial purposes, if you have cars and trucks, you want your staff to log in their mileage on those cars and trucks. This information is also used to send bills to customers connected to the projects. You must check and record your Trip Start and Trip End odometer readings. After you've keyed in all your data, you should be able to click the top right of the window and print a mileage report, either in detail or summary format.

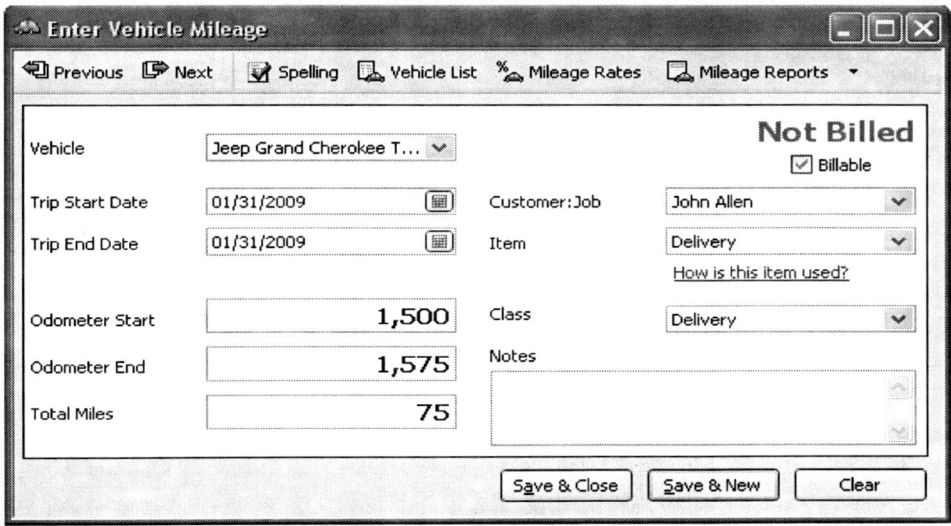

Activities:

- ❖ Click **Company menu**
- ❖ Click **Enter Vehicle Mileage**
- ❖ Vehicle: Select **Jeep Grand Cherokee Truck**
- ❖ Trip Start Date: Type **1/31/09**
- ❖ Trip End Date: Type **1/31/09**
- ❖ Odometer Start: Type **1,500**.
- ❖ Odometer End: Type **1,575**. Press **Tab**
- ❖ Total Miles: Accept **75**
- ❖ Checkmark **Billable** (top right)
- ❖ Customer: Job: Select **John Allen**
- ❖ Item: Select **Delivery**
- ❖ Class: Select **Delivery**
- ❖ Click **Save & Close** (bottom right)

Financial Results: Profit & Loss

In this chapter, we created a password for our financial file. I urge you to do the same on your own file. It's always good to make it difficult for intruders to invade your privacy. We introduced the depreciation expense by making a General Journal entry for 666.67, to reduce the value of the Truck asset. Every month, the Truck value is decreased and the depreciation expense account is increased by the same amount. If you did not select This Fiscal Year from the date drop-down arrow, your result might be different from the textbook's result.

Activities:

- ❖ Click **Reports menu**
- ❖ Click **Company & Financial**
- ❖ Click **Profit & Loss Standard**
- ❖ Date: Select **This Fiscal Year**
- ❖ From: Accept **1/1/09**
- ❖ To: Accept **12/31/09**
- ❖ **Net Income 999,183.33**
- ❖ Click **X** to close window

Quick Payroll 2009
Profit & Loss
January through December 2009

	◇ Jan - Dec 09 ◇
Ordinary Income/Expense	
Income	
Opening Balance Income	▶ 1,005,000.00 ◀
Total Income	1,005,000.00
Gross Profit	1,005,000.00
Expense	
Depreciation Expense	666.67
Opening Balance Expense	5,000.00
Travel Expense	150.00
Total Expense	5,816.67
Net Ordinary Income	999,183.33
Net Income	**999,183.33**

Financial: Balance Sheet

Anytime you depreciate an asset account, you reduce the account balance. As you continue to depreciate the asset account, the accumulated depreciation balance will continue to increase while the asset balance will continue to decrease by the same amount. So every month, you must check both the Profit & Loss and the Balance Sheet statements to make sure the amounts are pulling into the reports. Total Truck account has decreased by 666.67 and Total Assets is 2,244,183.33.

Activities:

- ❖ Click **Reports menu**
- ❖ Click **Company & Financial**
- ❖ Click **Balance Sheet Standard**
- ❖ Date: Select **This Fiscal Year**
- ❖ As of: Accept **12/31/09**
- ❖ Click **Collapse**
- ❖ **Total Assets 2,244,183.33**
- ❖ Click **X** to close window

```
                    Quick Payroll 2009
                     Balance Sheet
                  As of December 31, 2009
                              ◇ Dec 31, 09 ◇
     ASSETS
       Current Assets
         Checking/Savings
           Money Market Account   ▶   100,000.00 ◀
           USA Checking                799,850.00
           USA Payroll                 250,000.00
         Total Checking/Savings      1,149,850.00

         Accounts Receivable
           Accounts Receivable       1,005,000.00
         Total Accounts Receivable   1,005,000.00

         Other Current Assets
           Inventory Asset              50,000.00
         Total Other Current Assets     50,000.00

       Total Current Assets          2,204,850.00

       Fixed Assets
         Truck                          39,333.33
       Total Fixed Assets              39,333.33

     TOTAL ASSETS                    2,244,183.33
```

Review Principles of Journal Entries

There are five major accounts in accounting. However, sometimes accountants create minor accounts to explain the nature of these five accounts. For instance, asset is one of the five major accounts, but sometimes accountants create current assets, fixed assets, and other assets to explain how liquid these assets are.

Five major accounts:
- Assets
- Liabilities
- Equity
- Income
- Expenses

Debits and Credits:

Newcomers to the accounting profession would find this section a little hard to understand initially more than any other part of accounting. In fact, this is one of the most important sections of the entire book, because debit and credit are what happen to most numbers that enter the QuickBooks software. I'm going to give you the summary of debits and credits, and once you understand this simple principle, every facet of accounting job will so easy to you.

Debits and Credits Picture:

Increase(Debit)	Increase(Credit)
Assets	Liabilities
	Equity
Expenses	Income
Decrease (Credit)	Decrease (Debit)

Every accountant has this same picture you're looking at, burnt into his or her mind, and once you understand and can remember this picture, the rest of accounting is history! I'll explain the picture in a minute, but let me repeat what I said before: All accounts in the accounting profession are created from these five accounts. All you have to do is remember these five accounts, and any time you see an account, you just find out which account it was created from. Once you understand how to debit and credit these five accounts, you will understand how to debit and credit thousands of accounts you or anyone else can create from these five accounts. It's that easy!

Explanation to Debit and Credits Picture:

Increase (Debit)	Increase (Credit)
Assets	Liabilities
	Equities
Expenses	Income
Decrease (Credit)	Decrease (Debit)

- First, remember there are only five major accounts
- Assets and Expenses on the left
- Liabilities, Equities, and Income on the right
- On the Left side Increase is Debit
- On the right side Increase is Credit
- Increase on Assets and Expenses is Debit and the opposite is true
- Decrease on Assets and Expenses is Credit
- Increase on Liabilities, Equities and Income is Credit and the opposite is true
- Decrease on Liabilities, Equities and Income is Debit
- If you think Assets and Expenses increases you think Debit
- If you think Liabilities, Equities and Income increases you think Credit
- Can you close your eyes and see this picture? That's all you need
- Increase Debit. Increase Credit. That's it! And the opposite is true.

Using Debits and Credits Picture in Journal Entry:

Increase (Debit)	Increase (Credit)
Assets	Liabilities
	Equity
Expenses	Income
Decrease (Credit)	Decrease (Debit)

Assets and Equity:
You can get clues about a journal entry by talking to yourself about what happened. For example, you might say, "I put money in the checking account—Asset, which is on the left side," or "I took out a loan--Liability, which is on the right side."

What if you, as the owner, bring money into the business and put it in the bank account called USA Checking in the amount of 50,000?

You will increase USA Checking (an Asset) by 50,000 and will increase the Owner's accounts Equity). When you increase asset, you Debit it. And when you increase equity, you Credit it.

USA Checking   50,000
Owner's Investments   50,000

Assets and Expenses:

Now you have funds in the bank account USA Checking. What if it's the end of the month and you wrote a check from USA Checking to pay a telephone bill for 450? You will decrease USA Checking (an Asset) by 450 and will increase the telephone bill accounts (an Expense). When you decrease asset, you Credit it; and when you increase expense, you Debit it.

USA Checking   450
Telephone Expense   450

Assets and Liabilities:

What if go out and buy Inventory for 65,786 for your business, they give you a bill and you promised to pay the account within 30 days.

You will increase Inventory (an Asset) by 65,786 and also increase Accounts Payable (a Liability). When you increase asset you, Debit it; and when you increase liability, you Credit it.

Inventory Asset   65,786
Accounts Payable   67,786

Assets and Income:

What if one of your customers sends you a check for consulting services for 23,450 and you put it in USA Checking account?

You will increase USA Checking (an Asset) by 23,450 and will increase Consulting Income (an Income). When you increase asset, you Debit it; and when you increase income, you Credit it.

USA Checking   23,450
Consulting Income   23,450

Assets and Assets:

Up until now I've been talking about Assets and other accounts, now let's see what happened when you used asset to buy asset. For example, you went to a store and bought a computer for 3,500 with a check.

When you pay by check, you decreased USA Checking (an Asset) by 3,500 and increase Computer account (an Asset). When you decrease asset you, Credit it; and when you increase asset, you Debit it.

USA Checking   3,500
Computer   3,500

Examples of Accounts:
Click Lists menu. Click Chart of Accounts. Review some accounts examples.
  a. Examples of Assets: Cash, Checking account, Savings account, Accounts Receivables, Other Current Assets, Fixed (Long Term) Assets
  b. Examples of Liabilities: Accounts Payable, Credit Card, Other Current Liabilities, Long Term Liabilities
  c. Examples of Equity: Beginning Equity, Owner's Contribution, Owners Distribution, Retained Earnings, Other Equity accounts
  d. Examples of Income: Landscaping, Materials, Supplies, Subcontractors, Sales, Services, Uncategorized
  e. Examples of Expenses: Cost of Goods Sold, Materials, Supplies, Automobile, Insurance, Telephone, Taxes, Utilities, Uncategorized

To perform the journal entries, you click Company menu, then, click Make General Journal entries. You are now in the journal entry window.

Practice makes perfect!
The difference between you and I is time. I've been using the same principle I'm teaching you here for many years now—it's no magic at all. Believe me, as soon as you understand this simple principle, and use it over and over again, it will be as easy as ABC. I've just given you few examples, every other journal entries will follow similar pattern. You can use the same thought pattern I've used here to make practically any journal entries. Remember QuickBooks is designed to make these entries for you, all the hard work has been done, I'm just showing what is going on behind the scenes, should you want to make one these entries yourself. This stuff is very easy with practice!

Review Month-End Journal Entries

From time to time you may make journal entries such as when you bought asset or pay for expenses with your personal money. You have to make a journal entry to bring in that money into the business as Debit to Checking and Credit to Owners Contribution. However, in this section we are looking at monthly entries you have to make because business activities. You don't have to worry too much about accounting and journal entries; QuickBooks has done all the work for you. However, there are few entries you would have to do yourself and my job is to make sure you understand, step by step, how to make these few entries. Relax and have fun—this is so easy! I'll start here with the company related entries, when you get to the Banking menu, I'll explain those entries also. **You may test these journal entries only in the Testing Company file not in the Quick Payroll file**. There are four basic entries in this section:

Company basic entries:
- Depreciation
- Inventory Supplies
- Prepaid Expenses
- Payroll (aka Wages)

Depreciation:
As you manage your business with your fixed assets—truck, building or furniture—these assets are losing value. Accountants would say these assets are depreciating in value (the opposite of appreciating in value). Accounting rules allow you to reduce your income every month by the amount your asset is depreciating in value. Initially, you created a Truck account in the Chart of Account window for 40,000. Let's find out how QuickBooks made the journal entry. Click **Repots menu**. Click **Company & Financial**. Click **Balance Sheet Standard**. Double click **40,000** for Original Truck Price. Double click **40,000** again. Double click **GENJRNL** (left of 1st row). Look! QuickBooks made the following entries for you:

Truck: Original Truck Price   40,000
Opening Bal Equity   40,000

As we calculated somewhere in the previous pages, if your monthly depreciation amount is 666.67. Then your job is to make the following entries:

Deprecation Expense   666.67
Accumulated Depreciation-Truck   666.67

Inventory Asset:
When you set up your Inventory Parts in the Item List window under the List menu, QuickBooks made the following entries for Inventory Asset of 50,000.

Inventory Asset   50,000
Opening Bal Equity- Adjustment   50,000

As you continue to use the supplies, the number and the value will continue to go down. If you set the quantity box, QuickBooks should be able to track of your inventory balance on your Balance Sheet report. If you did not set the quantity box, QuickBooks will not track of your inventory, you have to go to the warehouse and count the remainder of your inventory. When you subtract what is left from what you started with, the difference is what you used. If you used 4,500 of Material Inventory, your job would be to make the following entries, but QuickBooks made the entries for you because you told QuickBooks to track your inventory.

Inventory: Materials		4,500
Cost of Good Sold: Materials	4,500	

Click **Reports menu**. Click **Company & Financial**. Click **Balance Sheet Standard**, you will see Inventory Asset has gone down by 4,500. Click **Reports menu**. Click **Company & Financial**. Click **Profit & Loss Standard**, Date: Select **This Fiscal Year**, you will see Cost of Good Sold has 4,500.

Prepaid Expenses:
If you own assets such as a Truck or Building, you should have insurance on those assets. Sometimes, the insurance company will prorate the insurance bill into monthly payments, which they can withdraw from your checking account by EFT (electronic fund transfer). In this case, you have no journal entry problem. However, if you wrote a one-time check for 10,500 to the insurance company for one year you must write the check in the Check Register, but you should first create an account called prepaid insurance in the Chart of Account window with 0.00 opening balance, and then pull that account into the check register. QuickBooks will then make the following entries for you:

USA Checking		10,500
Prepaid Insurance	10,500	

As each month passes by, you divide the annual lump sum of 10,500 into 12 and book the result of 875 every month. You will make the following monthly entries:

Insurance Expense	875.00	
Prepaid Insurance		875.00

Click **Reports menu**. Click **Company & Financial**. Click **Balance Sheet Standard**, you will see Prepaid Insurance has gone down by 875. Click **Reports menu**. Click **Company & Financial**. Click **Profit & Loss Standard**, Date: Select **This Fiscal Year**. You will see Insurance Expense has 875.00

Wages:
If you have December 31 as the end of your fiscal year—as most companies do— sometimes, that date will fall in the middle of the week, say, on a Tuesday. What if you have an employee who earns $20 an hour and worked from Monday, December 29, 2008 through Friday, January 2, 2009 the next year? You will accrue the Monday, Tuesday, and Wednesday in the 2008 financial statement, because the services have been performed but not paid for yet till Friday of 2009.

Your entry for the three days (Monday and Wednesday) that fell in 2008 financial statement, but were not paid for, will be 24 hours at 20 an hour.

Payroll Expense	480.00	
Payroll Liabilities		480.00

Summary:
These are the four basic end-of-the-period journal entries you will have to make in the Company menu. Any other journal entries that come along will follow one these four basic entries. All you have to do is follow the same thinking pattern and you will be OK. It is not hard once you take one of these examples and repeat it over and over again—be it Depreciation, Inventory Supplies, Prepaid Expenses, or Payroll Payable.

Chapter Summary

Most Company menu activities are office administration in nature: how to update the Company Information and how to set up and update password windows for users and administrator. We looked at the Make General Journal Entry window which is important because you will be using it frequently. If you pay a bill with a personal check, you will first use the Enter Bills window under Vendor menu; then make a Journal Entry to increase the checking account by debiting the checking account and increasing owner's contribution to the business by crediting owner equity. Finally, pay the bill with the amount you just posted to the checking account.

What we accomplished:
- Reviewed the Company submenus
- Reviewed the content of home page
- Identified the company snapshot
- Updated the company information
- Set up administrator and user passwords
- Edited and deleted users passwords
- Edited admin's password
- Setup and removed closing date
- Learned how to prepare a payroll budget
- Learned how to use the To-Do list, reminders & alert manager
- Made a general journal entry
- Completed the vehicle mileage window
- Processed financial statements
- Reviewed the principles of journal entries
- Reviewed month-end journal entries

Additional Financial activities:
- We made a Journal entry for 666.67

Optional Test 5

Questions: True/False

Answer the following questions by placing letter the T or F in the space provided before the question number.

_____ 1. If you want to change the name of a company on the Title bar, you must do so in Company Information submenu.

_____ 2. Change Your Password submenu is used to change Administrator's password not users.

_____ 3. When you set up a Closing Date/Password, QuickBooks will ask for your password before making any changes to a closed year.

_____ 4. Reminders are generated by QuickBooks based on the information on your database like invoice due dates.

_____ 5. When making a General Journal entry, if you want to increase an asset you credit it and when you want to decrease an asset you debit it.

_____ 6. When making a General Journal entry, if you want to increase a liability you credit it and when you want to decrease a liability you debit it.

_____ 7. Like reminders, Alerts are generated by QuickBooks and are always left in the list even when the activity due date is passed.

_____ 8. When completing a company information window, the e-mail box is essential because QuickBooks uses the e-mail in the send form window.

_____ 9. If you want to increase an income account you have to debit the account, and if you want to decrease an income account you have to credit.

_____ 10. When you want to increase an expense account you have to debit it and when you want to decrease an expense account you have to credit it.

Questions: Multiple Choices

Answer the following questions by placing letter A, B, C, or D in the space provided before the question number.

_____ 1. In creating a new budget, QuickBooks allows you to create which of the following budgets?
A. Profit & Loss
B. Balance Sheet
C. All of the above
D. None of the above

_____ 2. When a fixed asset used in business is losing market value due to wear and tear or obsolesces, it is said to be_____?
A. Appreciating
B. Contributing
C. Depreciating
D. Non-Contributing

_____ 3. If you don't want your daily tasks to fall through the cracks, like failing to pay for an invoice by the due date, you use which of the following tools?
A. Daily List
B. To Do List
C. All of the above
D. None of the above

_____ 4. If you want to increase an asset or increase an expense you do which of the following?
A. Debit it
B. Credit it
C. All of the above
D. None of the above

_____ 5. As you complete the Enter Vehicle Mileage submenu, which of the following about the vehicle is not included?
A. Customer: Job
B. Trip Start Date
C. Trip End Date
D. Vehicle Destination

____ 6. To change the QuickBooks company title, which of the following box in the company information window must be changed?
   A. Legal Name
   B. Contact Name
   C. Company Name
   D. Federal Tax ID Name

____ 7. Set Up Users' submenu under Company menu allows you to set up Password-related tasks, which of the following is not performed in the set up window?
   A. Add Users
   B. Edit Users
   C. Replace Users
   D. Delete Users

____ 8. After you have posted a depreciation expense for the month, the Balance Sheet statement will show it as a _____ from an asset account?
   A. Addition
   B. Subtraction
   C. Division
   D. Multiplication

____ 9. When you paid a lump sum one-year insurance premium you debit Prepaid and credit Checking, each month you reduce the Prepaid by the one month premium by crediting Prepaid and debiting_____?
   A. Insurance Prepaid
   B. Insurance Liability
   C. Insurance Equity
   D. Insurance Expense

____ 10. When you want to delete the administrator's password which of the following text boxes would be left blank for the process to work?
   A. New Password
   B. Confirm New Password
   C. Challenge Question
   D. All of the above

$

Chapter 6

Customers Menu

Objectives: After you've completed this chapter, you will be able to:

- ✓ Describe the Customer submenus
- ✓ Identify the Customer center contents
- ✓ Create new customers with details and opening balances
- ✓ Prepare invoices for your customers
- ✓ Receive payments from customers on outstanding invoices
- ✓ Create accounts receivable & sales graphs
- ✓ Process customer balance on pdf
- ✓ Run financial reports and compare your results

Review Customers Submenus

Most businesses sell goods and services to customers and collect payments from them. The purpose of the Customers menu is to help you complete all customer-related windows with the right information. When you want to create, edit or delete a customer, you should remember the Customers menu. When you get used to the Customer menu and its functions, navigating through the Customer windows will be easy. I cannot emphasize consistency enough in accessing Customer windows through the menu; this way you don't waste your time running back and forth from one window to another.

- Click **Customers menu**

The following submenus are located under the Customers menu:

- **Customer Center:** This is the door office to other customer windows. It holds all the information about each customer. The windows in the Customers Center will allow you to create, edit or delete customers. You can delete a new customer, but if sales and payments are connected to that customer, QuickBooks will not allow you to delete it. It is recommended that you make the customer inactive.

- **Create Estimates:** Your customer may request an estimate for a particular job or project; this way the customer can evaluate whether to choose you over other Vendors. Estimate is a precursor to an invoice, since the customer is going to review your invoice based on the estimated price of the items you previously quoted. So be sure your prices are correct; most customers don't like surprises.

- **Create Invoices:** Before you can sell anything to your customer, an invoice window should be completed. The customer invoice window is user-friendly and easy to navigate as long as you have completed the appropriate Lists menu windows; you can pull the right information into the customer's invoice.

- **Enter Sales Receipts:** When a customer pays immediately and the transaction is completed in one shot, it is best to use the sales receipts. With sales receipt, your customer is not going to owe you in the future; rather payment is made in full at the moment. You don't need an invoice an item again after you've completed the Sales Receipt.

- **Enter Statement Charges:** The job of this window is to accumulate charges until the end of the month. If you are performing consulting services for a customer, every time you incur a charge, you may enter the charge daily or wait until the end of the month. You enter the charges directly in the register and receive payment in the receive payment window as usual. At the end of the month, you will print a statement that shows all the charges.

- **Create Statements:** After you've entered all your charges, at the end of the month you are ready to send a statement to the customer. It is recommended that you make sure all charges from all departments are entered on the statements, if you have more than one department. Your customer would not like to see last month's activities on this month's statement.

- **Assess Finance Charges:** After you've sent invoices to your customers, not all the customers will pay off their invoices at the end of the month. After 30, 60 or 90 days, you will start charging late fees on those outstanding invoices at the percentage you preset in QuickBooks. You then run the Assess Finance Charges process to update customer balances with the late fees and a new invoice will be sent out next month with late fees included.

- **Receive Payments:** This is not receiving payment in the mail, but completing the Receive Payment window. It allows you to enter the payment for the right customer. I cannot overemphasize the importance of pulling the right customer for the right payment. You could assess late fees to the wrong customer because you have applied another's payment to the wrong customer. It is recommended to double check your work after this window is completed.

- **Create Credit Memo/Refunds:** If you sell merchandise to a customer, you may specify FOB Shipping point. This means the customer is responsible for the goods as soon as it leaves your dock. Another option is to specify FOB Destination, which means you are responsible for the goods until they arrive at the customer's dock. If this is the case, you will be issuing credit memos or refunds for all damaged goods in transit, because you are responsible for the goods until they arrive at the customer's dock. If you can, it is a good practice to avoid all FOB Destination arrangements.

- **Add Credit Card Processing:** A small business will be quick in receiving payment much faster if you can sign up for credit card processing. The only drawback is the fees from the credit card issuer, which may be exorbitant.

- **Enter Time:** If you have hourly employee, at the end of every week, you will fill out a Time Card for him or her in QuickBooks. There are two ways of recording time. The first one is the use of the Weekly Timesheet. It has a one-week period, Monday through Sunday, where you can enter the eight hours worked for one day. The second tool is the Time/Enter Single Activity. It allows you to complete a day's job by time clock.

- **Add Marketing and Customer Tools** You have to login to the internet to use this submenu.

- **Learn about Point of Sales** You have to login to the internet to use this submenu.

- **Item List:** We've discussed Item List under the Item menu. The Item List window allows you to create items that pull to other windows and reports.

- **Change Item Prices:** Item prices are not carved in stone; it changes from month to month or from year to year. QuickBooks has made it possible for you to change a list of product prices with a click of a button. It is recommended to use the percentage method of increasing prices across the board, so you don't have to manually increase prices on thousands of individual items.

Review Customer Center

Anytime you have a problem with a customer, the first place you should think about is the Customers menu, and the next place is the Customer Center. They have all the activities that pertain to a customer. If you're at the Home Page, you can access the Customer Center by clicking the Customers button. However, if you're at any other window, the best move is to click the Customers menu and then Customer Center. Let's review the contents of the Customer Center windows.

- Click **Customers menu**
- Click **Customer Center**

Activities buttons and windows: You will find the following activities when you open the Customer Center window

- New Customer & Job
- New Transaction
- Print

- Excel
- Word
- Customer & Job tab
- View down arrow
- Transaction tab
- Edit Customer
- Edit Notes
- Show down arrow
- Filter By down arrow
- Date down arrow

Report for this Customer: Customer reports are located at the right side of the window and they include the following:

- QuickReport
- Open Balance
- Show Estimates

Right Click: When you right click the left side of the Customer Center window, you will find the following options:

- Find
- Use
- Refresh
- Edit Customer: Job
- Add Job
- Make Customer: Job Inactive
- Re-sort List
- Hierarchical View
- Flat View
- Customize Columns
- Show Full Customer List only
- Create Invoice
- Create Estimates
- Show Estimates
- Receive Payments
- Make Deposits
- Enter Sales Receipts

- Enter Statement Changes
- Create Credit Memo/Refunds
- Create Statements
- Access Finance Charges
- Use Register

New Customer: James Adams

As soon as you've signed a contract with a customer, the next step is to load the customer data into the system. You should not waste time taking care of this task because you will be overwhelmed when you decide to send out invoices and you discover the customer is not available in QuickBooks. When creating a new customer, you should supply as much information as possible. The particular information you skip may be the one you'll need most on an invoice or report.

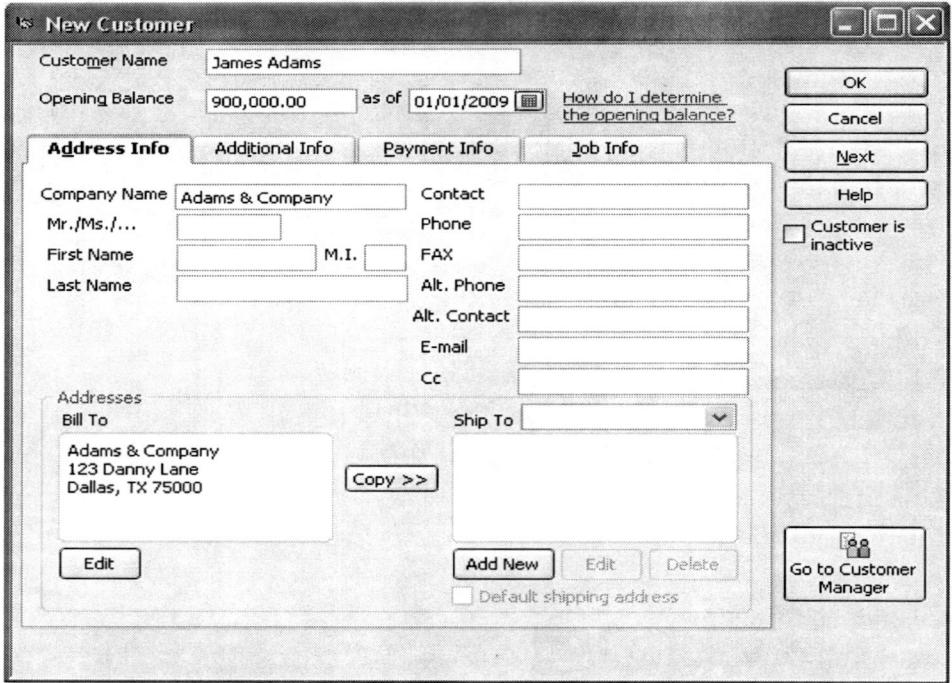

Activities:

- ❖ Click **Customers menu**
- ❖ Click **Customer Center**
- ❖ Right click in the window
- ❖ Click **New Customer**

❖ Customer Name: Type **James Adams**
❖ Opening Balance: Type **900,000** as of: Type **1/1/09**
❖ Company Name: Type **Adams & Company**
❖ Click in Bill To box. Accept **Adams & Company**. Press **Enter**
❖ Type **123 Danny Lane, Dallas, TX 75000**
❖ Click **OK**

Customer Detail: James Adams

In the Lists menu, we touched briefly on a customer's address information. In this section, we are going provide detailed information about a customer. Remember the more data you can provide about a customer, the more knowledgeable you are about that customer and the more reports you will be able to pull about that customer in the future. Additional Info tab and the Job Info tab are excellent places to furnish some vitally essential data about your customers.

Activities:

❖ Click **Customers menu**
❖ Click **Customer Center**
❖ Double click **James Adams**
❖ Contact: Type **Kenny Moore**
❖ Phone: Type **214-300-1111**
❖ Fax: Type **214-300-2222**
❖ E-mail: **kmoore@adamscompany.com**
❖ Click **Additional Info** tab

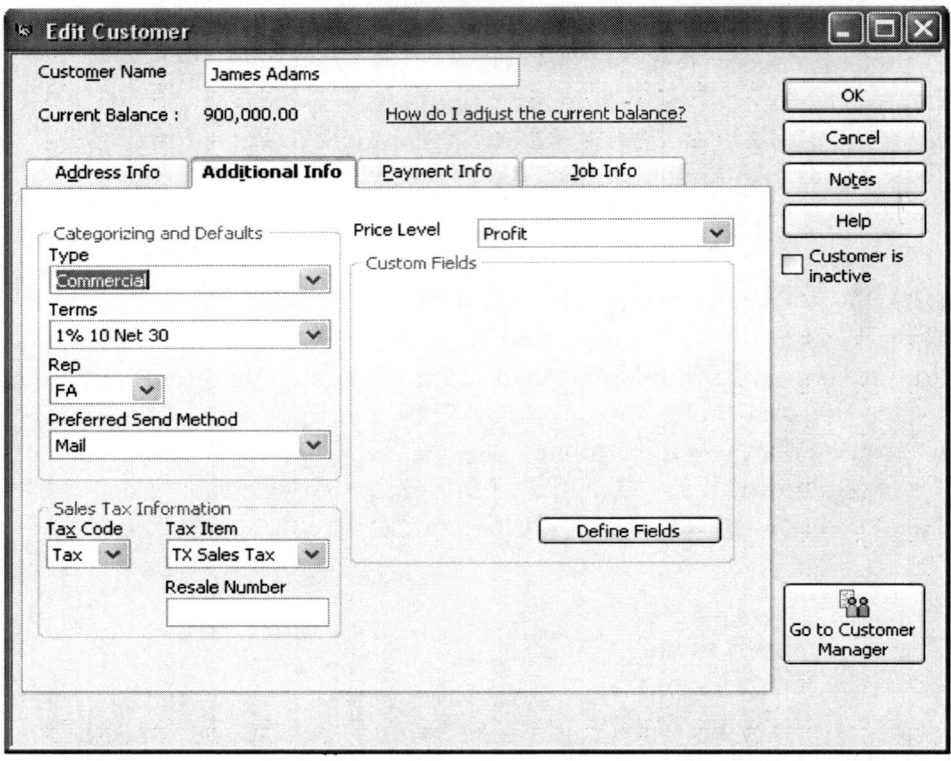

- ❖ Type Select **Commercial**
- ❖ Terms: Select **1% 10 Net 30**
- ❖ Rep: Select **FA**
- ❖ Preferred Send Method: Select **Mail**.
- ❖ Tax Code: Select **Tax**
- ❖ Tax Item: Select **TX Sales Tax**
- ❖ Price Level (top right): Select **Profit**
- ❖ Click **Payment Info** tab
- ❖ Account No: Type **Cust 123601**
- ❖ Credit Limit: Type **2,000,000**
- ❖ Preferred Payment Method: Type **Check**
- ❖ Click **Job Info** tab
- ❖ Job Status: Select **In Progress**
- ❖ Start Date: Type **1/1/09**
- ❖ Projected Date: Type **12/31/09**
- ❖ End Date: (Leave blank)
- ❖ Description: Type **Flower Beds**
- ❖ Job Type: Select **New Construction**
- ❖ Click **OK**

Create Invoice

An invoice must have the customer's name and address, with shipping and billing addresses if they are different. The terms of payment should be provided, along with a purchase order number. Product data are required to be accurate including the item name, item number, quantities, prices and sales tax amount. You must have inventory on hand from vendors before you invoice an Inventory Item. Otherwise, the only items you could invoice are labor or non-inventory items.

Activities:

- ❖ Click **Customers menu**
- ❖ Click **Create Invoices**
- ❖ Customer: Job: Select **James Adams**
- ❖ Class: Select **Landscaping**
- ❖ Date: Type **1/2/09**
- ❖ Invoice: Type **1001**
- ❖ P. O. No: Type **01012009**
- ❖ Terms: Accept **1% 10 Net 30**
- ❖ Click under Item: Select **Flowers**
- ❖ Click under Qty: Type **1000**
- ❖ Customer Message: Accept **Thank you for your business**
- ❖ Tax: Accept **TX Sales Tax (7.5%) 5,625**
- ❖ Checkmark **To be Printed** (bottom)
- ❖ Checkmark **To be e-mailed** (Very Important)
- ❖ Customer Tax Code: Accept **Tax**
- ❖ Balance Due: Accept **80,625.00**
- ❖ Click **Print Preview** (top right of the window)
- ❖ Click **Zoom In.** Click **Close**
- ❖ Click **Save & Close**

> Because P.O. numbers are very important, if you don't have any P.O use the date you received the email or other communication for the order.

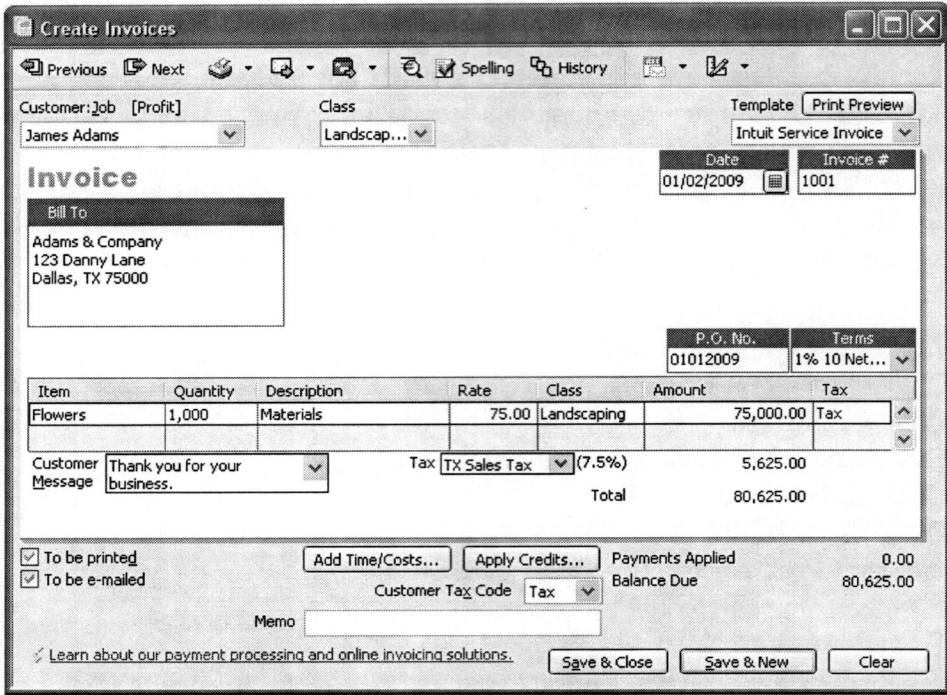

Receive Payment

When you receive a payment from your customer, you pull the customer's invoices and apply the check to the outstanding balances. Sometimes, one check will cover a number of invoices and, at other times, one check will cover just one invoice. Completing the Receive Payment window is easy, because as soon as you pull up the invoice, QuickBooks does the rest with the click of a button. If you deposited a check without creating an invoice first, be sure to create and receive the payment according to the deposit in the bank statement, that way it is simple to identify.

Activities:

- ❖ Click **Customers menu**
- ❖ Click **Receive Payments**
- ❖ Launch Web Browser? Click **Cancel**
- ❖ Receive From: Select **James Adams**
- ❖ Amount: Type **900,000**
- ❖ Customer Balance: Accept **980,625.00**
- ❖ Date: Type **1/15/09**
- ❖ Pmt Method: Select **Check**
- ❖ Check #: Type **4005**

❖ Accept **Checkmarks on 1/1/09 for 900,000**
❖ Click **Save & Close**

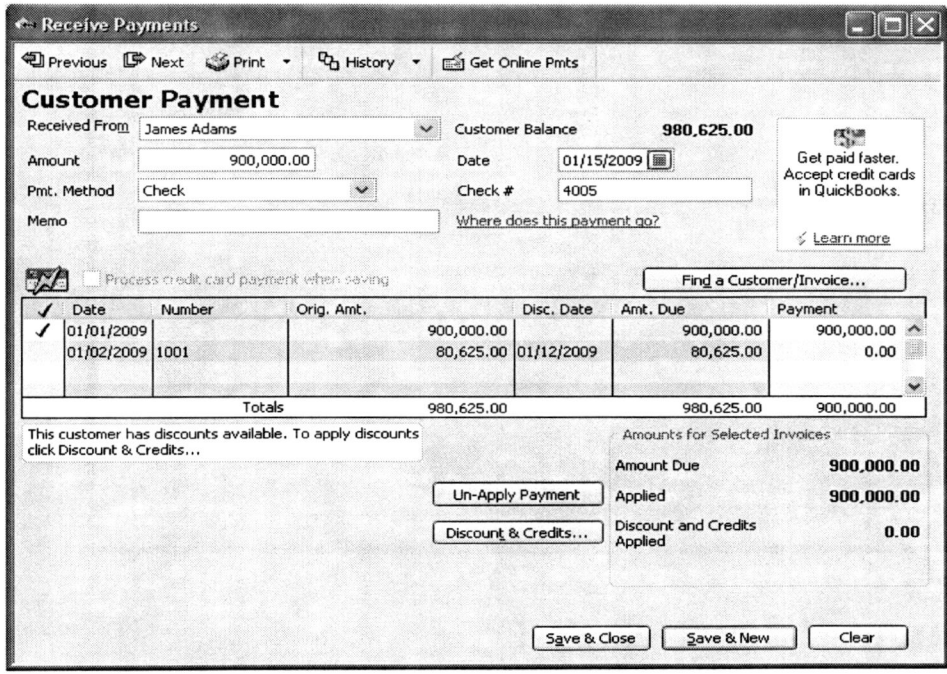

Accounts Receivable Graph

Customer invoice sales are tracked by QuickBooks and used to update the Accounts Receivable balance. Furthermore, Accounts Receivable can be presented in an aging format. The purpose of the Accounts Receivable Graph is to present the balances by aging format in a bar chart and by customer in a pie chart. If you want to get the details of the individual bar chart and pie chart, double click on it. Be sure the date range is exactly what you want; otherwise, your result will be incorrect.

Activities:

❖ Click **Reports menu**
❖ Click **Customers & Receivables**
❖ Click **Accounts Receivable Graph**
❖ Click **Date**..(top left of the window)
❖ Show Aging as of: Type **12/31/09**
❖ Click **OK**
❖ Click **X** to close Graph window

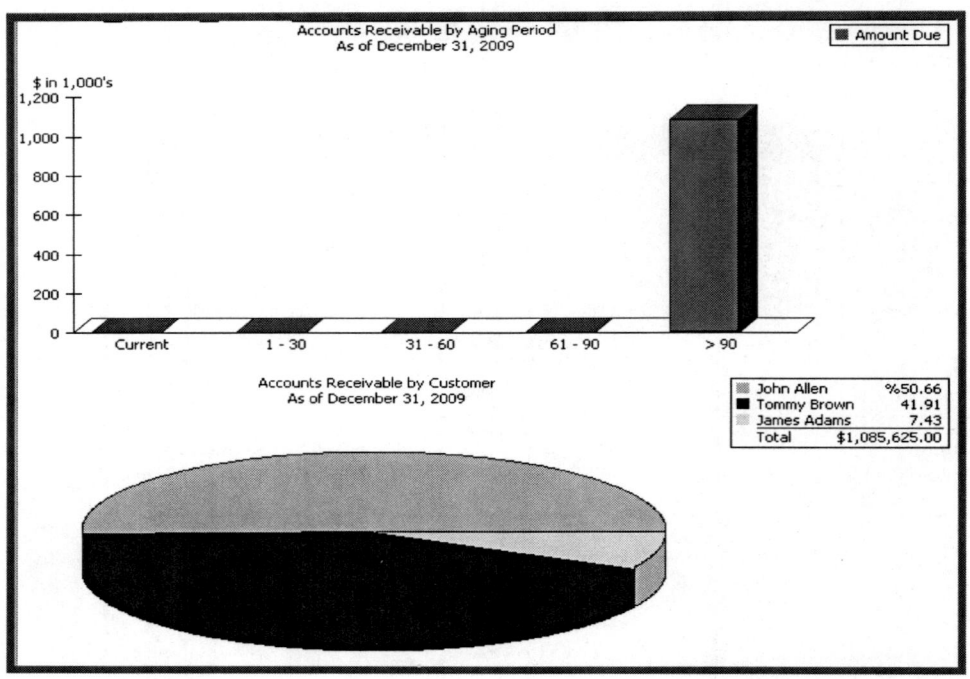

Customer Balance on PDF

If you want to increase your cash flow you must be on top of your account receivables. Some customers will pay you on time without being asked to do so. For other customers, you have to remind them of their outstanding balance before they will send you a check. You should run your aging summary report to see who is 30 days past due. As soon as a customer is 30 days past due, you should run the customer balance report as shown below and email it immediately. You can also open an invoice, save it as a PDF and email to a customer.

Quick Payroll 2009
Balance Details for James Adams
All Transactions

Type	Num	Date	Due Date	Aging	Amount	Open Balance
▶ Payment	4005	01/15/2009			-900,000.00	◀
Invoice	1001	01/02/2009	02/01/2009		80,625.00	80,625.00
Invoice		01/01/2009	01/01/2009		900,000.00	
Total					80,625.00	80,625.00

Activities:

- ❖ Click **Customers menu**
- ❖ Click **Customer Center**
- ❖ Click **James Adams** in the left window
- ❖ In the bottom right window
- ❖ Show: Select **Balance Details**
- ❖ Right click in the bottom right window
- ❖ Click **View as a Report**
- ❖ Dates: Select **This Fiscal Year**
- ❖ Click **File menu**
- ❖ Click **Save as PDF...**
- ❖ Save in: Select **Desktop**
- ❖ File name: Type **James Adams Balance Details**
- ❖ Click **Save**
- ❖ Click **X** to close Balance Details window
- ❖ Minimize all windows to see James Adams' pdf
- ❖ Double click **James Adams** pdf to open
- ❖ Click red **X** to close pdf
- ❖ Maximize QuickBooks

> You can also view a customer's report by right-clicking on the customer and clicking QuickReport at the bottom of the list.

Financial Results: Profit & Loss

You created new customers, invoices and received payments. Payments for invoices were received from customers. We invoiced inventory items and received payments from James Adams in the amount of 980,625.00. These activities affected the Profit & Loss statement by 1,924,183.33. Remember that QuickBooks call opening balances Uncategorized Income and Expenses, but you have to change them.

Activities:

- ❖ Click **Reports menu**
- ❖ Click **Company & Financial**
- ❖ Click **Profit & Loss Standard**
- ❖ Date: Select **This Fiscal Year**
- ❖ From: Accept **1/1/09**
- ❖ To: Accept **12/31/09**
- ❖ Click **Collapse**
- ❖ **Net Income 1,924,183.33**
- ❖ Click **X** to close window

```
                    Quick Payroll 2009
                    Profit & Loss
              January through December 2009
                                        ◇ Jan - Dec 09 ◇
        Ordinary Income/Expense
          Income
             Landscaping Services         75,000.00
             Opening Balance Income   ▶ 1,905,000.00 ◀
          Total Income                  1,980,000.00

          Cost of Goods Sold
             Materials                     50,000.00
          Total COGS                       50,000.00

        Gross Profit                    1,930,000.00

          Expense
             Depreciation Expense            666.67
             Opening Balance Expense       5,000.00
             Travel Expense                  150.00
          Total Expense                    5,816.67

        Net Ordinary Income            1,924,183.33

        Net Income                     1,924,183.33
```

Financial Results: Balance Sheet

When you sell goods and services, you send invoices to customers. If payments are not received at the same time the invoices are created, Accounts Receivable, a Balance Sheet account is affected. As customers make payments, you receive them in the Receive Payments window. If the Preferences windows are set up correctly, payments are sent automatically to Undeposited Funds. Undeposited Funds is now at 900,000 and the Total Assets balance is 3,174,808.33.

Activities:

- ❖ Click **Reports menu**
- ❖ Click **Company & Financial**
- ❖ Click **Balance Sheet Standard**
- ❖ Date: Select **This Fiscal Year**
- ❖ As of: Accept **12/31/09**
- ❖ Click **Collapse**
- ❖ **Total Assets 3,174,808.33**
- ❖ Click **X** to close window

```
                    Quick Payroll 2009
                     Balance Sheet
                  As of December 31, 2009
                                      ◇  Dec 31, 09  ◇
       ASSETS
         Current Assets
           Checking/Savings
             Money Market Account   ▶    100,000.00  ◀
             USA Checking                 799,850.00
             USA Payroll                  250,000.00
           Total Checking/Savings       1,149,850.00

           Accounts Receivable
             Accounts Receivable        1,085,625.00
           Total Accounts Receivable    1,085,625.00

           Other Current Assets
             Undeposited Funds            900,000.00
           Total Other Current Assets     900,000.00

         Total Current Assets           3,135,475.00

         Fixed Assets
           Truck                           39,333.33
         Total Fixed Assets               39,333.33

       TOTAL ASSETS                     3,174,808.33
```

Chapter Summary

Customers menu is about sales and receipt of payments from the customers. Your ending balance from previous books is your opening balance. If you have a few invoices, enter them individually through the Create Invoices window and for many invoices, enter the total amount per customer in the opening balance box.

What we accomplished:
- Reviewed the Customers submenus
- Reviewed customers center window
- Created new customers with details and opening balances
- Received payment from new customer James Adams
- Processed the accounts receivable graph
- Practiced customer balance report on pdf
- Processed financial statements

Additional financial activities:
- Opened sales for James Adams 900,000
- Created invoice #1001 for 80,625.00

- Received payment from James Adams for 900,000

Optional Test 6

Questions: True/False

Answer the following questions by placing letter the T or F in the space provided before the question number.

_____ 1. To delete an invoice that has not been paid, open the invoice in the Create Invoice window, click the Edit menu, and delete invoice.

_____ 2. With the Enter Statement Charges submenu, you cannot enter charges directly in the register and receive payment through the Receive Payment window.

_____ 3. When creating an invoice if you want to send the invoice by e-mail you must first enter the addresses of the company and the customer otherwise you will be asked to so.

_____ 4. When you're applying a Credit Memo to an invoice, it serves as an addition to the total invoice amount.

_____ 5. Once every month Finance Charges are assessed on outstanding invoices which are not yet due.

_____ 6. You can adjust item prices by amount or by percentage based on the current prices or unit cost.

_____ 7. You cannot copy previous Timesheet into current window, because QuickBooks will not allow you to do so.

_____ 8. It is possible to e-mail a single or batch of estimate or invoice right at the same window it is being created.

_____ 9. Invoice is created before an Estimate is created and forwarded to the customer not the other way around.

_____ 10. It is impossible to delete an invoice that a customer has paid for because this action will force QuickBooks to be out of balance.

Questions: Multiple Choices

Answer the following questions by placing letter A, B, C, or D in the space provided before the question number.

_____ 1. When you made a cash sale which of the following submenu is used to record such cash sale activity?
    A. Estimate
    B. Invoice
    C. Sales Receipt
    D. Statement Charges

_____ 2. Finance charges on outstanding invoices can be calculated from which of the following dates except...
    A. Due date
    B. Invoice date
    C. Billed date
    D. Call date

_____ 3. From time to time, you may want to change Item Prices, which of the following items will QuickBooks allows you to change its prices?
    A. Inventory
    B. Non Inventory
    C. All of the above
    D. None of the above

_____ 4. You may want to review your sales data by looking at the accounts receivable graph, which of the following graph format is available?
    A. Statistical chart
    B. Trending chart
    C. Pie chart
    D. All of the above

_____ 5. In completing a Customer Detail Information window, which of the following tab is not required to be completed?
    A. Address Info
    B. Payment Info
    C. Job Info
    D. Company Info

_____ 6. When completing the Additional Info tab in the Customer Information
window, which of the following is not a Term Listing?
   A. 1% 10 Net 30
   B. 30 Net 10 1%
   C. Due on receipt
   D. Net 30

_____ 7. After you have created an invoice, which of the following activities will
QuickBooks allows you to perform on the same invoice window?
   A. Edit
   B. Void
   C. Delete
   D. All of the above

_____ 8. After you have created a Credit/Refund memo, QuickBooks will allow you
to select which of the following options?
   A. Retain it as an available credit
   B. Give a refund by sending check
   C. Apply it to an invoice
   D. All of the above

_____ 9. If you want to delete an invoice that has been paid for by customer you
perform which of the following activities?
   A. Delete invoice
   B. Delete payment
   C. Verify amount is deleted in checking account
   D. All of the above

_____10. It is necessary to print a Customer Transaction report for your customer, to
do this you open the Customer Center, click on a customer, click the
Print button top of the window and select which of the following report?
   A. Customer List
   B. Financial List
   C. Customer & Job Transaction List
   D. None of the above

$

Chapter 7

Vendors Menu

Objectives: After you've completed this chapter, you will be able to:

- ✓ Explain the Vendors submenus
- ✓ Identify the Vendor center contents
- ✓ Create vendors with opening balances
- ✓ Create inventory bill
- ✓ Pay inventory bill
- ✓ Enter office bill
- ✓ Pay office bill
- ✓ Process the Forms 1099 & 1096
- ✓ Run the account payable graph
- ✓ Process vendor balance on pdf
- ✓ Run financial reports and compare your results

Review Vendor Submenus

Vendor management is crucial to the success of your business. Vendors want your money more than you can imagine, and controlling them and their bills is essential to your bottom line and your cash flow. The Vendors menu is the gateway to vendor-related activities and reports. You want to ask for estimates and bids to select the most cost-effective vendors to work with. You should take discounts from your vendors when offered. If I were to show you the math on the savings when you take discounts from your vendors, it would be outstanding, and no bank can come close in lending you money at that rate.

- Click **Vendors menu**

The following submenus are found under the Vendors menu:

- **Vendor Center:** The center allows you to see the summary of vendor activities in one window, including address, credit limit, account number, contact information, e-mail address, phone number, fax number and terms of payment.

- **Enter Bills:** Before you pay your bill, you are encouraged to first enter the bill in the Enter Bills window. You will be able to enter the vendor name, date, amount, terms, expense account or items as the case may be. Make it a practice to first enter bills before writing checks, that way at any point in time, you can see outstanding or unpaid bills.

- **Pay Bills:** Before you pay a bill remember to subtract any discounts from the vendor for early payments which is a reduction on cost of goods sold or cost of purchases. After you've entered the bills in the Enter Bills window, you come to the Pay Bills window, pull up the same bill you've just entered, and pay it. When you open the Pay Bills window, all unpaid bills are displayed in front of you. Select the bill or bills you want to pay and click Pay Now.

- **Sales Tax:** When you sell products to your customers, if you collect sales tax, at the end of the tax period, you must remit the collection to the appropriate government agency. You come to the Sales Tax submenu to pay the bills and perform other sales tax activities, including adjust sales tax due, and review sales tax liabilities.

- **Create Purchase Orders:** If you set up your reorder point correctly in the Edit menu, Preferences, QuickBooks will prompt you when you reach the reorder point. At that time, you will come to the Create Purchase Orders window to fill out the inventories you want from your vendors. Be sure to click the To Be e-mail box so you can e-mail your Purchase Orders to the vendors, which is more cost-effective than using the postal service.

- **Receive Item and Enter Bill:** After the Purchase Order is e-mailed to the vendor, items you requested are shipped to you immediately. Because the vendors ship the items and enclosed a bill, you are going to receive the items and at the same time Enter the Bills. You must make absolutely certain that you key in the invoice number when you enter bill so that you don't pay duplicate bills.

- **Receive Items:** If the vendor forgot to enclose the bills when shipping the items, you have to go to the Receive Items window, pull up the vendor, and receive the items. In this case, the Ref No. must be left blank because you do not have the bill number from the vendor. This is important to remember.

- **Enter Bill for Received Items:** After you've received the Items, and later received the bill from the vendor, it is now time to enter the bill number on the Ref No. line. This is necessary because you do not want to issue two or more checks on the same bill.

- **Inventory Activities:** This is where you manage your inventory quantities. You will be able to enter new items, adjust quantity/value on hand, and take a physical inventory count of your products

- **Print 1099s/1096:** Some of your vendors will qualify for Form 1099 or Form 1096, especially your subcontractors. You must click the "Vendor Eligible of 1099" in the Additional Info tab when creating or editing the vendor information. To activate the Form 1099/1096, you must set up the Edit menu, Preferences and Tax: 1099 window.

- **Item List:** You can access the Item List through the Vendor menu. This window allows you to create new items, and edit or delete old items. At the bottom of the window are the following activities: Items, Activities, Reports and Excel. Don't forget to always right click in any list window to see what activities are available for you. When you right click in the Item List window, you will get almost the same submenus as if you had clicked the Vendor menu.

Review Vendor Center

It is easier to access the Vendor Center if you're already in the Home Page by clicking the Vendors button. Depending on the nature of your business, you may have fewer vendors than customers. Though the Customer and Vendor Centers windows are similar, generally there are more activities in the Customer Center window than the Vendor Center window. Let's review the contents of the Vendor Center window.

- Click **Vendors menu**
- Click **Vendor Center**

Activities buttons and windows: You will find the following activities when you open the Vendor Center window

- New Vendor
- New Transaction
- Print
- Excel
- Word
- Vendor tab
- View down arrow
- Transaction tab
- Edit Vendor
- Edit Notes
- Show down arrow
- Filter By down arrow
- Date down arrow

Report for this Vendor: Vendor reports are located at the right side of the window and they include the following:

- QuickReport
- Open Balance

Right Click: When you right click the left side of the Vendor Center window, you will find the following options:

- Find
- Use
- Refresh

- Edit Vendor
- New Vendor
- Make Vendor Inactive
- Show Full Customer List Only
- Write Checks
- Enter Bills
- Pay Bills
- Enter Credit Card Charges
- Create Purchase Orders
- Receive Items & Enter Bills
- Receive Items
- Enter Bill for Received Items

Cost of Goods Sold Vendor

Most of the time, the Vendor Name and Company Name boxes are the same, if there is any reason both boxes are not the same, then make sure you provide the correct company name. QuickBooks uses the Company Name to populate the Name & Address and the "Print on Check as" boxes. In essence, the Company Name box is more legitimate than the Vendor Name, since you will see that name on a check being sent to a vendor. Provide any opening balance amount and remember QuickBooks calls this an Uncategorized Expense unless you change the account name.

Activities:

- ❖ Click **Vendors menu**
- ❖ Click **Vendor Center**
- ❖ Right click in the window
- ❖ Select **New Vendor**
- ❖ Vendor Name: Type **US Supplies**
- ❖ Opening Balance: Type **10,000** as of: Type **1/1/09**
- ❖ Company Name: Type **US Supplies**. Press **Tab**
- ❖ Name and Address: Accept **US Suppliers**. Press **Enter**
- ❖ Type **1234 Downing Rd, Dallas, TX 75000**
- ❖ Click **Additional Info** tab
- ❖ Account No: Type **Vend 123456**
- ❖ Type: Select **Supplier**
- ❖ Terms: Select **2% 10 Net 30**
- ❖ Credit Limit: Type **500,000**

> You can right click a vendor and click QuickReport at the bottom of the list to see the vendor account details.

❖ Tax ID: Type **99-1234566**
❖ Checkmark **Vendor eligible for 1099**
❖ Click **OK**

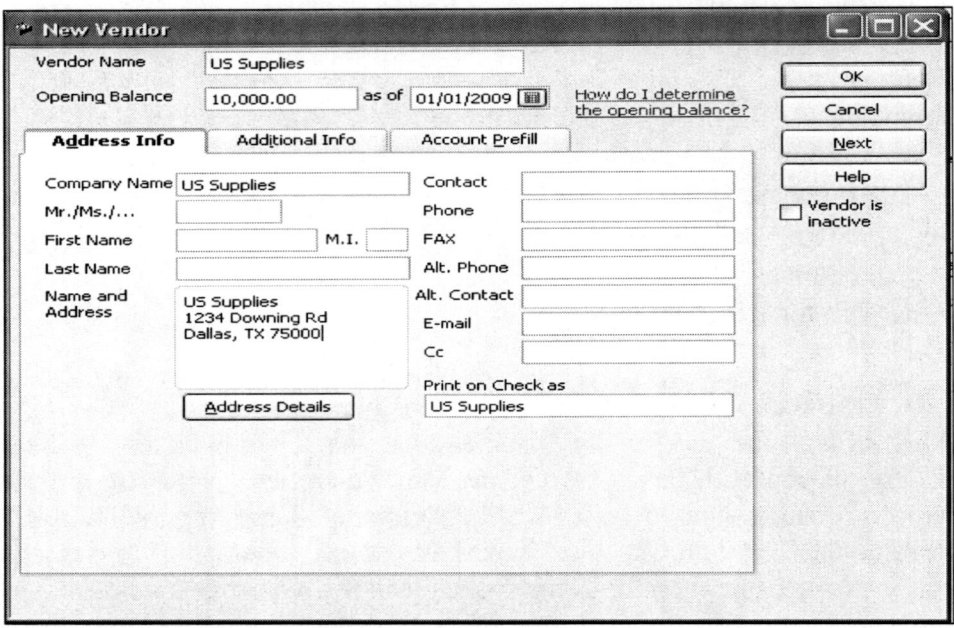

Operating Expenses Vendor

It is essential to provide vendor data and information as detailed as possible, because the vendor profile in this window is globally pulled to other windows and reports. The vendor's physical address should be double checked after entry, since other departments, especially the shipping department depend on its accuracy. Telephone and fax numbers should not be overlooked either, and must be updated frequently as information changes and becomes available. When you have a customer who is also a vendor, you have to modify the names such as John Doe Customer or Sales for customer and John Doe Vendor or Billing for vendor.

Activities:

❖ Click **Vendors menu**
❖ Click **Vendor Center**
❖ Double click **Telephone America**
❖ Company Name: Type **Telephone America**
❖ Click **in Name and Address box:**
❖ Accept **Telephone America**. Press **Enter**

- ❖ Type **4700 Welling Circle.** Press **Enter**
- ❖ Type **Dallas, TX.75000**
- ❖ Contact: Type **Susan Sanchez**
- ❖ Phone: Type **214-800-6000**
- ❖ Fax: Type **214-800-6001**
- ❖ E-mail: Type **ssanchez@ telamerica.com**
- ❖ Click **Additional Info** tab
- ❖ Account No: Type **Vend 123745**
- ❖ Type: Select **Utilities**
- ❖ Term: Select **Due on receipt**
- ❖ Credit Limit: Type **100,000**
- ❖ Click **Account Prefill** tab
- ❖ Select account to pre-fill: Select **Telephone Expense**
- ❖ Click **OK**

Payroll Services Vendors

Some payroll-related vendors are government agencies and others are private companies. Government agencies include the United States Treasury and state and local government agencies in charge of collecting sales tax. In the private sector, these are banks and other financial institutions. Most of the time, a company can contract with these financial institutions to manage employees and employer funds and, therefore, have fiduciary responsibilities to the funds entrusted in their care.

Activities:

- ❖ Click **Vendors menu**
- ❖ Click **Vendor Center**
- ❖ Right click in the window. Click **New Vendor**
- ❖ Vendor Name: Type **HMO of America**
- ❖ Opening Balance: Type **0.00** as of: Type **1/1/09**
- ❖ Contact: Type **Kathy Manning**
- ❖ Phone: Type **214-700-7000**
- ❖ Fax: Type **214-700-8000**
- ❖ E-mail: Type **kmanning@hmo.com**
- ❖ Click **Next**
- ❖ Vendor Name: Type **Money Mgt of America**
- ❖ Opening Balance: Type **0.00** as of: Type **1/1/09**
- ❖ Contact: Type **Tony Casey**
- ❖ Phone: Type **214-600-6000**
- ❖ **Fax: Type 214-600-7000**

- ❖ E-mail: Type **tcasey@mma.com**
- ❖ Click **Next**
- ❖ Vendor Name: Type **US Treasury**
- ❖ Opening Balance: Type **0.00** as of: Type **1/1/09**
- ❖ Contact: Type **Joe Lekey**
- ❖ Phone: Type **214-700-1040**
- ❖ Fax: Type **214-600-1040**
- ❖ E-mail: Type **jlekey@ustreasury.gov.** Click **Next**
- ❖ Vendor Name: Type **TX – Unemployment**
- ❖ Opening Balance: Type **0.00** as of: Type **1/1/09.** Click **OK**

Create Cost of Goods Sold Bill

When you create an inventory bill and the goods are received, it is important to enter the reference number in the box provided. In order to avoid paying a bill twice, this is essential. If you have already created a bill with a reference number, QuickBooks will not allow you to create another bill with the same number, but will prompt you that the number already exists in the database. This forces you to cancel the bill and prevents duplicate payment.

Activities:
- ❖ Click **Vendors menu**
- ❖ Click **Enter Bill**
- ❖ Click **Bill**
- ❖ Vendor: Select **US Supplies**
- ❖ Date: Type **1/2/09**
- ❖ Ref: Type **Ussup 200901**
- ❖ Bill Due: Accept **2/1/09**
- ❖ Terms: Accept **2% 10 Net 30**
- ❖ Discount Date: Accept **1/12/09**
- ❖ Click **Items** tab
- ❖ Click under Item (bottom left of the window): Select **Flowers**
- ❖ Qty: Type **500.** Press **Tab**
- ❖ Amount: Accept **25,000**
- ❖ Click **Save & Close**

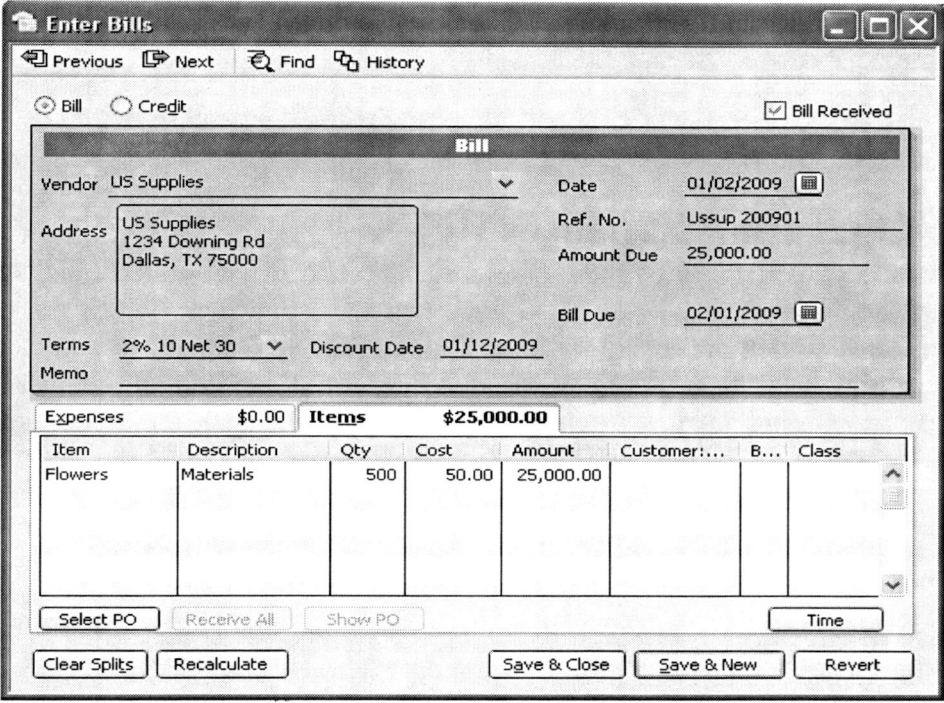

Pay Cost of Goods Sold Bill

When a bill has been recorded and goods are received, you ordinarily pay by the due date. However, before you pay the bill, find out if there's a cash discount for early payment. Pay on time to take advantage of any discounts; otherwise, you pay the bill by the due date. Make it a habit to make payments from previously recorded bills. This policy will prevent you from paying an invoice twice, since the payment window will have no invoice to pay.

Activities:
   ❖ Click **Vendors menu**
   ❖ Click **Pay Bills**
   ❖ Show bills(top left): Click **Show all bills**
   ❖ Checkmark the **two US Supplies bills** boxes
   ❖ Total Amount Due: Accept **40,000**
   ❖ Total Disc Used: Accept **700**
   ❖ Total Amount to Pay: Accept **34,300**
   ❖ Payment Date: Type **1/2/09**
   ❖ Payment Method (bottom left): Accept **Check**
   ❖ Click **To be printed**

* Payment Account: Accept **USA Checking** (bottom)
* Ending Balance: Accept **765,550.00**
* Click **Pay Selected Bills**
* Click **Done**

Enter Operating Expenses Bill

You have two types of bills, inventory bills and office related bills. At the bottom of the Enter Bills window, you have two tabs, Expenses, which are office bills, and Items, which are inventory bills. QuickBooks will default to one of these tabs depending on the type of vendor or what item for which you are going to pay. When you're entering inventory-related bills, you should click the Items tab and when you're entering office-related bills, click the Expenses tab.

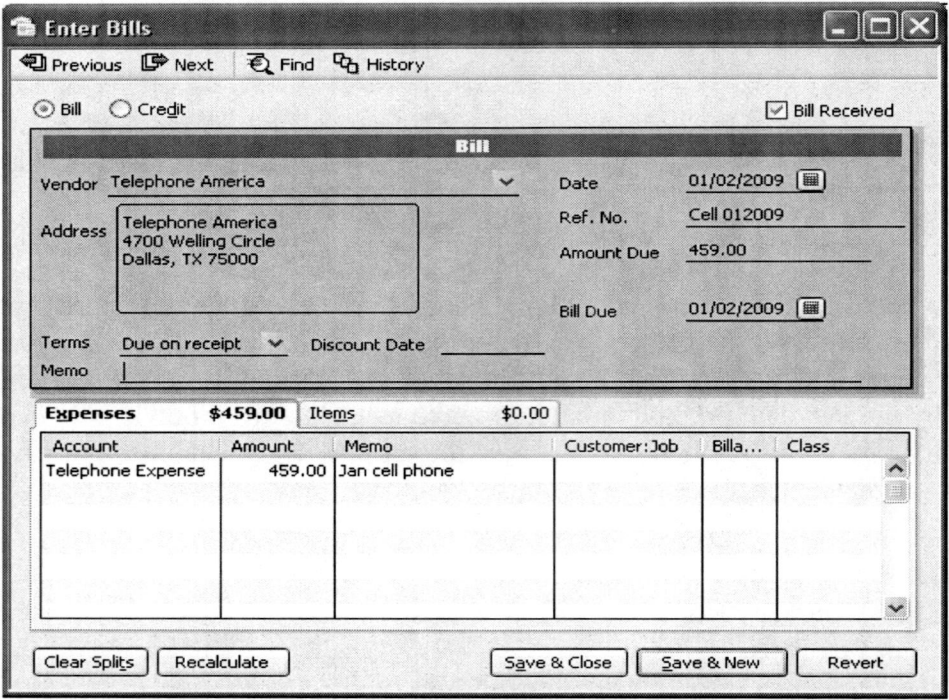

Activities:
* Click **Vendors menu**
* Click **Enter Bills**
* Click **Bill** (top left of the window)
* Vendor: Select **Telephone America**
* Date: Type **1/2/09**

- ❖ Ref. No.: Type **Cell 012009**
- ❖ Amount Due: Type **459.00**
- ❖ Bill Due: Accept **1/2/09**
- ❖ Term: Accept **Due on receipt**
- ❖ Click **Expenses** tab
- ❖ Click under Account (left of the window)
- ❖ Select **Telephone Expense**
- ❖ Amount: Accept **459.00**
- ❖ Memo: Type **Jan cell phone**
- ❖ Click **Save & Close** (bottom right of the window)

Pay Operating Expenses Bill

After you've entered office-related bills into QuickBooks, the totals of individual bills are matched with totals on the vendor reports. Payments to vendors are processed in the Pay Bills window, and bills are pulled up according to the cutoff date, mainly at the end of the month. You can view all bills by clicking the Show All Bills, but be sure to select those bills that came before the due date, unless you are paying the bills in advance to take advantage of discounts from the vendor.

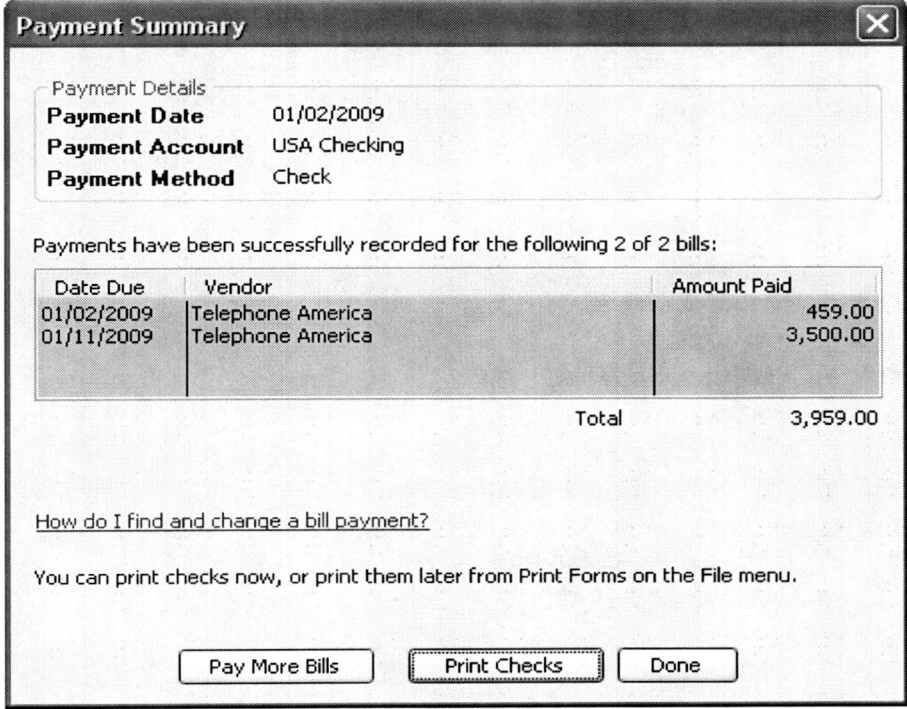

Activities:

- ❖ Click **Vendors menu**
- ❖ Click **Pay Bills**
- ❖ Click **Show all bills**
- ❖ Checkmark the **two Telephone America bills**
- ❖ Total Amt. Due: Accept **5,459.00**
- ❖ Total Amt To Pay: Accept **3,959.00**
- ❖ Payment Date: Type **1/2/09**
- ❖ Payment Method: Accept **Check**.
- ❖ Click **To be printed**
- ❖ Payment Account: Accept **USA Checking**
- ❖ Ending Balance: Accept **761,591**
- ❖ Click **Pay Selected Bills**
- ❖ Click **Done**

Process Form 1099 & 1096

When you're setting up your new vendors, some will qualify to receive Form 1099, especially your subcontractors. Their window should have a checkmark to receive Form 1099. Remember, if you did not check this box for the respective vendor, QuickBooks will not issue Form 1099 to that vendor. At the end of the year, you must run the Form 1099 report; you may select the "Only 1099 Vendors" window. Be sure to select Last Calendar Year for the Dates window.

Activities:

- ❖ Click **Vendors menu**
- ❖ Click **Print 1099/1096**
- ❖ Click **Run Report under #1**
- ❖ Click **X** to close window
- ❖ Click **Map Accounts under #2**
- ❖ Click **X** to close window
- ❖ Click **Run Report under #3**
- ❖ Dates (top left): Select **This Calendar Year**
- ❖ (Actually you should be looking at the "Last Calendar Year")
- ❖ 1099 Option: Accept **Only 1099 vendors**
- ❖ **Look! US Supplies has 33,600**
- ❖ Click **X** to close
- ❖ Click **Print 1099s under #4**
- ❖ Please specify date range: Accept **Last Calendar Year**
- ❖ Click **OK**

- ❖ Click **OK** on the problem message window
- ❖ No activities for last year to report
- ❖ Click **Close**

Accounts Payable Graph

As you pay your bills, QuickBooks tracks your payments and updates the Accounts Payable balance. If you want to see how long you have owed a certain bill, the best place to come is the Accounts Payable Graph. The graph presents Accounts Payable balances by aging in a bar chart and by customer in a pie chart. Double click the Bar Chart to see the details of the bar chart and double click the pie chart to see the details of the pie chart.

Activities:

- ❖ Click **Reports menu**
- ❖ Click **Vendors & Payables**
- ❖ Click **Accounts Payable Graph**
- ❖ Click **Date**..(top left of the window)
- ❖ Show Aging as of: Type **12/31/09.**
- ❖ Click **OK**
- ❖ Click **X** to close Graph window

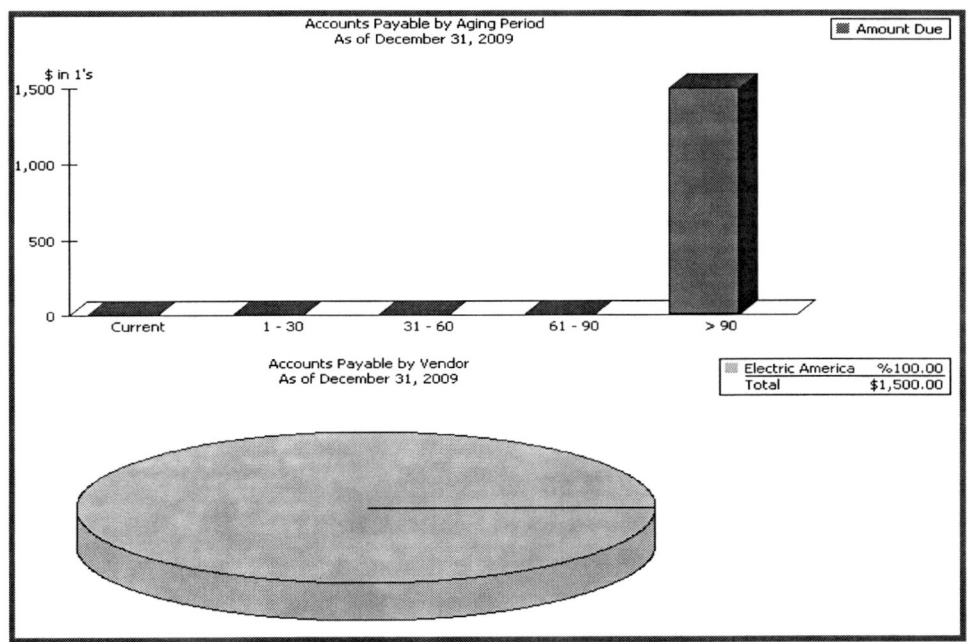

Vendor Balance on PDF

Sometimes, a vendor may call you for payment on a particular invoice. You have to research the invoice to see if it has been paid or not. If the invoice has been paid you have to run, print, and enclose the vendor balance details to the vendor. The report will show the check number and the date of payment. You may also run this report any time you are paying a vendor on an outstanding balance. That way the vendor can see what invoice is outstanding and what matching check amount is enclosed. You can also open a bill, save it as a PDF and email to a customer.

Quick Payroll 2009
Balance Details for Electric America
January through December 2009

Type	◇	Num	◇	Date	◇	Due Date	◇	Aging	◇	Amount	◇	Open Balance	◇
Jan - Dec 09													
▶ Bill				01/01/2009		01/11/2009		354		1,500.00		1,500.00	◀
Jan - Dec 09										1,500.00		1,500.00	

Activities:

* ❖ Click **Vendors menu**
* ❖ Click **Vendor Center**
* ❖ Click **Electric America** in the left window
* ❖ In the bottom right window
* ❖ Show: Select **Balance Details**
* ❖ Right click in the bottom right window
* ❖ Click **View as a Report**
* ❖ Dates: Select **This Fiscal Year**
* ❖ Click **File menu**
* ❖ Click **Save as PDF...**
* ❖ Save in: Select **Desktop**
* ❖ File name: Type **Electric America Balance Details**
* ❖ Click **Save**
* ❖ Click **X** to close Balance Details window
* ❖ Minimize all windows to see Electric America's pdf
* ❖ Double click **Electric America** pdf to open
* ❖ Click red **X** to close PDF
* ❖ Maximize QuickBooks

Financial Results: Profit & Loss

In the Vendors menu, we created inventory and office-related bills, including telephone expenses for Telephone America in the amount of 459.00 which was paid together with another outstanding bill. Most vendor activities are reflected in the Cost of Goods Sold and Expenses sections of the Income Statement, while Checking and Accounts Payable are reflected on the Balance Sheet. You should review both the Profit & Loss and Balance Sheet reports after completing the vendor activities.

Quick Payroll 2009
Profit & Loss
January through December 2009

	◇ Jan - Dec 09 ◇
Ordinary Income/Expense	
Income	
Opening Balance Income	▶ 1,905,000.00 ◀
Landscaping Services	75,000.00
Total Income	1,980,000.00
Cost of Goods Sold	
Materials	50,000.00
Discount Received	-700.00
Total COGS	49,300.00
Gross Profit	1,930,700.00
Expense	
Opening Balance Expense	15,000.00
Depreciation Expense	666.67
Telephone Expense	459.00
Travel Expense	150.00
Total Expense	16,275.67
Net Ordinary Income	1,914,424.33
Net Income	**1,914,424.33**

- ❖ Click **Reports menu**
- ❖ Click **Company & Financial**
- ❖ Click **Profit & Loss Standard**
- ❖ Date: Select **This Fiscal Year**
- ❖ From: Accept **1/1/09**
- ❖ To: Accept **12/31/09**
- ❖ Click **Collapse**
- ❖ **Net Income 1,914,424.33**
- ❖ Click **X** to close window

Financial Results: Balance Sheet

When you buy goods and services from vendors, they send you bills for those goods and services. If payments are not made at the same time, the bills become accounts payable, and a Balance Sheet account is affected. In this chapter, cash decreased when we partially paid US Supplies and Telephone America for goods and services and Accounts Payable was increased for the remainder of the unpaid bills. Inventory also increased to 25,000.

Activities:

- ❖ Click **Reports menu**
- ❖ Click **Company & Financial**
- ❖ Click **Balance Sheet Standard**
- ❖ Date: Select **This Fiscal Year**
- ❖ As of: Accept **12/31/09**
- ❖ Click **Collapse**
- ❖ **Total Assets 3,161,549.33**
- ❖ Click **X** to close window

Quick Payroll 2009
Balance Sheet
As of December 31, 2009

	Dec 31, 09
ASSETS	
Current Assets	
Checking/Savings	
Money Market Account	▶ 100,000.00 ◀
USA Checking	761,591.00
USA Payroll	250,000.00
Total Checking/Savings	1,111,591.00
Accounts Receivable	
Accounts Receivable	1,085,625.00
Total Accounts Receivable	1,085,625.00
Other Current Assets	
Undeposited Funds	900,000.00
Inventory Asset	25,000.00
Total Other Current Assets	925,000.00
Total Current Assets	3,122,216.00
Fixed Assets	
Truck	39,333.33
Total Fixed Assets	39,333.33
TOTAL ASSETS	**3,161,549.33**

Chapter Summary

Anytime you have a problem with a vendor, the first place to look is the Vendors menu and the next place is the Vendor Center. It has all the activities that pertain to a vendor. If you're at the Home Page, you can access the Vendor Center by clicking the Vendors button. However, if you're at any other window, the best move is to click the Vendors menu and then Vendor Center.

What we accomplished:
- Reviewed the Vendors submenus
- Reviewed Vendor Center contents
- Created vendors with opening balances
- Created an inventory bill
- Paid an inventory bill
- Created an office bill
- Paid an office bill
- Generated Forms 1099 & 1096
- Generated accounts payable graph
- Processed vendor report on pdf
- Processed financial statements

Additional financial activities:
- Opened Bill for US Supplies 10,000
- Created inventory for US Supplies 25,000
- Paid US Supplies 34,.300
- Received bill from Telephone America 459
- Paid Telephone America 3,959

Optional Test 7

Questions: True/False

Answer the following questions by placing letter the T or F in the space provided before the question number.

_____ 1. QuickBooks will not allow you to edit, void, and delete a bill in the same window it was created.

_____ 2. Discount received from a vendor for early payment of a bill is regarded as a deduction from Cost of Goods Sold not an addition to income.

_____ 3. In the Vendor Center window, by clicking a vendor, the Print button and Vendor Transaction List, it is impossible to see all the bills and payments for that one vendor.

_____ 4. When you create a new vendor and enter the opening balance, QuickBooks calls it Uncategorized Expense.

_____ 5. It is possible to send a bill to a vendor by e-mail in the same window it is created since you want to pay them immediately.

_____ 6. When making a payment to a vendor you can choose to take a discount or a credit on a bill but not both.

_____ 7. It is absolutely important to enter vendor's reference number in the Enter Bill window to avoid paying a bill twice.

_____ 8. You are required to provide all information on a vendor in the Enter Bill window before saving the bill.

_____ 9. It is impossible to delete a bill after it has been paid because QuickBooks does not want to change the financial information.

_____ 10. Completing the Reference Number box is very essential to avoid duplicate payments, you can do so in the Enter Bill window but not in the Receive Item window.

Questions: Multiple Choices

Answer the following questions by placing letter A, B, C, or D in the space provided before the question number.

_____ 1. The Vendors menu does not have a lot of submenu, which of the following is not a Vendor submenu?
    A. Enter Bills
    B. Enter Credits
    C. Pay Bills
    D. Purchase Orders

_____ 2. When you right-click in the Vendor Center window, which of the following is an impossible task because it is unavailable for selection?
    A. New Vendor
    B. Edit Vendor
    C. Delete Vendor
    D. Make Vendor Inactive

_____ 3. Ship To is the place designated for the vendor to deliver the goods, which of the following windows do you not expect to see the Ship To box?
    A. Enter Bills
    B. Purchase Orders
    C. All of the above
    D. None of the above

_____ 4. QuickBooks allows you to send documents to your vendor, which of the following windows is not allowed to be sent by e-mail?
    A. Enter Bills
    B. Purchase Orders
    C. Sales Tax Liability
    D. Sales Tax Revenue Summary

_____ 5. Accounts Payable graph is used by QuickBooks to present unpaid bills information by which of the following?
    A. Aging Period
    B. Vendor
    C. All of the above
    D. None of the above

_____ 6. Which of the following QuickBooks worksheet is used to count and adjust the quantity of stock you have in the warehouse?
   A. Quantity/Value on Hand
   B. Physical Inventory Worksheet
   C. All of the above
   D. None of the above

_____ 7. In the Enter Bill window, the bill due date is calculated by using which of the following data?
   A. Paid Amount
   B. Terms Date
   C. Canceled Date
   D. Delete Date

_____ 8. When you want to pay your Sales Tax Liabilities to a government agency which report are you more likely to print?
   A. Pay Bills report
   B. Pay Sales Tax report
   C. All of the above
   D. None of the above

_____ 9. If you have a customer who is also a vendor, QuickBooks will not allow you to enter the same name both as a customer and a vendor, except you modify the names to_____
   A. John Doe Sales
   B. John Doe Billing
   C. All of the above
   D. It is impossible to modify the names

_____ 10. When creating an invoice for a customer you use only the Item tab in the lower window, but when creating a bill for a vendor, what kind of tabs are available for use?
   A. Expense
   B. Items
   C. Both Expense and Items
   D. None of the above

$

Chapter 8

Employees Menu

Objectives: After you've completed this chapter, you will be able to:
- ✓ Describe the Employees submenu
- ✓ Identify the Employees center contents
- ✓ Identify payroll listing
- ✓ Set up free payroll subscription
- ✓ Set up payroll & employee preferences
- ✓ Create timesheets
- ✓ Create paychecks
- ✓ Edit paychecks
- ✓ Create payroll accounts
- ✓ Make liability payments to vendors
- ✓ Run payroll QuickReports
- ✓ Run financial reports and compare results

Review Employees Submenus

If you do not subscribe for the QuickPayroll service, you can still run the Payroll & Employees windows, but with manual calculation. It's one thing to run your business and deal with other businesses; it is another to deal with government agencies. It's a bad business practice to collect payroll taxes from employees and not remit them to the government. Therefore, the Employees menu is considered a very important regulatory issue. If you treat it that way, you have nothing to worry about! Sometimes, you may not want to process your payroll yourself, so finding a payroll service company is a good alternative. It is a matter of cost benefit analysis; you do what is profitable for your company.

- Click **Employees menu**

The following submenus are found under the Employees menu:

- **Employee Center:** The center lets you create new employees, edit, find and delete employees. It has other activities that help you manage your employees, such as completing the Timesheet and printing reports.

- **Enter Time:** For hourly employees, you must fill out or enter their time before they are paid. Open the Use Weekly Timesheet to enter a week's hours on each line. The timesheet is then processed for payment.

- **Pay Employees:** This allows you to select all the employees you want to pay for that period. Complete the pay period and the check date boxes. Make sure the bank account box is Payroll account or any other accounts designated to pay employees.

- **Edit/Void Paychecks:** You should know as long as you have not released a check, it can be edited or voided. And if you have just created a check, you can delete it and create another one.

- **Payroll Taxes and Liabilities:** This submenu allows you to pay payroll liabilities, adjust payroll liabilities, and deposit refund of liabilities. What if an employee decides to reduce his or her 401(k) contribution from $100 to $40. You open the "Review Paycheck" window and run $60 401(k) contribution to see how much the company contributes. Then go to the Adjust Payroll Liabilities window, adjust that amount for the company, and adjust $60 for the employee. If you erroneously sent a 401(k) to a vendor when an employee has already cancelled contribution, adjust the payroll liabilities as you did above and have the vendor refund the paycheck. Then use the "Deposit Refund Liabilities" window to enter the refund back to the Payroll checking account.

- **Payroll Tax Forms & W-2s:** QuickBooks will not allow you to process this submenu if you did not subscribe to QuickPayroll services.

- **Payroll Service Options:** This function allows you to go online to learn about payroll options, order payroll service, and enter payroll service key.

- **Payroll Setup:** This submenu allows you to complete the payroll set up for your company. Once you have activated the setup through the Help window, you're set to start the set up process.

- **Manage Payroll Items:** Here, you are able to set up new payroll items and view and edit the payroll item list. You will practice extensively with these windows.

Review Employee Center

As noted earlier, most of the buttons in the Employees menu will be activated if you complete the payroll setup process through the Help window. If you are at the Home Page, you can access the Employee Center by clicking on the Employees button located at the left of the window. Let's review the contents of the Employee Center window.

- Click **Employees menu**
- Click **Employee Center**

Activities buttons and windows: You will find the following activities when you open the Employee Center window:

- New Employee
- Related Activities
- Print
- Enter Time
- Excel
- Word
- Employees tab
- Transaction tab
- Payroll tab

- View down arrow
- Edit Employee
- Edit Notes
- Show down arrow
- Date down arrow

Report for this Employee: Employee reports are located at the right side of the window and they include the following:

- QuickReport
- Payroll Summary
- Paid Time Off Report
- Payroll Transaction Detail
- Learn About Payroll

Right Click: When you right click the left side of the Employee Center window, you will find the following options:

- Find
- Use
- Refresh
- Edit Employee
- New Employee
- Employee Default
- Delete Employee
- Make Employee Inactive
- Customize Columns
- Show Full Customer List Only

Payroll Listing

Compensation List:
Hourly
Overtime Hourly
Double-time Hourly
Hourly Sick
Hourly Vacation
Salary
Salary Sick
Salary Sick Cashout
Salary Vacation
Salary Vacation Cashout
Salary Leave Paid
Salary Leave Unpaid
Bonus
Commission
Piecework
Reported Paycheck Tip

Additions & Deductions to Compensation:
From time to time, especially when an employee is leaving the company, you would have to deal with some payroll items, which are outstanding balances to close out the outgoing employee's accounts. You can use the analysis below to find out what to do when you have similar situations.

Hourly employee's outstanding balances do not require additional payroll items, you just key in the outstanding hours and the employee's hourly rate and the amount are generated. However, with salary employees because they are not paid hourly you have to create additional payroll items. The hours below are used to calculate the amount payable to each item. It does not mean you're paying hourly amount to a salary employee.

Additions to compensation: Amount is "In addition to" the salary
1. Sick Cashout: Outstanding unused sick hours for a salary employee
Example: You pay Salary 80 hours and Sick Cashout 5 hours. Total 85 hours
2. Vacation Cashout: Outstanding unused vacation hours for a salary employee
Example: You pay Salary 80 hours and Vacation Cashout 7 hours. Total 87 hours
3. Paid Leave: This is the number hours an officer can be on leave and still be paid
Example: You pay Salary 80 hours and Paid Leave 10 hours. Total 90 hours

Deductions from compensation: Amount is "Split" with the salary
1. Sick: This is the normal hours a salary employee may use for sick time.
Example: You pay Salary 75 hours and Sick 5 hours. Total 80 hours (Always)
2. Vacation: This is the normal hours a salary employee may use for vacation time
Example: You pay Salary 73 hours and Vacation 7 hours. Total 80 hours (Always)
3. Unpaid Leave: If Paid Leave is used up and employee takes off, it's Unpaid Leave
Example: You pay Salary 80 hours and Unpaid Leave -10 hours. Total 70 hours

Insurance Benefits List:
Health (Pre tax)
Dental (Pre tax)
Vision (Pre tax)
Health Saving Account (Taxable)
Medical Care FSA (Pre tax)
Dependent Care FSA (Pre tax)
S-Corporation Medical (Pre tax)
Group Term Life (Pre tax)
Other Insurance (Pre tax)

Retirement Benefits List:
401k Emp
401k Co. Match
403b Emp
403b Co. Match
408k SEP Emp
408k SEP Co. Match
Simple IRA Emp
Simple IRA Co. Match

Misc—Additions and Deductions List:
Cash Advance (Addition)
Cash Advance Repayment (Deduction)
Union Dues (Deduction)
Charitable Donation (Deduction)
Mileage Reimbursement (Addition)
Wage Garnishment (Deduction)
Taxable Fringe Benefits (Addition)
Non Taxable Fringe Benefits (Addition)
Car Allowance (Addition)
Housing Allowance (Addition)

Travel Allowance (Addition)
Education Refund (Addition)
Miscellaneous Additions (Addition)
Miscellaneous Deductions (Deduction)

Payment Schedule List:
As needed (Daily)
Once per week (Weekly)
Every other week (Biweekly)
Twice a month (Semi monthly)
Once per month (Monthly)
Every 3 months (Quarterly)
Once per year (Annually).

Federal Taxes List:
Federal Withholding
Federal Unemployment (FUTA)
State Unemployment (SUTA)   *
Social Security Emp (FICA)   *
Social Security Comp (FICA)   *
Medicare Emp   *
Medicare Comp   *
Advanced Earned Income Credit (AEIC)

Schedule for Tax Payment List:
Federal 940 (Quarterly, most used)
Federal 941/944 (Quarterly, most used)
State Unemployment (Quarterly, most used)

Free Payroll Subscription

If you want to use QuickBooks Payroll to calculate your payroll figures and print the forms that go the government agencies, it is advisable to subscribe to the QuickBooks Payroll. However, if you just want to calculate the payroll numbers and have an accountant complete your government forms, then you can still use QuickBooks Payroll, but you cannot process the forms. Before the payroll setup, you will see just a few submenus, but after the setup, you will have more submenus.

Activities:

- ❖ Click **Employees menu**
- ❖ Look! You have few submenus
- ❖ Click **Help menu**
- ❖ Click **QuickBooks Help**
- ❖ Click **Search** tab (top right corner of the window)
- ❖ In the box: Type **manual calculation**
- ❖ Click the **Forward Arrow**
- ❖ Click "**Set your company file to use manual calculations**"
- ❖ In the lower window. **Scroll down**
- ❖ Click "**Set my company file to use manual calculations**"
- ❖ Click **OK** to "You must now calculate…"
- ❖ You're now setup for manual processing
- ❖ Click red **X** to close Help window

Set Up Payroll Introduction

After you have completed the setup process, your next step is to click the Employees menu to review the number of submenus available to you. At this point, you should click the Payroll Setup submenu, and in a few seconds, you will be taken to the QuickBooks Payroll Setup window. The window title is "Welcome to QuickBooks Payroll Setup," and the arrow to the left of the window will point to the "Introduction" link. Review the Welcome window and click Continue.

Activities:

- ❖ Click **Employees menu**
- ❖ **Look! You have more submenus than before**
- ❖ Click **Payroll Setup**
- ❖ Welcome to QuickBooks Payroll Setup
- ❖ **Arrow** points to **Introduction** (left of the window)
- ❖ Click **Continue** (bottom right of the window)

> If you don't see more than 3 submenus, shut down QuickBooks and re-enter. If you still don't see more than 3 submenus re-run the process the second time.

Welcome to QuickBooks Payroll Setup

We'll walk you through setting up the basics of payroll by asking you questions and giving you guidance along the way. When you're done with setup, you'll be ready to start using QuickBooks Payroll-- customized just for you!

Before you begin:

1. Review the payroll setup checklist.
2. Gather all the documents and information ahead of time that you'll need to answer the interview questions.

Company Set Up

Compensation and Benefits setup are the initial items in the process. You should have the Employee handbook or the Employee Payroll Policy to find what items are included as compensation and benefits. The basic compensation items are the hourly wage and overtime, salary, bonus, commission, tips and piecework. In general during the setup, you include the percentage of bonus or commission if this is a fixed percentage companywide. But if bonus and commission percentage varies with department or by employee, you should leave out the rate.

Activities:

- ❖ Company Setup: Compensation and Benefits
- ❖ Click **Continue** (bottom left of the window)
- ❖ Checkmark **Salary**
- ❖ Checkmark **Hourly wage and overtime**
- ❖ Checkmark **Bonus, award, or one-time compensation**
- ❖ Checkmark **Commission**
- ❖ Checkmark **Tips**
- ❖ Checkmark **Piecework**. Click **Next** (bottom right)
- ❖ Tell us about commissions

- ❖ Click **Dollar amount per units…**Click **Next**
- ❖ Tell us how you track tips
- ❖ Checkmark **Reported paycheck tips…**
- ❖ Click **Finish**
- ❖ Review your compensation list. Click **Continue**

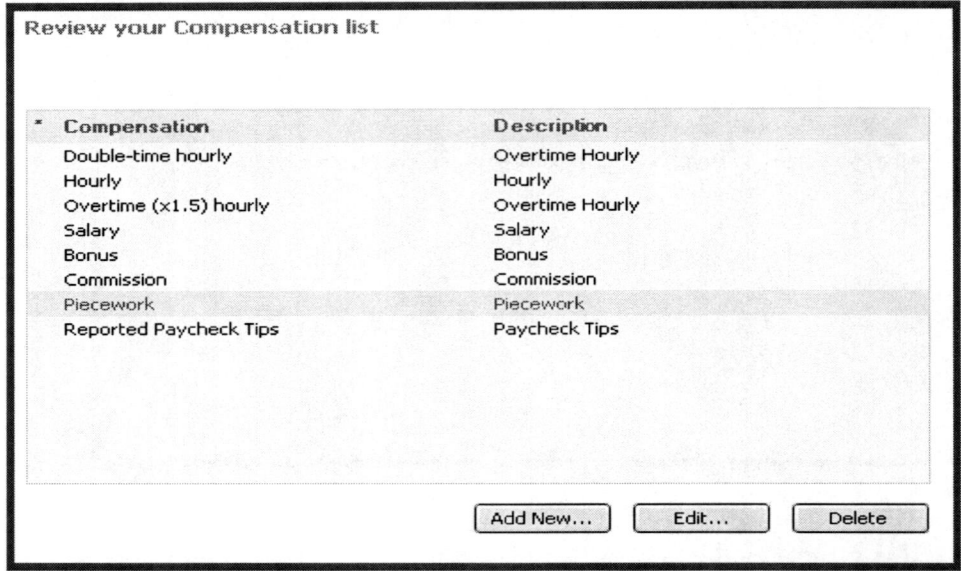

Employee Benefits: Insurance

Employee's payroll setup would not be complete without the insurance benefits items. Some insurance benefits are 100 percent paid by employees and some are paid by the company. However, the majority of insurance benefits are shared by employee and employer. Almost all insurance benefits are pretax benefits. That is, the insurance premium is deducted first from the employee's paycheck before the remainder is taxed. Check the employees' payroll policy for details.

Activities:

- ❖ Set up employee benefits
- ❖ Click **Continue**
- ❖ Checkmark **Health Insurance**
- ❖ Checkmark **Dental Insurance**
- ❖ Checkmark **Vision Insurance**
- ❖ Checkmark **Group Term Life**
- ❖ Checkmark **Health Savings Account**

- ❖ Checkmark **S Corp Medical**
- ❖ Checkmark **Other Insurance**
- ❖ Checkmark **Medical Care FSA**
- ❖ Checkmark **Dependent Care FSA**
- ❖ Click **Next**

Employee Benefits: Payment Schedule 1

The insurance payment schedule is very important because it lets QuickBooks know when you plan to pay your liabilities to the vendors. There are several time frames you may choose to pay the premium to the vendor. Mostly, every company chooses the quarterly payment schedule, because it forces you to pay all your vendors at the same time, including the government agencies. A company may choose to pay the premium on a monthly basis.

Activities:

- ❖ Tell us about health insurance
- ❖ Click **Employee pays for all of it**
- ❖ Click **Payment is deducted BEFORE**…Click **Next**
- ❖ Payee (Vendor): Select **HMO of America**
- ❖ Payment frequency: Click **Quarterly** on the: Select **31**
- ❖ Click **Next**
- ❖ Tell us about dental Insurance
- ❖ Click **Employee pays for all of it**
- ❖ Click **Payment is deducted BEFORE**…Click **Next**
- ❖ Payee (Vendor): Select **HMO of America**
- ❖ Payment frequency: Click **Quarterly** on the: Select **31**
- ❖ Click **Next**
- ❖ Tell us about vision insurance
- ❖ Click **Employee pays for all of it**
- ❖ Click **Payment is deducted BEFORE**…Click **Next**
- ❖ Payee (Vendor): Select **HMO of America**
- ❖ Payment frequency: Click **Quarterly** on the: Select **31**
- ❖ Click **Next**
- ❖ Set up payment schedule for S-Corp medical insurance
- ❖ Accept **I don't need a regular payment schedule…**
- ❖ Click **Next**

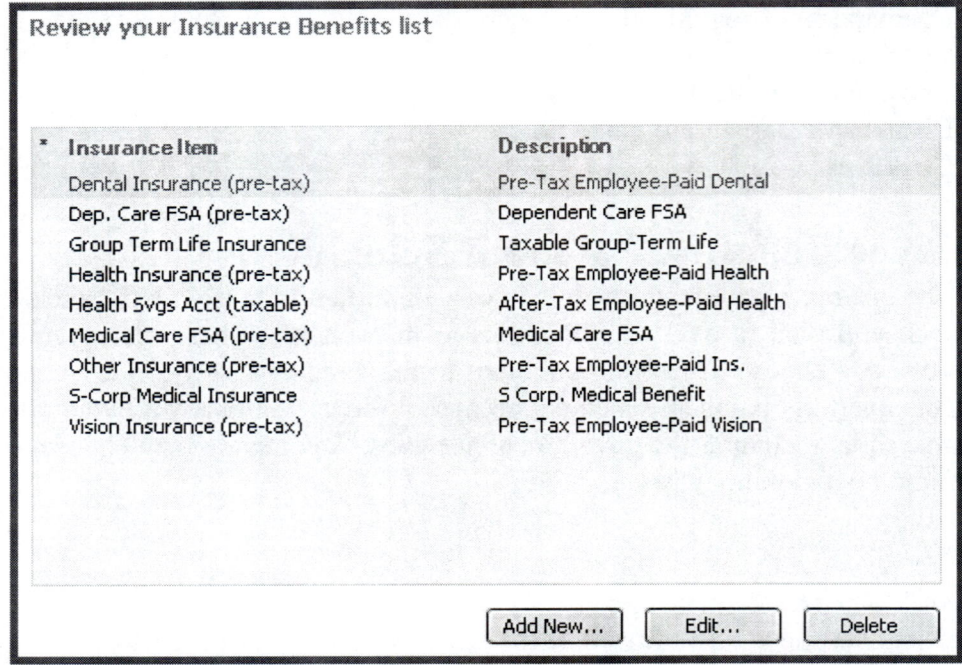

Employee Benefits: Payment Schedule 2

Managing benefits payment schedule is a strict task, because every payment must be on time. To select a vendor, probably an HMO, invite a few companies to bid for your business. You want to choose a company that likes to receive the premium quarterly instead of monthly. At least you get to use the premium for 60 days before releasing it to the vendor. You will need a handbook to see if employees are paying the entire premium or not.

- ❖ Tell us about the Medical Care FSA insurance plan
- ❖ Click **Employee pays for all of it.** Click **Next**
- ❖ Payee (Vendor): Select **HMO of America**
- ❖ Payment frequency: Click **Quarterly** on the: Select **31**
- ❖ Click **Next**
- ❖ Tell us about the Dep. Care FSA insurance plan
- ❖ Click **Employee pays for all of it.** Click **Next**
- ❖ Payee (Vendor): Select **HMO of America**
- ❖ Payment frequency: Click **Quarterly** on the: Select **31**
- ❖ Click **Next**
- ❖ Tell us about any other insurance you provide
- ❖ Click **Employee pays for all of it**

* Click **Payment is deducted BEFORE**…Click **Next**
* Payee (Vendor): Select **HMO of America**
* Payment frequency: Click **Quarterly** on the: Select **31**
* Click **Next**
* Tell us about the Health Saving Account plan
* Click **Employee pays for all of it.** Click **Next**
* Payee (Vendor): Select **HMO of America**
* Payment frequency: Click **Quarterly** on the: Select **31**
* Click **Next**
* Set up the payment schedule for Group Term Life Insurance
* Payee (Vendor): Select **HMO of America**
* Frequency: Click **Quarterly** on the: Select **31**
* Click **Finish**
* Review your Insurance Benefits list
* Click **Continue**

Employee Benefits: Retirement

Cost/benefit analysis will help to determine if you want to use the same company for both the insurance benefit and retirement benefit. Some companies manage both retirement and insurance, but others specialize as an insurance or retirement management company. You can consolidate your activities with one company if you are able to receive substantial discounts by letting one company handle both the retirement and the insurance businesses.

* Tell us about your company retirement benefits
* Checkmark **401(k)**
* Checkmark **Simple IRA**
* Checkmark **403(b)**
* Checkmark **408(k)(6) SEP.** Click **Next**
* Set up the payment schedule for 401(k)
* Payee (Vendor): Select **Money Mgt of America**
* Payment Frequency: Click **Quarterly** on the: Select **31**
* Click **Next**
* Set up the payment schedule for 403(b).
* Payee (Vendor): Select **Money Mgt of America**
* Payment Frequency: Click **Quarterly** on the: Select **31**
* Click **Next**
* Set up the payment schedule for 408(k)(6) SEP.
* Payee (Vendor): Select **Money Mgt of America**

- ❖ Payment Frequency: Click **Quarterly** on the: Select **31**
- ❖ Click **Next**
- ❖ Set up the payment schedule for Simple IRA.
- ❖ Payee (Vendor): Select **Money Mgt of America**
- ❖ Payment Frequency: Click **Quarterly** on the: Select **31**
- ❖ Click **Finish**.
- ❖ Review your Retirement Benefits List
- ❖ Click **Continue**

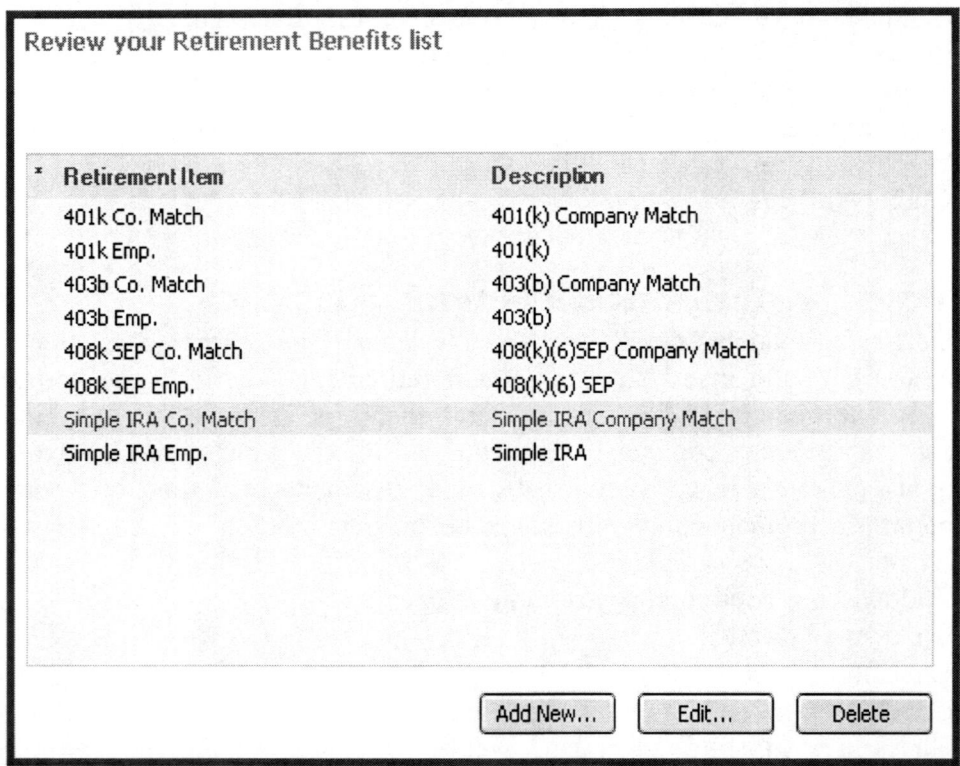

Review your Retirement Benefits list

Retirement Item	Description
401k Co. Match	401(k) Company Match
401k Emp.	401(k)
403b Co. Match	403(b) Company Match
403b Emp.	403(b)
408k SEP Co. Match	408(k)(6)SEP Company Match
408k SEP Emp.	408(k)(6) SEP
Simple IRA Co. Match	Simple IRA Company Match
Simple IRA Emp.	Simple IRA

[Add New...] [Edit...] [Delete]

Employee Benefits: Paid Time Off

At this point, it's a question of finding out if your company pays for sick and vacation time off or not. Most companies pay for sick and vacation time off, but small mom and pop businesses may not afford to do so for everyone. Check the personnel policy to find out. In general, when a company pays for sick time off, it also pays for vacation time off. But the question is in the accrual. Some companies have a "use it or lose it" policy, while others roll over to the next year if you don't use it all this year.

Activities:

- ❖ Set up paid time off:
- ❖ Checkmark **Paid sick time off**
- ❖ Checkmark **Paid vacation time off**
- ❖ Click **Finish**
- ❖ Review your Paid Time Off list
- ❖ Click **Continue**

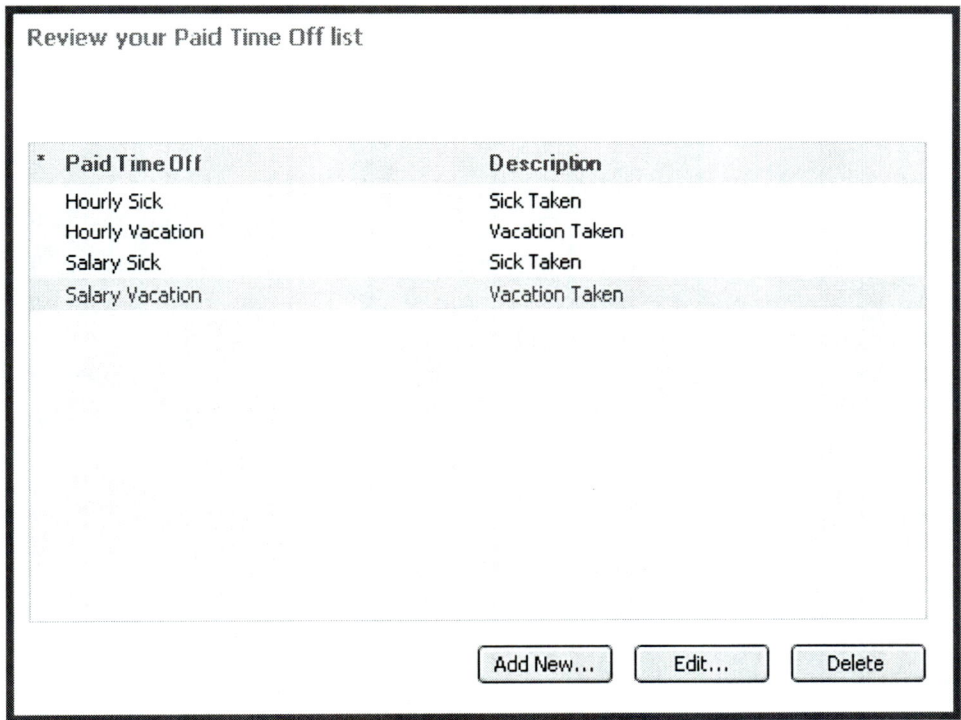

Review your Paid Time Off list

* Paid Time Off	Description
Hourly Sick	Sick Taken
Hourly Vacation	Vacation Taken
Salary Sick	Sick Taken
Salary Vacation	Vacation Taken

Add New...   Edit...   Delete

Employee Benefits: Additions & Deductions

The Paycheck Details window has two main sections. The first is the Earnings box and the other is the Other Payroll Items. Any payroll items not selected as Earnings are pulled into the Other Payroll Items box. Employee payroll items other than Earnings are classified as "addition to" or "deduction from" Earnings. For example, cash advances and mileage reimbursements are additions (extra money) to Earnings. and wage garnishment, union dues and donation are deduction from Earnings.

Activities:

- ❖ Set up additions and deductions window
- ❖ Checkmark **Cash Advance**
- ❖ Checkmark **Taxable fringe benefits**
- ❖ Checkmark **Mileage reimbursement**
- ❖ Checkmark **Miscellaneous addition**
- ❖ Checkmark **Wage garnishment**
- ❖ Checkmark **Union dues**
- ❖ Checkmark **Donation to charity**
- ❖ Checkmark **Miscellaneous deduction**
- ❖ Click **Next**

Employee Benefits: Payment Schedule

Setting up the payment schedule for additions and deductions is the same as the compensation, insurance and retirement benefits. You choose a vendor that will receive the payments and then decide if you want to make your payments on a monthly or quarterly basis. However, the vendor that handles your insurance benefits should also handle addition and deduction items that are insurance-related, and the same vendor that handles retirement benefits should also handle addition and deduction items that are retirement-related.

Activities:

- ❖ Set up the payment schedule for taxable fringe benefits
- ❖ Payee (Vendor): Select **Money Mgt of America**
- ❖ Payment Frequency: Click **Quarterly** on the: Select **31**
- ❖ Click **Next**
- ❖ Set up the payment schedule for donation to charity
- ❖ Payee (Vendor): Select **Money Mgt of America**
- ❖ Payment Frequency: Click **Quarterly** on the: Select **31**
- ❖ Click **Next**
- ❖ Set up the payment schedule for union dues
- ❖ Payee (Vendor): Select **Money Mgt of America**
- ❖ Payment Frequency: Click **Quarterly** on the: Select **31**
- ❖ Click **Next**
- ❖ Set up the payment schedule for wage garnishment
- ❖ Payee (Vendor): Select **Money Mgt of America**
- ❖ Payment Frequency: Click **Quarterly** on the: Select **31**
- ❖ Click **Next**

- ❖ Set up the payment schedule for miscellaneous deduction
- ❖ Payee (Vendor): Select **Money Mgt of America**
- ❖ Payment Frequency: Click **Quarterly** on the: Select **31**
- ❖ **Click Finish**
- ❖ Review your Additions and Deductions list
- ❖ Click **Continue**

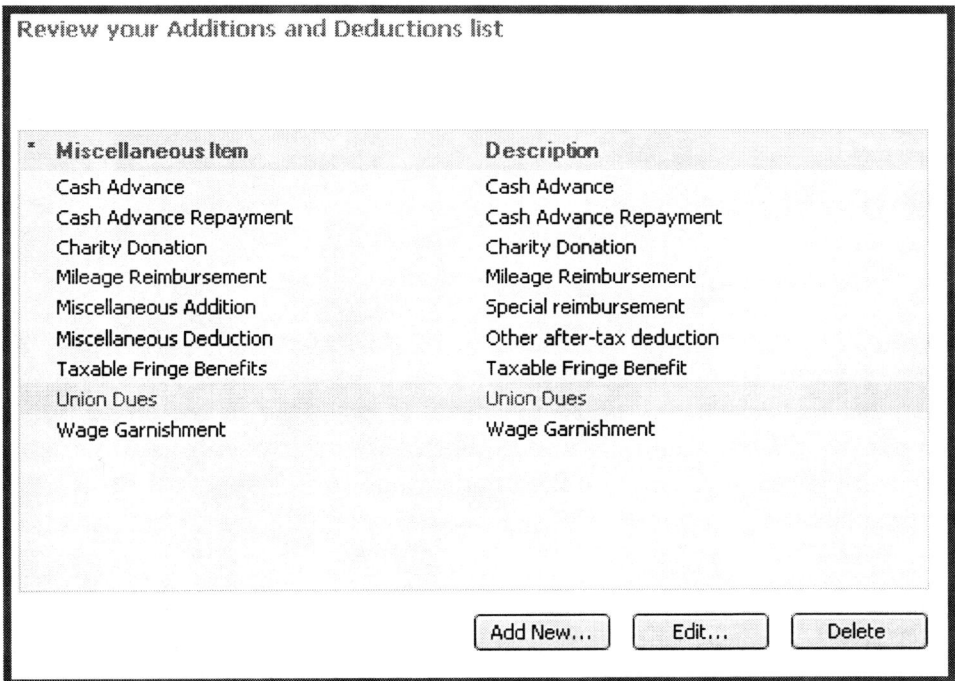

Employee List: Fate Acres

Up to this point, you have been setting up global items, or items that can be used for any employee. Here, you are going to set up specific items that are related to one particular employee. Employee information varies with each individual; however, you should include as much information for an employee as possible. It is pertinent to find employee information when you need it. For example, the contact information should be included for each employee.

Activities:

- ❖ Set up your employees
- ❖ Click **Continue**
- ❖ Click **Fate Acres** in the window

- ❖ Click **Edit** (bottom of the window)
- ❖ Home Address: Type **123 Danny Lane**
- ❖ City: Type **Dallas**
- ❖ State: Press **T** twice to select **TX**
- ❖ Zip Code: Type **75000**.
- ❖ Click **Next**
- ❖ Enter Fate Acres's hiring information
- ❖ Employee type: Select **Regular**
- ❖ Social Security #: Accept **999-45-6789**
- ❖ Hire date: Type **12/31/2008 (Must be 2008** Very Important**)**
- ❖ Birth date: Accept **1/1/1977**
- ❖ Gender: Accept **Female**
- ❖ Click **Next**

Employee List: Compensation

Here, you are going to set up Fate's compensation information. Since we have set up global payroll items, this is the time to pull in as much payroll items that relate to Fate as possible. It is easier when you want to pay Fate to see all payroll items needed to pay her. Fate is an hourly employee and her hourly wage is 50 per hour. To calculate her overtime pay, multiply the hourly wage by 1.5 to get 75 per hour. Since we know Fate's commission is 10% of her bi-weekly earnings, add that percentage.

Activities:

- ❖ Tell us about wages and compensation for Fate Acres
- ❖ Payment frequency: Select **Every other week (Biweekly)**
- ❖ Click **Employee is paid hourly**
- ❖ Hourly wage: Type **50**
- ❖ Checkmark **Overtime (x1.5)**. Amount: Type **75**
- ❖ Checkmark **Bonus**. Amount: **Leave Blank**
- ❖ Checkmark **Commission**. Amount: **Type 10%**
- ❖ Click **Next**

Overtime rate is calculated by multiplying the hourly wage 50 by 1.5 to get 75.

Tell us about wages and compensation for Fate Acres

Pay frequency   Every other week (Biweekly) ▼

What regular compensation does Fate Acres receive?

◉ **Employee is paid hourly**

○ Employee is paid on salary

○ Employee does not have any base compensation

Hourly wage   50.00

	Regular wages	Amount	Description
☐	Double-time hourly		$ per hour
☑	Overtime (x1.5) hourly	$75.00	$ per hour
☑	Bonus		default amount
☑	Commission	10%	commission rate or amount
☐	Piecework		piecework rate

One of the ways I pay this employee isn't on this list. What should I do?

[Cancel]   [< Previous] [Next >]

UPS10.3.1174

Employee List: Insurance

To set up Fate's benefits, we look at her employment file to see what the company agrees to pay. In her file, you determined that Fate is covered for health, dental and vision insurance. You also determined that the company matches up to 5% if Fate contributes 5% or more of her biweekly pay to the 401(k) plan. If she contributes less than 5%, such as 3%, the company matches only 3%. In addition, we saw that Fate signed for union dues and charitable donation.

❖ Tell us about benefits for Fate Acres
❖ Checkmark **401(k) Emp**
❖ Checkmark **Dental Insurance**
❖ Checkmark **Health Insurance**
❖ **Scroll down to other items**
❖ Checkmark **Vision Insurance**
❖ Checkmark **401k Co Match**. Amount: Type **5%.** (Very Important)
❖ Checkmark **Taxable Fringe Benefit**
❖ Checkmark **Cash Advance**
❖ Checkmark **Mileage Reimbursement**
❖ Checkmark **Miscellaneous Addition**

* ❖ Checkmark **Cash Advance Repayment**
* ❖ Checkmark **Charity Donation**
* ❖ Checkmark **Health Svgs Acct (taxable)**
* ❖ Checkmark **Miscellaneous Deduction**
* ❖ Checkmark **Union Dues**
* ❖ Click **Wages Garnishment**
* ❖ Click **Next**

Employee List: Sick and Vacation

You will be setting up sick and vacation time for Fate. Pay particular attention to the per paycheck selection. The company agrees to put four hours in her sick bank per paycheck not per month and four hours in her vacation bank per paycheck. To make Fate's accrued hours not pass the four hours, multiple the 4 hours by 26 or 104 for the maximum number of hours she can accrue for the year. If Fate decides to sign up for direct deposit, she has to complete the direct deposit form.

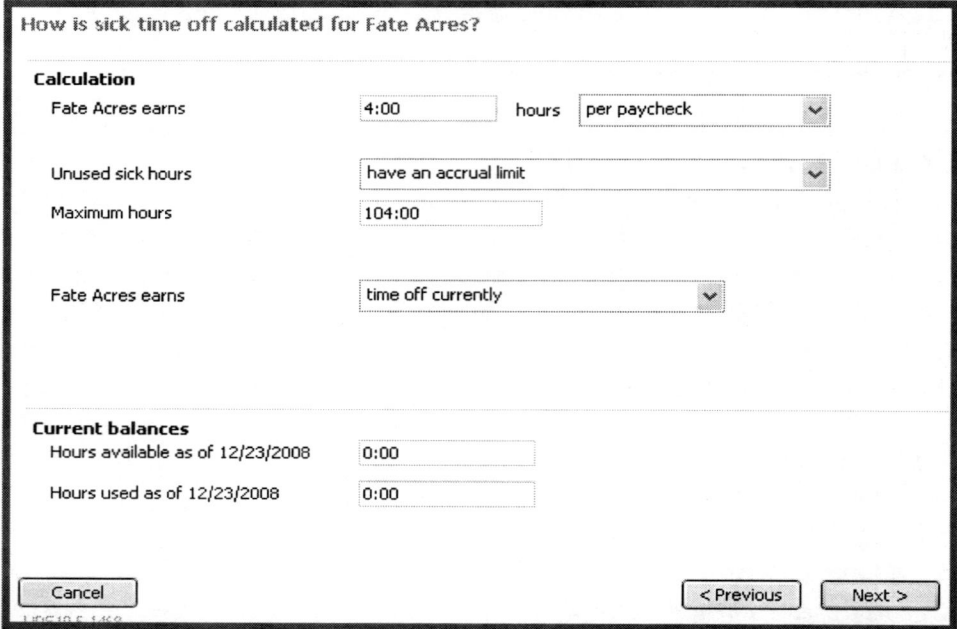

Activities:
* ❖ How is sick time off calculated for Fate Acres
* ❖ Fate Acres earns: Type **4.** Hours: Select **per paycheck**
* ❖ Unused sick hours: Select **have an accrual limit**
* ❖ Maximum hours: Type **104**

- ❖ Fate Acres earns: Select **time off currently**
- ❖ Hours available as of…: Type **0.00**
- ❖ Hours used as of…: Type **0:00**
- ❖ Click **Next**
- ❖ How is vacation time off calculated for Fate Acres
- ❖ Fate Acres earns: Type **4.** Hours: Select **per paycheck**
- ❖ Unused sick hours: Select **have an accrual limit**
- ❖ Maximum hours: Type **104**
- ❖ Fate Acres earns: Select **time off currently**
- ❖ Hours available as of…: Type **0.00**
- ❖ Hours used as of…: Type **0:00**
- ❖ Click **Next**
- ❖ Set up Fate Acres direct deposit information
- ❖ Click **Pay Fate Acres by Direct Deposit**
- ❖ How many accounts: Click **One account**
- ❖ Bank name: Type **JP Morgan Chase**
- ❖ Account No.: Type **999999999** (Nine 9s)
- ❖ Routing No.: Type **021000021** (Nine numbers)
- ❖ Account Type: Select **Checking.** Click **Next**

Employee List: Taxes

Nothing is more important in setting up an employee's payroll than the state and federal taxes. Federal taxes depend on a lot of items including filing status and number of allowances. For Fate, her filing status is married and her allowance is two. Whatever you do, make sure that Medicare, Social Security and Federal Unemployment boxes are checked. QuickBooks will guide you during the company setup to see if employees in your state pay state unemployment taxes or not.

Activities:

- ❖ Tell us where Fate Acres is subject to taxes
- ❖ State subject to withholding: Select **TX-Texas**
- ❖ State subject to unemployment tax: Select **TX-Texas**
- ❖ While working for you…Click **No**
- ❖ Click **Next**
- ❖ Enter federal tax information for Fate Acres
- ❖ Filing Status: Select **Married**
- ❖ Allowances: Type **2**
- ❖ Extra Withholding: Type **0.00**
- ❖ Nonresident Alien Withholding: Accept **Does not apply**

❖ Checkmark **Subject to Medicare**
❖ Checkmark **Subject to Social Security**
❖ Checkmark **Federal Unemployment**
❖ Click **Next**
❖ Enter State tax information for Fate Acres
❖ Checkmark **Subject to TX-Unemployment**
❖ Is this employee subject to any special local taxes…?
❖ Click **No**
❖ Click **Finish**
❖ Review your Employee list
❖ Click **Continue**

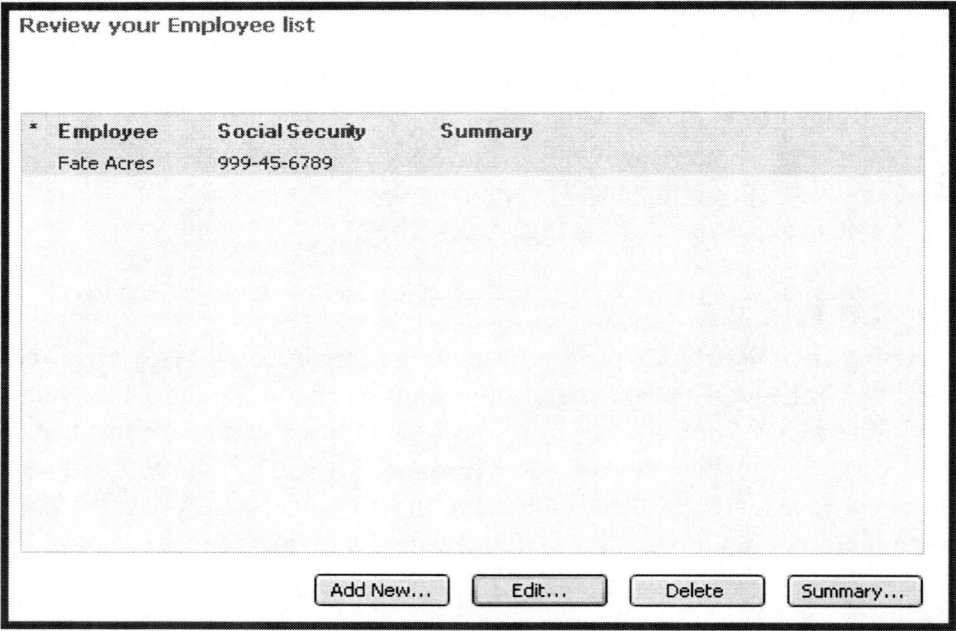

Set Up Payroll Taxes

After reviewing the Employee List window above, you clicked continue to review the federal taxes that were set up for you by QuickBooks. You will be prompted with an error message if you did not provide the EIN (Employer Identification Number). The EIN was provided during the Company Information update in chapter five. If there are error prompts, you must exit to provide the needed information before continuing. Therefore, the EIN is a required number when it comes to the payroll process.

Activities:

* ❖ Set up your payroll taxes
* ❖ Click **Continue**
* ❖ Here are the federal taxes we set up for you
* ❖ Click **Continue**
* ❖ TX – Cashier, Texas Workforce Commission payments
* ❖ TX – Unemployment Company Rate: Type **2.7.** Press **Tab**
* ❖ Click **Finish**
* ❖ Review your state taxes
* ❖ Click **Continue**

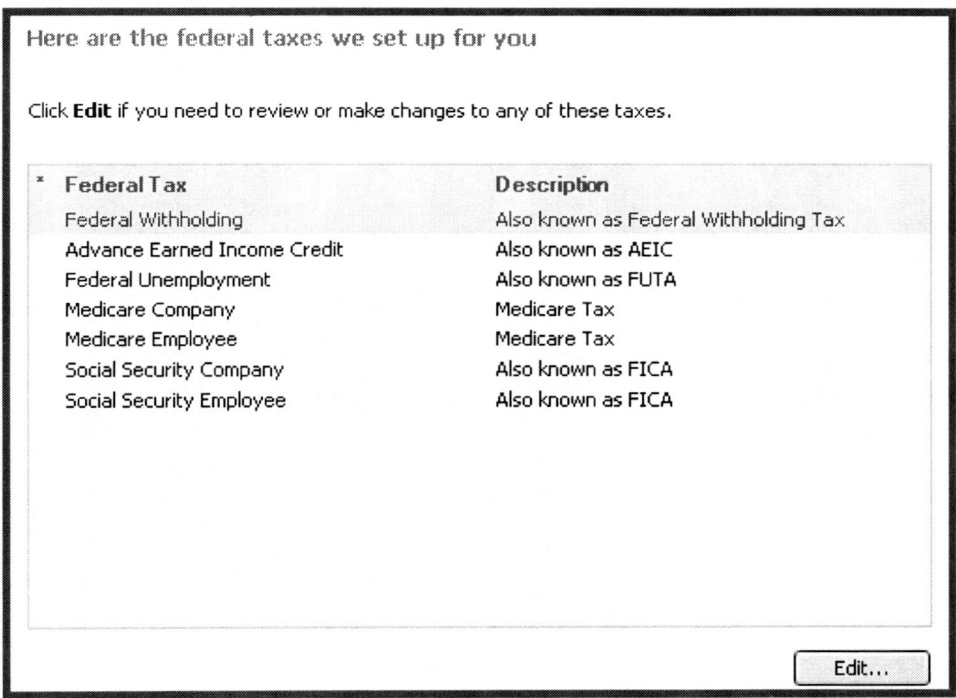

Here are the federal taxes we set up for you

Click **Edit** if you need to review or make changes to any of these taxes.

* Federal Tax	Description
Federal Withholding	Also known as Federal Withholding Tax
Advance Earned Income Credit	Also known as AEIC
Federal Unemployment	Also known as FUTA
Medicare Company	Medicare Tax
Medicare Employee	Medicare Tax
Social Security Company	Also known as FICA
Social Security Employee	Also known as FICA

Edit...

Set Up Federal Payroll Taxes

If you checkmarked Medicare, Social Security and Federal Unemployment boxes as instructed in the previous section, you should provide QuickBooks with the payee when the check is issued. In this section, you will accept the United States Treasury as defaulted in the text box. Most companies choose quarterly as the payment frequency instead of monthly or semi-annually. At least you get to carry those funds on your books for three months before remitting to the agency.

Activities:

- ❖ Set up your payment schedule for Federal 940
- ❖ Payee: Accept **United States Treasury**
- ❖ Payment (deposit) frequency: Accept **Quarterly (usual frequency)**
- ❖ Click **Next**
- ❖ Set up payment schedule for Federal 941/944
- ❖ Payee: Accept **United States Treasury**
- ❖ Payment (deposit) frequency: Select **Quarterly**
- ❖ Click **Next**
- ❖ Set up payment schedule for TX Unemployment Insurance
- ❖ Payee: Accept **Cashier, Texas Workforce Commission**
- ❖ TX Workforce Commission Acct No: Type **99-999999-9** (Six 9s in the middle)
- ❖ Payment deposit) frequency: Accept **Quarterly (usual frequency)**
- ❖ Click **Finish**
- ❖ Review your Schedule Payment lists
- ❖ Click **Continue**

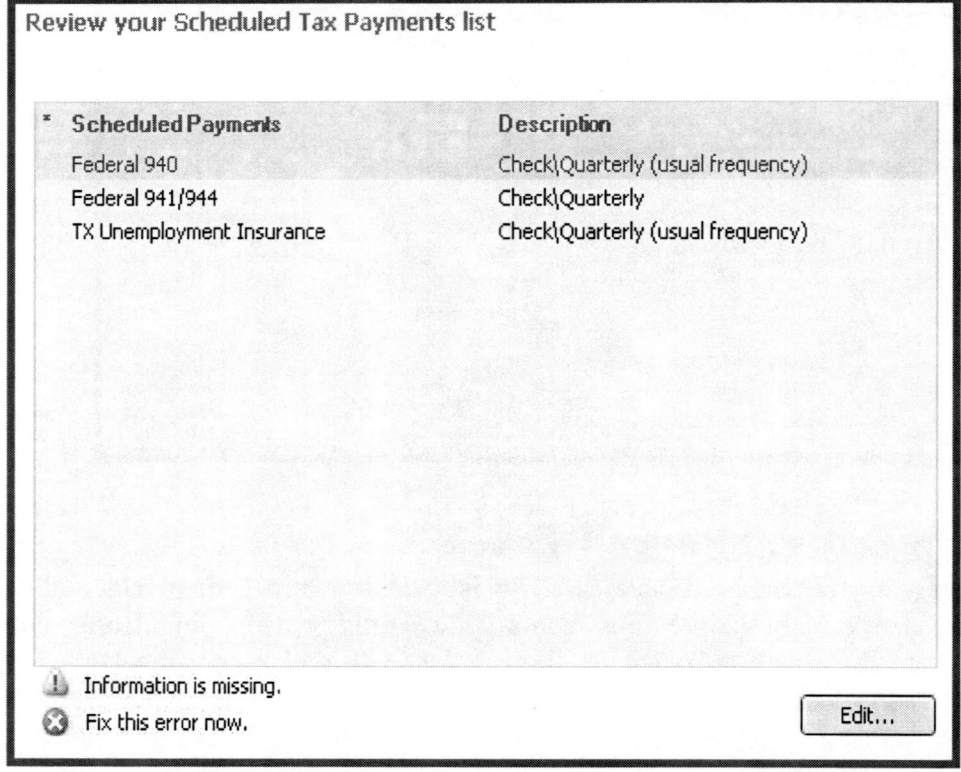

Set Up Payroll History

Setting up the Payroll History is the hardest task in the payroll process. For this reason, a lot of companies avoid it by starting their payroll process at the beginning of the year, January 1 and so should you. If you happen to be in a situation where you are switching payroll software or you want to start payroll in-house instead of using an outside company, you must wait until the beginning of the year. Setting up the payroll history is not too hard, but it is better to start with a clean slate.

❖ Enter payroll history for the current year
❖ Click **Continue**
❖ Determine if you need to enter payroll history
❖ Click **2009.** Click **No** (If available). Or Click **OK**
❖ Click **Continue**
❖ Setup is complete
❖ **Arrow** is pointed to **Finishing Up**
❖ (Congratulations!)
❖ Click **Go to Payroll Center**

Setup is complete

Now that your payroll is set up, you can start paying employees using the Payroll Center. The Payroll Center is where you manage the most common payroll tasks, including paying employees, paying tax and other payroll-related liabilities and preparing your payroll tax filings.

To continue to the Payroll Center, click **Go to Payroll Center** below.

UPS33.1438

[Go to Payroll Center]

Browse Payroll Item Listing

Managing your payroll items is very vital because from time to time, you will be required to add or edit payroll items. QuickBooks will not allow you to delete a payroll item if the item has been used somewhere, especially in creating a paycheck. In the Payroll Listing window, you can edit an individual item, but remember you have to click through the windows for that item as if you are newly creating it. You can also print a report of an item, which is very vital if you want to see what transactions are posted to that item. Also, you can print a report for all the payroll items.

Activities:

- ❖ To find out what items you've created
- ❖ Click **Employees menu**
- ❖ Click **Manage Payroll Items**
- ❖ Click **View/Edit Payroll Item List**
- ❖ Click **No** to "Would you like to learn more?"
- ❖ Maximize window
- ❖ To edit an item
- ❖ Right click on **Salary**
- ❖ Click **Edit Payroll Item**
- ❖ Click **X** to close window
- ❖ To print payroll listing
- ❖ Click **Reports menu**
- ❖ Click **Employees & Payroll**
- ❖ Click **Payroll Item Listing** (bottom of list)
- ❖ Click **No** to "Would you like to learn more?"
- ❖ Click **Print** (top of the window)
- ❖ Click **Preview** (right of the window). Click **Zoom In**
- ❖ Click **Close** or Print if printer is ready
- ❖ Click **X** to close Print Report window
- ❖ Click small **X** below red X to close Payroll Item Listing report

> Before you delete a payroll item or any other items or accounts in QuickBooks, you must right click on the item or account and click QuickReport at the bottom of the list to view the content of the item or account. You can only delete empty items or accounts.

Create Timesheets

If you plan on paying an hourly employee, you must receive a timesheet from the employee for audit purposes. Never pay an hourly employee without a timesheet. Most hourly employees are paid biweekly; in that case, you will receive two timesheets for each week, Monday through Sunday, with a total of 80 hours. Choose the date range that corresponds with the date on the timesheet from the drop-down window. If the company tracks time against what job was done, you must complete the customer name and the service item.

Activities:

- ❖ Click **Employees menu**
- ❖ Click **Employee Center**
- ❖ Double click **Fate Acres**
- ❖ Change tabs: Select **Payroll & Compensation Info**
- ❖ Checkmark **Use time data to create paychecks** (under Earnings box)
- ❖ Click **OK** to close window
- ❖ Click **Employees menu**
- ❖ Click **Enter Time**
- ❖ Click **Use Weekly Timesheet**
- ❖ Name: Select **Fate Acres.** Press **Tab**
- ❖ Week of: Click **Button**
- ❖ Click arrow **to December 2008**
- ❖ Click **31** (For Dec 29 to Jan 4,2009)
- ❖ Click under Customer: Job: Select **James Adams**
- ❖ Service Item: Select **Delivery**
- ❖ Payroll Item: Select **Hourly**
- ❖ From Monday(M) 29 to Friday(F) 2: Type **8**. Total **40**
- ❖ Uncheck **Billable?** (Very Important)
- ❖ Click **Save & New**
- ❖ Name: Select **Fate Acres**
- ❖ Click **Next** button (top of the window)
- ❖ Week of: Accept Jan 5 to Jan 11, 2009)
- ❖ Click **Copy Last Sheet** (bottom left)
- ❖ Click **Save & Close** (bottom right)
- ❖ Click **Edit men.** Click **Calculator**
- ❖ **Minimize Calculator to the Taskbar**

> We're making it an even number 80hrs; actually you should be paying 8 hours for Friday and then 40 hrs from 5th to 11th for a total of 48 hours for the two weeks she worked.

Create Paychecks

After you've completed the timesheet, the next step is to pay the employee. You key in the end of the period date and the date of the check; both are required boxes before a check is issued to an employee. If QuickBooks prompts you with "You're not signed up yet…Do you want to learn more?," click No. When you enter the Pay Employee window, you will confirm the 80 hours you entered for the employee and click the Create Paychecks button.

Activities:

- ❖ Click **Employees menu**
- ❖ Click **Pay Employees**
- ❖ Click **No** to "You aren't sign up…Would you like to learn more…?"
- ❖ Pay Period Ends: Highlight box. Type **1/11/09**. Press **Tab**
- ❖ Click **Yes** to "If you're using time tracking…"
- ❖ Check Date: Type **1/11/09**
- ❖ Bank Account: Select **USA Payroll**
- ❖ Bank Account Balance: Accept **250,000**
- ❖ Checkmark **Fate Acres** (left of the window).
- ❖ Hourly: Accept **80:00**. Total Hours: Accept **80:00**
- ❖ Click **Continue**
- ❖ Click **Create Paychecks**
- ❖ Click **Close** on the Confirmation window

Edit Paychecks

After you click Create Paycheck, the process is completed. Go the Employee Center window to pull up the check for reviewing and editing. Bear in mind a lot more corrections are made in the Review Paycheck window as shown below. The objective is to add all the payroll items for that employee you have identified. For example, you will provide the quantity for commission or bonus if they are based on a percentage of certain amounts other than the earnings.

Activities:

- ❖ Click **Employees menu**. Click **Employee Center**
- ❖ Click **Fate Acres** (left of the window)
- ❖ Double click **Paycheck for 1/11/09** (right)
- ❖ Bank Account: Accept **USA Payroll**
- ❖ Click **Paycheck Details** (bottom right)
- ❖ Accept click on **Unlock Net Pay** (bottom right)
- ❖ Complete window with information on the next page

It's essential to create the payment schedule and distribute to all employees starting from the last Monday in December, separated by pay periods equal to 52wks

12/29/08—	1/4/09
1/5/09—	**1/11/09**
1/12/09—	1/18/09
1/19/09—	**1/25/09**
1/26/09—	2/1/09
2/2/09—	**2/8/09**
2/9/09—	2/15/09
2/16/09—	**2/22/09**
2/23/09—	3/1/09
3/2/09—	**3/8/09**

The bold dates are the paydays, the end of the period, and the pay check dates

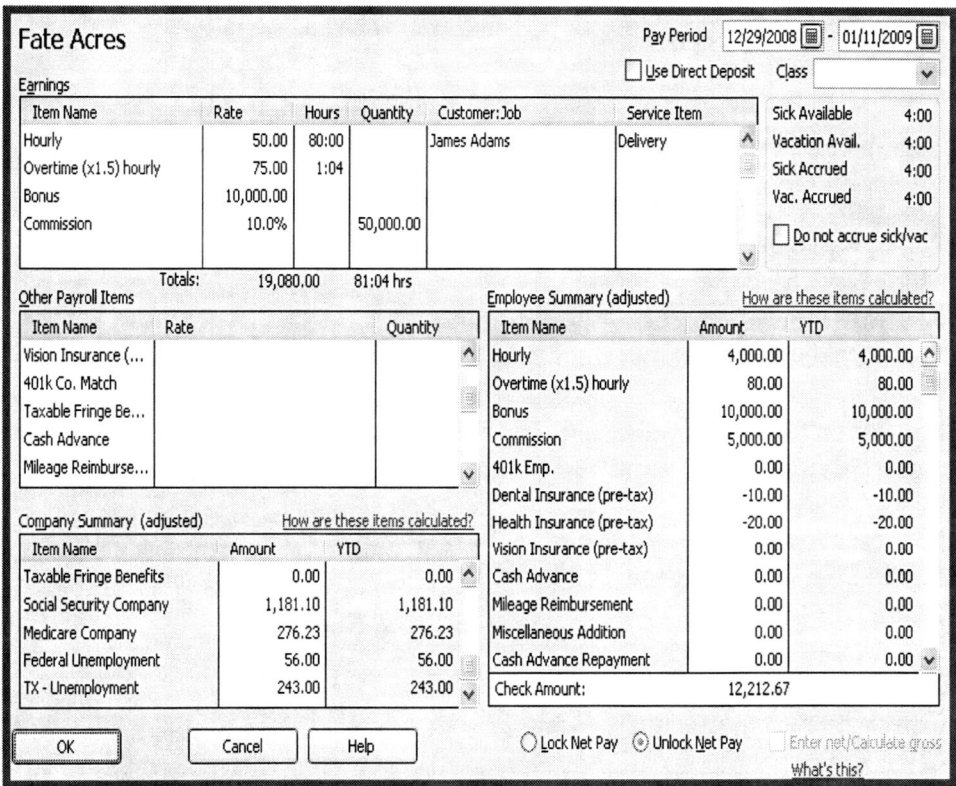

Paycheck Details

Here are the details of entries for the Review Paycheck window. If an item is already default, go to the next item. Click in the Earnings box to pull up the items. Be sure to type the number under the right title (rate, hours or quantity) as required. You need to delete the 401(k) default percentage; otherwise, QuickBooks will use it to calculate the amount for the Company Summary box. Keep your eyes on the check total to make sure it matches with the total below, and you need to use the QuickBooks calculator to confirm the Company totals as shown below.

Activities Details:

- ❖ Earning:
- ❖ Hourly. Rate: 50. Hours: 80
- ❖ Click under Hourly. Select Overtime. Rate: 75. Hours: 1:04 (with colon)
- ❖ Select Bonus. Rate: 10,000
- ❖ Select Commission. Rate: 10%. Quantity: 50,000
- ❖

* Other Payroll Items: (Type as positive will show as negative)
* Dental. Rate: 10
* Health. Rate: 20
* 401k Co. Match. Rate: blank (delete 5%). Press **Tab**
*
* Company Summary (adjusted)
* Social Security. Amount: 1,181.10
* Medicare. Amount: 276.23
* Federal Unemployment. Amount: 56.00
* TX – Unemployment. Amount: 243.00
*
* Employee Summary (adjusted) (right of the window)
* Accept default figures and add these
* **Scroll down**
* Federal Withholding. Amount: 5,380.00
* Social Security. Amount: 1181.10
* Medicare. Amount: 276.23
*
* Check Amount: **12,212.67**
* Company Summary (left): **1,756.33**
* Click **OK**
* Click **Save & Close** on check window
* Click **Yes** to "You have changed the transaction…"

> Because the Company Summary does not have total amount, you must use the calculator you minimized on the taskbar to confirm the number you entered is correct. Very Important!

Run QuickReport

QuickReport is something you have to understand and be able to use as often as possible to proof your work. As you become acclimated to QuickBooks, you will be able to access the QuickReport from many windows. You can access QuickReport from the Employee Center window, under the Report menu, but you must click an employee first, and in the Payroll Item list window, but you must click an item first. You want to see how much you paid Fate for the year; therefore, we clicked "This Calendar Year." Always keep your eyes on the date range.

Activities:

* Click **Employees menu**
* Click **Employee Center**
* Click **Fate Acres** (left of the window)
* Click **Reports menu**
* Click **QuickReport**

> You can auto-view QuickReport on any item or account by right clicking on the account and selecting QuickReport at the bottom of the list

- ❖ Towards the bottom of the submenus
- ❖ Dates: Select **This Calendar Year**
- ❖ Look! Fate Acres has **12,212.67**
- ❖ Click **X** to close window

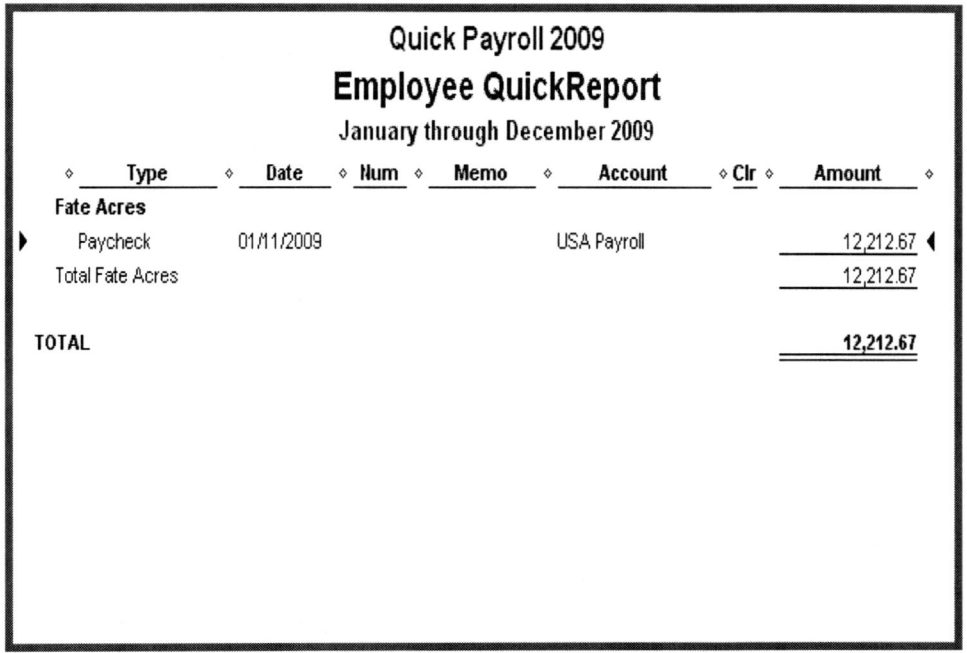

Run Payroll Transaction Report

You should get familiar with the Payroll transaction report. If you run the report by payee, it gives you the summary of your activities by payee. You see a snapshot of what checks were issued to both employees and vendors. If you run the detailed report, which most people do, you get to see the individual payments you made to employees by date and vendors by date. It's pertinent to review the detailed report to see how federal and state calculations are done, especially the wage base.

Activities:

- ❖ Click **Reports menu**
- ❖ Click **Employees & Payroll**
- ❖ Click **Payroll Transaction by Payee**
- ❖ Dates: Select **This Calendar Year**
- ❖ Total Payroll check is **12,212.67**
- ❖ Click **X** to close window

```
                        Quick Payroll 2009
                    Payroll Transactions by Payee
                    January through December 2009
       ◇   Date   ◇      Name    ◇    Type   ◇  ◇  Account  ◇     Amount     ◇
      Fate Acres
   ▶    01/11/2009    Fate Acres      Paycheck      USA Payroll      -12,212.67 ◀
        Total Fate Acres                                            -12,212.67

    TOTAL                                                          -12,212.67
```

Add Employee: Personal Info

In addition to setting up an hourly employee, you should learn how to set up a salary employee. The process and the basic information are almost the same with minor variations with an hourly employee. Review employee's personnel file to collect these basic personal data. When adding a new employee, you should click the Continue button until you get to the employee window, or checkmark the setup boxes until you get to the Employee List, since you cannot jump to the Employee List.

Activities:

- ❖ Click **Employees menu**
- ❖ Click **Payroll Setup**
- ❖ Arrow is pointed to **Introduction** (left of the window)
- ❖ **Continue to click Next until you see "Set up your employees" #3 step**
- ❖ Click **Continue**
- ❖ Review your Employee list
- ❖ Click **Add New**…(bottom of the window)
- ❖ First name: Type **Jerry**
- ❖ Last name: Type **Jordan**
- ❖ Home address: Type **456 Kenton St**
- ❖ City: Type **Dallas**

- ❖ State: Press **T** twice to select **Texas**
- ❖ Zip Code: Type **75000**
- ❖ Click **Next**
- ❖ Employee type: Select **Officer**
- ❖ Social Security #: **999-12-3456**
- ❖ Hire date: Type **12/31/08** (Must be 2008)
- ❖ Birth date: Type **1/1/1971**
- ❖ Gender: Select **Male**
- ❖ Click **Next**

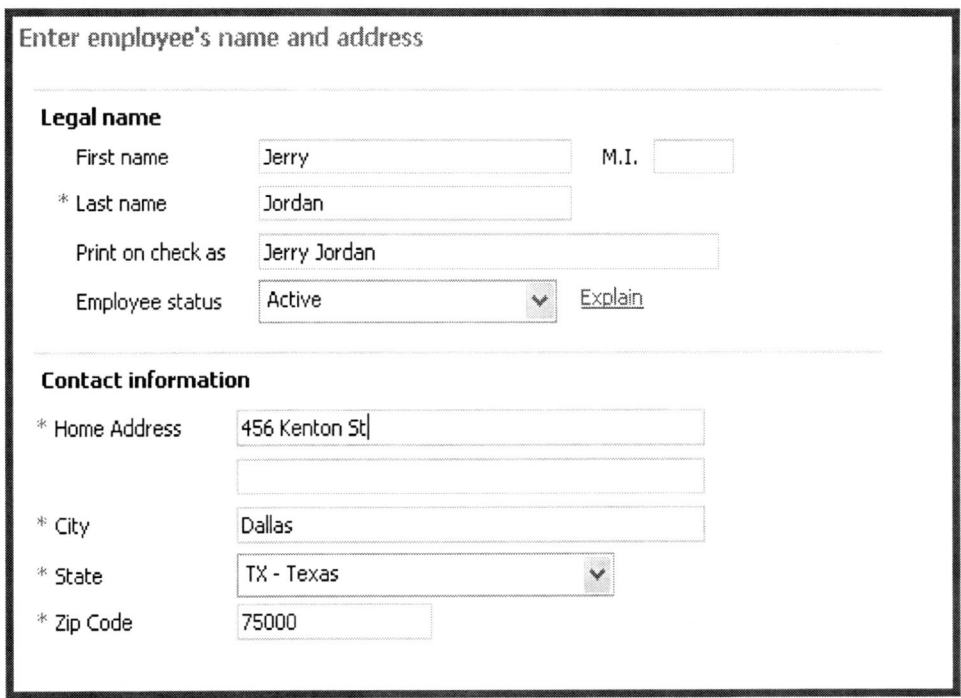

Add Employee: Compensation

The pay frequency is the same with an hourly employee; choose the biweekly option, which is the most used option. However, top management and board directors may opt for monthly compensation. When you click "Employee is paid on salary" option, be sure to provide the annual amount and the per-year option. Also provide bonus and commission information, if necessary. These details are very important for QuickBooks to calculate employees' payroll compensation.

Activities:

- ❖ Tell us about wages and compensation for Jerry Jordan
- ❖ Payment frequency: Accept **Every other week (Biweekly)**
- ❖ Click **Employee is paid on salary**
- ❖ Salary amount: Type **100,000.** Per: Accept **Year**
- ❖ Checkmark **Bonus**
- ❖ Checkmark **Commission**. Amount: **10%**
- ❖ Click **Next**

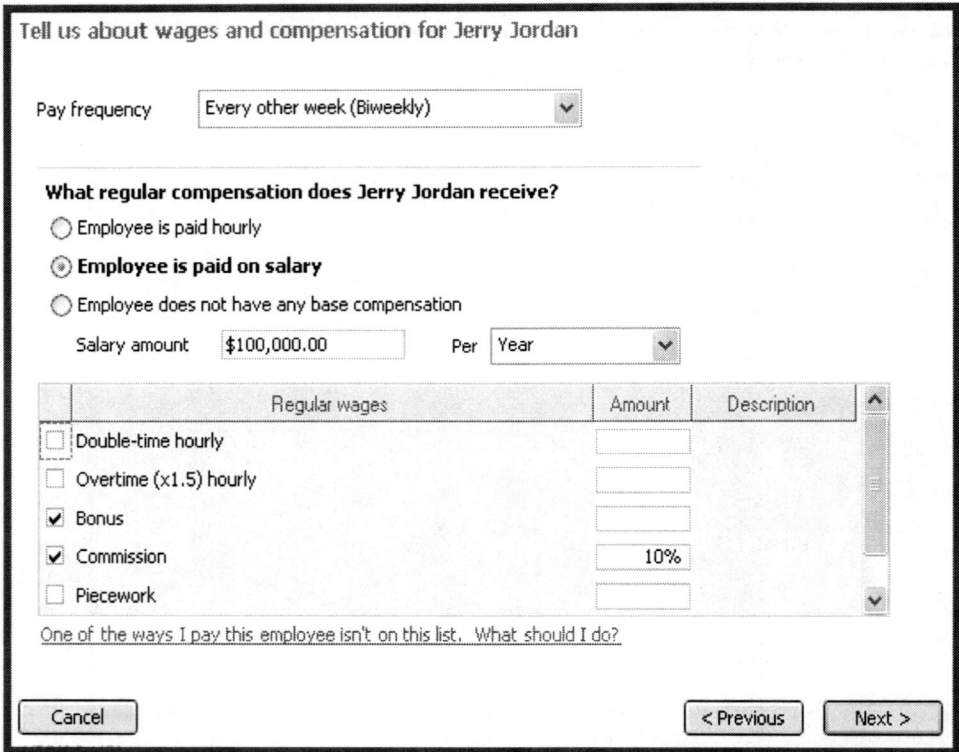

Add Employee: Insurance

In general, a salary employee may have more payroll benefit items than an hourly employee; therefore, you should review the employee's file to pick up all the benefits that are stipulated on the employment agreement. One mistake most people make in using the payroll windows is not scrolling down to find other items. Always keep your eyes on the scroll bar to pull more items that are required to complete the payroll windows. Be sure to type 5% for 401(k) company match.

Activities:

- ❖ Tell us about benefits for Jerry Jordan
- ❖ Checkmark **401(k) Emp**
- ❖ Checkmark **Dental Insurance**
- ❖ Checkmark **Health Insurance**
- ❖ **Scroll down to other items**
- ❖ Checkmark **Vision Insurance**
- ❖ Checkmark **401k Co Match**. Amount: Type **5%** (Very Important)
- ❖ Checkmark **Taxable Fringe Benefit**
- ❖ Checkmark **Cash Advance**
- ❖ Checkmark **Mileage Reimbursement**
- ❖ Checkmark **Miscellaneous Addition**
- ❖ Checkmark **Cash Advance Repayment**
- ❖ Checkmark **Charity Donation**
- ❖ Checkmark **Health Svgs Acct (taxable)**
- ❖ Checkmark **Miscellaneous Deduction**
- ❖ Checkmark **Union Dues**
- ❖ Click **Wages Garnishment**
- ❖ Click **Next**

Add Employee: Sick & Vacation

As we move toward a cashless society, most employees are choosing direct deposit. You will need to set up this correctly for the process to work. You will receive a completed form from an employee that contains all the necessary banking information to complete the direct deposit requirements. The bank account's number is mostly nine digits, and the routing number, also a requirement, contains nine digits, too.

Activities:

- ❖ How is sick time off calculated for Jerry Jordan
- ❖ Jerry Jordan earns: Type **4** hours: Select **per paycheck**
- ❖ Unused sick hours: Select **have an accrual limit**
- ❖ Maximum hours: Type **104**
- ❖ Jerry Jordan earns: Select **time off currently**
- ❖ Hours available as of…: Type **0:00**
- ❖ Hours used as of…: Type **0:00**
- ❖ Click **Next**

How is sick time off calculated for Jerry Jordan?

Calculation

Jerry Jordan earns   `4:00`   hours   `per paycheck` ▼

Unused sick hours   `have an accrual limit` ▼

Maximum hours   `104:00`

Jerry Jordan earns   `time off currently` ▼

Current balances

Hours available as of 12/23/2008   `0:00`

Hours used as of 12/23/2008   `0.00`

- ❖ How is vacation time off calculated for Jerry Jordan
- ❖ Jerry Jordan earns: Type **4** hours: Select **per paycheck**
- ❖ Unused sick hours: Select **have an accrual limit**
- ❖ Maximum hours: Type **104**
- ❖ Jerry Jordan earns: Select **time off currently**
- ❖ Hours available as of…: Type **0:00**
- ❖ Hours used as of…: Type **0:00**
- ❖ Click **Next**
- ❖ Set up Jerry Jordan direct deposit information
- ❖ Click **Pay Jerry Jordan by Direct Deposit**
- ❖ How many accounts: Click **One account**
- ❖ Bank name: Type **JP Morgan Chase**
- ❖ Account No.: Type **999999000** (Nine 6s and 3 zeros)
- ❖ Routing No.: Type **021000021** (Nine numbers)
- ❖ Account Type: Select **Checking**
- ❖ Click **Next**

Add Employee: Taxes

When you review a salary employee's personnel file, you will be able to find all the information you need to complete the state and federal tax data. The file should contain the filing status and number of allowances. Otherwise, you would have the employee fill out Form W-4 with a signature, if he or she has not already done so. The most important payroll items in this section are Medicare, Social Security, and Federal Unemployment. Be sure that these boxes are checked.

Activities:

- ❖ Tell us where Jerry Jordan is subject to taxes
- ❖ State subject to withholding: Select **TX-Texas**
- ❖ State subject to unemployment tax: Select **TX-Texas**
- ❖ While working for you…Click **No**
- ❖ Click **Next**
- ❖ Enter federal tax information for Jerry Jordan
- ❖ Filing Status: Select **Married**
- ❖ Allowances: Type **3**
- ❖ Extra Withholding: Type **0.00**
- ❖ Nonresident Alien Withholding: Select **Does not apply**
- ❖ Checkmark **Subject to Medicare**
- ❖ Checkmark **Subject to Social Security**
- ❖ Checkmark **Federal Unemployment**
- ❖ Click **Next**

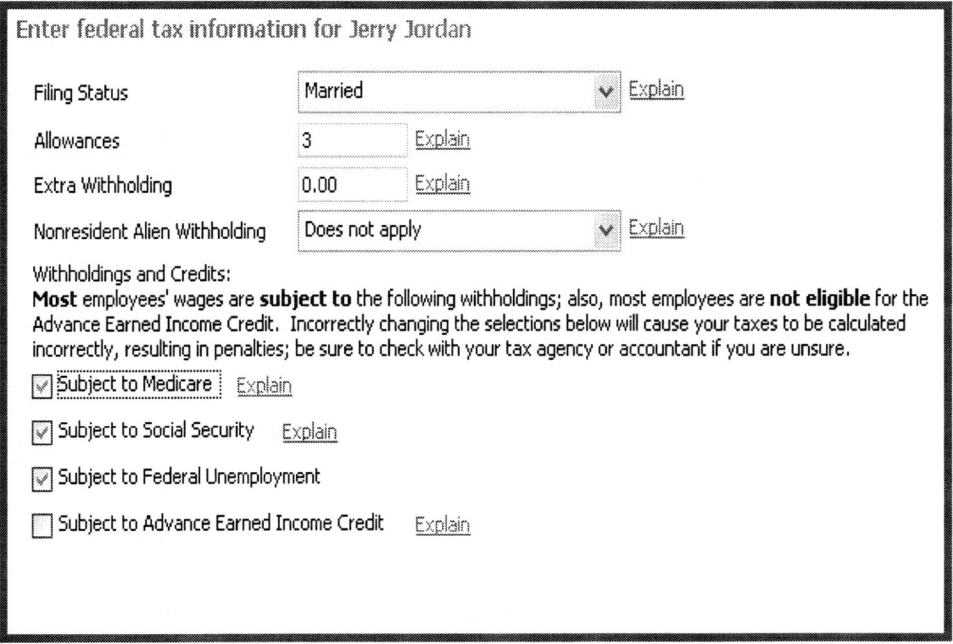

❖ Enter state tax information for Jerry Jordan
❖ Checkmark **Subject to TX-Unemployment**
❖ Is this employee subject to any special local taxes?
❖ Click **No**
❖ Click **Finish**
❖ Review your Employee list
❖ Click **Continue** till you reach **Go To Payroll Center**
❖ Click **Go To Payroll Center**

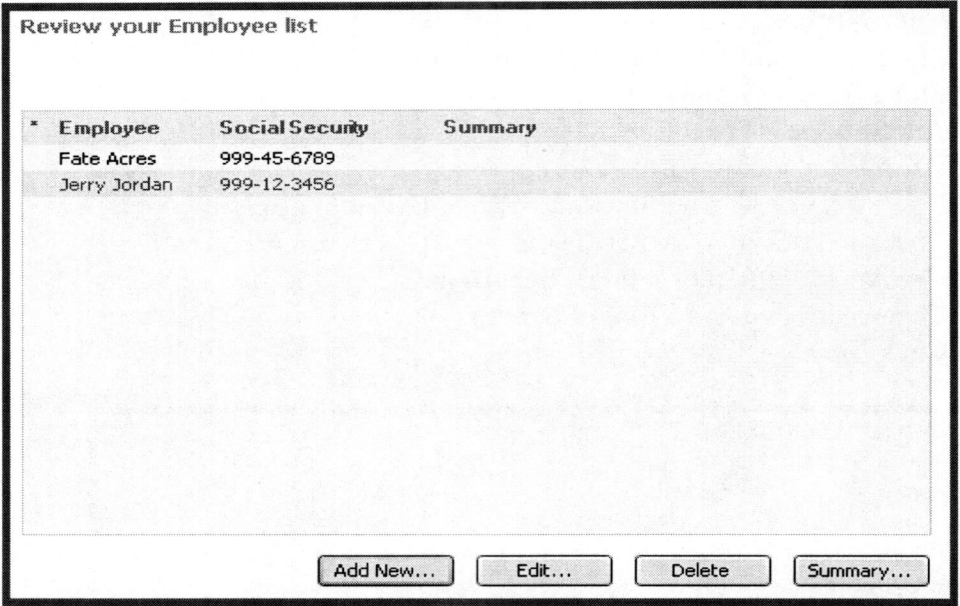

Create Paychecks

After you've completed a salary employee's personal, compensation, benefits and tax windows, the next step is to get ready to pay the employee using the correct pay period. Before you create a check, you should update the Edit Employee window to allow it to use time data. You need to click the Payroll and Compensation Info tab and checkmark the box, "Use time data to create paychecks." This is to ensure that QuickBooks will pull in an employee's time data to his or her paycheck.

Activities:
❖ Click **Employees menu**
❖ Click **Employee Center**
❖ Double click **Jerry Jordan**

❖ Change tab: Select **Payroll & Compensation Info**
❖ Checkmark **Use time data to create paychecks**
❖ Click **OK** to close window
❖ Click **Employees menu**
❖ Click **Pay Employees**
❖ Pay Period Ends: Highlight box. Type **1/11/09.** Press **Tab**
❖ Click **Yes** to "If you're using time tracking…"
❖ Check Date: Type **1/11/09**
❖ Bank Account: Select **USA Payroll**
❖ Bank Account Balance: Accept **237,787.33**
❖ Checkmark **Jerry Jordan** (left of the window). Only Jerry Jordan
❖ Click **Continue**
❖ Click **OK** to "Time data has not been…""
❖ Click **Create Paychecks**
❖ Click **Close** on Confirmation window

Edit Paychecks

After you've provided the correct pay period and the check date, click "Create Paycheck" and the paycheck is created automatically. That is half the story, because you have to open the check you just created to include additional payroll items and edit the paycheck. The purpose is to make sure the employee is getting paid correctly. You cannot be allowed to edit a paycheck unless you click the "Unlock Net Pay" button located at the bottom right of the paycheck window.

❖ Click **Employees menu**
❖ Click **Employee Center**
❖ Click **Jerry Jordan** (left of the window)
❖ Double click **Paycheck for 1/11/09** (right of the window)
❖ Bank Account: Accept **USA Payroll**
❖ Click **Paycheck Detail** (bottom right of the window)
❖ Accept click on **Unlock Net Pay** (bottom right of the window)
❖ Complete window with information on the next page

Jerry Jordan					Pay Period	12/29/2008 ▦	-	01/11/2009 ▦

☐ Use Direct Deposit   Class [▾]

Earnings

Item Name	Rate	Hours	Quantity	Customer:Job	Service Item		
Salary	3,846.15						Sick Available 4:00
Bonus	20,000.00						Vacation Avail. 4:00
Commission	10.0%		100,000.00				Sick Accrued 4:00
							Vac. Accrued 4:00

☐ Do not accrue sick/vac

	Totals:	33,846.15	0:00 hrs

Other Payroll Items

Item Name	Rate	Quantity
401k Emp.		
Dental Insurance (...		-10.00
Health Insurance (...		-20.00
Vision Insurance (...		
401k Co. Match		

Employee Summary (adjusted)   How are these items calculated?

Item Name	Amount	YTD
Cash Advance	0.00	0.00
Mileage Reimbursement	0.00	0.00
Miscellaneous Addition	0.00	0.00
Cash Advance Repayment	0.00	0.00
Charity Donation	0.00	0.00
Health Svgs Acct (taxable)	0.00	0.00
Miscellaneous Deduction	0.00	0.00
Union Dues	0.00	0.00
Wage Garnishment	0.00	0.00
Federal Withholding	-10,501.00	-10,501.00
Social Security Employee	-2,096.60	-2,096.60
Medicare Employee	-490.33	-490.33

Company Summary (adjusted)   How are these items calculated?

Item Name	Amount	YTD
Taxable Fringe Benefits	0.00	0.00
Social Security Company	2,096.60	2,096.60
Medicare Company	490.33	490.33
Federal Unemployment	56.00	56.00
TX - Unemployment	243.00	243.00

Check Amount:	20,728.22

[OK]   [Cancel]   [Help]   ○ Lock Net Pay ⦿ Unlock Net Pay   ☐ Enter net/Calculate gross

What's this?

Paycheck Details

Here are the details for Jerry's paycheck. You will need to type the 80 hours for Salary for Jerry, but remember you are not paying him by the hour. QuickBooks uses the hour to calculate any additional payroll items. For example, if Jerry took two hours of sick time for the period, you will need to split the 80 hours by typing 78 for the salary line and 2 for the Salary Sick item. That way Jerry will end up getting the same total biweekly salary he's been getting, but this time it will be split between Salary and Salary Sick.

Activities Details:

- ❖ Earning:
- ❖ Salary. Rate: Accept 3,846. Hours: 80
- ❖ Select Bonus. Rate: 20,000
- ❖ Select Commission. Rate: 10%. Quantity: 100,000
- ❖

* Other Payroll Items: (Type as positive will as negative)
* Dental. Rate: 10
* Health. Rate: 20
* 401k Co. Match. Rate: blank (delete 5%). Press **Tab**
*
* Company Summary (adjusted)
* Social Security. Amount: 2,096.60
* Medicare. Amount: 490.33
* Federal Unemployment. Amount: 56.00
* TX – Unemployment. Amount: 243.00
*
* Employee Summary (adjusted) (right of the window)
* Accept default figures and add these
* **Scroll down**
* Federal Withholding. Amount: 10,501.00
* Social Security. Amount: 2,096.60
* Medicare. Amount: 490.33
*
* Check Amount: **20,728.22**
* Company Summary (left): **2,885.93** (confirm with QuickBooks calculator)
* Click **OK**
* Click **Save & Close** on check window
* Click **Yes** to "You have changed the transaction…"

Pay Payroll Liabilities

Paying employees will automatically create payroll taxes and liabilities, payable to the taxing agencies. Because you set up to pay your liabilities quarterly, you will be paying your outstanding liabilities on March 31, 2009 and the check will probably be the same date unless processed on a different date. As the Payroll Liabilities window opens, you will checkmark the entries you want to pay. Be sure the total "Amount to pay" includes all the liabilities you want to pay for the period.

Activities:

* Click **Employees menu**
* Click **Payroll Taxes and Liabilities**
* Click **Pay Payroll Liabilities**
* Dates: From: Type **12/15/08** (must be 2008) To: Type **3/31/09**. Click **OK**
* Checkmark **To be printed**
* Click **Review liability check to enter…**

❖ Bank Account: Accept **USA Payroll**
❖ Check Date: Type **3/31/09**
❖ **Checkmark on liabilities with numbers**
❖ Scroll down for other items
❖ Total Balance: Accept **24,627.52**
❖ Total Amt. To Pay: Accept **24,627.52**
❖ Ending Bank Balance: Accept **192,431.59**
❖ Click **Create** (top right of the window).
❖ Click **Save & Close** on the check window

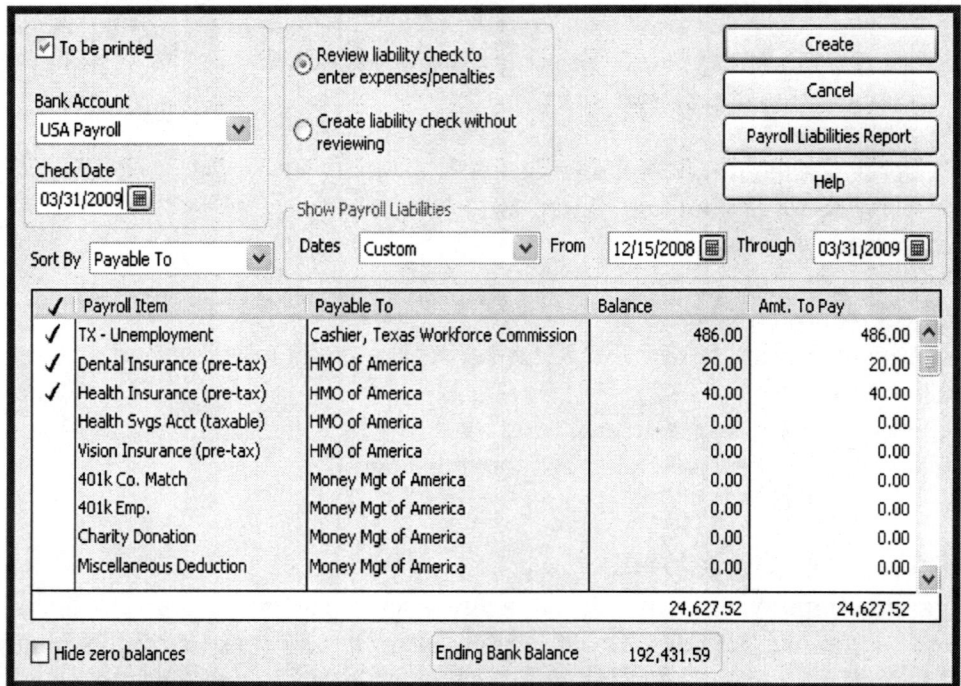

Run QuickReport

After paying Jerry, you quickly run a QuickReport for him to verify the report is showing the same amount on the paycheck window. You will not get the same result unless you select the right date range for Jerry. And to open up the QuickReport, you must click on Jerry in the Employee Center; otherwise, the report will not be activated. As shown below, the same amount, 20,728.22, was paid to Jerry for the period. It's very essential to confirm all your payroll numbers.

Activities:

- ❖ Click **Employees menu**
- ❖ Click **Employees Center**
- ❖ Click **Jerry Jordan** (left of the window)
- ❖ Click **Reports menu**
- ❖ Towards the bottom of the submenus
- ❖ Click **QuickReport**
- ❖ Dates (top left of the window): Select **This Calendar Year**
- ❖ Look! Jerry Jordan has **20,728.22**
- ❖ Click **X** to close window

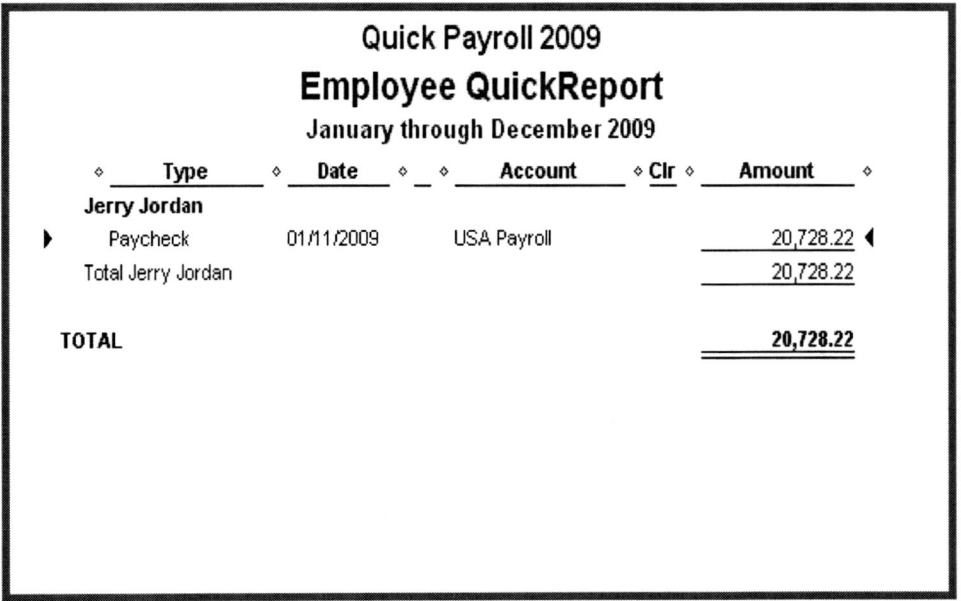

Quick Payroll 2009

Employee QuickReport

January through December 2009

Type	Date	Account	Clr	Amount
Jerry Jordan				
▶ Paycheck	01/11/2009	USA Payroll		20,728.22 ◀
Total Jerry Jordan				20,728.22
TOTAL				**20,728.22**

Run Payroll Transaction Report

After you have run the QuickReport and the numbers look good, your next job is to quickly run the Payroll Transaction report. You want to verify all the activities so far. You want to see Fate's and Jerry's paychecks in the report. You want to make sure they match the check you issued. Scan the report to look for the taxes you paid at the end of the quarter on March 31, 2009. Match the numbers on this report with the amounts on the checks you issued to the various government agencies.

Activities:

- ❖ Click **Reports menu**
- ❖ Click **Employees & Payroll**
- ❖ Click **Payroll Transaction by Payee**
- ❖ Dates (top left of the window): Select **This Calendar Year**
- ❖ Total Payroll check is **57,568.41**
- ❖ Click **X** to close window

Quick Payroll 2009

Payroll Transactions by Payee

January through December 2009

Date	Name	N...	Type	Memo	Account	Amount
Cashier, Texas Workforce Commission						
03/31/2009	Cashier, Texas Wo...		Liability Check	99-999999-9	USA Payroll	-486.00
Total Cashier, Texas Workforce Commission						-486.00
HMO of America						
03/31/2009	HMO of America		Liability Check		USA Payroll	-60.00
Total HMO of America						-60.00
United States Treasury						
03/31/2009	United States Trea...		Liability Check	99-1234567	USA Payroll	-24,081.52
Total United States Treasury						-24,081.52
Fate Acres						
01/11/2009	Fate Acres		Paycheck		USA Payroll	-12,212.67
Total Fate Acres						-12,212.67
Jerry Jordan						
01/11/2009	Jerry Jordan		Paycheck		USA Payroll	-20,728.22
Total Jerry Jordan						-20,728.22
TOTAL						**-57,568.41**

Create Timesheets

You are going to pay employees for the second period. You'll see how easy the payroll process is after you've completed the setup. The only real work is the setup and once that is taken care, processing biweekly paychecks to employees is very simple. To process Fate's paycheck for the second period, enter her timesheet into the system and with a click, her check is generated. Here, you're going to create her timesheet. Remember, she must have two timesheets for two weeks.

Activities:

- ❖ Click **Employee menu**
- ❖ Click **Enter Time**
- ❖ Click **Use Weekly Timesheet**
- ❖ Name: Select **Fate Acres**
- ❖ Week of: Click **Previous or Next** to **Jan 5 to Jan 11, 2009**
- ❖ Click **Next** (top of the window) to **Jan 12 to Jan 18, 2009**
- ❖ Click **Copy Last Sheet**
- ❖ Click **Save & New**
- ❖ Name: Select **Fate Acres**
- ❖ Click **Next** (top of the window) to **Jan 19 to Jan 25, 2009**
- ❖ Click **Copy Last Sheet**
- ❖ Click **Save & Close**

Create Paychecks

You only create timesheets for hourly employees, but for salary employees, you do almost nothing to create the paycheck. To pay salary employees, open the Pay Employees window and complete the Pay Period and Check Date boxes, which may or may not be the same. Next, checkmark all the employees you want to pay for this period, and then click Create Paychecks at the bottom of the window. The check is automatically generated behind the scenes.

Activities:

- ❖ Click **Employees menu**
- ❖ Click **Pay Employees**
- ❖ Pay Period Ends: Type **1/25/09**
- ❖ Check Date: Type **1/25/09**
- ❖ Bank Account: Select **USA Payroll**
- ❖ Bank Account Balance: Accept **192,431.59**
- ❖ Checkmark **Fate Acres** (left of the window).
- ❖ Hourly: Accept **80**
- ❖ Total Hours: Accept **80:00**
- ❖ Checkmark **Jerry Jordan**
- ❖ Click **Continue**
- ❖ Click **OK** to "Time data has not been entered…"
- ❖ Click **Create Paychecks** (bottom of the window)
- ❖ Click **Close** on Confirmation window

Edit Paychecks

Once you click Create Paychecks, the process is done immediately. The next action is to display the Review Paycheck window, and make minor changes. Unless you click the "Unlock Net Pay" at the bottom right of the window, QuickBooks will not allow you to edit the paycheck. Look at the top right of the check to confirm the pay period dates.

Activities:

- ❖ Click **Employees menu**
- ❖ Click **Employee Center**
- ❖ Click **Fate Acres** (left of the window)
- ❖ Double click 1st **Paycheck for 1/25/09** (right of the window)
- ❖ Bank Account: Accept **USA Payroll**
- ❖ Click **Paycheck Details** (bottom right of the window)
- ❖ Complete window with information on the next page

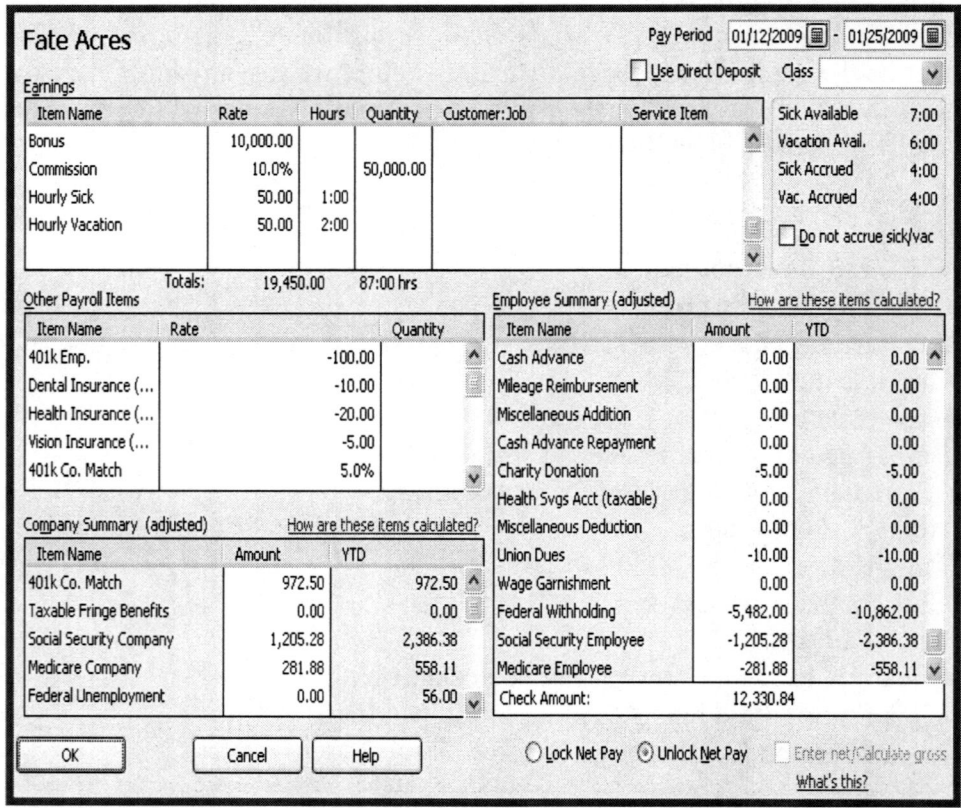

Paycheck Details

Complete the paycheck window with the details below as you've done earlier.

Activities Details:

Earning:

- ❖ Hourly. Rate: 50. Hours: 80
- ❖ Click under Hourly. Select Overtime. Rate: 75. Hours: 4
- ❖ Select Bonus. Rate: 10,000
- ❖ Select Commission. Rate: 10%. Quantity: 50,000
- ❖ Hourly Sick. Rate: 50. Hours: 1
- ❖ Hourly Vacation. Rate: 50. Hours: 2
- ❖
- ❖ Other Payroll Items: (Type as positive will show as negative)
- ❖ 401k Emp. Rate: 100
- ❖ Dental. Rate: 10
- ❖ Health. Rate: 20
- ❖ Vision. Rate: 5
- ❖ 401k Co. Match. Rate: 5%
- ❖ Charity Donation. Rate: 5
- ❖ Union Dues. Rate: 10
- ❖
- ❖ Company Summary (adjusted)
- ❖ 401k Co. Match. Amount: Accept 972.50
- ❖ Social Security. Amount: 1,205.28
- ❖ Medicare. Amount: 281.88
- ❖ Federal Unemployment. Amount: 0
- ❖ TX – Unemployment. Amount: 0
- ❖
- ❖ Employee Summary (adjusted) (right of the window)
- ❖ Accept default figures and add these
- ❖ Scroll down
- ❖ Federal Withholding. Amount: 5,482.00
- ❖ Social Security. Amount: 1,205.28
- ❖ Medicare. Amount: 281.88
- ❖
- ❖ Check Amount: **12,330.84**
- ❖ Company Summary: **2,459.66.** Click **OK**
- ❖ Click **Save & Close** on check window
- ❖ Click **Yes** to "You have changed the transaction…"

> There is no total amount for Company Summary. Be sure to confirm your total with the calculator on the taskbar.

Edit Paychecks

It was easy to pay an hourly employee, but it's even easier to pay a salary employee. Because there are no timesheets, just repeat the process of paying the same amount unless there are minor changes. Like Fate's paycheck, you have to double click on Jerry's check in the Employee Center to open the check already generated. Click on the Paycheck Details on the bottom right of the window to open the details for editing. Unlock the check and complete the paycheck.

Activities:

- ❖ Click **Employees menu**
- ❖ Click **Employee Center**
- ❖ Click **Jerry Jordan** (left of the window)
- ❖ Double click 1st **Paycheck for 1/25/09** (right of the window)
- ❖ Bank Account: Accept **USA Payroll**
- ❖ Click **Paycheck Detail** (bottom right of the window)
- ❖ Complete window with information on the next page

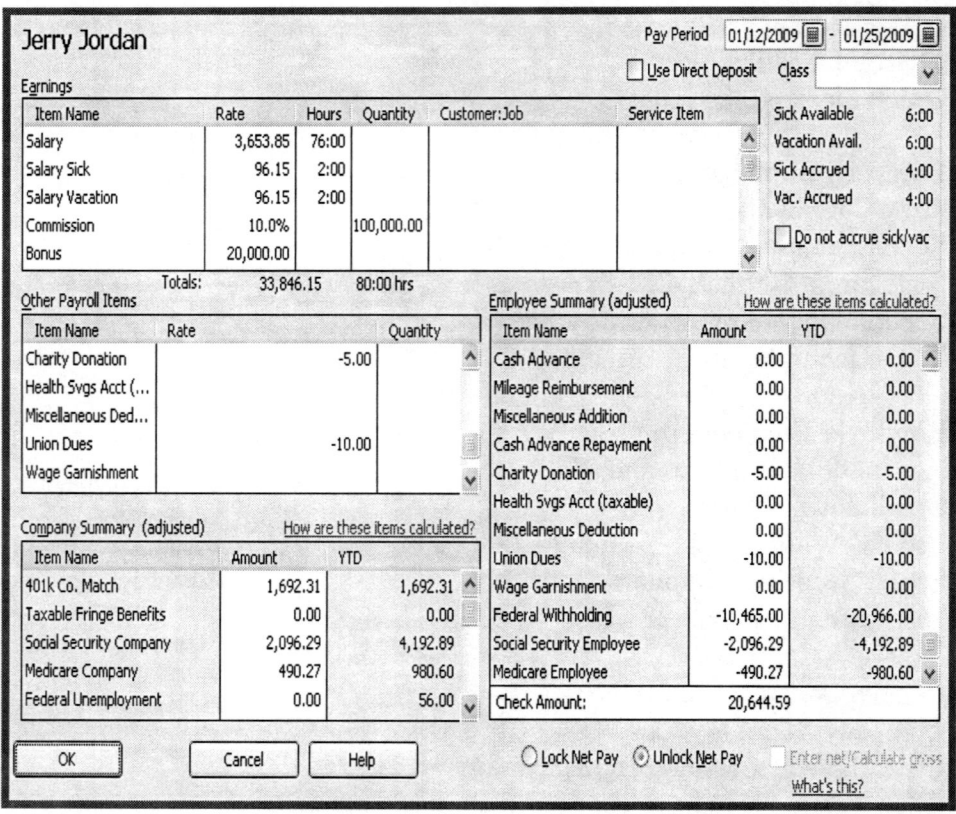

Paycheck Details

Also, complete the paycheck window with the details below. In the salary section, type the hours first and the rate is populated for you.

❖ Earning:
❖ Salary. Hours: Type 76
❖ Salary Sick. Hours: Type 2
❖ Salary Vacation. Hours: Type 2
❖ Select Commission. Rate: 10%. Quantity: 100,000
❖ Select Bonus. Rate: 20,000
❖
❖ Other Payroll Items: (Type as positive will show as negative)
❖ 401k Emp. Rate: 100
❖ Dental. Rate: 10
❖ Health. Rate: 20
❖ Vision. Rate: 5
❖ 401k Co. Match. Rate: 5%
❖ Charity Donation. Rate: 5
❖ Union Dues. Rate: 10
❖
❖ Company Summary (adjusted)
❖ 401k Co. Match. Amount: Accept 1,692.31
❖ Social Security. Amount: 2,096.29
❖ Medicare. Amount: 490.27
❖ Federal Unemployment. Amount: 0.00
❖ TX – Unemployment. Amount: 0.00
❖
❖ Employee Summary (adjusted) (right of the window)
❖ Accept default figures and add these
❖ Scroll down
❖ Federal Withholding. Amount: 10,465.00
❖ Social Security. Amount: 2,096.29
❖ Medicare. Amount: 490.27
❖
❖ Check Amount: **20,644.59**
❖ Company Summary: **4,278.87**. Click **OK**
❖ Click **Save & Close** on check window
❖ Click **Yes** to "You have changed the transaction…"

> Note! You have to reduce a salaried staff's 80 hrs by the sick and vacation hours since a salary person is on a fixed amount per month.

> Don't forget to always confirm your total amount.

Pay Payroll Liabilities

As you did previously, every time you pay employees, automatically payroll liabilities are generated. You are going through these processes to understand the steps involved in payroll processing, and also to realize how easy the actual work is after you have completed the payroll setup. Again, open the Payroll Liabilities window, and select the liabilities you want to pay, making sure the figure in "Amount to Pay" column has everyone you want to pay.

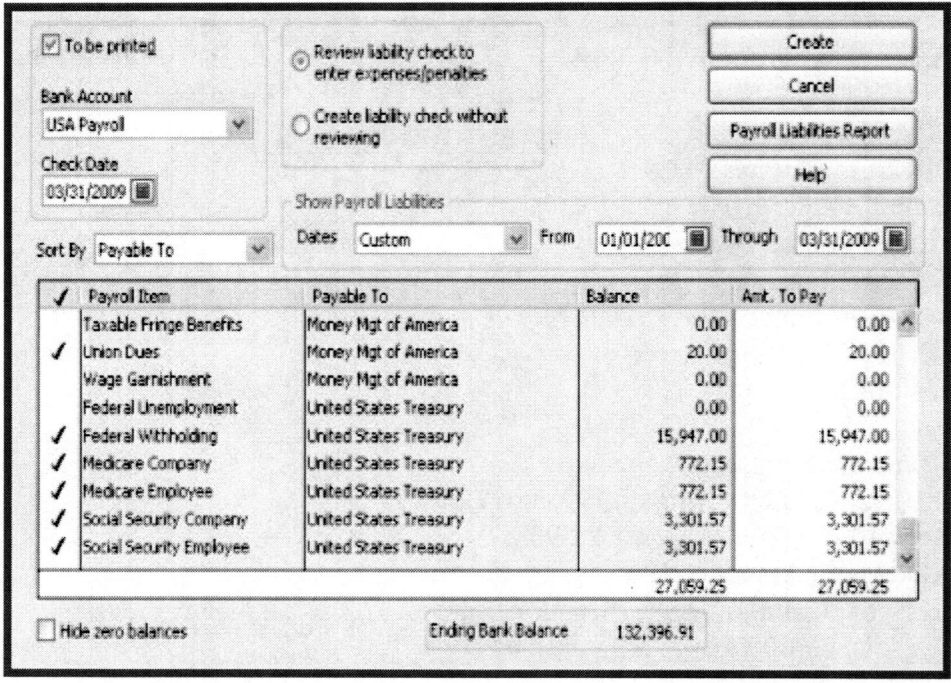

Activities:

- ❖ Click **Employees menu**
- ❖ Click **Payroll Taxes and Liabilities**
- ❖ Click **Pay Payroll Liabilities**
- ❖ Dates: From: Type **1/1/09** Through: Type **3/31/09**
- ❖ Click **OK**
- ❖ Checkmark **To be printed**
- ❖ Click **Review liability check to enter...**
- ❖ Bank Account: Accept **USA Payroll**
- ❖ Check Date: Type **3/31/09**
- ❖ Dates: From: Accept **1/1/09**. To: Type **3/31/09**

❖ **Checkmark on all liabilities with numbers**
❖ Total Balance: Accept **27,059.25**
❖ Total Amt. To Pay: Accept **27,059.25**
❖ Ending Bank Balance: Accept **132,396.91**
❖ Click **Create** (top right of the window)
❖ Click **Save & Close**

Run QuickReport: Fate Acres

Yes, it's all about reports. You've paid Fate Acres again. Now, you will quickly pull up her QuickReport to review the numbers. Everything looks fine; the numbers on the report are exactly what you expected, which is the same amount on the checks. You must have selected the right date range, of course. Remember you could access the QuickReport in the Employee Center window or through the Report menu. Just choose what route you want to follow; what matters is consistency.

Quick Payroll 2009
Employee QuickReport
January through December 2009

Type	Date	Account	Amount
Fate Acres			
Paycheck	01/11/2009	USA Payroll	12,212.67 ◀
Paycheck	01/25/2009	USA Payroll	12,330.84
Total Fate Acres			24,543.51
TOTAL			**24,543.51**

Activities:
❖ Click **Employees menu**
❖ Click **Employee Center**
❖ Click **Fate Acres** (left of the window)
❖ Click **Reports menu**
❖ Click **QuickReport**
❖ Towards the bottom of the submenus
❖ Dates (top left of the window): Select **This Calendar Year**
❖ Look! Fate Acres has **24,543.51**
❖ Click **X** to close window

Run QuickReport: Jerry Jordan

You ran a QuickReport for Fate Acres, and now, Jerry Jordan needs one, too. Running these reports is fun and necessary. You do not know how much time it costs you to correct your mistakes if you don't find them earlier. And the best time to find your mistakes is after you have just written the check. It is very easy to open the checks and edit or even delete them now rather than later. Therefore, reviewing payroll reports and confirming your numbers is the key to being successful in the payroll business.

Activities:
- ❖ Click **Employees menu**
- ❖ Click **Employees Center**
- ❖ Click on **Jerry Jordan** (left of the window)
- ❖ Click **Reports menu**
- ❖ Click **QuickReport**
- ❖ Towards the bottom of the submenus
- ❖ Dates (top left of the window): Select **This Calendar Year**
- ❖ Look! Fate Acres has **41,372.81**
- ❖ Click **X** to close window

Quick Payroll 2009
Employee QuickReport
January through December 2009

Type	Date	Account	Amount
Jerry Jordan			
Paycheck	01/11/2009	USA Payroll	20,728.22
Paycheck	01/25/2009	USA Payroll	20,644.59
Total Jerry Jordan			41,372.81
TOTAL			**41,372.81**

Run Payroll Transaction Report

It's getting easier and easier. You ran the QuickReport, and the checks are confirmed. The next step is to run the Payroll Transaction report to make sure the numbers are looking good. You want to see the same checks you paid employees and even more importantly, you want to review the checks you paid the government agencies and other payroll vendors. You see Cashier Texas Workforce Commission, HMO of America, Money Management of America and United States Treasury with the respective amount. Everything looks good!

Quick Payroll 2009
Payroll Transactions by Payee
January through December 2009

Date	Name	Type	Memo	Account	Amount
Cashier, Texas Workforce Commission					
03/31/2009	Cashier, Texas Wo...	Liability Check	99-999999-9	USA Payroll	-486.00 ◀
Total Cashier, Texas Workforce Commission					-486.00
HMO of America					
03/31/2009	HMO of America	Liability Check		USA Payroll	-60.00
03/31/2009	HMO of America	Liability Check		USA Payroll	-70.00
Total HMO of America					-130.00
Money Mgt of America					
03/31/2009	Money Mgt of Ame...	Liability Check		USA Payroll	-2,894.81
Total Money Mgt of America					-2,894.81
United States Treasury					
03/31/2009	United States Trea...	Liability Check	99-1234567	USA Payroll	-24,081.52
03/31/2009	United States Trea...	Liability Check	99-1234567	USA Payroll	-24,094.44
Total United States Treasury					-48,175.96
Fate Acres					
01/11/2009	Fate Acres	Paycheck		USA Payroll	-12,212.67
01/25/2009	Fate Acres	Paycheck		USA Payroll	-12,330.84
Total Fate Acres					-24,543.51
Jerry Jordan					
01/11/2009	Jerry Jordan	Paycheck		USA Payroll	-20,728.22
01/25/2009	Jerry Jordan	Paycheck		USA Payroll	-20,644.59
Total Jerry Jordan					-41,372.81
TOTAL					**-117,603.09**

Activities:

- ❖ Click **Reports menu**
- ❖ Click **Employees & Payroll**
- ❖ Click **Payroll Transaction by Payee**
- ❖ Dates (top left of the window): Select **This Calendar Year**
- ❖ Total Payroll check is **117,603.09**
- ❖ Click **X** to close window

Salary Sick Cashout

From time to time, an employee might be terminated or decide to leave the company. A final paycheck will be issued to the employee, accrued sick and vacation hours would have to be paid to the employee. For an hourly employee, select the Hourly Sick and Vacation. However, for a salary employee, create another payroll item. This will mean more money to the salary employee, not the normal split we did earlier. The item will be selected in the Other Payroll Item box.

Activities:

- ❖ Click **Employees menu**
- ❖ Click **Manage Payroll Items**
- ❖ Click **View/Edit Payroll Item List**
- ❖ Right click in the window. Click **New**
- ❖ Click **Custom Setup.** Click **Next**
- ❖ Click **Addition.** Click **Next**
- ❖ Name used…: Type **Salary Sick Cashout.** Click **Next**
- ❖ Expense account: Accept **Payroll Expenses.** Click **Next**
- ❖ Tax Tracking type: Select **Compensation.** Click **Next**
- ❖ Taxes: Accept **Checkmarks on all items.** Click **Next**
- ❖ Calculate based on quantity: Click **Neither.** Click **Next**
- ❖ Default rate and limit: Accept **0.00**
- ❖ Click **Finish**

Salary Vacation Cashout

The same goes for the Salary Vacation, which is a new payroll item that is created and selected in the Other Payroll Item box. The Sick and Vacation Cashout will increase the salary pay for the employee. Once you understand this process, you can apply the same process to other situations. All you have to ask yourself is, "Does it increase or decrease the earnings?" If it increases earnings, use the Addition to earnings and if it decreases earnings, use the Deduction from earnings.

Activities:

- ❖ You're back in the Payroll Item list window
- ❖ Right click in the window
- ❖ Click **New**
- ❖ Click **Custom Setup**
- ❖ Click **Next**
- ❖ Click **Addition.** Click **Next**

- ❖ Name used…: Type **Salary Vacation Cashout**. Click **Next**
- ❖ Expense account: Accept **Payroll Expenses**. Click **Next**
- ❖ Tax Tracking type: Select **Compensation**. Click **Next**
- ❖ Taxes: Accept **Checkmarks on all items.** Click **Next**
- ❖ Calculate based on quantity: Click **Neither**. Click **Next**
- ❖ Default rate and limit: Accept **0.00**
- ❖ Click **Finish**

Salary Leave Paid

During employment negotiations, a salary employee might get the company to agree to Paid Leave. This is outside the Salary Sick and Vacation hours. It means an employee can take off from work and still get paid. If the paid leave hours are not used it's an additional money to the paycheck. In the Salary Sick and Vacation, it is a split with 80 hours, but in the Paid Leave, it is 80 hours plus the Paid Leave hours.

Activities:

- ❖ You're back in the Payroll Item list window
- ❖ Right click in the window
- ❖ Click **New**
- ❖ Click **Custom Setup**
- ❖ Click **Next**
- ❖ Click **Addition.** Click **Next**
- ❖ Name used…: Type **Salary Leave Paid**. Click **Next**
- ❖ Expense account: Accept **Payroll Expenses**. Click **Next**
- ❖ Tax Tracking type: Select **Compensation**. Click **Next**
- ❖ Taxes: Accept **Checkmarks on all items.** Click **Next**
- ❖ Calculate based on quantity: Click **Neither**. Click **Next**
- ❖ Default rate and limit: Accept **0.00**
- ❖ Click **Finish**

Salary Leave Unpaid

When a salary employee has used up all of his or her hours: sick, vacation and paid leave, and still for some reason wants to take off from work, this is the opposite of the Paid Leave. The amount for hours will be deducted from the total biweekly salary. One of the most important issues in the setup process is the account to use. In other payroll items, you selected Payroll Liability as the liability account. But in Unpaid Leave, select Payroll Asset, because the money is going to be deducted from the employee's paycheck back to the company payroll account.

Activities:

- ❖ You're still in the Payroll Item list window
- ❖ Right click in the window
- ❖ Click **New**
- ❖ Click **Custom Setup.** Click **Next**
- ❖ Click **Deduction.** Click **Next**
- ❖ Name used…: Type **Salary Leave Unpaid**. Click **Next**
- ❖ Enter name of agency: (Blank)
- ❖ Liability account: Select **Payroll Asset.** (Very Important). Click **Next**
- ❖ Tax Tracking type: Select **Compensation.** Click **Next**
- ❖ Taxes: Accept **Checkmarks on all items.** Click **Next**
- ❖ Calculate based on quantity: Click **Neither.** Click **Next**
- ❖ Default rate and limit: Accept **0.00**
- ❖ Click **Finish**

Released Staff: Timesheet

If an hourly employee is terminated or the employee decides to leave the company, a final timesheet is prepared for the final check. You would need a timesheet for the days he or she worked. There is nothing complicated about it. Select the same pay period as you have done in the past and with a few clicks, the paychecks is generated. Don't forget to use the Copy Last Sheet button to copy the previous period's timesheet instead of retyping the entire timesheet again. Then delete the day(s) not worked, if needed.

Activities:

- ❖ Click **Employees menu**
- ❖ Click **Enter Time**
- ❖ Click **Use Weekly Timesheet**
- ❖ Name: Select **Fate Acres**
- ❖ Week of: Click **Previous/Next** to **Jan 19 to Jan 25, 2009**
- ❖ Click **Next** to Week of: **Jan 26 to Feb 1, 2009**
- ❖ Click **Copy Last Sheet**
- ❖ Click **Save & New** (bottom right of the window)
- ❖ Name: Select **Fate Acres**
- ❖ Week of: Click **Next** (top of the window) to **Feb 2 to Feb 8, 2009**
- ❖ Click **Copy Last Sheet**
- ❖ Delete **8** hours for F (Friday) 8. Press **Tab**
- ❖ Total (hours): Accept **32**

❖ Uncheck **Billable**
❖ Click **Save & Close**

Released Staff: Time Activity

Besides the Timesheet, you may use the Time Activity window to record hours for an hourly employee. The major difference is that you import the time activity directly into the paycheck window for payment. It is essential to checkmark the Billable box and select Hourly for the Payroll Item; that way QuickBooks knows where to post it. You will need to enter the customer and the service to make sure the time is billed to the right customer.

Activities:

❖ Click **Employees menu**
❖ Click **Enter Time**
❖ Click **Time/Enter Single Activity**
❖ Date: Type **2/5/09** (The 4th day of the week she worked)
❖ Name: Select **Fate Acres**
❖ Customer: **James Adams**
❖ Service: **Delivery**
❖ Duration: Type **1:30** (use colon)
❖ Checkmark **Billable**
❖ Payroll Item: Select **Hourly**
❖ Click **Save & Close**

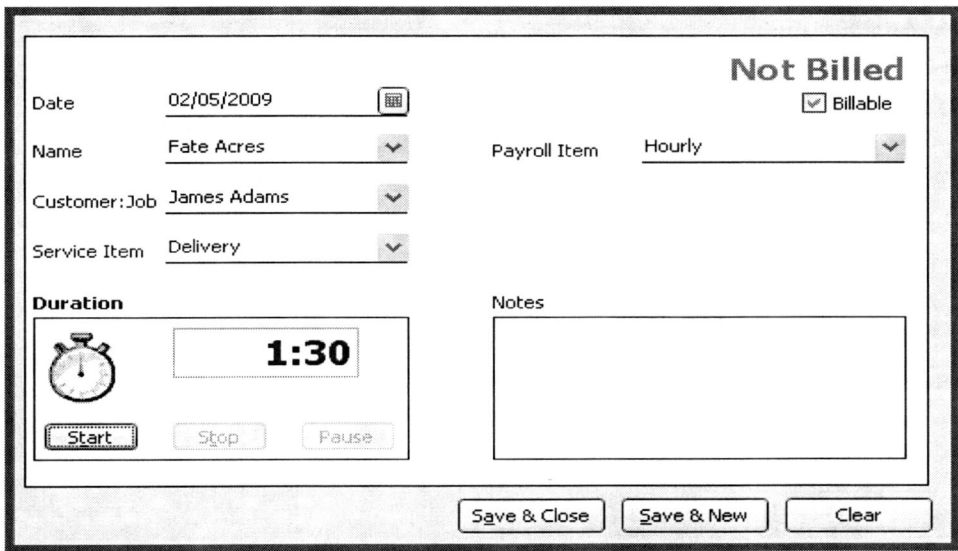

Released Staff: Create Paychecks

There's nothing magic about the final check payment. However, be sure that all the hours the employee worked are included in the paycheck. You will see from the practice below that the time activity hours are imported into the paycheck. If you don't see the activity hours, it may that be you did not checkmark Billable, or you did not click Yes to "You're using tracking…" Remember that the time tracking is set up in the Preference window under the Edit menu.

- ❖ Click **Employees menu**
- ❖ Click **Pay Employees**
- ❖ Pay Period Ends: Highlight box. Type **2/8/09.** Press **Tab**
- ❖ Click **Yes** to "You're using time tracking…"
- ❖ Check Date: Type **2/8/09**
- ❖ Bank Account: Select **USA Payroll**
- ❖ Checkmark **Fate Acres** (left of the window).
- ❖ Hourly: Accept **73:30**
- ❖ Total Hours: Accept **73:30**
- ❖ Checkmark **Jerry Jordan**
- ❖ Click **Continue**
- ❖ Click OK to "Time data has not been…"
- ❖ Click **Create Paychecks** (bottom of the window)
- ❖ Click **Close** on Confirmation window

Released Staff: Edit Paycheck

You have created the Timesheet and completed the Time Activity window. It's time to pay the hourly employee. It's always the same process.. Just select the pay period, the check date and the employees you want to pay; then click the Create Paycheck, and the check is created automatically. Fate's paycheck is displayed below. As you can see, the Timesheet total and the Time Activity hours are imported into the paycheck for a total of 73:30 hours. You can confirm this window with data from other sources namely, Timesheet and the Time Activity.

Activities:
- ❖ Click **Employees menu**
- ❖ Click **Employee Center**
- ❖ Click **Fate Acres** (left of the window)
- ❖ Double click 1st **Paycheck for 2/8/09** (right of the window)
- ❖ Bank Account: Accept **USA Payroll**

❖ Click **Paycheck Details** (bottom right of the window)
❖ Complete window with information on the next page

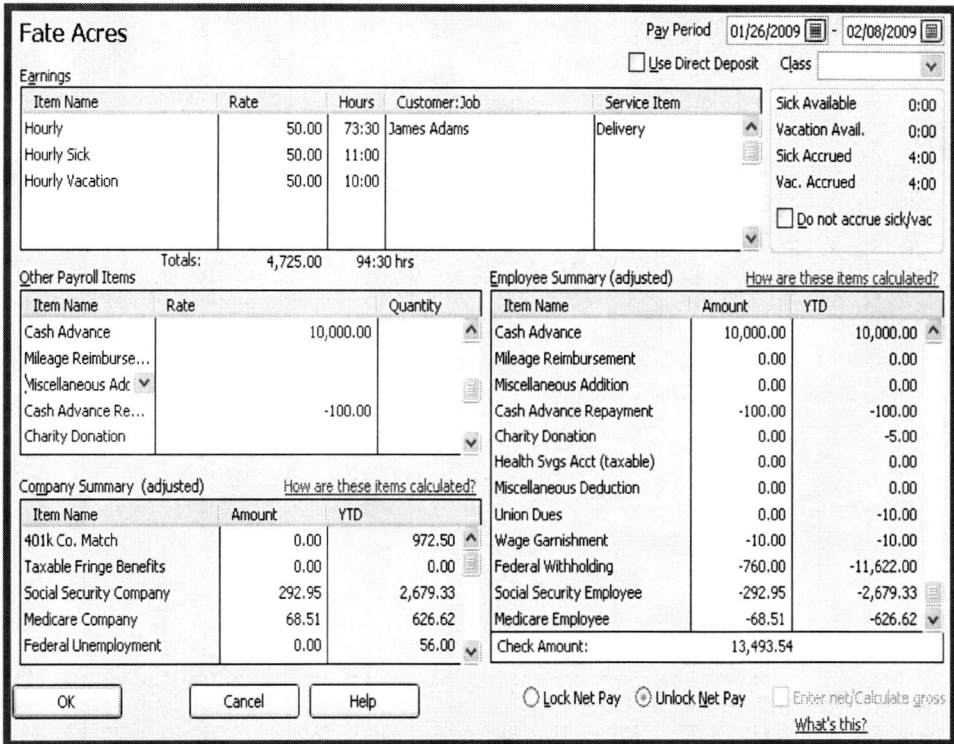

Released Staff: Paycheck Details

Below are the details for Fate's paycheck. Complete the paycheck and confirm the check total and the company summary total shown in bold below.

Earning:
❖ Hourly. Rate: 50. Hours: 73:30
❖ Hourly Sick. Rate: 50. Hours: 11
❖ Hourly Vacation. Rate: 50. Hours: 10
❖
❖ Other Payroll Items:
❖ 401k Co. Match. Rate: balance (Delete 5%). Press **Tab**
❖ Cash Advance. Rate: 10,000
❖ Cash Advance Repayment. Rate: 100
❖ Wage garnishment. Rate: 10
❖

❖ Company Summary (adjusted)
❖ Social Security. Amount: 292.95
❖ Medicare. Amount: 68.51
❖ Federal Unemployment. Amount: 0
❖ TX – Unemployment. Amount: 0
❖
❖ Employee Summary (adjusted)
❖ Accept default figures and add these
❖ Scroll down
❖ Federal Withholding. Amount: 760.00
❖ Social Security. Amount: 292.95
❖ Medicare. Amount: 68.51
❖
❖ Check Amount: **13,493.54**
❖ Company Summary: **361.46**
❖ Click **OK**
❖ Click **Save & Close** on check window
❖ Click **Yes** to "You have changed the transaction…"

> Be sure to confirm Company Summary total with the calculator.

Released Staff: Edit Paychecks

You can see how easy this payroll stuff is. The hourly employee's process is almost the same as the salary employee. The only difference is in cashing out accrued sick and vacation hours. First, you use the Salary Sick item under the Salary to split the 80 hours with the Cashout hours to determine the amount of the Cashout. Write it down and delete the entry to bring the salary hours back to 80. Second, pull in the Salary Sick Cashout in the Other Payroll Items box and type the amount you wrote down as shown below for 480.77. Then you're done.

❖ Click **Employees menu**
❖ Click **Employee Center**
❖ Click **Jerry Jordan** (left of the window)
❖ Double click 1st **Paycheck for 2/8/09** (right of the window)
❖ Bank Account: Accept **USA Payroll**
❖ Click **Paycheck Details** (bottom right of the window)
❖ Complete window with information on the next page

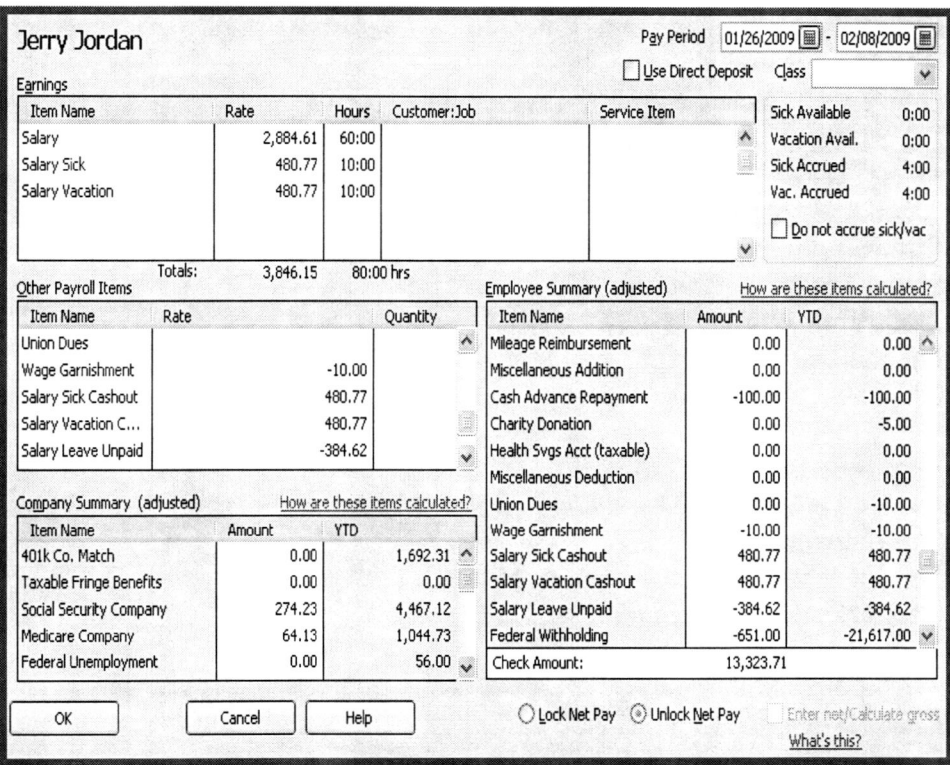

Released Staff: Paycheck Details

Here is detail for Jerry's paycheck. Jerry has 10 hours for sick, 10 hours for vacation and 8 hours for unpaid leave, a total of 28 hours. First calculate the amount for each item, then delete the unpaid leave and subtract in other payroll items.

❖ Earning:
❖ Salary. Hours: Type 52
❖ Salary Sick: Hours: 10
❖ Salary Vacation: Hours: 10
❖ Salary Sick: Hours 8. Rate: Accept 384.62
❖ Delete the entire line for Salary Sick 8 hours
❖ Salary. Hours: Type 60. Rate Accept 2,884.61
❖
❖ Other Payroll Items:
❖ 401k Co. Match. Rate: blank (Delete 5%). Press **Tab**
❖ Cash Advance. Rate: 10,000

> You use the 52, 10, 10, 8, to make the total hours 80 and the total amount must be 3,846.15. Then you pull up all three items in the other payroll items box.

❖ Cash Advance Repayment. Rate: 100
❖ Wage garnishment. Rate: 10
❖ Salary Sick Cashout: 480.77 (as calculated above)
❖ Salary Vacation Cashout: 480.77 (as calculated above)
❖ Salary Leave Unpaid. Rate: 384.62 (as calculated above) (type as positive)
❖
❖ Company Summary (adjusted)
❖ Social Security. Amount: 274.23
❖ Medicare. Amount: 64.13
❖ Federal Unemployment. Amount: 0.00
❖ TX – Unemployment. Amount: 0.00
❖
❖ Employee Summary (adjusted)
❖ Accept default figures and add these
❖ Scroll down
❖ Federal Withholding. Amount: 651.00
❖ Social Security. Amount: 274.23
❖ Medicare. Amount: 64.13
❖
❖ Check Amount: **13,323.71**
❖ Company Summary: **338.36.** Click **OK**
❖ Click **Save & Close** on check window
❖ Click **Yes** to "You have changed the transaction…"

> Confirm your total with a calculator manually.

Released Staff: Pay Payroll Liabilities

You've paid hourly and salary employees; as usual the payroll liabilities are generated behind the scenes. Every time you pay employees, you pay the accompanying liabilities, but the checks are not printed until the end of the quarter as promised in the setup process. Another option is to wait until the end of the quarter to run the liabilities checks at one time. Either way is OK as long as the total matches the total on the Payroll Summary report.

Activities:

❖ Click **Employees menu**
❖ Click **Payroll Taxes and Liabilities**
❖ Click **Pay Payroll Liabilities**
❖ Dates: From: Type **1/1/09** Through: Type **3/31/09**
❖ Click **OK**
❖ Checkmark **To be printed**

❖ Click **Review liability check to enter…**
❖ Bank Account: Accept **USA Payroll**
❖ Check Date: Type **3/31/09**
❖ Dates: From: Accept **1/1/09**. To: Type **3/31/09**.
❖ **Checkmark on all liabilities with numbers**
❖ Total Balance: Accept **2,830.64**
❖ Total Amt. To Pay: Accept **2,830.64**
❖ Ending Bank Balance: Accept **102,749.02**
❖ Click **Create** (top right of the window).
❖ Click **Save & Close**

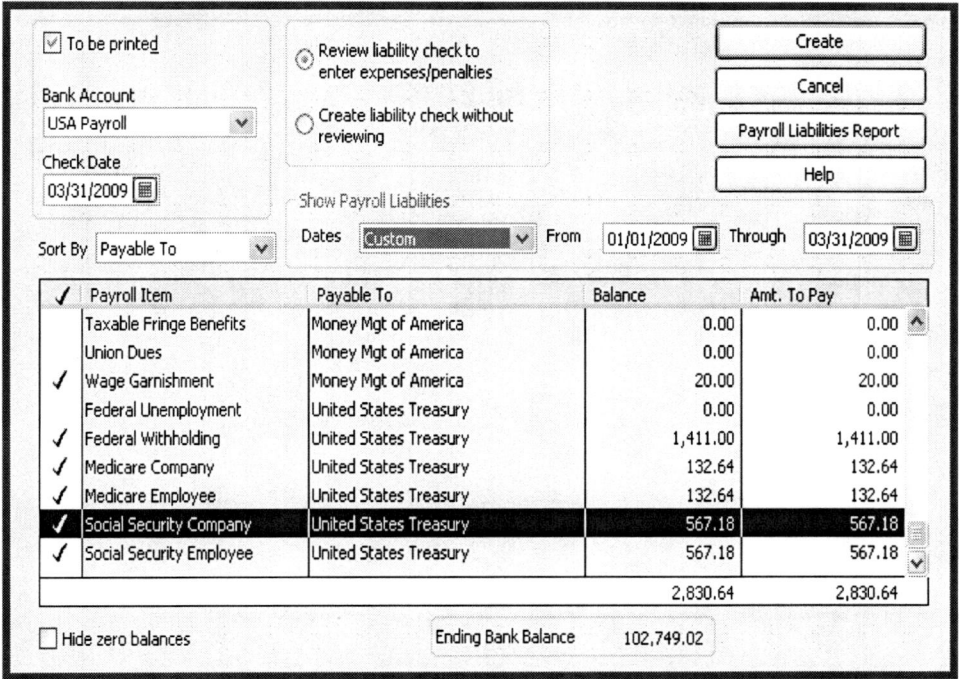

QuickReport: Fate Acres

After you've processed the hourly employees' paychecks, pull up the QuickReport to see what amounts are reflected on the report. Once the amounts are confirmed, you know that your activities are correct. You can see the report has all the checks that were issued to Fate Acres, lined up by date. If the amounts did not match, check the date range to make sure you've selected the correct range. After that, double click on the amount in the QuickReport and you will be taken to the check window for review.

Activities:

- ❖ Click **Employees menu**
- ❖ Click **Employee Center**
- ❖ Click **Fate Acres** (left of the window)
- ❖ Click **Reports menu**
- ❖ Towards the bottom of the submenus
- ❖ Click **QuickReport**
- ❖ Dates (top left of the window): Select **This Calendar Year**
- ❖ Look! Fate Acres has **38,037.05**
- ❖ Click **X** to close window

Quick Payroll 2009
Employee QuickReport
January through December 2009

Type	Date	Account	Amount
Fate Acres			
Paycheck	01/11/2009	USA Payroll	12,212.67
Paycheck	01/25/2009	USA Payroll	12,330.84
Paycheck	02/08/2009	USA Payroll	13,493.54
Total Fate Acres			38,037.05
TOTAL			**38,037.05**

QuickReport: Jerry Jordan

You ran the same QuickReport for Jerry Jordan to confirm his numbers. Like Fate's report, all the checks paid to Jerry are listed in this window. Remember, you ran this report because you've issued checks to employees. However, you can use the same report to look for an employee's check if someone calls you and said his or her check is not correct. Pull up the check and make the necessary correction, and the situation is taken care of in little time.

Activities:

- ❖ Click **Employees menu**
- ❖ Click **Employees Center**
- ❖ Click on **Jerry Jordan** (left of the window
- ❖ Click **Reports menu**
- ❖ Towards the bottom of the submenus
- ❖ Click **QuickReport**
- ❖ Dates (top left of the window): Select **This Calendar Year**
- ❖ Look! Fate Acres has **54,696.52**
- ❖ Click **X** to close window

Quick Payroll 2009
Employee QuickReport
January through December 2009

◇	Type	◇	Date	◇	Account	◇	Amount	◇
Jerry Jordan								
▶	Paycheck		01/11/2009		USA Payroll		20,728.22 ◀	
	Paycheck		01/25/2009		USA Payroll		20,644.59	
	Paycheck		02/08/2009		USA Payroll		13,323.71	
	Total Jerry Jordan						54,696.52	
TOTAL							**54,696.52**	

Run Payroll Transaction Report

To get the total picture of everything that happened for the period in one mirror, you should look at the Payroll Transaction report. It displays all the activities, including the checks issued to the vendor namely government agencies, both state and federal and health and retirement management companies. The intent is the same: to confirm the amounts on checks are correct. You might as well open a file for this report because you would want to keep a hard copy for audit purposes.

Activities:

- ❖ Click **Reports menu**
- ❖ Click **Employees & Payroll**
- ❖ Click **Payroll Transaction by Payee**

- ❖ Dates (top left of the window): Select **This Calendar Year**
- ❖ Total Payroll check is **147,250.98**
- ❖ Click **X** to close window

Quick Payroll 2009
Payroll Transactions by Payee
January through December 2009

◇ Date ◇	◇ Name ◇	◇ Type ◇	◇ Memo ◇	◇ Account ◇	◇ Amount ◇
03/31/2009	HMO of America	Liability Check		USA Payroll	-70.00
Total HMO of America					-130.00
Money Mgt of America					
03/31/2009	Money Mgt of Ame...	Liability Check		USA Payroll	-2,894.81
03/31/2009	Money Mgt of Ame...	Liability Check		USA Payroll	-20.00
Total Money Mgt of America					-2,914.81
United States Treasury					
03/31/2009	United States Trea...	Liability Check	99-1234567	USA Payroll	-24,081.52
03/31/2009	United States Trea...	Liability Check	99-1234567	USA Payroll	-24,094.44
03/31/2009	United States Trea...	Liability Check	99-1234567	USA Payroll	-2,810.64
Total United States Treasury					-50,986.60
Fate Acres					
01/11/2009	Fate Acres	Paycheck		USA Payroll	-12,212.67
01/25/2009	Fate Acres	Paycheck		USA Payroll	-12,330.84
02/08/2009	Fate Acres	Paycheck		USA Payroll	-13,493.54
Total Fate Acres					-38,037.05
Jerry Jordan					
01/11/2009	Jerry Jordan	Paycheck		USA Payroll	-20,728.22
01/25/2009	Jerry Jordan	Paycheck		USA Payroll	-20,644.59
02/08/2009	Jerry Jordan	Paycheck		USA Payroll	-13,323.71
Total Jerry Jordan					-54,696.52
TOTAL					**-147,250.98**

Payroll Item Reports

As you become acclimated with QuickBooks Payroll you will run into other reports of your choice that help you to synthesize your work. We've mentioned the Payroll Summary reports, but other helpful payroll reports are the Payroll Item Listing report and the Payroll Item Detail reports. The listing report will show you some default information that QuickBooks generated behind the scenes. It's very important to update yourself on these payroll data.

Activities:

- ❖ To print payroll item detail
- ❖ Click **Reports menu**
- ❖ Click **Employees & Payroll**
- ❖ Click **Payroll Item Detail**
- ❖ Date: Select **This Calendar Year**
- ❖ Click **Print** (top of the window)
- ❖ Click **Preview** (right of the window)
- ❖ Click **Zoom In**
- ❖ Click **Close** or Print if printer is ready
- ❖ Click **X** to close Print Report window
- ❖
- ❖ To print payroll listing report
- ❖ Click **Reports menu**
- ❖ Click **Employees & Payroll**
- ❖ Click **Payroll Item Listing** (bottom of list)
- ❖ Click **Print** (top of the window)
- ❖ Click **Preview** (right of the window)
- ❖ Click **Zoom In**
- ❖ Click **Close** or Print if printer is ready
- ❖ Click **X** to close Print Report window

Financial Results: Profit & Loss

If you have employees, whether you choose to run your payroll in-house or sign up with an outside vendor, you can see the effects of payroll activities on your Profit & Loss statements. In this chapter, we completed the Employees window for hourly, as well as salaried, personnel. We processed paychecks for employees, government agencies and payroll-related management companies.

Activities:

- ❖ Click **Reports menu**
- ❖ Click **Company & Financial**
- ❖ Click **Profit & Loss Standard**
- ❖ Date: Select **This Fiscal Year**
- ❖ From: Accept **1/1/09**
- ❖ To: Accept **12/31/09**
- ❖ Click **Collapse**
- ❖ Net Income **1,786,588.73**
- ❖ Click **X** to close window

```
                    Quick Payroll 2009
                     Profit & Loss
              January through December 2009
                                    ◇ Jan - Dec 09 ◇
    Ordinary Income/Expense
       Income
          Opening Balance Income   ▶ 1,905,000.00 ◀
          Landscaping Services          75,000.00
       Total Income                  1,980,000.00

       Cost of Goods Sold
          Materials                     50,000.00
          Discount Received               -700.00
       Total COGS                       49,300.00

    Gross Profit                     1,930,700.00

       Expense
          Opening Balance Expense       15,000.00
          Depreciation Expense             666.67
          Payroll Expenses             127,835.60
          Telephone Expense                459.00
          Travel Expense                   150.00
       Total Expense                    144,111.27

    Net Ordinary Income              1,786,588.73

    Net Income                       1,786,588.73
```

Financial Results: Balance Sheet

As you issue the payroll checks from the Payroll Checking account, the Balance Sheet statement is affected. If you paid employees and the Payroll Checking is still the same, that's a red flag you have issued payroll checks from the wrong account. If the checks are available, zero them out and re-issue checks from the right account; otherwise, you will need a journal entry to move money to the payroll account. Payroll Checking balance is now 102,749.02 and Total Assets is now 3,033,713.73.

Activities:
   ❖ Click **Reports menu**
   ❖ Click **Company & Financial**
   ❖ Click **Balance Sheet Standard**
   ❖ Date: Select **This Fiscal Year**
   ❖ As of: Accept **12/31/09**
   ❖ Click **Collapse**
   ❖ Total Assets **3,033,713.73**
   ❖ Click **X** to close window

```
                        Quick Payroll 2009
                        Balance Sheet
                     As of December 31, 2009
                                          ◇  Dec 31, 09  ◇
        ASSETS
          Current Assets
            Checking/Savings
              Money Market Account      ▶   100,000.00  ◀
              USA Checking                   761,591.00
              USA Payroll                    102,749.02
            Total Checking/Savings          964,340.02

            Accounts Receivable
              Accounts Receivable         1,085,625.00
            Total Accounts Receivable     1,085,625.00

            Other Current Assets
              Payroll Asset                  19,415.38
              Undeposited Funds             900,000.00
              Inventory Asset                25,000.00
            Total Other Current Assets      944,415.38

          Total Current Assets           2,994,380.40

          Fixed Assets
            Truck                            39,333.33
          Total Fixed Assets               39,333.33

        TOTAL ASSETS                     3,033,713.73
```

Chapter Summary

You have completed the Payroll Cycle. You saw how easy it is to process timesheets and pay employees and vendors once the payroll setup is completed. When you repeatedly practice the process, it will become second nature to you. This chapter took you from the setup windows through check processing to printing reports. Once you understand the basic cycle, it is only a matter of repeating the same process every two weeks.

What we accomplished:
- Reviewed the Employees submenus
- Reviewed the Employee center contents
- Practiced how to set up free payroll subscription
- Completed the payroll & employees preferences setup
- Created hourly and salary employees
- Created hourly employee Timesheet
- Paid hourly and salary employees
- Paid payroll liabilities to vendors
- Ran payroll reports
- Processed financial statements

Additional Financial activities:
- We paid the following liabilities:
- Cashier, TX Workforce Commission 486.00
- HMO of America 130.00
- Money Management of America 2,914.81
- United States Treasury 50,986.60
- Fate Acres (employee) 38,037.05
- Jerry Jordan (employee) 54,696.52
- Total payments 147,250.98

Optional Test 8

Questions: True/False
Answer the following questions by placing letter the T or F in the space provided before the question number.

_____ 1. During Payroll Item setup process Overtime Rate will default as one and one-half of the hourly rates.

_____ 2. When processing a payroll check for an employee you must make sure both the employee and the company pay the same amount for Social Security and Medicare.

_____ 3. During an employee paycheck processing, you will notice that Federal Withholding is paid by the employee while Federal Unemployment is paid by the company.

_____ 4. You go through the Employee menu to setup employee preferences, you are not allowed to setup employee preferences through the Edit menu.

_____ 5. After you issued a check to an employee but has not been cashed yet, it is impossible to delete that check because QuickBooks is strict about it.

_____ 6. You may not be able to process employees' checks manually and calculate the taxes by hand unless you are registered with QuickPayroll.

_____ 7. Sick and Vacation leaves are accrued until used not expensed immediately whether used or not.

_____ 8. It is a government mandate that only the employer can process employee payroll check, an outside payroll company is not allowed to perform the task

_____ 9. When creating a timesheet QuickBooks will allow you to copy the last timesheet to the current window.

_____ 10. After you have created an employee QuickBooks will allow you to delete it, even if it has a balance or used in at least one transaction.

Questions: Multiple Choices

Answer the following questions by placing letter A, B, C, or D in the space provided before the question number.

_____ 1. Health and Dental insurance premium are Payroll Items on an employee's paycheck, how do they affect the gross income?
A. As Additions
B. As Deductions
C. All of the above
D. None of the above

_____ 2. All of the following are Payroll Items on an employee's paycheck, which of these is a deduction from employee's paycheck?
A. Social Security Company
B. Medicare Company
C. Federal Unemployment
D. None of the above

_____ 3. All of the following are Payroll Items on an employee's paycheck, which of following is paid by the employer?
A. Social Security Employee
B. Medicare Employee
C. Federal Withholding
D. None of the above

_____ 4. Which of the following is not a Payroll Item used in calculating employee wages when processing payroll checks?
A. Hourly
B. Annual
C. Commission
D. Hourly Tips

_____ 5. A company's payroll policy will determine how and when it processes its payroll checks, which of the following is a pay period option?
A. Biweekly
B. Semimonthly
C. Monthly
D. All of the above

_____ 6. An employee must select a filing status before a payroll check is issued, all of the following are available in QuickBooks except…
   A. New Employee
   B. Single
   C. Married
   D. Don't Withhold

_____ 7. Before making a payroll-related Journal Entries, you must create payroll accounts, which of the following is a Payroll Type of account?
   A. Income
   B. Cost of Goods Sold
   C. Expense
   D. Other Income

_____ 8. In completing the Employee Information window there are three Change tabs selection available, which of these is not a Change tab selection?
   A. Personal Info
   B. Payroll and Compensation Info
   C. Employment Info
   D. All of the above are available

_____ 9. Payroll sheet is used to collect information about how many hours an employee actually worked. Which of these sheets is used by QuickBooks?
   A. Check Sheet
   B. Daily Sheet
   C. Work Sheet
   D. Time Sheet

_____ 10. After an employee has been created and a check has been issued to this employee, you can perform all of the following activities except…
   A. Edit the employee
   B. Delete the employee
   C. Make the employee inactive
   D. Copy Employee

$

Chapter 9

Online Payroll

Objectives: After you've completed this chapter, you will be able to:

- ✓ Explain the Payroll submenus
- ✓ Setup employees
- ✓ Create paychecks
- ✓ Make payments
- ✓ Process tax forms
- ✓ Update settings
- ✓ Process reports

Review Online Payroll Submenus

Online payroll is a complete system used in processing employees' paychecks, make liability payment, and process related forms. This is one of the most user-friendly payroll systems I've ever seen. As with any other system, you must know what you're doing and the possible outcome to be effective and efficient in using this package. This textbook will make using the payroll system a lot easier.

The following activities tabs are found on the Online Payroll window:

- **Home:** Anytime you login, you will be defaulted to the home page, where you can read the alerts. It will tell you about pertinent events and schedules you need to be aware of. The home page has a "Things To Do" section, which contains three major areas: create payments, make tax payments, and file tax forms.

- **Employees:** Employees' names are listed in alphabetical order, and you can zero in on an employee by clicking on the related alphabet. At the bottom right of the window are the following buttons: new, edit, delete, and report. When you click on the report button, it takes you to the paychecks by employee window, where you can use the transaction date drop down window to pull this year or last year checks. You use the related reports button located at the top right of the window to see all the employees reports

- **Paychecks:** The paychecks window allows you to create checks by selecting the pay period you desire. The window has the listing of all the checks you've made recently with dates and amounts. A view paycheck history link is located at the bottom right of the recent checks box, which you can use to open the transaction (paycheck) list by date. You can use the related activities box to print paychecks, print paystubs, buy blank checks, and export payroll.

- **Payments:** When you want to make liability payments to vendors, the payment window is your destination. It allows you to checkmark the desired vendor and process the payment. The top of the payment window is a listing of upcoming payments. The bottom right of the box has a view/pay link which takes you to the actual check for edit or payment. Below the upcoming payments box is the recent payments box. The top right of the window has related activities on edit payment setup, set up e-pay, print liability checks, make custom payment, and enter liability refunds.

- **Tax Forms:** The tax form window has the listings of forms due soon and recent forms. The top right of the window has related activities on prepare any form, select Form 941 or 944, buy W-2 form, and view all due dates.

- **Settings:** If you think of making changes to your setups, think settings. You should get used to the links in this window. The employees and paychecks box is essential, because it allows you to make changes to the following settings: employees, compensation, payments and deductions, paid time off plans, and pay schedules. Other boxes in the setting window are: printing, electronic payments, tax and other liability payments, exporting to QuickBooks or Quicken, and general.

- **Reports:** The report window has submenus including memorized, paychecks and payments, recent activities, lists, all (lists) alphabetical, activity log, how do I..., and request a new report. You will need to scroll through the window to view all the reports displayed on the window.

Free Trial Online Payroll

Intuit, the maker of the online payroll software allows you a three month free trial subscription, after which it starts charging you the amount it stipulates on its website. I have no doubt once you try this package, you will like it and will continue to stay with it for a long time. It is one of the easiest, most efficient software I've ever seen. It is very comprehensive and yet user-friendly. You will like it enough to recommend it to your company if it's not already using it. **If you choose to cancel, you must do so within the time allowed. At the end of this chapter, I will give you the steps to canceling your subscription without fees if you choose to do so.**

Activities:

- ❖ Type **www.payroll.intuit.com**
- ❖ In the Intuit Online Payroll box. Click **Learn More**
- ❖ Click **Start for Free**
- ❖ Thank you for choosing Intuit Online Payroll
- ❖ Click **Continue with FREE Trial**
- ❖ Startup Interview. Create a Login. **Complete the box**
- ❖ **Correct email address to receive subscription & cancellation notices**
- ❖ Customize Intuit Online Payroll. **Complete box**
- ❖ What is the name of the business? ──────────────➤
- ❖ Finish Setup. **Complete the box**
- ❖ Subscription Setup. **Review price**
- ❖ Credit Card Information. **Complete the box**
- ❖ Subscription is complete
- ❖ Congratulations! Intuit Online Payroll is ready to use
- ❖ Welcome to the Payroll Setup Interview. Click **Continue**
- ❖ **Date of Subscription**_____ Please write the date!

> Important !!!
> What is the name of the business? Type your first name and "& Company."

Steps to payroll processing

First cycle
- ❖ Setup company
- ❖ Setup employees
- ❖ Pay employees
- ❖ Make liability payments (If due)
- ❖ Process tax forms (If available)
- ❖ Run reports

Pay period cycle
- ❖ Update settings with new payroll items
- ❖ Update related employees with new payroll items
- ❖ Pay employees
- ❖ Make liability payments (If due)
- ❖ Process tax forms (If available)
- ❖ Run reports

Company Information

This is where you supply the basic information about your company. The name and address of your company should match the name and address on your EIN application. The basic information includes the following: name, street, city, state, and zip code. If you have not paid an employee in the past, click no, I'm paying my first employee of the year.

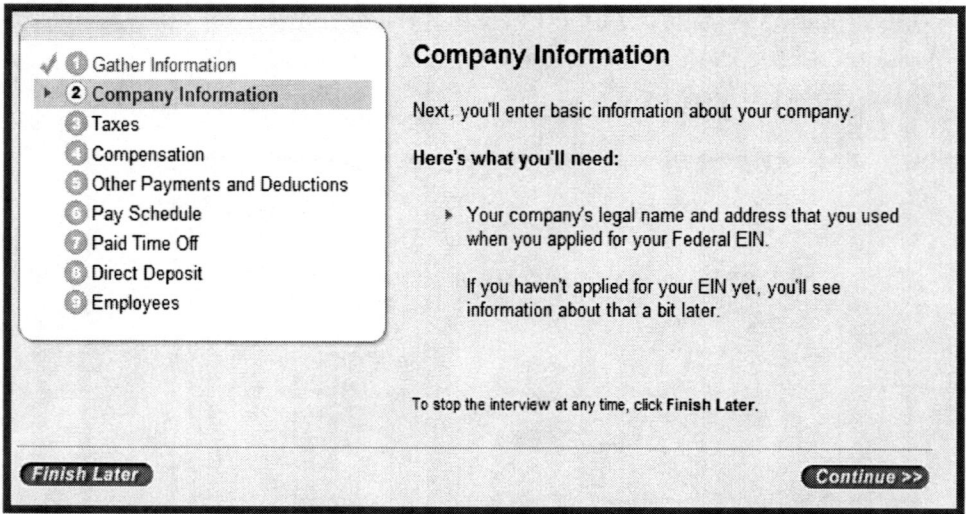

Activities:

- ❖ Welcome to the Payroll Setup Interview. Click **Continue**
- ❖ What will I need? Click **Continue**
- ❖ Company Information. Click **Continue**
- ❖ Legal Name: Your name **& Company**
- ❖ Street: Type **123 Adam Lane**
- ❖ City: Type **Dallas**
- ❖ State: Select **TX**
- ❖ Zip: Type **75000**
- ❖ Click **No I'm paying my first employee of the year**
- ❖ Date of Paycheck: Type **1/1/2008 (Must be 2008)**
- ❖ Click **Continue**

Federal Taxes

Before you pay the federal taxes, you must set the federal taxes windows. You will be selecting the United States Treasury and supply your EIN number if you have one. After you're completed the rates for medicare, social security, and federal unemployment will be listed in the window.

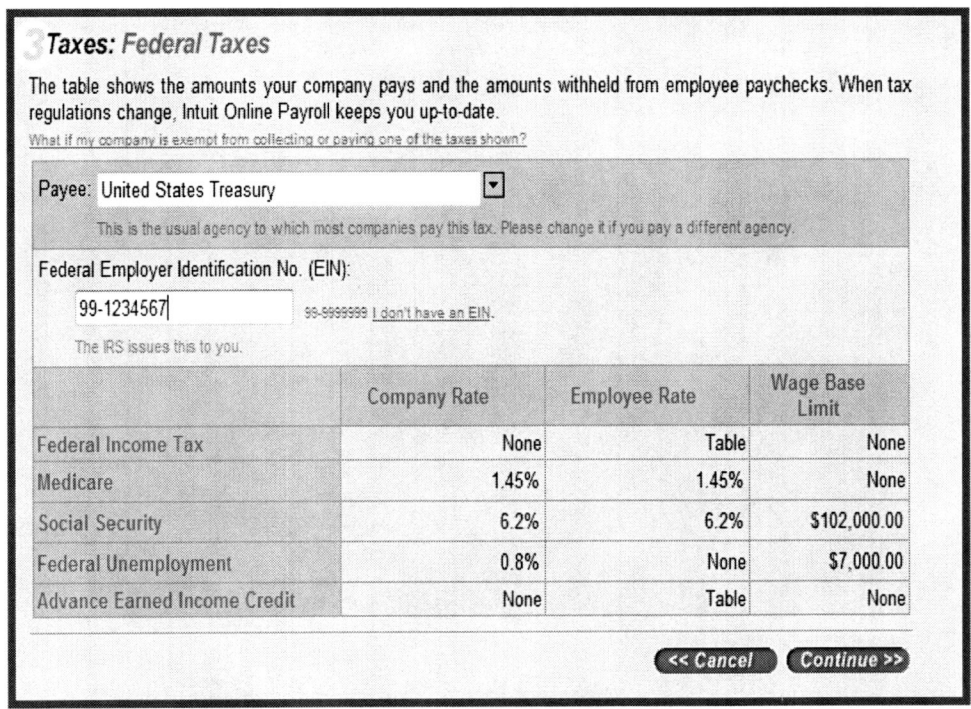

3 Taxes: *Federal Taxes*

The table shows the amounts your company pays and the amounts withheld from employee paychecks. When tax regulations change, Intuit Online Payroll keeps you up-to-date.

What if my company is exempt from collecting or paying one of the taxes shown?

Payee: United States Treasury

This is the usual agency to which most companies pay this tax. Please change it if you pay a different agency.

Federal Employer Identification No. (EIN):

99-1234567   99-9999999 I don't have an EIN.

The IRS issues this to you.

	Company Rate	Employee Rate	Wage Base Limit
Federal Income Tax	None	Table	None
Medicare	1.45%	1.45%	None
Social Security	6.2%	6.2%	$102,000.00
Federal Unemployment	0.8%	None	$7,000.00
Advance Earned Income Credit	None	Table	None

<< Cancel   Continue >>

Activities:

❖ Federal Taxes. Click **Continue**
❖ Federal Employer Identification No (EIN): Type **99-1234567**
❖ Click **Continue**

State and Local Taxes

With state and local taxes window, you must choose the state where the company is based or located for tax purposes. When you select the state, online payroll system defaults the payee's name. You have to enter the account number you received from the state as required for the process to be completed.

Activities:

❖ State and Local Taxes. Click **Continue**
❖ State: Select **Texas** (Very Important). Click **OK**. Click **Continue**
❖ Payee: Accept **Cashier, Texas Workforce Commission**
❖ TX Workforce Commission Acct No: Type **99-999999-9** (9 nine digits)
❖ Click **Continue**
❖ Taxes: State and Local Taxes. Click **Continue**

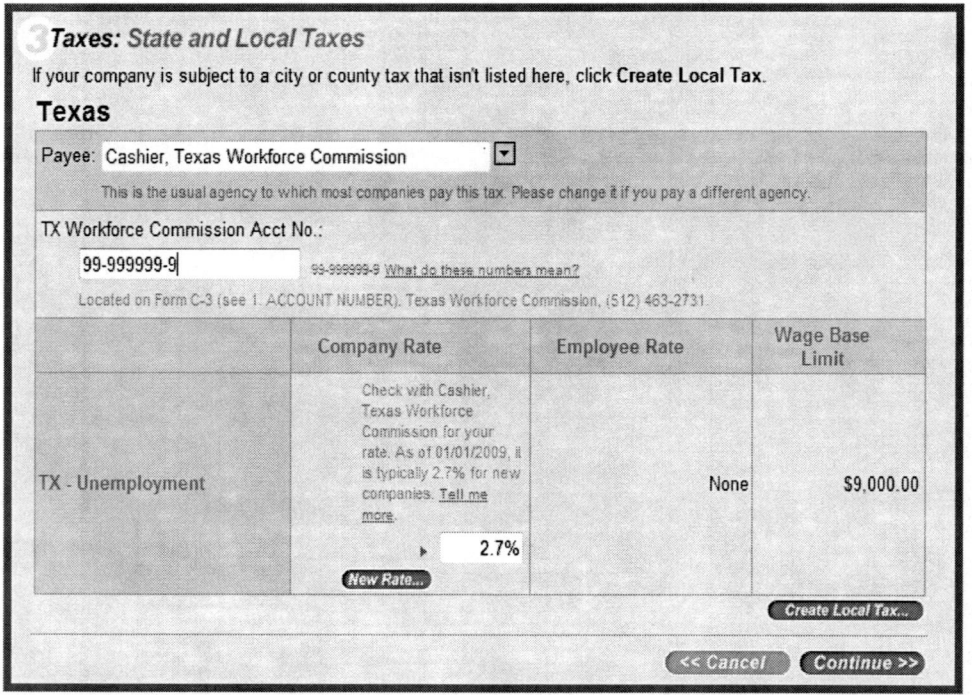

Tax Payments and Schedules

Whatever you do keep the tax payment schedule somewhere you can always see it. Better yet, online payroll has made it easy by alerting you of the due dates after you have completed the setup process. You will be selecting the following schedules: federal 940 (quarterly, most used), federal 941/944 (quarterly, most used), and state unemployment (quarterly, most used)

Activities:

- ❖ Tax Payments and Schedules. Click **Continue**
- ❖ Taxes: Tax Payments. Click **Continue**
- ❖ Payment Name: Accept **Federal 940**
- ❖ Payment Method: Click **Check/Other**
- ❖ How often do you pay? Accept **Quarterly (usual frequency).**Click **Continue**

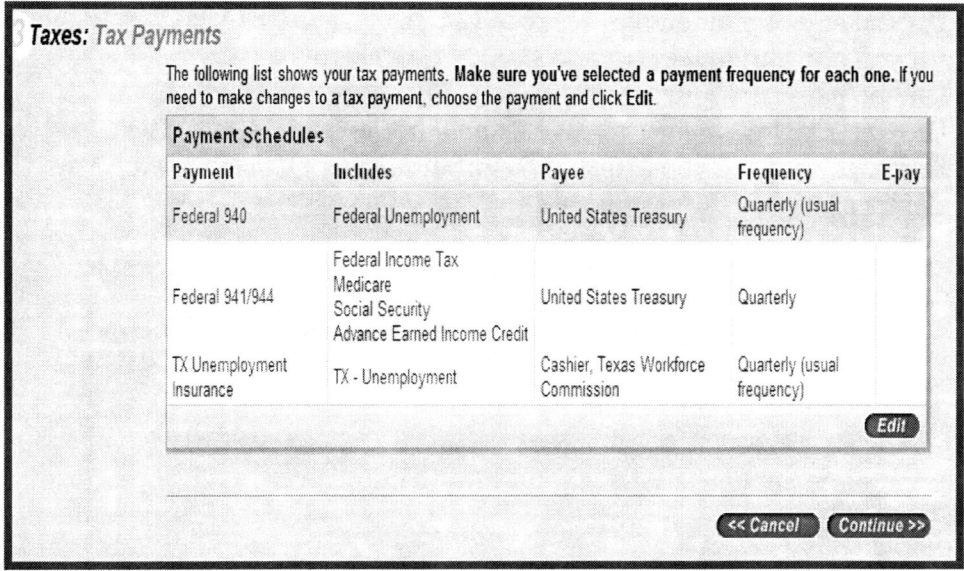

- ❖ Payment Name: Accept **Federal 941/944**
- ❖ Payment Method: Click **Check/Other**
- ❖ How often do you pay…? Select **Quarterly**. Click **Continue**
- ❖ Payment Name: Accept **TX Unemployment Insurance**
- ❖ Payment Method: Click **Check/Other**
- ❖ How often do you pay…? Accept **Quarterly**. Click **Finish**
- ❖ Taxes: Tax Payments. Click **Continue**

Compensation

You will be selecting items that match the employment contract.   For example, you select hourly for the hourly employees and salary for the salaried employees.   Compensation items include the following: salary, hourly, overtime hourly, double-time hourly, bonus, commission, piecework, allocated tips, cash tips, paycheck tips, expense allowance, taxable fringe benefits, other compensation.

Activities:

- ❖ Compensation. Click **Continue**
- ❖ Do you have any hourly employees? Click **Yes**
- ❖ Do you have any salaried employees? Click **Yes**. Click **Next**
- ❖ Do you ever pay your employees a bonus…? Click **Yes**
- ❖ Do you pay commission…? Click **Yes**
- ❖ How is it calculated? Accept **Dollar amount**. Click **Next**
- ❖ Do you any of your employees receive tips? Click **Yes**
- ❖ Click **Your employees turn in tips**…Click **Next**
- ❖ Do you pay employees according to the quantity…? Click **No**
- ❖ Do your employees ever receive taxable fringe benefits…? Click **Yes**
- ❖ Payment Name: Type **Mileage Reimbursement.** Click **Finish**
- ❖ Compensation. Click **Continue**

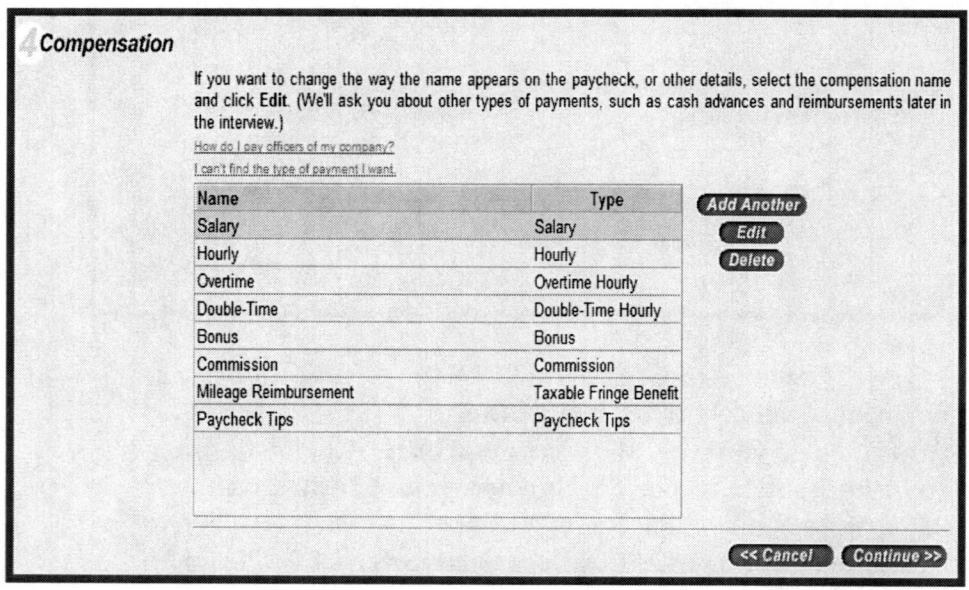

Other Payments and Deductions: Insurance

These are the insurance items you will select from and the pre-tax items are essential and must be selected: health (pre-tax), dental (pre-tax), vision (pre-tax), dependent care fsa (pre-tax), s-corp medical benefits (pre-tax), medical care fsa (pre-tax), group term life (pre-tax), other insurance (pre-tax), flexible spending account (taxable), and health savings account (taxable).

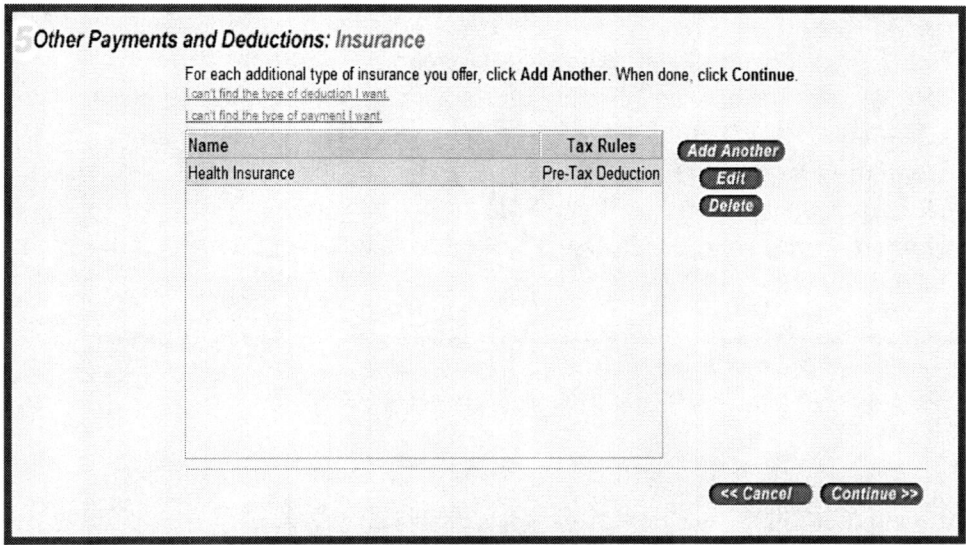

Activities:

- ❖ Other Payments and Deductions-Insurance. Click **Continue**
- ❖ Do you provide any insurance benefits…? Click **Yes**. Click **Next**
- ❖ Click **Health Insurance**. Click **Next**
- ❖ Click **Pre-Tax Employee-Paid Health**. Click **Next**
- ❖ Deduction Name: Accept **Health Insurance**
- ❖ Default Rate or Amount: Type **20.00**
- ❖ Default Annual Limit: Type **480.00**. Click **Next**
- ❖ Payee: Select **Add New**
- ❖ Name: Type **HMO of America**. Click **Quick Add**
- ❖ Account Number: Type **HMO 123456**. Click **Finish**
- ❖ Payment Name: Accept **HMO of America**
- ❖ How often do you pay…? Select **Quarterly**
- ❖ On what day is this payment due? Click **On the last day of the quarter**
- ❖ Click **Finish**
- ❖ Other Payments and Deductions: Insurance. Click **Continue**

Other Payments and Deductions: Retirement

Most retirement items are pre-tax, especially when the item has a company match with it. When you set up an IRA and Roth 401(k) with a bank or broker yourself outside your company it is considered after-tax. You will select from the following items: 401(k), 401(k) Match, 403(k), 403(k) Match, 408(k), 408(k) Match, Simple IRA, Simple IRA Match, IRA (after-tax), roth 401(k)(after-tax).

Activities:

- ❖ Other Payments and Deductions-Retirement. Click **Continue**
- ❖ Do you provide any retirement benefits…? Click **Yes.** Click **Next**
- ❖ Click **401 (k).** Click **Next**
- ❖ Deduction Name: Accept **401 (k)**
- ❖ Default Rate or Amount: Type **0.00**
- ❖ Default Annual Limit: Accept **15,500.00.** Click **Next**
- ❖ Payee: Select **Add New**

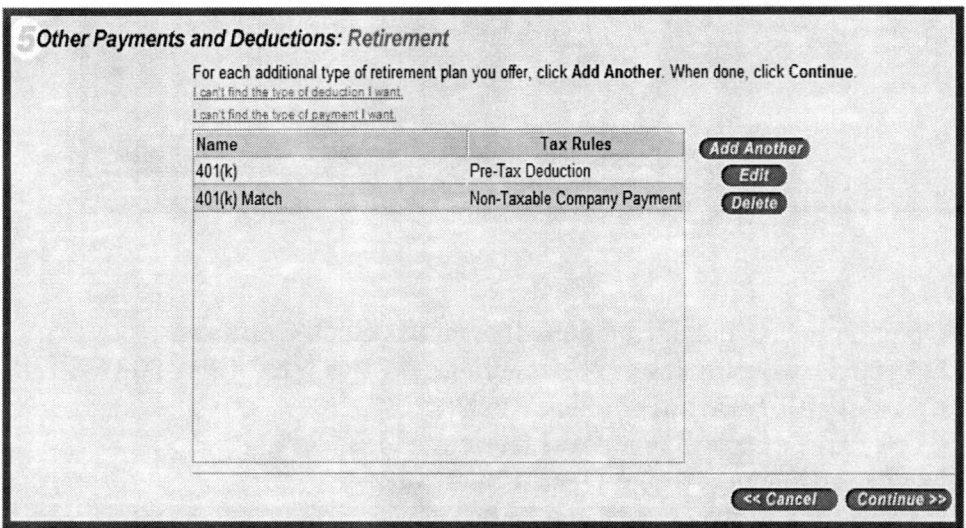

- ❖ Name: Type **Money Mgt of America.** Click **Quick Add**
- ❖ Account Number: Type **MMA 123456.** Click **Finish**
- ❖ Payment Name: Accept **Money Mgt of America**
- ❖ How often do you pay…? Select **Quarterly**
- ❖ On what day is this payment due? Click **On the last day of the quarter**
- ❖ Click **Finish**
- ❖ Other Payments and Deductions: Retirement. Click **Add Another**
- ❖ Click **401 (k) Match.** Click **Next**

- ❖ Payment Name: Accept **401 (k)**
- ❖ Default Rate or Amount: Type **5%**
- ❖ Default Annual Limit: Type **15,500.00**. Click **Next**
- ❖ Payee: Select **Money Mgt of America**
- ❖ Account Number: Type **MMA 101456.** Click **Finish**
- ❖ Liability: Accept **401 (k) Match**
- ❖ Do you want to group this..? Click **Yes**. Click **Finish**
- ❖ Other Payments and Deductions: Retirement. Click **Continue**

Other Payments and Deductions: Miscellaneous

Miscellaneous payments and deductions are items that are not either insurance or retirement related. They are deductions or additions from compensation and they include the following: cash advance(addition), cash advance repayment(deduction), union dues(deduction), charitable donation(deduction), mileage reimbursement (addition), wage garnishment(deduction), taxable fringe benefits(addition), non taxable fringe benefits(addition), car allowance(addition), housing allowance (addition), travel allowance(addition), education refund(addition), miscellaneous additions(addition), and miscellaneous deductions(deduction). You can see the list is endless. Use this process to classify other items that may come your way.

Activities:

- ❖ Other Payments and Deductions-Miscellaneous. Click **Continue**
- ❖ Are there any remaining types of payments…? Click **Yes**. Click **Next**
- ❖ Click **Union Dues.** Click **Next**
- ❖ Deduction Name: Accept **Union Dues**
- ❖ How is it calculated? Click **Dollar amount**
- ❖ Default Rate or Amount: Type **10.00**
- ❖ Default Annual Limit: Type **240.00**. Click **Next**
- ❖ Payee: Select **Add New**
- ❖ Name: Type **National Union.** Click **Quick Add**
- ❖ Account Number: Type **NU 123456.** Click **Finish**
- ❖ Payment Name: Accept **National Union**
- ❖ How often do you pay…? Select **Quarterly**
- ❖ On what day is this payment due? Click **On the last day of the quarter**
- ❖ Click **Finish**
- ❖ Other Payments and Deductions: Miscellaneous. Click **Continue**

If you can't find a pre-tax deductible: you go to settings tab, payments and deductions, insurance benefit, health insurance, pre-tax employee-paid health and change the name to what you want.

If you can't find an after-tax deductible: you go to settings tab, payments and deductions, miscellaneous payment and deduction, generic after-tax deduction and change the name to what you want.

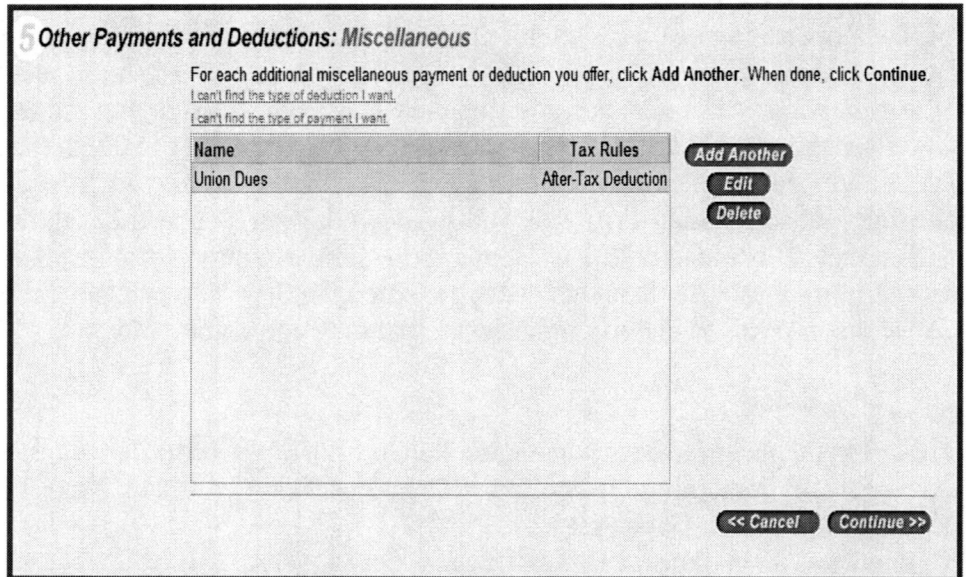

Pay Schedule

You will setup the pay schedule before you can issue checks to employees. The following are the pay schedule listing: daily(as needed), week(once per week), biweekly(every other week), semi monthly(twice a month), monthly(once per month), quarterly(every 3 months), and annually(once per year).

Activities:

- ❖ Pay schedule. Click **Continue**
- ❖ Pay Schedule Name: Type **Biweekly**
- ❖ Click **Every other week**. First Check Date: Type **1/1/2009**
- ❖ Click **On the last day of each pay period.** Click **Save**
- ❖ Pay Schedule. Click **Continue**

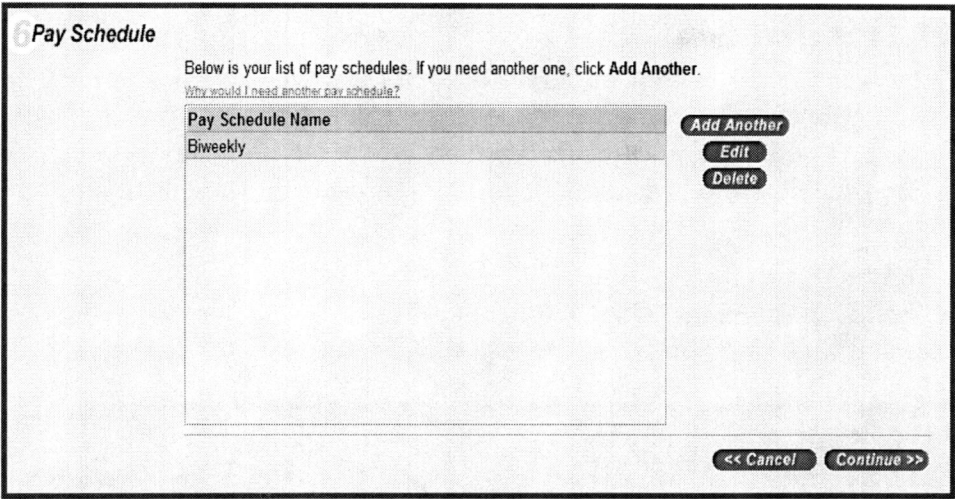

Paid Vacation Time

If the company offers paid vacation, you would consult the employment contract to see how many hours are agreed with each employee and enter that number multiplied by 26 paydays for the maximum balance.

Activities:

- ❖ Paid Vacation Time. Click **Continue**
- ❖ My company offers paid time off, such as vacation. Click **Yes**
- ❖ Name: Accept **Vacation**
- ❖ Employees earn: Type **4:00.** Select **hours per paycheck** (Very Important)
- ❖ Maximum Balance: Type **104.** Click **Continue**

Paid Sick Time

Most companies offer paid sick time. Check with the employment contract for each employee to determine the number of hours per paycheck. Enter that number and multiply by 26 paydays for the maximum balance.

Activities:

- ❖ Paid Sick Time. Click **Continue**
- ❖ My company offers another type of paid time off... sick time. Click **Yes**
- ❖ Name: Accept **Sick**
- ❖ Employees earn: Type **4:00.** Select **hours per paycheck** (Very Important)
- ❖ Maximum Balance: Type **104.** Click **Continue**

Direct Deposit Setup

You will not be setting up direct deposit, however, it is one of the easiest windows to complete. To add direct deposit, go to the settings tab and click set up direct deposit. You have not set up direct deposit for your company if in the settings tab window, you still see set up direct deposit or complete direct deposit setup link.

Activities:

- ❖ Direct Deposit Setup. Click **Continue**
- ❖ Do you want to set up Direct Deposit now? Click **No**. Click **Finish**

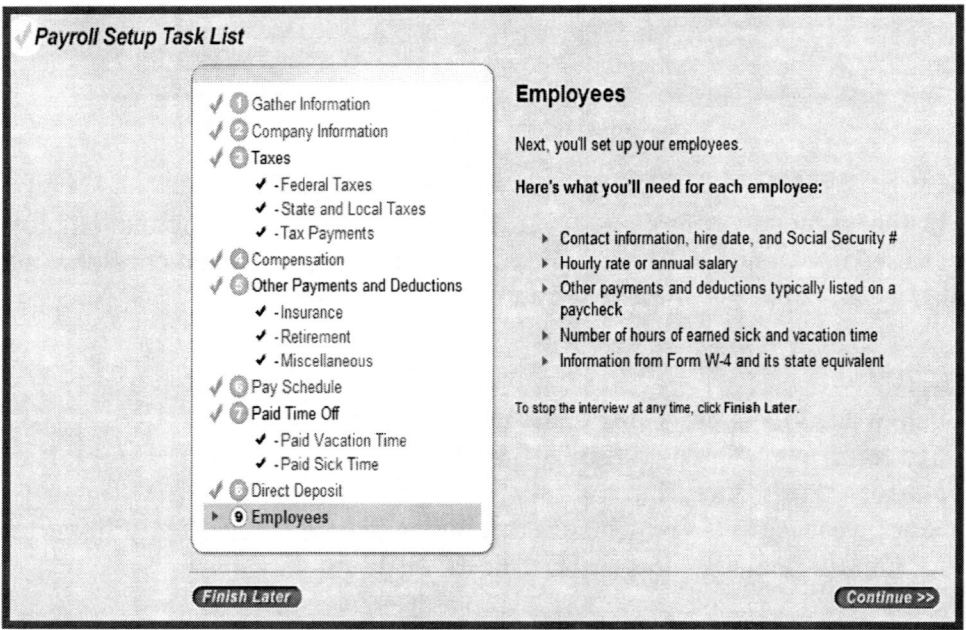

Add Employee

You will supply basic information for each employee, including their name, address, and hiring date. Other information you will complete include compensation and payments and deductions.

Activities:

- ❖ Employees. Click **Continue**
- ❖ Full Name…: Type **Fate Acres**. Press **Tab**
- ❖ Display Name As: Accept **Fate Acres**
- ❖ Print on Check As: Accept **Fate Acres.** Click **Next**

- ❖ Street: Type **123 Danny Lane**
- ❖ City: Type **Dallas**. State: Select **TX**
- ❖ Zip: Type **75000**.   Country: Type **USA**. Click **Next**
- ❖ Social Security: Type **999-12-3456**
- ❖ Hire Date: Type **1/1/2008 (Must be 2008)**
- ❖ Date of Birth: Type **1/1/1977**
- ❖ Gender: Select **Female**. Click **Next**
- ❖ Is this employee paid by the hour? Click **Yes**
- ❖ Under Hourly Name
- ❖ Select **Hourly**. Rate: Type **50.00**. Hours: Type **80**
- ❖ Select **Overtime**. Rate: Type **75.00** Hours: **Leave blank**. Click **Next**
- ❖ Do you pay this employee a salary? Click **No**. Click **Next**

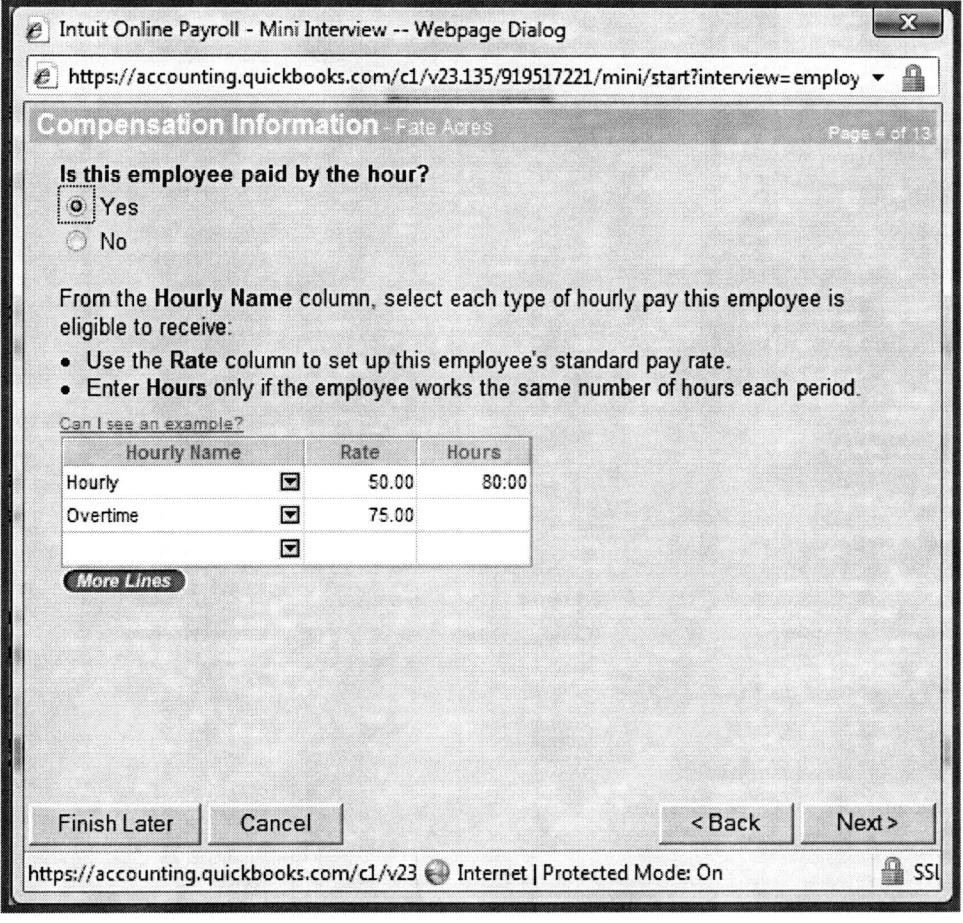

- ❖ Under Compensation Name
- ❖ Select **Bonus**. Rate or Amount: **Leave blank**
- ❖ Select **Commission**. Rate or Amount: **Leave blank**
- ❖ Select **Mileage Reimbursement.** Rate or Amt: **Leave blank.** Click **Next**

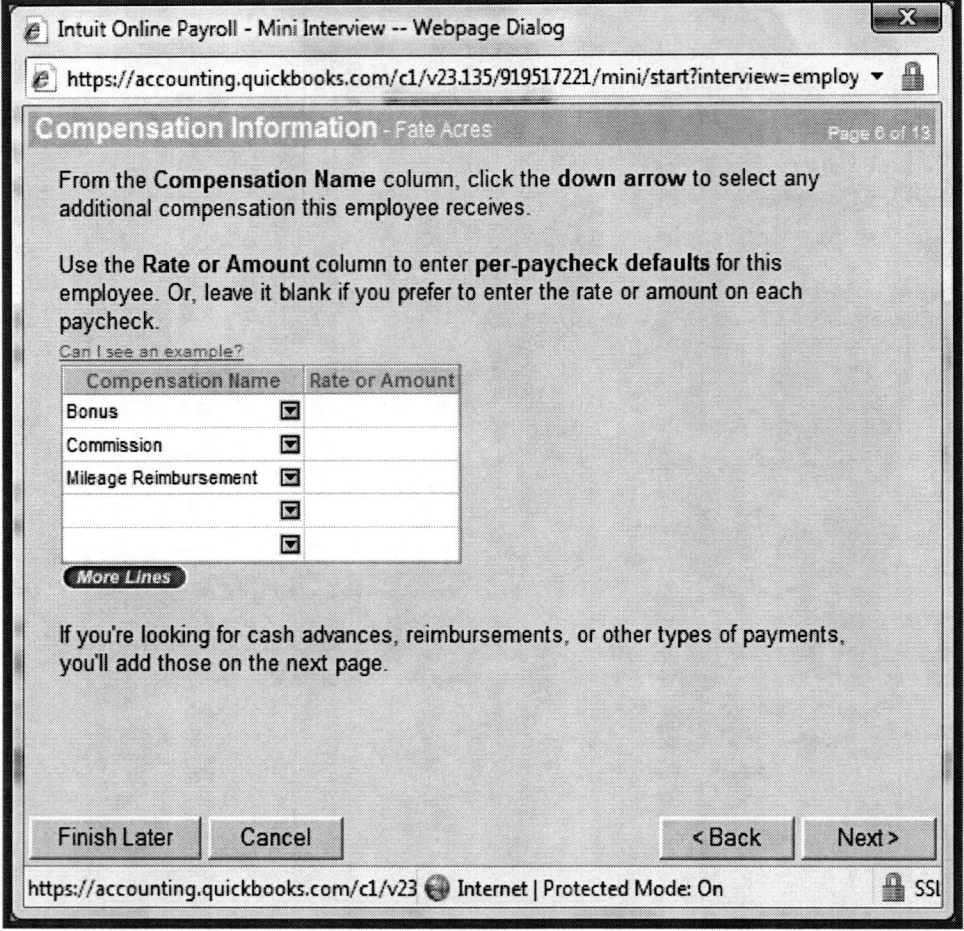

- ❖ Under Pmt or Deduct Name
- ❖ Select **401 (k)**
- ❖ Select **401 (k) Match**
- ❖ Select **Health Insurance**
- ❖ Select **Union Dues.** Click **Next**
- ❖ Checkmark **This employee is eligible for Vacation time**
- ❖ Employee earns: Accept **4:00**. Select **hours per paycheck**
- ❖ Maximum Balance: Accept **104**

- ❖ Opening Balance: Type **0.00** as of Type **1/1/2009**
- ❖ Hourly Rate: Accept **50.00**. Click **Next**
- ❖ Checkmark **This employee is eligible of Sick time**
- ❖ Employee earns: Accept **4:00**. Select **hours per paycheck**
- ❖ Maximum Balance: Accept **104**
- ❖ Opening Balance: Type **0.00** as of Type **1/1/2009**
- ❖ Hourly Rate: Accept **50.00**. Click **Next**

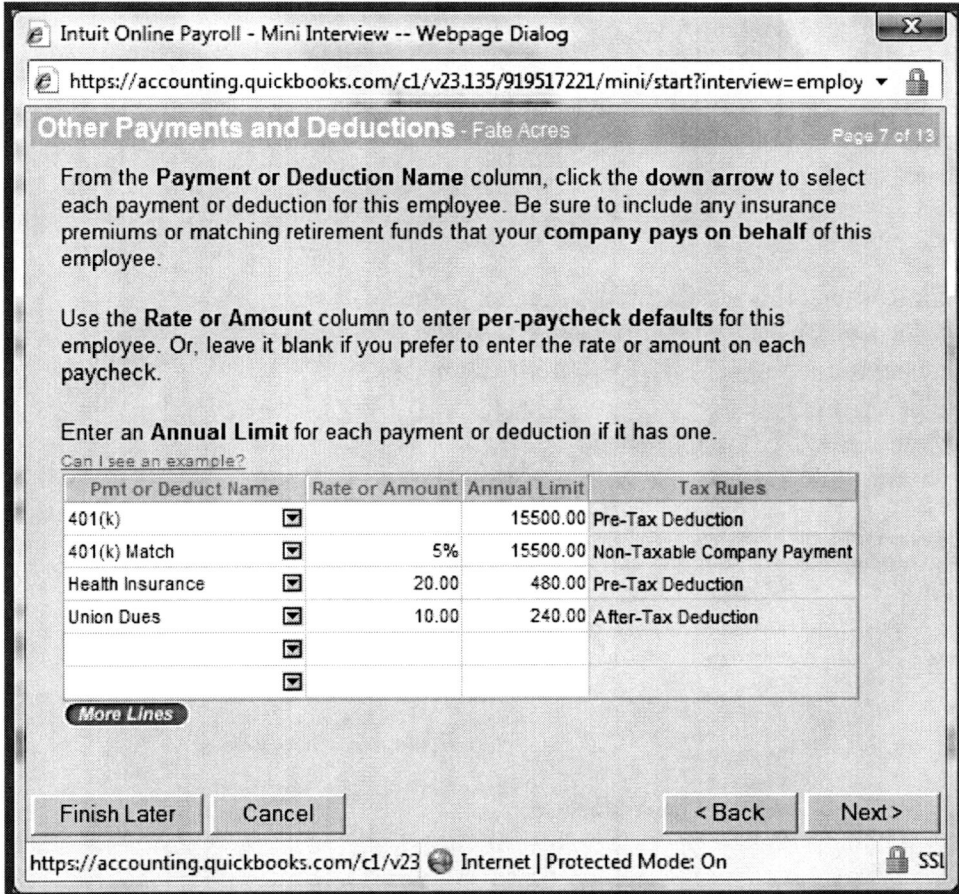

Federal Tax Information

There are several key federal tax data that are required and they include the following: filing status, allowance, extra withholding, social security, medicare, and federal unemployment tax.

Activities:

- ❖ Filing Status: Select **Married**
- ❖ Allowance: Type **2**
- ❖ Extra Withholding: Type **0.00**
- ❖ Nonresident Alien Withholding: Accept **Does not apply**
- ❖ Checkmark **Subject to Medicare and Social Security**
- ❖ Checkmark **Subject to Federal Unemployment. Click Next**

State Tax Information

The state where the employee worked will determine the state taxes that are levied against the employee's paycheck, therefore selecting the right state is very imperative for tax purposes.

Activities:

- ❖ State subject to withholding: Accept **Texas**
- ❖ State works in: Accept **Texas. Click Next**
- ❖ Checkmark **Subject to TX-Unemployment**
- ❖ Click **Finish**
- ❖ Employees. Click **Continue**
- ❖ Congratulations! Click **Go To Home Page**

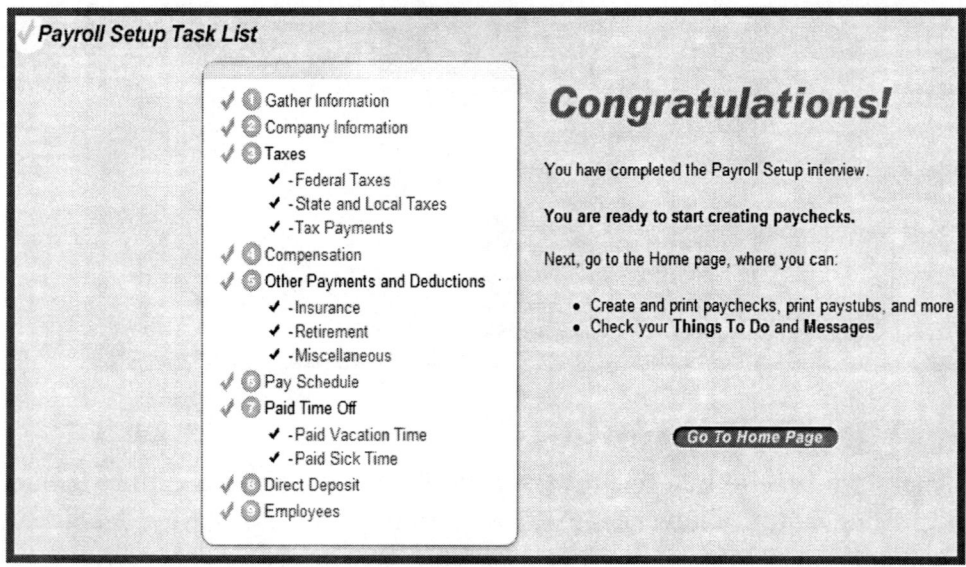

Add New Payroll Item

There are two cycles to payroll processing. The first cycle is the setup process and the second cycle is the monthly maintenance process. During the monthly maintenance phase, you add new items, update employees with new items, pay employees, pay liability vendors, process tax forms and run reports. Let's start with adding new item called dental insurance.

Activities:

- ❖ Click **Settings** tab
- ❖ Click **Payments and deductions** link
- ❖ Click **New** (bottom right)
- ❖ Click **Insurance benefit.** Click **Next**
- ❖ Click **Dental Insurance.** Click **Next**
- ❖ Click **Pre-Tax Employee-Paid Dental**. Click **Next**
- ❖ Deduction Name: Accept **Dental Insurance**
- ❖ Default Rate or Amount: Type **10.00**
- ❖ Default Annual Limit: Type **260.00**. Click **Next**
- ❖ Payee: Select **HMO of America**
- ❖ Account Number: Type **HMO 456789**. Click **Finish**
- ❖ Do you want to group…? Click **Yes**. Click **Finish**

Edit Old Payroll Item

During the month, you may discover certain rates or account names need to be changed. You go to the settings tab and choose the area you want to update and after completing the windows you click the save button where necessary.

Activities:

- ❖ Click **Settings** tab
- ❖ Click **Payments and deductions** link
- ❖ Double click **Health Insurance**
- ❖ Default Rate: Accept **20.00**
- ❖ Default Annual limit: Type **520.00**
- ❖ Click **Save**
- ❖ Double click **Union Dues**
- ❖ Default Rate: Accept **10.00**
- ❖ Default Annual limit: Type **260.00**
- ❖ Click **Save**

Update Employee Payroll Items

Any time you add new items or make changes to the items, you check the affected employees to make sure they have the have been updated with the new items. Here you will be adding dental insurance to Fate.

Activities:

- ❖ Click **Employees** tab
- ❖ Double click **Fate Acres**
- ❖ Scroll down to **Payments and Deductions**
- ❖ Click **More Lines**
- ❖ Select **Dental Insurance**
- ❖ Click **Save** (bottom right)

Pay Employee

After you have verified the affected employees have the new item, you are ready to process the weekly, biweekly or monthly paychecks. Not necessary, but you might want to check if the employees are all listed in the employee list window.

Activities:

- ❖ Click **Employees** tab
- ❖ You're going to pay Fates Acres
- ❖ Make sure employee is in the window

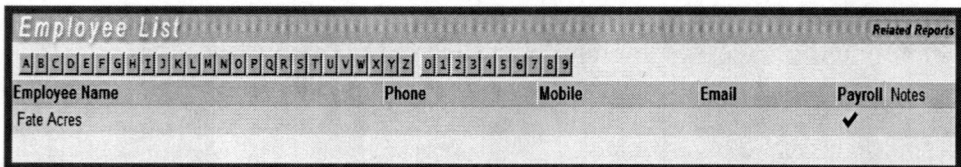

- ❖ Click **Paychecks** tab
- ❖ Pay Period: Select **1/2/2009 – 1/15/2009**
- ❖ Check Date: Accept **1/15/2009**. Click **Continue**
- ❖ Checkmark **Fate Acres**. Click **Edit & Create** (Next to 80:00)
- ❖ Scroll down to **Compensation** box. Click **Edit...**
- ❖ Hourly: Accept **80:00**
- ❖ Overtime: Type **1:04** (with colon)
- ❖ Bonus: Type **5,000**
- ❖ Commission: Type **10,000**
- ❖ Scroll down to **After-Tax Payments and Deductions**. Click **Edit...**

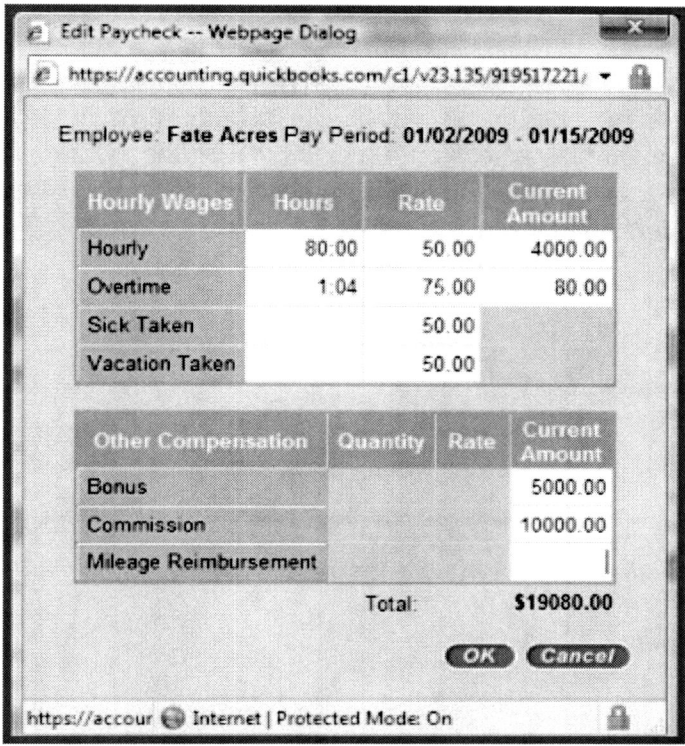

- ❖ Union Dues: Delete **10.00**. Click **OK**
- ❖ Right of the window. **Non-Taxable Company Payment**. Click **Edit**
- ❖ 401 (k) Match. Delete **5%**. Click **OK**
- ❖ Total Check is **12,212.67**
- ❖ Click **Save** (bottom right)

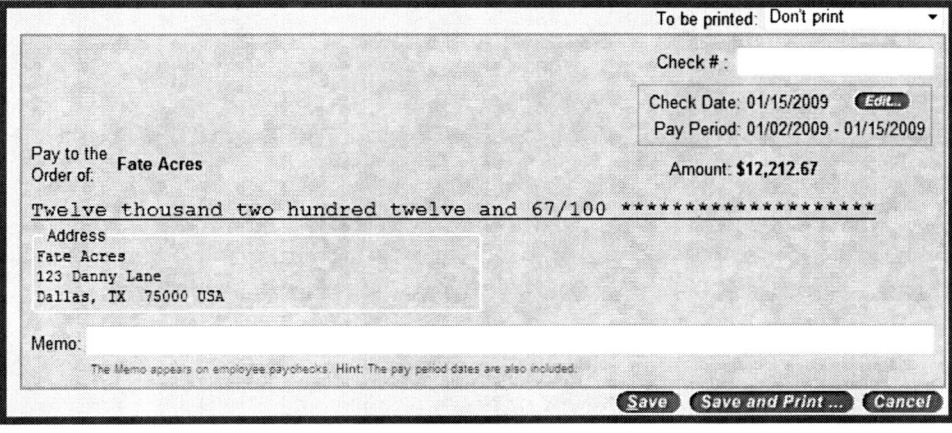

Run Reports

At this time you want to run the various reports to make sure the number are accurate. You want to see the employees' paychecks and the payment totals to the federal and state governments are what you expected. Run the vacation and sick report to see the balances are correct. The main purpose of reports is to verify your work to confirm the numbers are correctly reported.

Activities:

- ❖ Click **Reports** tab
- ❖ Click **Payroll Summary by Employee**
- ❖ From: Type **1/2/09**. To: Type **1/15/09**. Click **Run Report**
- ❖ Review report

Quick Payroll
Payroll Summary by Employee
January 2-15, 2009

Employee	Payment or Deduction	Hours	Amount
Fate Acres	**Compensation**		
SSN: 999-12-3456	Hourly	80:00	4,000.00
Fed Married/2/Does not apply/0.00	Overtime	1:04	80.00
	Bonus		5,000.00
	Commission		10,000.00
	Total Compensation	81:04	$19,080.00
	Pre-Tax Deductions		
	Dental Insurance		-10.00
	Health Insurance		-20.00
	Total Pre-Tax Deductions	0:00	$ -30.00
	Employee-Paid Taxes		
	Federal Income Tax		-5,380.00
	Medicare		-276.23
	Social Security		-1,181.10
	Total Employee-Paid Taxes	0:00	$ -6,837.33
	Net Pay	81:04	$12,212.67

- ❖ Click **Reports** tab
- ❖ Click **Payroll Summary Total**
- ❖ From: Type **1/2/09**. To: Type **1/15/09**. Click **Run Report**
- ❖ Review report
- ❖ Click **Reports** tab
- ❖ Click **Paychecks by Employee**
- ❖ From: Type **1/2/09**. To: Type **1/15/09**. Click **Run Report**
- ❖ Review report

Quick Payroll
Paychecks by Employee
January 2-15, 2009

Date	Type	Num	Memo/Description	Employee	Net Pay
Fate Acres					
01/15/2009	Paycheck			Fate Acres	12,212.67
Total for Fate Acres					**$12,212.67**
TOTAL					**$12,212.67**

- ❖ Click **Reports** tab
- ❖ Click **Payroll Liability Summary**
- ❖ From: Type **1/2/09.** To: Type **1/15/09.** Click **Run Report**
- ❖ Review report

Quick Payroll
Payroll Liability Balances Summary
January 2-15, 2009

	Jan 2-15, 2009	Balance
Federal Income Tax	5,380.00	$5,380.00
Federal Unemployment	56.00	$56.00
Medicare	276.23	$276.23
Medicare Company	276.23	$276.23
Social Security	1,181.10	$1,181.10
Social Security Company	1,181.10	$1,181.10
TX - Unemployment	243.00	$243.00
Health Insurance	20.00	$20.00
Dental Insurance	10.00	$10.00
TOTAL	**$8,623.66**	**$8,623.66**

Add New Employee

From time to time you will receive a file for a new employee that needs to be setup in the system for the next paycheck cycle. You complete the windows as you did earlier. You will be setting up Jerry Jordan, a salaried employee.

Activities:

- ❖ Click **Employees** tab
- ❖ Click **New** (bottom right)
- ❖ Full Name: Type **Jerry Jordan.** Press **Tab**
- ❖ Display Name As: Accept **Jerry Jordan**
- ❖ Print in Check As: Accept **Jerry Jordan.** Click **Next**
- ❖ Street: Type **456 Kenton Street**
- ❖ City: Type **Dallas**. State: Select **TX**
- ❖ Zip: Type **75000**. Country: Type **USA**. Click **Next**
- ❖ Social Security #: Type **999-45-6789**
- ❖ Hire Date: Type **1/1/2009**
- ❖ Date of Birth: Type **1/1/1971**
- ❖ Gender: Select **Male**. Click **Next**

Compensation Information

The employee's file will give you his or her compensation details. Both hourly and salaried employees will have 40 hours in the window if they work full time. You must double check the hourly or salary amount you entered are correct. Over and under payment in compensation window cannot be tolerated.

Activities:

- ❖ Is this employee paid by the hour? Click **No**. Click **Next**
- ❖ Do you pay this employee a salary? Click **Yes**
- ❖ Salary Name: Select **Salary**
- ❖ Annual Amount: Type **100,000**
- ❖ Hours per week: Accept **40:00**. Click **Next**

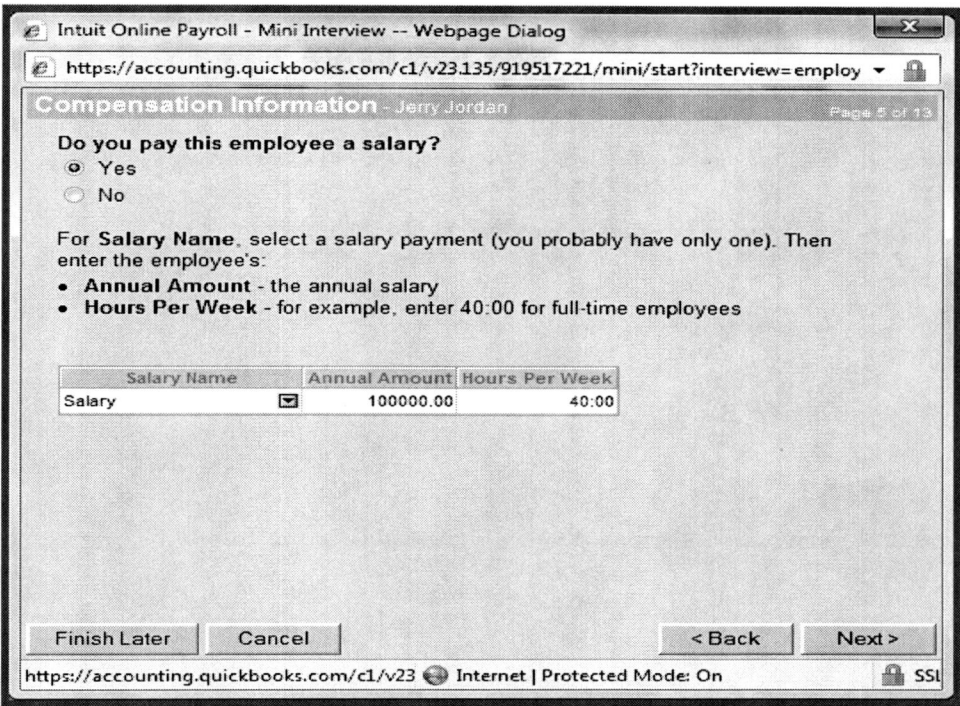

- ❖ Compensation Name box
- ❖ Select **Bonus**. Rate: **Leave blank**
- ❖ Select **Commission**. Rate: **Leave blank**
- ❖ Select **Mileage Reimbursement.** Rate: **Leave blank**. Click **Next**

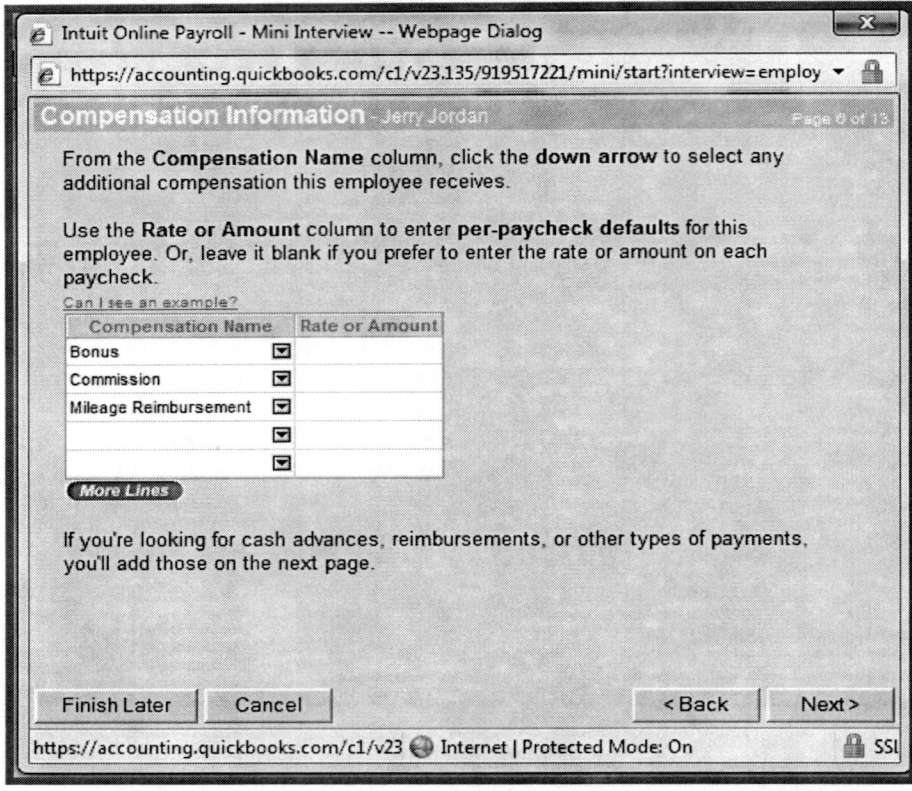

- ❖ Pmt and Deduct Name box
- ❖ Select **401 (k).** Rate **Leave blank**
- ❖ Select **401 (k) Match.** Rate: Accept **5%**
- ❖ Select **Health Insurance.** Rate: Accept **20.00**
- ❖ Select **Dental Insurance.** Rate: Accept **10.00**
- ❖ Select **Union Dues.** Rate: Accept **10.00.** Click **Next**

If you can't find a non-taxable compensation/payment, you go to settings tab, miscellaneous payments and deductions, generic non-taxable payment, and change the name to what you want.

If you can't find a taxable compensation/payment, you go to settings tab, miscellaneous payments and deductions, generic reimbursement, and change the name to what you want.

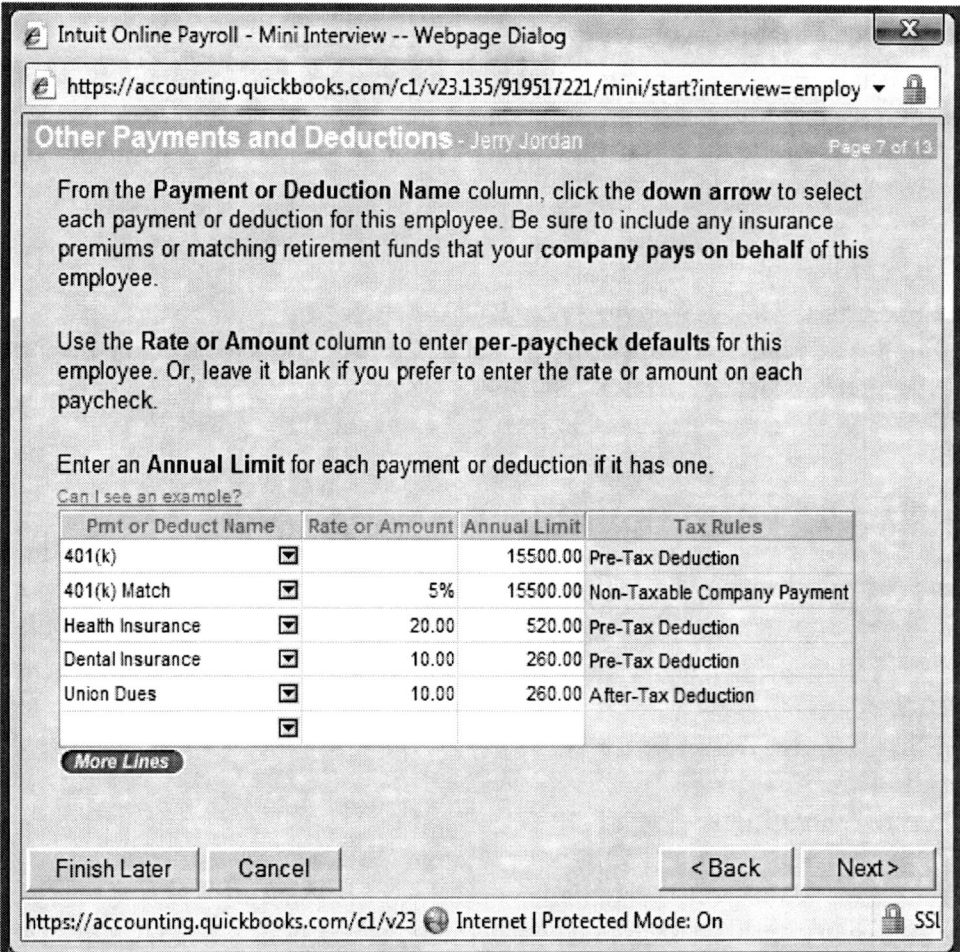

Paid Vacation Time

After the compensation numbers are completed, the next step is to complete the overtime window. Check the employment contract for details. A new employee will have a 0.00 for the opening balance.

Activities:

- ❖ Checkmark **This employee is eligible for Vacation time**
- ❖ Employee earns: Accept **4:00**. Select **hours per paycheck** (Very Important)
- ❖ Maximum Balance: Accept **104:00**
- ❖ Opening Balance: Type **0.00**. as of: Type **1/1/2009**. Click **Next**

Paid Sick Time

You also need to complete the sick window. Most companies offer both vacation and sick. When you run your report and you did not see vacation and sick figures an employee, it is a red flag you've omitted the setup. Again, the opening balance sick for any employee is 0.00.

Activities:

- ❖ Checkmark **This employee is eligible for Sick time**
- ❖ Employee earns: Accept **4:00**. Select **hours per paycheck** (Very Important)
- ❖ Maximum Balance: Accept **104:00**
- ❖ Opening Balance: Type **0.00**. as of: Type **1/1/2009**. Click **Next**

Federal Tax Information

In the federal tax information window, the most essential items are the filing status and the allowance. The employee would have completed the W-4 and a copy is found in the employment file that show has filing status and allowance details.

Activities:

- ❖ Filing Status: Select **Married**
- ❖ Allowance: Type **3**
- ❖ Extra Withholding: Type **0.00**
- ❖ Non Resident Alien Withholding: Accept **Does not apply**
- ❖ Checkmark **Subject to Medicare and Social Security**
- ❖ Checkmark **Subject to Federal Unemployment.** Click **Next**

State Tax Information

You must find out the employee's state of residency for tax purposes and complete the window as required.

Activities:

- ❖ State subject to withholding: Accept **Texas**
- ❖ State works in: Accept **Texas**. Click **Next**
- ❖ Checkmark **Subject to TX-Unemployment**
- ❖ Click **Finish**

Pay Employee

When you have completed the personal and tax related windows, it is time to pay employees and the paychecks tab is opened and completed. You will need to edit the paycheck details to match the items and the amounts you are paying for the period. You edit the paycheck to match employees' requests.

Activities:

- ❖ Click **Paychecks** tab
- ❖ Pay Period: Select **1/2/2009 – 1/15/2009**
- ❖ Check Date: Accept **1/15/2009**. Click **Continue**
- ❖ Checkmark **Jerry Jordan.** Click **Edit & Create**
- ❖ Scroll down to **Compensation** box. Click **Edit...**
- ❖ Bonus: Type **20,000**
- ❖ Commission: Type **10,000**. Click **OK**
- ❖ Scroll down to **After-Tax Payments and Deductions**. Click **Edit...**
- ❖ Union Dues: Delete **10.00**. Click **OK**
- ❖ Right of the window. **Non-Taxable Company Payments**. Click **Edit**
- ❖ 401(k) Match. Delete **5%**
- ❖ Total Check is **20,728.22**
- ❖ Click **Save** (bottom right)

> The compensation box will have the following:
> Salary: 3,846.15
> Bonus: 20,000
> Commission: 10,000

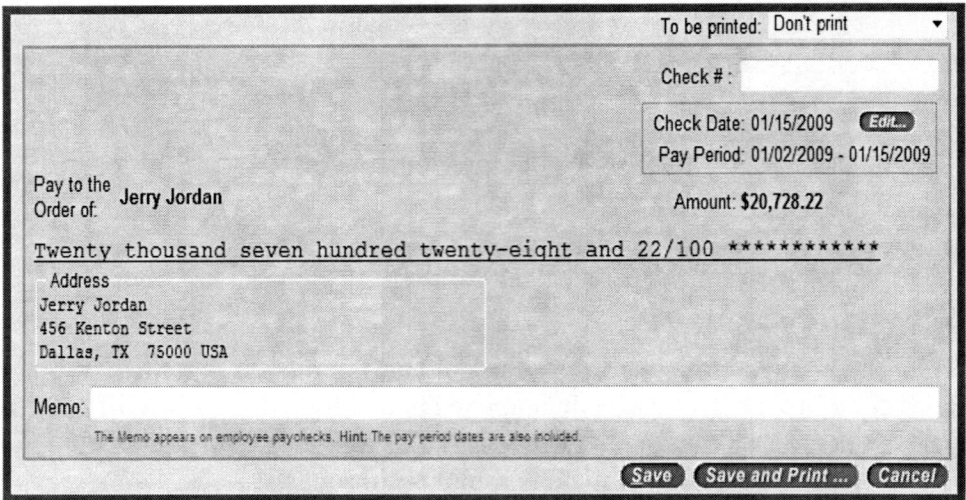

Run Reports

There are so many reports to run; you just have to process the ones that confirm your totals to verify your activities. The basic reports include the following: payroll summary by employee, payroll summary total, paychecks by employee, and the payroll liability summary.

Activities:

- ❖ Click **Reports** tab
- ❖ Click **Payroll Summary by Employee**
- ❖ From: Type **1/2/09.** To: Type **1/15/09.** Click **Run Report**
- ❖ Review report
- ❖ Click **Reports** tab
- ❖ Click **Payroll Summary Total**
- ❖ From: Type **1/2/09.** To: Type **1/15/09.** Click **Run Report**
- ❖ Review report
- ❖ Click **Reports** tab
- ❖ Click **Paychecks by Employee**
- ❖ From: Type **1/2/09.** To: Type **1/15/09.** Click **Run Report**
- ❖ Review report

Quick Payroll
Paychecks by Employee
January 2-15, 2009

Date	Type	Num	Memo/Description	Employee	Net Pay
Fate Acres					
01/15/2009	Paycheck			Fate Acres	12,212.67
Total for Fate Acres					**$12,212.67**
Jerry Jordan					
01/15/2009	Paycheck			Jerry Jordan	20,728.22
Total for Jerry Jordan					**$20,728.22**
TOTAL					**$32,940.89**

- ❖ Click **Reports** tab
- ❖ Click **Payroll Liability Summary**
- ❖ From: Type **1/2/09.** To: Type **1/15/09.** Click **Run Report**
- ❖ Review report

Quick Payroll
Payroll Liability Balances Summary
January 2-15, 2009

	Jan 2-15, 2009	Balance
Federal Income Tax	15,881.00	$15,881.00
Federal Unemployment	112.00	$112.00
Medicare	766.56	$766.56
Medicare Company	766.56	$766.56
Social Security	3,277.70	$3,277.70
Social Security Company	3,277.70	$3,277.70
TX - Unemployment	486.00	$486.00
Health Insurance	40.00	$40.00
Dental Insurance	20.00	$20.00
TOTAL	**$24,627.52**	**$24,627.52**

Add New Item: Vision Insurance

Vision as an insurance benefit paid by the employee must be approved also by the employee. The premium amount is multiplied by 26 pay period or 52 weeks to get the 130.00 annual limit.

Activities:

* Click **Settings** tab
* Click **Payments and deductions** link
* Click **New** (bottom right)
* Click **Insurance benefit**. Click **Next**
* Click **Vision Insurance.** Click **Next**
* Click **Pre-Tax Employee-Paid Vision**. Click **Next**
* Deduction Name: Accept **Vision Insurance**
* Default Rate or Amount: Type **5.00**
* Default Annual Limit: Type **130.00.** Click **Next**
* Payee: Select **HMO of America**
* Account Number: Type **HMO 120123**. Click **Finish**
* Do you want to group…? Click **Yes**. Click **Finish**

Add New Item: Charity Donation

Charity donation is also approved and paid by the employee and therefore must be documented. The employee will fill out a form to stipulate the amount and designate a charitable organization to receive the funds.

Activities:

* You're in **Other Payments and Deductions** window
* Click **New** (bottom right)
* Click **Miscellaneous payment or deduction**. Click **Next**
* Click **Charity Donation**. Click **Next**
* Deduction Name: Accept **Charity Donation**
* Default Rate or Amount: Type **5.00**
* Default Annual Limit: Type **130.00.** Click **Next**
* Payee: Select **Money Mgt of America**
* Account Number: Type **MMA 120140**. Click **Finish**
* Do you want to group…? Click **Yes**. Click **Finish**

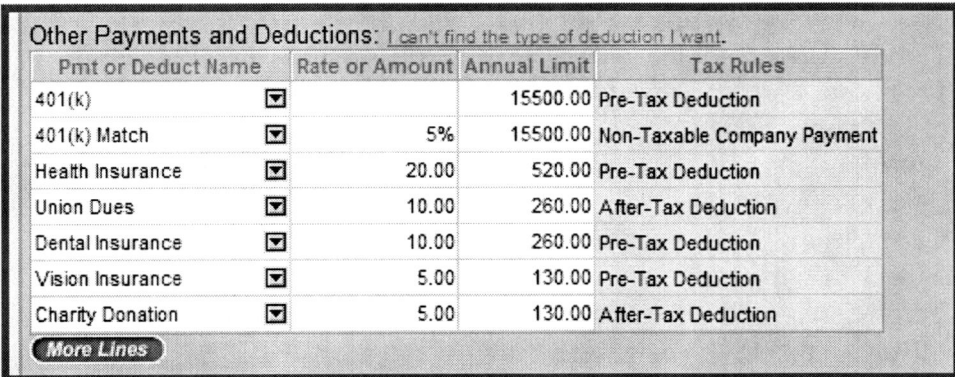

Other Payments and Deductions List	Related Reports
Name	**Ty**
401(k)	401(k)
401(k) Match	401(k) Compan
Dental Insurance	Pre-Tax Emplo
Health Insurance	Pre-Tax Emplo
Vision Insurance	Pre-Tax Emplo
Charity Donation	Charity Donatio
Union Dues	Union Dues

Update Employee Payroll Items

After the payroll items are completed in the setting tab window, the next step is to update the affected employees' windows with the new items. In this case you will pull in vision and charitable donation into Fate's window.

Activities:

- ❖ Click **Employees** tab
- ❖ Double click **Fate Acres**
- ❖ Scroll to **Other Payments and Deductions**
- ❖ Click **More Lines**
- ❖ Select **Vision Insurance.** Rate: Accept **5.00.** Annual: Accept **130.00**
- ❖ Select **Charity Donation.** Rate: Accept **5.00.** Annual: Accept **130.00**
- ❖ Click **Save** (bottom right)

Other Payments and Deductions: I can't find the type of deduction I want.

Pmt or Deduct Name		Rate or Amount	Annual Limit	Tax Rules
401(k)	▼		15500.00	Pre-Tax Deduction
401(k) Match	▼	5%	15500.00	Non-Taxable Company Payment
Health Insurance	▼	20.00	520.00	Pre-Tax Deduction
Union Dues	▼	10.00	260.00	After-Tax Deduction
Dental Insurance	▼	10.00	260.00	Pre-Tax Deduction
Vision Insurance	▼	5.00	130.00	Pre-Tax Deduction
Charity Donation	▼	5.00	130.00	After-Tax Deduction

(More Lines)

- ❖ Double click **Jerry Jordan**
- ❖ Scroll to **Other Payments and Deductions**
- ❖ Click **More Lines**
- ❖ Select **Vision Insurance.** Rate: Accept **5.00.** Annual: Accept **130.00**
- ❖ Select **Charity Donation**. Rate: Accept **5.00.** Annual: Accept **130.00**
- ❖ Click **Save** (bottom right)

Pmt or Deduct Name	Rate or Amount	Annual Limit	Tax Rules
401(k)	▼	15500.00	Pre-Tax Deduction
401(k) Match	▼ 5%	15500.00	Non-Taxable Company Payment
Health Insurance	▼ 20.00	520.00	Pre-Tax Deduction
Dental Insurance	▼ 10.00	260.00	Pre-Tax Deduction
Union Dues	▼ 10.00	260.00	After-Tax Deduction
Vision Insurance	▼ 5.00	130.00	Pre-Tax Deduction
Charity Donation	▼ 5.00	130.00	After-Tax Deduction

Other Payments and Deductions: I can't find the type of deduction I want.

(More Lines)

Pay Employee: Fate Acres

We are in a new cycle; you have added new items or updated old ones, and have pulled in those items into the affected employee's window, the next step is to pay employee through the paycheck tab window.

Activities:

- ❖ Click **Paychecks** tab
- ❖ Pay Period: Select **1/16/2009 – 1/29/2009**
- ❖ Check Date: Accept **1/29/2009.** Click **Continue**
- ❖ Checkmark **Fate Acres.** Click **Edit & Create** (Next to 80:00)
- ❖ Scroll down to **Compensation** box. Click **Edit…**
- ❖ Hourly. Hours: **80:00.** Rate: **50.** Current Amount: **4,000**
- ❖ Overtime. Hours: Type **4:00.** Rate: 75. Current: 300
- ❖ Sick Taken. Hours: Type **1.** Rate: 50. Current: 50
- ❖ Vacation Taken. Hours: Type **2.** Rate: 50. Current: 100
- ❖ Bonus: Type **10,000**
- ❖ Commission: Type **5,000**
- ❖ Mileage Reimbursement: Type **25.** Click **OK**
- ❖ Scroll down to **Pre-Tax Deductions.** Click **Edit…**
- ❖ 401(k). Current: Type **100.** Click **OK**
- ❖ Total Check is **12,330.84**
- ❖ Click **Save** (bottom right)

> The compensation window has these current amounts:
>
> Hourly 4,000.00
> Overtime 300.00
> Sick Taken 50.00
> Vacation Taken 100.00
> Bonus 10,000.00
> Commission 5,000.00
> Mileage Reimb 25.00

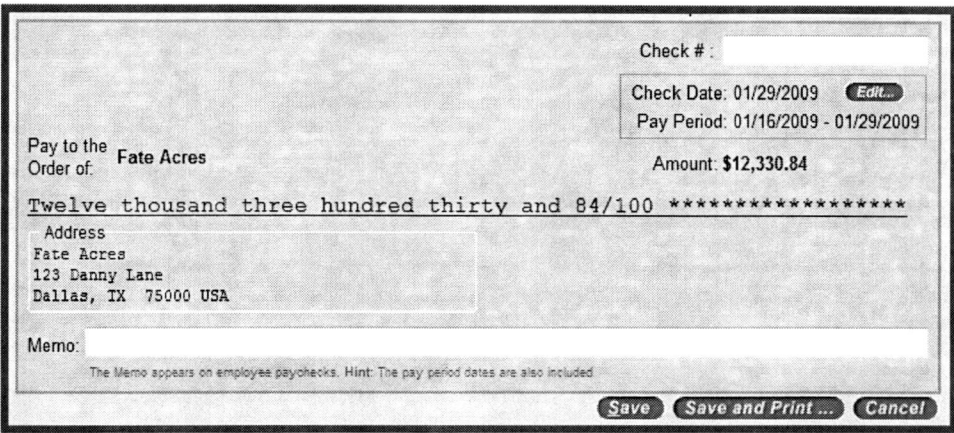

Pay Employee: Jerry Jordan

You have two employees to pay; and you have processed Fate's paycheck. The next step is to pay Jerry Jordan. Because Jerry is a salaried employee, the system calculates his salary amount and defaults it in the window.

Activities:

- ❖ Checkmark **Jerry Jordan.** Click **Edit & Create**
- ❖ Scroll down to **Compensation** box. Click **Edit...**
- ❖ Sick Taken. Hours: Type **2**
- ❖ Vacation Taken. Hours: Type **2**

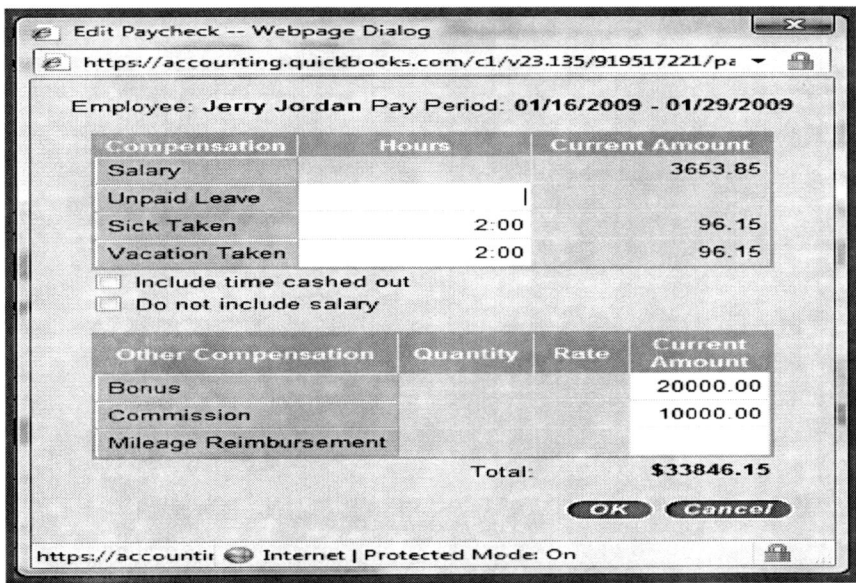

❖ Bonus: Type **20,000**
❖ Commission: Type **10,000**. Click **OK**
❖ Scroll down to **Pre-Tax Deductions**. Click **Edit...**
❖ 401(k). Current: Type **100**. Click **OK**
❖ Total Check is **20,644.59**
❖ Click **Save** (bottom right)

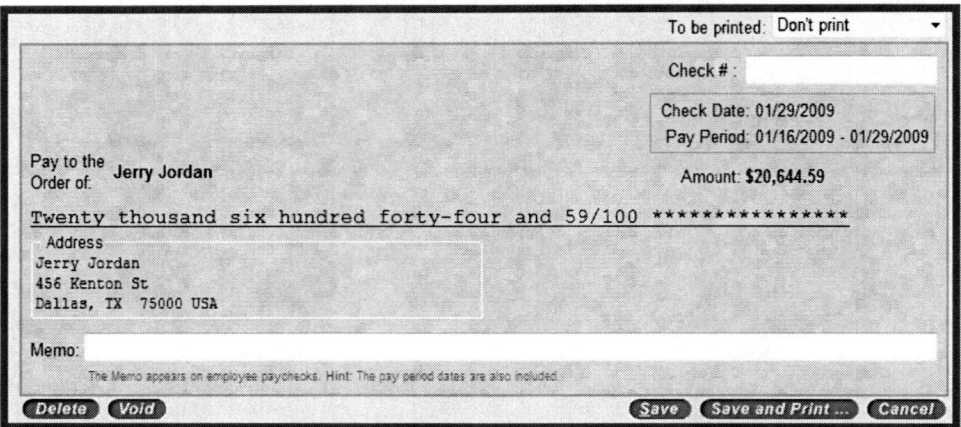

Run Reports

After you've paid all the employees, the next steps are to pay vendors, process tax forms. But we'll skip these two and assume they are not available for the practice, but they might be available depending on the date you're processing payroll. You will run the four basic reports to verify you numbers.

Activities:

❖ Click **Reports** tab
❖ Click **Payroll Summary by Employee**
❖ From: Type **1/2/09.** To: Type **1/29/09**. Click **Run Report**
❖ Review report
❖ Click **Reports** tab
❖ Click **Payroll Summary Total**
❖ From: Type **1/2/09.** To: Type **1/29/09**. Click **Run Report**
❖ Review report
❖ Click **Reports** tab
❖ Click **Paychecks by Employee**
❖ From: Type **1/2/09**. To: Type **1/29/09**. Click **Run Report**
❖ Review report
❖ Click **Reports** tab

- ❖ Click **Payroll Liability Summary**
- ❖ From: Type **1/2/09.** To: Type **1/29/09.** Click **Run Report**
- ❖ Review report

Run Vacation Report

For the remainder of this chapter we will look at what happens when an employee is no longer with the company. First we run various reports to gather employee balance. One of those reports is the vacation report. You want to see how many vacation hours are still remaining.

Activities:

- ❖ Click **Reports** tab
- ❖ Click **Vacation Plan Detail by Employee**
- ❖ From: Type **1/2/09**. To: Type **1/29/09**. Click **Run Report**
- ❖ Review report

Quick Payroll
Vacation Plan Detail by Employee
As of January 29, 2009

Date	Reason	Hours	Balance
Fate Acres			
01/15/2009	Earned on paycheck	4:00:00	4:00:00
01/29/2009	Taken on Paycheck	-2:00:00	2:00:00
01/29/2009	Earned on paycheck	4:00:00	6:00:00
Total for Fate Acres		6:00:00	
Jerry Jordan			
01/15/2009	Earned on paycheck	4:00:00	4:00:00
01/29/2009	Taken on Paycheck	-2:00:00	2:00:00
01/29/2009	Earned on paycheck	4:00:00	6:00:00
Total for Jerry Jordan		6:00:00	
TOTAL		12:00:00	

Run Sick Report

You also need to run the sick report to ascertain the balances for each employee. As we will see in a minute you might have to pay for those remaining hours to the employees.

Activities:

- ❖ Click **Reports** tab
- ❖ Click **Sick Plan Detail by Employee**
- ❖ From: Type **1/2/09**. To: Type **1/29/09**. Click **Run Report**
- ❖ Review report

Quick Payroll
Sick Plan Detail by Employee
As of January 29, 2009

Date	Reason	Hours	Balance
Fate Acres			
01/15/2009	Earned on paycheck	4:00:00	4:00:00
01/29/2009	Taken on Paycheck	-1:00:00	3:00:00
01/29/2009	Earned on paycheck	4:00:00	7:00:00
Total for Fate Acres		7:00:00	
Jerry Jordan			
01/15/2009	Earned on paycheck	4:00:00	4:00:00
01/29/2009	Taken on Paycheck	-2:00:00	2:00:00
01/29/2009	Earned on paycheck	4:00:00	6:00:00
Total for Jerry Jordan		6:00:00	
TOTAL		13:00:00	

Add New Item: Wage Garnishment

Let's go through the cycle one more time: you add new items or update old ones, you update employees with the new items, you pay employees, you pay vendors, you process tax forms, and you run reports. Here you're going to add a new item called wage garnishment.

Activities:

* ❖ Click **Settings** tab
* ❖ Click **Payments and deductions** link
* ❖ Click **New** (bottom right)
* ❖ Click **Miscellaneous payment or deduction**. Click **Next**
* ❖ Click **Wage Garnishment.** Click **Next**
* ❖ Deduction Name: Accept **Wage Garnishment**
* ❖ How is it calculated? Click **Dollar amount**
* ❖ Default Rate or Amount: Type **10.00**
* ❖ Default Annual Limit: Type **260.00.** Click **Next**
* ❖ Payee: Select **Money Mgt of America**
* ❖ Account Number: Type **MMA 456123**. Click **Finish**
* ❖ Do you want to group…? Click **Yes**. Click **Finish**

Add New Item: Cash Advance & Repayment

Next, you are going to add another new item called cash advance and cash advance repayment. Keep an eye on some items that have opposites such as: loan and loan repayment. Anytime you set up an item where you pay and have to take it back every month, then you will have the item and the item repayment.

Activities:

* ❖ You're still in the **Other Payments and Deductions List** window
* ❖ Click **New** (bottom right)
* ❖ Click **Miscellaneous payment or deduction**. Click **Next**
* ❖ Click **Cash Advance**. Click **Next**
* ❖ Payment Name: Accept **Cash Advance**
* ❖ Default Rate or Amount: Type **0.00**
* ❖ Default Annual Limit: Type **0.00**. Click **Next**
* ❖ Click **Finish**
* ❖ Click **New** (bottom right)
* ❖ Click **Miscellaneous payment or deduction**. Click **Next**
* ❖ Click **Cash Advance Repayment**. Click **Next**

❖ Payment Name: Accept **Cash Advance Repayment**
❖ Default Rate or Amount: Type **0.00**
❖ Default Annual Limit: Type **0.00.** Click **Next**
❖ Click **Finish**

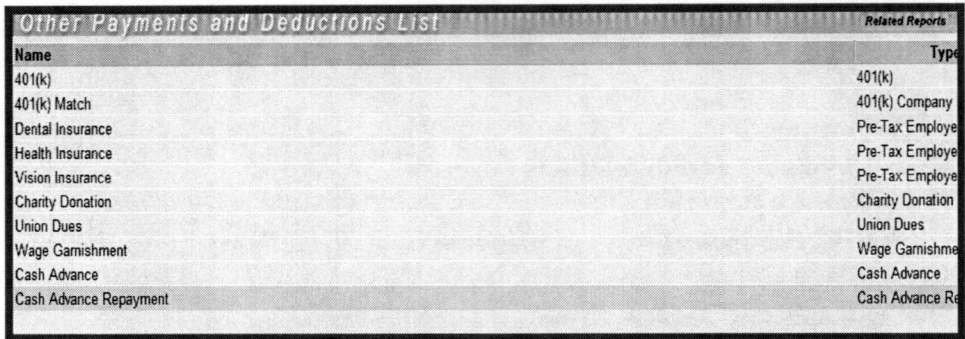

Name	Type
401(k)	401(k)
401(k) Match	401(k) Company
Dental Insurance	Pre-Tax Employe
Health Insurance	Pre-Tax Employe
Vision Insurance	Pre-Tax Employe
Charity Donation	Charity Donation
Union Dues	Union Dues
Wage Garnishment	Wage Garnishme
Cash Advance	Cash Advance
Cash Advance Repayment	Cash Advance Re

Update Employee Payroll Items

You have created new items, it is time to update the affected employee with the new items. In this case you will pull in the new items namely: cash advance, cash advance repayment, and wage garnishment.

Activities:

❖ Click **Employees** tab
❖ Double click **Fate Acres**
❖ Scroll to **Other Payments and Deductions**
❖ Click **More Lines**
❖ Select **Cash Advance**
❖ Select **Cash Advance Repayment**
❖ Click **More Lines**
❖ Select **Wage Garnishment**
❖ Click **Save** (bottom right)

Other Payments and Deductions: I can't find the type of deduction I want.		Rate or Amount	Annual Limit	Tax Rules
401(k)	▼		15500.00	Pre-Tax Deduction
401(k) Match	▼	5%	15500.00	Non-Taxable Company Payment
Health Insurance	▼	20.00	520.00	Pre-Tax Deduction
Union Dues	▼	10.00	260.00	After-Tax Deduction
Dental Insurance	▼	10.00	260.00	Pre-Tax Deduction
Vision Insurance	▼	5.00	130.00	Pre-Tax Deduction
Charity Donation	▼	5.00	130.00	After-Tax Deduction
Cash Advance	▼			Non-Taxable Payment
Cash Advance Repaymen	▼			After-Tax Deduction
Wage Garnishment	▼	10.00	260.00	After-Tax Deduction
	▼			

More Lines

- ❖ You're still in the **Employee List** window
- ❖ Double click **Jerry Jordan**
- ❖ Scroll to **Other Payments and Deductions**
- ❖ Click **More Lines**
- ❖ Select **Cash Advance**
- ❖ Select **Cash Advance Repayment**
- ❖ Click **More Lines**
- ❖ Select **Wage Garnishment**
- ❖ Click **Save** (bottom right)

Other Payments and Deductions: I can't find the type of deduction I want.		Rate or Amount	Annual Limit	Tax Rules
401(k)	▼		15500.00	Pre-Tax Deduction
401(k) Match	▼	5%	15500.00	Non-Taxable Company Payment
Health Insurance	▼	20.00	520.00	Pre-Tax Deduction
Dental Insurance	▼	10.00	260.00	Pre-Tax Deduction
Union Dues	▼	10.00	260.00	After-Tax Deduction
Vision Insurance	▼	5.00	130.00	Pre-Tax Deduction
Charity Donation	▼	5.00	130.00	After-Tax Deduction
Cash Advance	▼			Non-Taxable Payment
Cash Advance Repaymen	▼			After-Tax Deduction
Wage Garnishment	▼	10.00	260.00	After-Tax Deduction
	▼			

More Lines

Pay Employee: Fate Acres

After you've created new items and updated employees with the new items, it's time to pay employees. You select the pay period and you click continue. In the next window, you will checkmark the employee and click the edit/create beside the name.

Activities:

❖ Click **Paychecks** tab
❖ Pay Period: Select **1/30/2009 – 2/12/2009**
❖ Check Date: Accept **2/12/2009**. Click **Continue**
❖ Checkmark **Fate Acres.** Click **Edit & Create** (Next to 80:00)
❖ Scroll down to **Compensation** box. Click **Edit...**
❖ Hourly. Hours: Type **73:30** (with colon)
❖ Sick Taken. Hours: Type **11**
❖ Vacation Taken. Hours: Type **10.** Click **OK**

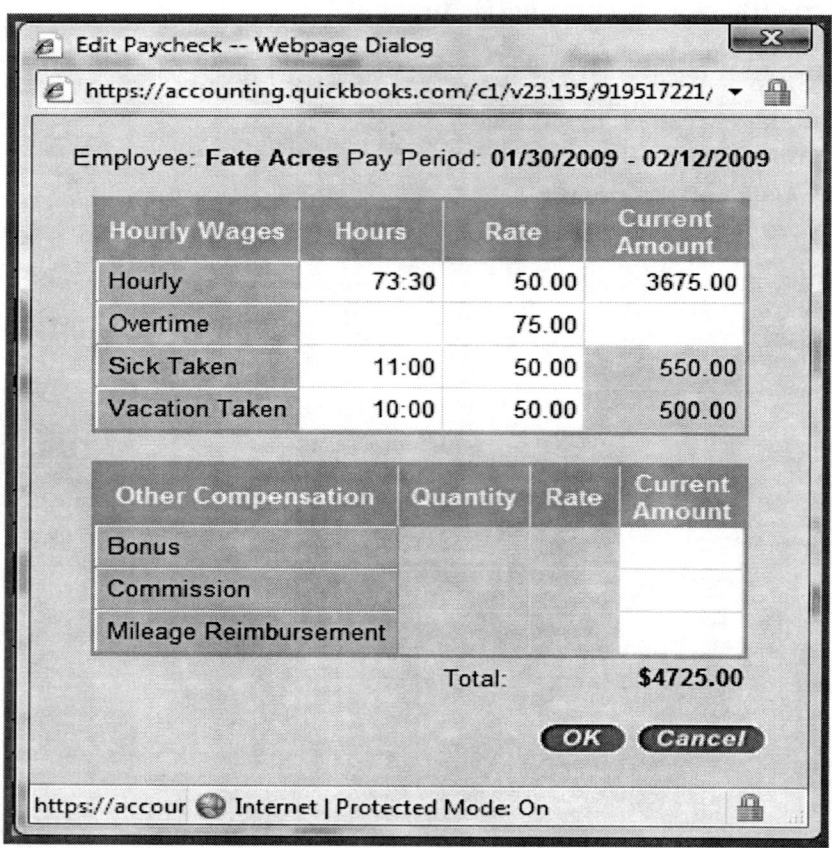

Edit Paycheck -- Webpage Dialog

https://accounting.quickbooks.com/c1/v23.135/919517221/

Employee: **Fate Acres** Pay Period: **01/30/2009 - 02/12/2009**

Hourly Wages	Hours	Rate	Current Amount
Hourly	73:30	50.00	3675.00
Overtime		75.00	
Sick Taken	11:00	50.00	550.00
Vacation Taken	10:00	50.00	500.00

Other Compensation	Quantity	Rate	Current Amount
Bonus			
Commission			
Mileage Reimbursement			

Total: $4725.00

OK   Cancel

https://accour   Internet | Protected Mode: On

❖ Scroll down to **Pre-Tax Deductions**. Click **Edit...**
❖ Health. Delete **20**
❖ Dental. Delete **10**
❖ Vision. Delete **5.** Click **OK**
❖ Scroll down to **After-Tax Payment and Deductions.** Click **Edit...**
❖ Cash Advance. Type **10,000**
❖ Union Dues. Delete **10**
❖ Charity Donations. Delete **5**
❖ Cash Advance Repayment. Type **100**
❖ Wage Garnishment. Accept **10**. Click **OK**

❖ Right side of the window. **Non-Taxable Company Payment**. Click **Edit…**
❖ 401(k) Match. Delete **5%**. Press **Tab**. Click **OK**
❖ Total check is **13,493.54**
❖ Click **Save** (bottom right)

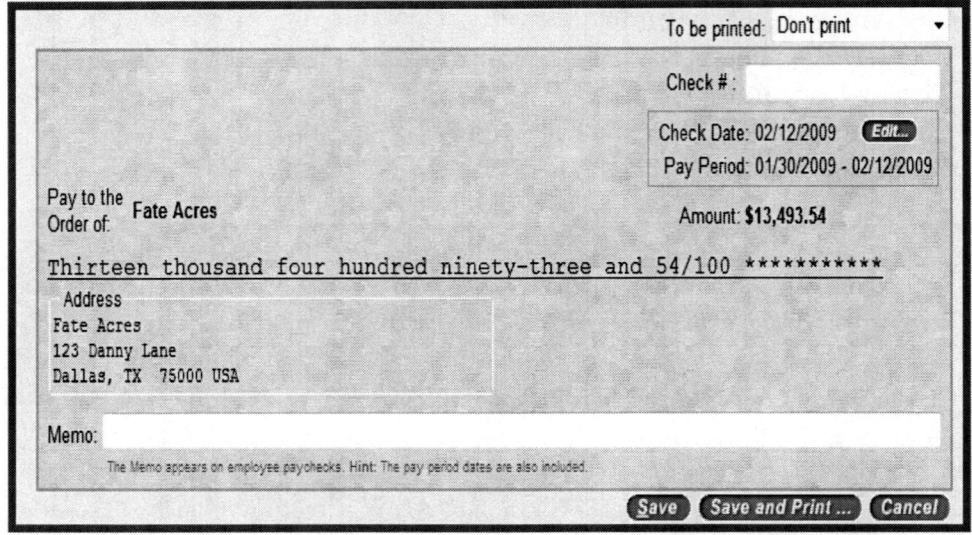

Pay Employee: Jerry Jordan

You've paid Fate Acres, the next employee is Jerry Jordan. After you checkmarked Jerry, you click edit & create which takes you to the check window where you edit the check to match your expectations. Unpaid Leave is the sick leave you took outside your normal accrue hours on emergency, hence it's a subtraction.

Activities:

❖ You're still in the **Create Paychecks** window
❖ Checkmark **Jerry Jordan.** Click **Edit & Create**
❖ Scroll down to **Compensation** box. Click **Edit…**
❖ Unpaid Leave. Hours: Type **8**
❖ Click **Include time cashed out** (Very Important)
❖ Sick Cashed Out: Type **10**
❖ Vacation Cashed Out: Type **10**. Click **OK**

Note! Cash outs are not income to a salaried employee. They are used to zero out the sick and vacation report balances and are also subtracted from the salary amount. Add the cash outs to the salary to get the full monthly salary amount.

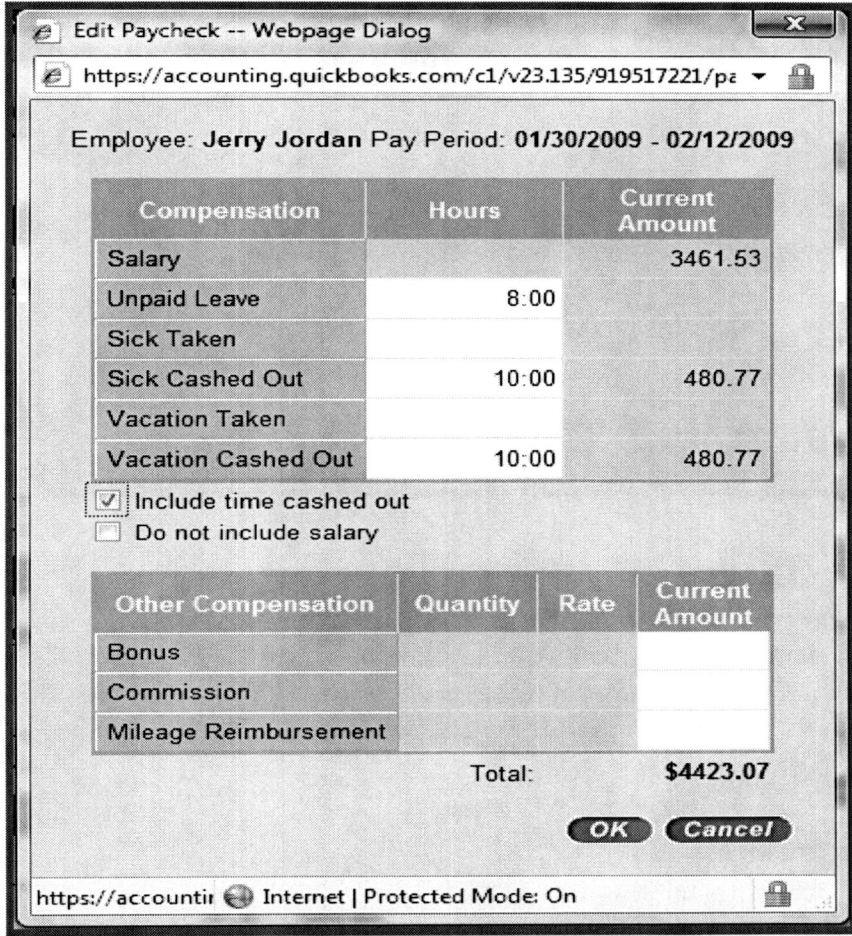

- ❖ Scroll down to **Pre-Tax Deductions**. Click **Edit...**
- ❖ Health Insurance. Delete **20**
- ❖ Dental Insurance. Delete **10**
- ❖ Vision Insurance. Delete **5**. Click **OK**
- ❖ Scroll down to **After-Tax Payment and Deduction**. Click **Edit...**
- ❖ Cash Advance. Current: Type **10,000**
- ❖ Union Dues. Delete **10**
- ❖ Charity Donation. Delete **5**
- ❖ Cash Advance Repayment. Type **100**
- ❖ Wage Garnishment. Accept **10**. Click **OK**
- ❖ Right of the window. **Non-Taxable Company Payment**. Click **Edit...**
- ❖ 401 (k) Match. Delete **5%**
- ❖ Total check is **13,323.71**
- ❖ Click **Save** (bottom right

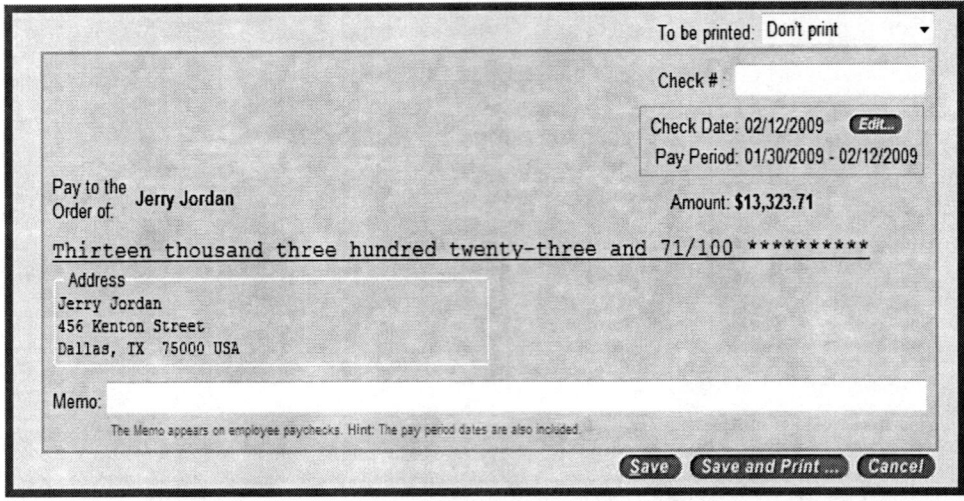

Pay Liabilities

You've paid employees, the next step is to pay vendors. The payment tab window will default the payments that are due based on the payment schedules you selected during setup. If you want to edit a check to pay or not pay, you double click on the vendor itself and this opens the check window for editing.

Activities:

- ❖ Click **Payments** Tab
- ❖ This is where you make payment
- ❖ Under **Payments** column
- ❖ Double click **HMO of America**
- ❖ Review window details
- ❖ Click **Cancel**
- ❖ You may review other payments

You checkmark the "Send By" box in the payments window to select all the vendors. To pay a single vendor you checkmark it.

Liability Payments Center

Upcoming Payments

	Send By ?	Payment	Period	Status ?	Amount
☐	3/31/09	HMO of America	Q1 2009	Not Due Yet	130.00
☐	3/31/09	Money Mgt of America	Q1 2009	Not Due Yet	2896.06
☐	3/31/09	National Union	Q1 2009	Not Due Yet	20.00
☐	4/30/09	Federal 941/944	Q1 2009	Not Due Yet	50874.61
☐	4/30/09	TX Unemployment Insurance	Q1 2009	Not Due Yet	486.00
☐	2/1/10	Federal 940	2009	Not Due Yet	112.00
				Total Selected:	0.00

View/Pay

Run Reports

We will skip the next step, process tax forms, because the forms may not be ready. Otherwise you click the tax forms tab and process the forms; it is very easy to complete the process. Remember these are just a few of the reports you can run. Preview some of these reports at your convenience and see what they look like and what numbers are reported. You will be running the four basic reports in this section.

Activities:
❖ Click **Reports** tab
❖ Click **Payroll Summary by Employee**
❖ From: Type **1/2/09**. To: Type **2/12/09**. Click **Run Report**
❖ Review report
❖ Click **Reports** tab
❖ Click **Payroll Summary Total**
❖ From: Type **1/2/09**. To: Type **2/12/09**. Click **Run Report**
❖ Review report
❖ Click **Reports** tab
❖ Click **Paychecks by Employee**
❖ From: Type **1/2/09.** To: Type **2/12/09.** Click **Run Report**
❖ Review report
❖ Click **Reports** tab
❖ Click **Payroll Liability Summary**
❖ From: Type **1/2/09**. To: Type **2/12/09**. Click **Run Report**
❖ Review report

Quick Payroll
Payroll Liability Balances Summary
January 2 - February 12, 2009

	Jan 2-31, 2009	Feb 1-12, 2009	Balance
Federal Income Tax	31,828.00	1,411.00	$33,239.00
Federal Unemployment	112.00	0.00	$112.00
Medicare	1,538.71	132.64	$1,671.35
Medicare Company	1,538.71	132.64	$1,671.35
Social Security	6,579.27	567.18	$7,146.45
Social Security Company	6,579.27	567.18	$7,146.45
TX - Unemployment	486.00	0.00	$486.00
Dental Insurance	40.00		$40.00
Health Insurance	80.00		$80.00
Vision Insurance	10.00		$10.00
401(k)	200.00		$200.00
401(k) Match	2,666.06		$2,666.06
Charity Donation	10.00		$10.00
Union Dues	20.00		$20.00
Wage Garnishment		20.00	$20.00
TOTAL	**$51,688.02**	**$2,830.64**	**$54,518.66**

Pay Employee: Prior Year

Tax forms have not been processed because all paychecks were made in the current year. You will create a check for Fate Acres for last year so you can have a check to pay and tax forms to process.

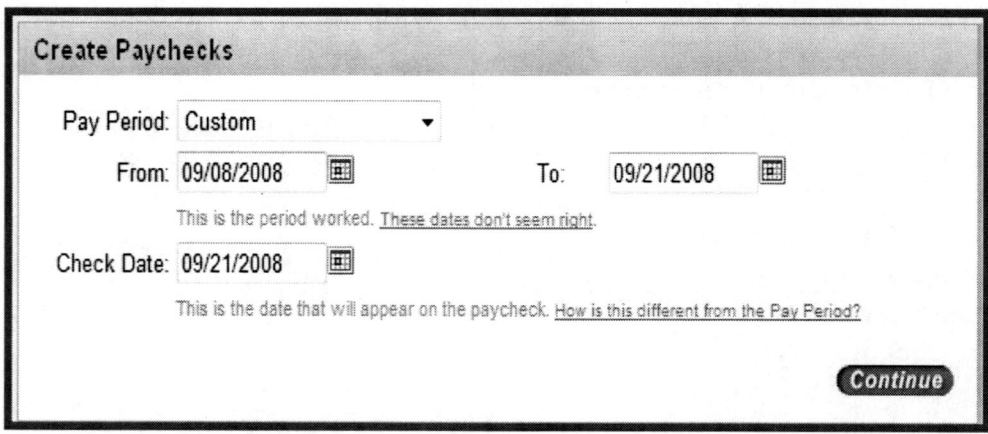

Activities:

- ❖ Click **Paychecks** tab
- ❖ Pay Period: Select **Custom**
- ❖ From: Type **9/8/08.** To: Type **9/21/08**
- ❖ Check Date: Accept **9/21/08.** Click **Continue**
- ❖ Checkmark **Fate Acres**. Click **Edit & Create** (next to 80:00)
- ❖ Non Taxable Company Payments (right of the window). Click **Edit…**
- ❖ 401 (k) Match. Press **Delete on 5%.** Click **OK**
- ❖ Click **Save** (bottom right of the window)

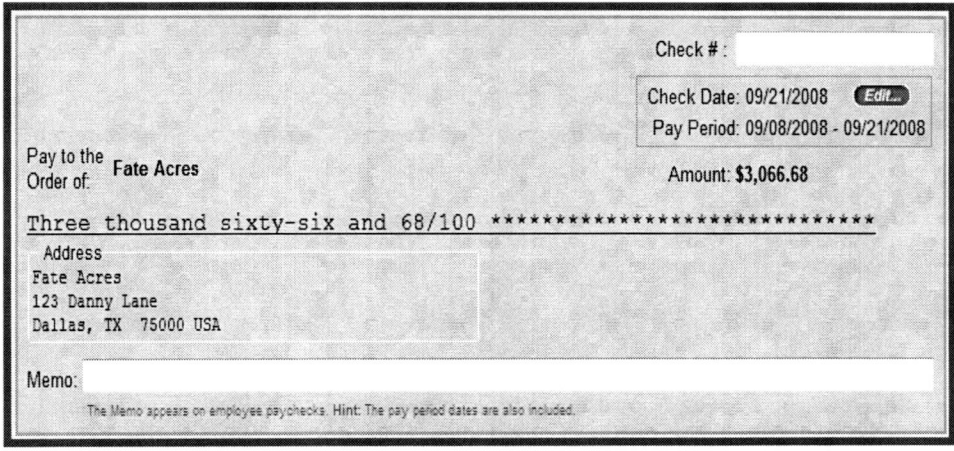

Pay Vendors: Prior Year

Now you've paid an employee for last year, you should have payments due to payroll vendors including the federal and state governments. Once you click the payments tab, overdue payments will be checkmarked and ready for payment.

Activities:

- ❖ Click **Payments** tab
- ❖ Look! You have overdue payments
- ❖ Click **View/Pay** (bottom right of Upcoming Payments box)
- ❖ Look! All checks are displayed for payment
- ❖ Click **Make Payment** (top right)
- ❖ Click **Done.**

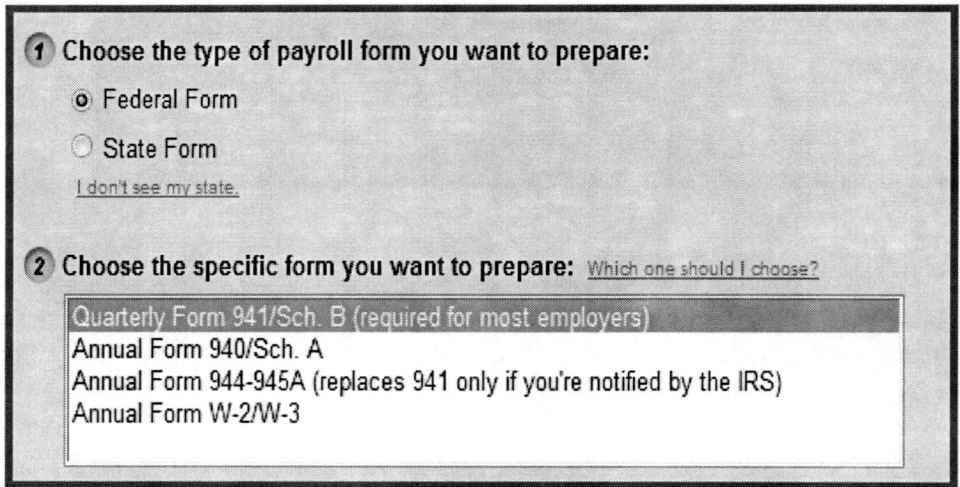

5 regular payments created ($1,344.65)				
Payment	**Period**	**Method**	**Status ?**	**Amount**
HMO of America	Q3 2008	Check	To Print	35.00
Money Mgt of America	Q3 2008	Check	To Print	15.00
National Union	Q3 2008	Check	To Print	10.00
Federal 941/944	Sep 2008	Check	To Print	1176.65
TX Unemployment Insurance	Q3 2008	Check	To Print	108.00
			Total:	$1,344.65

Print Checks...

Tax Forms Prior Year: 941/Sch B

After paychecks to employees and payments to vendors were made, there are tax forms now available for processing. The first tax form is the Federal Tax Form-941/Sch B

1 Choose the type of payroll form you want to prepare:

○ Federal Form

○ State Form

I don't see my state.

2 Choose the specific form you want to prepare: Which one should I choose?

Quarterly Form 941/Sch. B (required for most employers)
Annual Form 940/Sch. A
Annual Form 944-945A (replaces 941 only if you're notified by the IRS)
Annual Form W-2/W-3

Activities:

❖ Click **Tax Forms** tab
❖ Click **Prepare any form** under Related Activities (top right)
❖ In #1. Click **Federal Form**
❖ In #2. Click **Quarterly Form 941/Sch. B**. Click **Next**
❖ In #3. Select **3rd Qtr (Jul, Aug, Sept) 2008**. Click **Continue**

- ❖ Are you required to file…Click **Yes**
- ❖ Select the state…Select **TX**
- ❖ Do you want to allow…Click **No**
- ❖ Do you want to enter…Click **No**. Click **Continue**
- ❖ Review tax form
- ❖ Click **Finished**

Form **941** for 2008:	**Employer's QUARTERLY Federal Tax Return**			970106

Form **941** for 2008: (Rev. October 2008)

Employer's QUARTERLY Federal Tax Return
Department of the Treasury — Internal Revenue Service

OMB No. 1545-0029

(EIN)
Employer identification number   99-1234567

Report for this Quarter of 2008 (Check one.)
- ☐ 1: January, February, March
- ☐ 2: April, May, June
- ☒ 3: July, August, September
- ☐ 4: October, November, December

Name (not your trade name):   Quick Payroll

Trade name (if any):

Address: PO Box 60507

Aurora   IL   60507

Part 1: Answer these questions for this quarter.

1 Number of employees who received wages, tips, or other compensation for the pay period
including: Mar. 12 (Quarter 1), June 12 (Quarter 2), Sept. 12 (Quarter 3), Dec. 12 (Quarter 4) · · · **1** _____ 1

2 Wages, tips, and other compensation · **2** _____ 3,965.00

3 Income tax withheld from wages, tips, and other compensation · · · · · · · · · · · · · · · **3** _____ 570.00

4 If no wages, tips, and other compensation are subject to social security or Medicare tax · · · · · · · ☐ Check and go to line 6.

5 Taxable social security and Medicare wages and tips:

		Column 1		Column 2
5a	Taxable social security wages . . .	3,965.00	x .124 =	491.66
5b	Taxable social security tips	_____	x .124 =	_____
5c	Taxable Medicare wages & tips . . .	3,965.00	x .029 =	114.99

5d Total social security and Medicare taxes (Column 2, lines 5a + 5b + 5c = line 5d) · · · · · · **5d** _____ 606.65

6 Total taxes before adjustment (lines 3 + 5d = line 6) · **6** _____ 1,176.65

7 TAX ADJUSTMENTS. Read instructions for line 7 before completing lines 7a through 7g.

Tax Forms Prior Year: Annual Form 940/Sch. A

You've processed Federal quarterly form successfully, the next form is the Annual Form 940-Sch. A.

Activities:

- ❖ Click **Tax Forms** tab
- ❖ Click **Prepare any form** under Related Activities (top right)
- ❖ In #1. Click **Federal Form**
- ❖ In #2. Click **Quarterly Form 940/Sch. A**. Click **Next**
- ❖ In #3. Select **2008**. Click **Continue**
- ❖ Do you want to allow…Click **No**
- ❖ Do you want to enter…Click **No**. Click **Continue**
- ❖ Review tax form
- ❖ Click **Finished**

Form **940** for 2008: **Employer's Annual Federal Unemployment (FUTA) Tax Return**   850106
Department of the Treasury — Internal Revenue Service
OMB No. 1545-0028

(EIN)
Employer identification number   99-1234567

Name (not your trade name)   Quick Payroll

Trade name (if any)

Address   PO Box 60507

Aurora   IL   60507

Type of Return (Check all that apply)

☐ a. Amended
☐ b. Successor employer
☐ c. No payments to employees in 2008.
☐ d. Final: Business closed or stopped paying wages

Read the separate instructions before you fill out this form. Please type or print within the boxes.

Part 1: Tell us about your return. If any line does NOT apply, leave it blank.

1 If you were required to pay your state unemployment tax in

  1a One state only, enter the state abbreviation · · · · · · ·   1a TX
      - OR -
  1b More than one state (You are a multi-state employer) · · · · · · · · · · · · · · · · ·   1b ☐ Check here. Fill out Schedule A.

2   Line 2 is not applicable for 2008 ·   2

Part 2: Determine your FUTA tax before adjustments for 2008. If any line does NOT apply, leave it blank.

3   Total payments to all employees ·   3   _____ 4,000.00

4   Payments exempt from FUTA tax· · · · · · · · · · · · ·   4   _____ 35.00

    Check all that apply: 4a ☒ Fringe benefits   4c ☐ Retirement/Pension   4e ☐ Other
                           4b ☐ Group-term life insurance   4d ☐ Dependent care

5   Total of payments made to each employee in excess of $7,000 · · · · ·   5

6   Subtotal (line 4 + line 5 = line 6) ·   6   _____ 35.00

Tax Form Prior Year: Annual Form 944/945A

The next Annual federal form to process is the Annual Form 944/945A. Be sure to checkmark you're required to file.

Activities:

- ❖ Click **Tax Forms** tab
- ❖ Click **Prepare any form** under Related Activities (top right)
- ❖ In #1. Click **Federal Form**
- ❖ In #2. Click **Annual Form 944/945A**. Click **Next**
- ❖ In #3. Select **2008**. Click **Continue**
- ❖ Are you required to file…Click **Yes**
- ❖ Select state…Select **TX**
- ❖ Do you want to allow…Click **No**
- ❖ Do you want to enter…Click **No**. Click **Continue**
- ❖ Review tax form
- ❖ Click **Finished**

Form **944** for 2008: **Employer's ANNUAL Federal Tax Return**
Department of the Treasury — Internal Revenue Service

(EIN)
Employer identification number 99-1234567

Name (not your trade name) Quick Payroll

Trade name (if any)

Address PO Box 60507

Aurora IL 60507

OMB No. 1545-2007

Who Must File Form 944

You must file annual Form 944 instead of filing quarterly Forms 941 only if the IRS notified you in writing.

QBM944P1 1/2008

Read the separate instructions before you complete Form 944. Type or print within the boxes.

Part 1: Answer these questions for 2008.

1 Wages, tips, and other compensation	1	3,965.00
2 Income tax withheld from wages, tips, and other compensation	2	570.00
3 If no wages, tips, and other compensation are subject to social security or Medicare tax	3	☐ Check and go to line 5.

4 Taxable social security and Medicare wages and tips:

	Column 1		Column 2
4a Taxable social security wages	3,965.00	x .124 =	491.66
4b Taxable social security tips		x .124 =	
4c Taxable Medicare wages & tips	3,965.00	x .029 =	114.99
4d Total social security and Medicare taxes (Column 2, lines 4a + 4b + 4c = line 4d)		4d	606.65
5 Total taxes before adjustments (lines 2 + 4d = line 5)		5	1,176.65

Tax Form Prior Year: W-2/W-3

The final Annual federal form to process is the Annual Form 944/945A. Be sure to click no to do you want to e-file?

Activities:

- ❖ Click **Tax Forms** tab
- ❖ Click **Prepare any form** under Related Activities (top right)
- ❖ In #1. Click **Federal Form**
- ❖ In #2. Click **Annual Form W-2/W-3**. Click **Next**
- ❖ In #3. Select **2008**. Click **Continue**
- ❖ Do you want to e-file…Click **No**
- ❖ What kind of payee…Accept **941**
- ❖ Do you have any employees…Click **No**
- ❖ Do you have any Statutory…Click **No**. Click **Continue**

- ❖ Review **Form W-2 B22 C (Acres)**
- ❖ Click **Forms W-2 Copy D, A, and 1**
- ❖ Click **Form W-3** for Social Security Administration
- ❖ Click **Cancel**

Tax Form Prior Year: State

There is a state tax form that needs to be processed. Whatever you do, never skip the state tax forms, sometimes, most tax payers do.

Activities:

- ❖ Click **Tax Forms** tab
- ❖ Click **Prepare any form** under Related Activities (top right)
- ❖ In #1. Click **State Form**
- ❖ In #2. Click **C-3 Employer's Quarterly Report**. Click **Next**
- ❖ In #3. Select **3rd Qtr (Jul, Aug, Sept) 2008**. Click **Continue**
- ❖ Choose the County for…Select **Dallas**
- ❖ Choose the County where…Select **Dallas**. Click **Continue**
- ❖ Review state tax form
- ❖ Click **Finished**

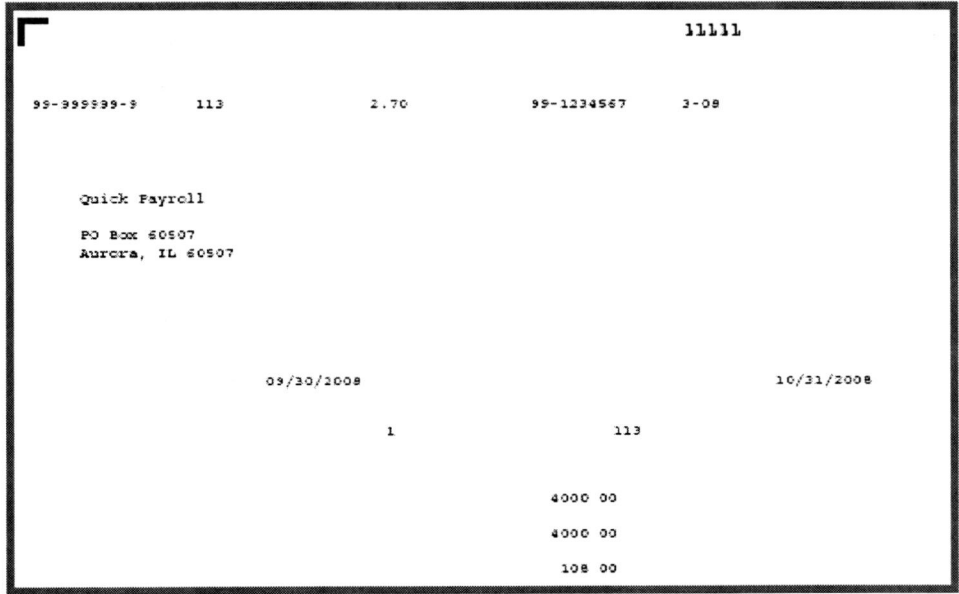

Find Payee

From time to time you may want to know if a vendor or an employee was paid. There are many way to do this; another easy way to find the payee and the window will display all the checks that have been paid to the company or individual.

Activities:

- ❖ Click **Payments** tab
- ❖ Click **Find** (Next to the Report tab)
- ❖ Search: Select **Payee**
- ❖ Find: Type **Jerry Jordan**
- ❖ Click **Close**

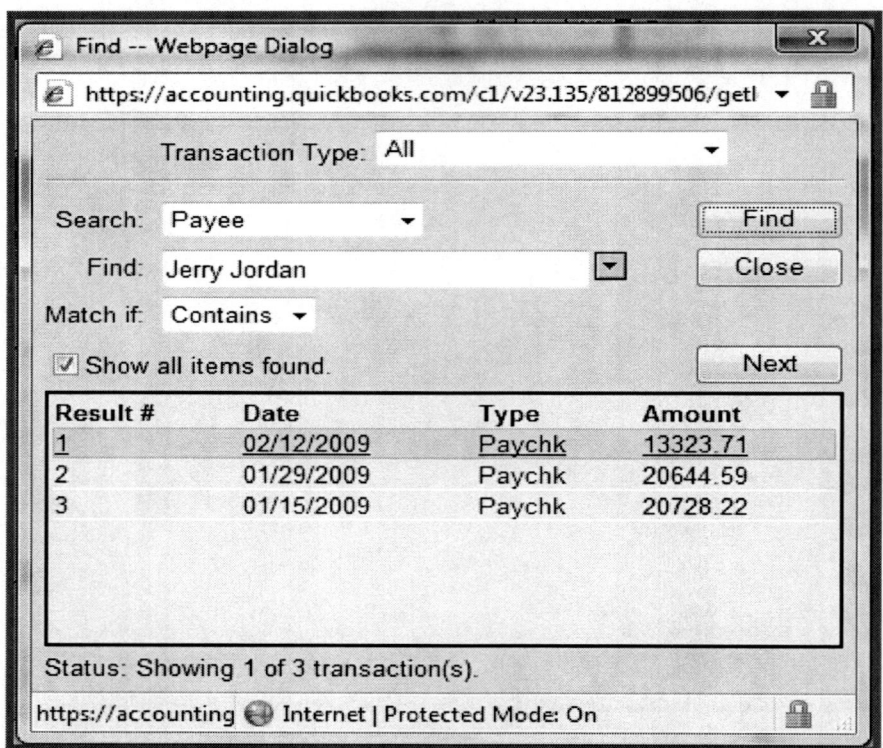

Cancel Subscription

After completing this course, there is no doubt this online payroll system will be your number software in payroll processing and you will recommend it to your company since you've practiced payroll on it. Should you choose to cancel your subscription the following are the step you use to complete the process.

Activities:

- ❖ Congratulations! On the job well done.
- ❖ Click **my account** (next to the Reports tab)
- ❖ Click **My Subscription**
- ❖ Click **Cancel My Subscription** (right of the window)
- ❖ Scroll to the bottom
- ❖ Click **Complete Cancellation**
- ❖ Log off on Online Payroll and open QuickBooks Payroll 2009 file
- ❖ Open the email address you used during subscription
- ❖ Double click **Online Payroll: Subscription Cancellation**
- ❖ **Print cancellation notice for your file**
- ❖ **Date of Cancellation_____** Please write the date!

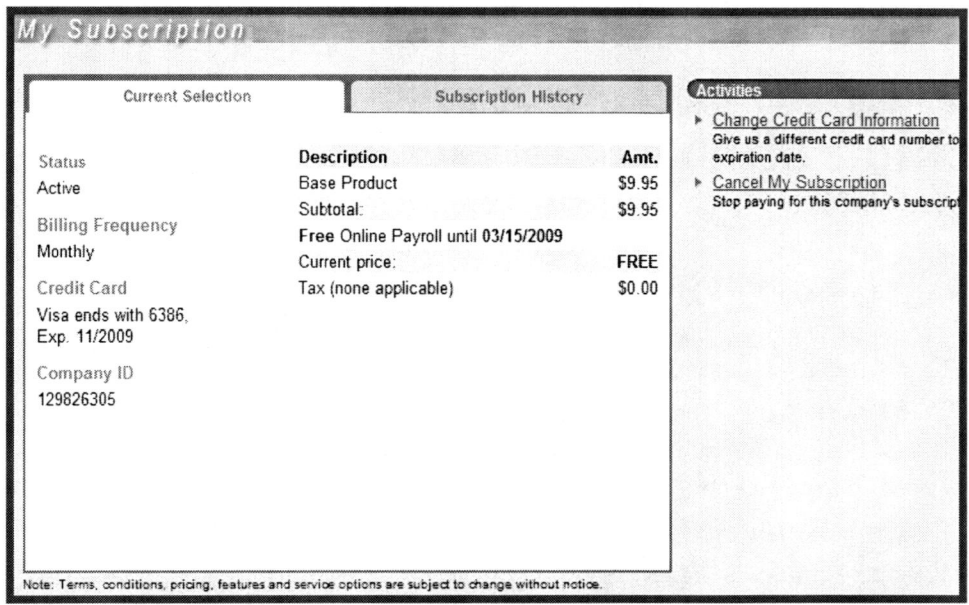

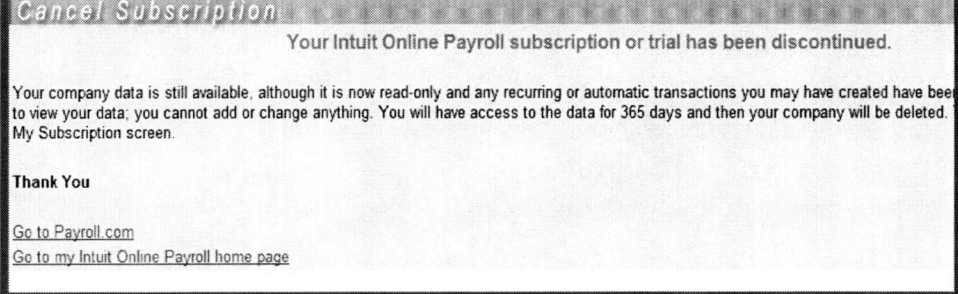

Chapter 10

Banking Menu

Objectives: After you've completed this chapter, you will be able to:

- ✓ Explain the Banking submenus
- ✓ Write checks
- ✓ Record credit card charges
- ✓ Process single or multiple checks
- ✓ Generate register reports
- ✓ Process register QuickReport
- ✓ Edit, sort, and split entries in the register
- ✓ Make deposits to checking account
- ✓ Complete the transfer funds process
- ✓ Make journal entries
- ✓ Reconcile the bank statements
- ✓ Run financial reports and compare your results
- ✓ Explain the bank reconciliation steps
- ✓ Identify the bank reconciliation journal entries

Review Banking Submenus

As you work through this book, you will discover that there are windows you have like to use over and again. On one occasion, I saw a client writing deposit slips by hand, when all he had to do was go to the Deposit window, click the Print down arrow at the top of the window, and click Print Deposit Slip

- Click **Banking menu**

The following activities are found under the Banking menu:

- **Write Checks:** Before you use this window, be sure that you have completed the vendor list; that is, you have listed all your vendors, because the Write Checks window will need the vendor's name on the checks. You may also add the vendor as you write the checks. It's pertinent to identify the expense account or the item name for which you are writing the check. The Write Checks window will also show you the checking account you are writing the check from and the current balance. Make sure you select the correct checking account and that you have enough balance to cover the amount of the check you're writing.

- **Order Checks & Envelopes:** If you plan to write a large number of checks and to automate the check writing process in your QuickBooks software, it would be wise to order checks and envelopes from QuickBooks. This submenu will allow you to set up a check reorder reminder. QuickBooks will prompt you to reorder checks as soon as you reach that check number.

- **Enter Credit Card Charges:** If you are going to have volumes of credit card charges or activities, this is one of the key windows you need to understand. During reconciliation, it's cost effective to download your credit card charges into the credit card register rather than enter credit card charges individually. The Credit Card Charges window will give you the name of the credit card and the current balance. Be sure to select the right credit card name.

- **Use Register:** You can write a check directly from the check register window or straight from the Write Check window as we discussed above. Using the check register is faster, because you don't have to deal with all the details as in the Write Checks window. You will need to select or type the right check number.

- **Make Deposits:** The Making Deposit window is easy is to use; the checks you collected from the customers are now listed in the Make Deposit window. In making a deposit, you are transferring the money to the Undeposited Funds account in the Chart of Accounts. After the deposit process is completed, the Undeposited Funds account will be zero, and the checking account where you deposited the checks will be higher.

- **Transfer Funds:** Transferring funds does not mean the funds have been moved physically to the receiving account. You must write a check, call the bank, or go online to actually complete the process of moving the money to the right account. You can check the balances of the sending and receiving accounts before and after the process in the Chart of Accounts to make sure the results are what you intended. The sending account is decreased and the receiving account is increased.

- **Reconcile:** Every month, you will use the reconcile window to balance or match the amount in your QuickBooks file with the amount in the bank. If there is any difference, you will have to make a journal entry to make QuickBooks agree with the bank account. If the bank overpaid a check this month, you will credit the checking account and debit Other Expense and call the bank refund your account with the overpayment. Next month, when the bank refunds your money, debit the checking account and credit Other Income.

- **Online Banking:** More companies are conducting businesses online, and you should do the same. Check with your bank to see what is required to allow to you to pay and receive money online.

- **Loan Manager:** After you have created your loan account in the Chart of Accounts, you can come to the Loan Manager window to give complete details of the loan. The Loan Manager will allow you to add more loans and review loan summary and payment schedules. One of the best features is the "What if Scenarios," which allows you to play what will happen if your loan amount, loan percentage (term), payment amount or payment period changes.

- **Other Names List:** This window allows you to create names that are not related to other windows. Names such as Transfer From Checking, Transfer To Checking, Transfer From Savings, Transfer To Savings and ATM Withdrawal are created in this window. You can think of other names; any odd names you're not used to or you don't know will go with the Chart of Accounts or Item Lists windows.

Write Check

Many companies are now receiving more funds electronically and by credit card than any from any other medium of exchange. Though many people still write checks, those are increasingly being turned into electronic checks. Therefore, the checks are being cashed without the actual checks being presented to the recipient's bank. QuickBooks will always default your bank balance on the check window. This is very significant so that you don't have to click over to your checking account for the balance before writing checks.

Activities:

- ❖ You're back in QuickBooks Payroll 2009 file
- ❖ Click **Banking menu**
- ❖ Click **Write Checks**
- ❖ Bank Account: Accept **USA Checking**
- ❖ Ending Balance: Accept **761,591.00**
- ❖ Date: Type **1/15/09**
- ❖ Pay to the Order of: Click **Down arrow**. Scroll up
- ❖ Click **Add New.** Click **Vendor**. Click **OK**
- ❖ Vendor name: Type **American Auto Services**. Click **OK**
- ❖ Amount: Type **150.** Press **Tab**
- ❖ Click **Expenses** tab
- ❖ Click under **Account** (left of the window):
- ❖ Select **Repairs/Maint under Automobile Expense**.   Press **Tab**
- ❖ Amount: Accept **150**. Under Memo: Type **Auto Services**
- ❖ Customer: Job: Select **James Adams**
- ❖ Uncheck **Billable**
- ❖ Checkmark **To be Printed** (right)
- ❖ Click **Save & Close**

Record Credit Card

As we move toward a cashless society, most future purchases will be in the form of Credit Card charges. There are two ways of entering Credit Card charges: the first is to manually enter single credit card charge into the window; the second and fastest way of entering credit card charges is to download the transactions into your Quickbooks account. If you have many pages of transactions each month, you should consider the online download. The benefit more than offsets the cost of setting it up with an Internet provider.

Activities:

- ❖ Click **Banking menu**
- ❖ Click **Enter Credit Card Charges**
- ❖ Credit Card: Accept **Visa Credit Card**
- ❖ Click **Purchase/Charge**
- ❖ Purchase From: Select **American Auto Services**
- ❖ Date: Accept **1/15/09**
- ❖ Ref No.: Type **Vcc 10075**
- ❖ Amount: Type **24**
- ❖ Click **Expenses** tab
- ❖ Click under **Account** (left of the window)
- ❖ Select **Fuel under Automobile Expenses**. Press **Tab**
- ❖ Amount: Accept **24.** Memo: Type **Gas**
- ❖ Customer: Job: Select **James Adams**
- ❖ Uncheck **Billable**
- ❖ Click **Save & Close**

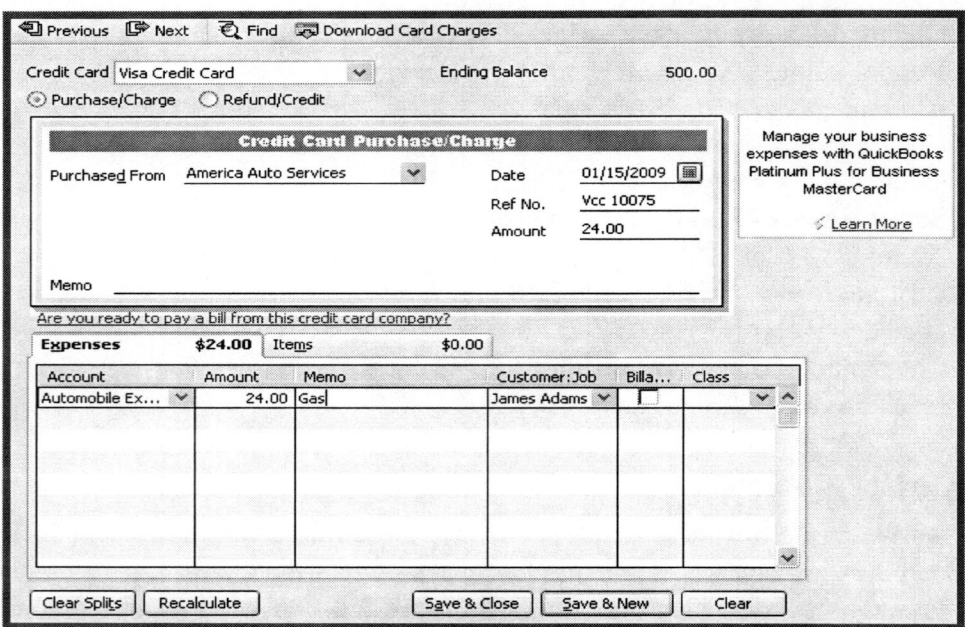

Print Single Checks

From time to time, you may want to write a single check to a vendor. Especially in a cash-on-delivery situation, you will be forced to write a single check in the check register. As always, you must make sure you are printing from the right bank account using the next check serial number. All you have to do is pull up the single check with the right date. Then click Print from the Print drop-down window at the top of the window.

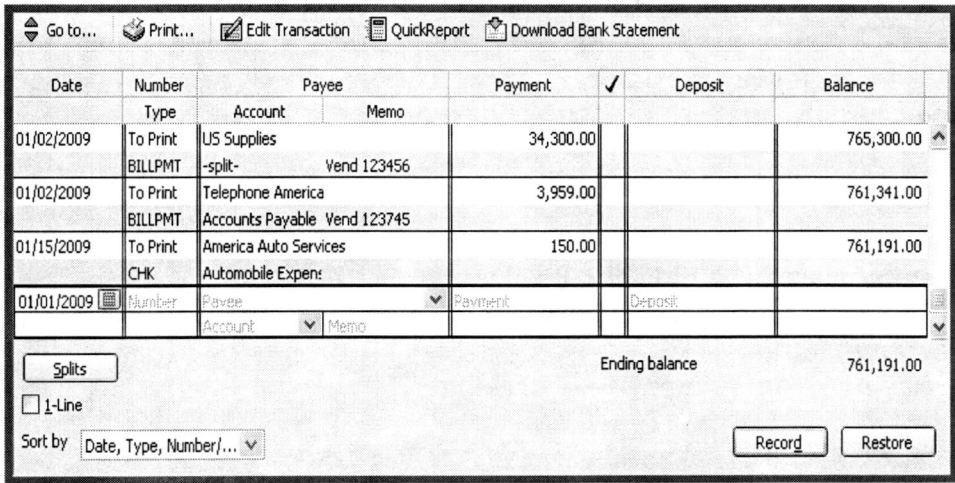

Activities:

- ❖ Click **Banking menu**
- ❖ Click **Use Register**
- ❖ Select Account: Select **USA Checking**. Click **OK**
- ❖ On the last line. Date: Type **1/1/09**
- ❖ Number: Accept **1002**
- ❖ Payee: Select **American Auto Services**
- ❖ Amount: Type **250**
- ❖ Account: Click **Repairs/Maint under Automobile Expense**
- ❖ Double click **CHK** in the Number/Type
- ❖ Uncheck **To be printed** (right)
- ❖ No (top right of the window): Accept **1002**
- ❖ Click **Print down arrow** (top left of the window)
- ❖ Select **Print…**
- ❖ Printed Check Number: Type **1002**. Click **OK**
- ❖ Check Style: Accept **Voucher** (left of the window)
- ❖ Click **Cancel**
- ❖ Click **Save & Close**

Print Batch Checks

Most companies have a particular day of the month when they process all checks, except the payroll checks that are processed twice a month. On that day, all checks to vendors are processed simultaneously. Normally, you open the Check Register and Preview the windows and print a check. However, using the batch processing function will save time and money when you have more than one check to print. If you have hundreds of checks, batch processing is the only way to go.

Activities:

- ❖ You're still in USA Checking register window
- ❖ Double click **BILLPMT for US Supplies for 34,300.00**
- ❖ Click **Print down arrow** (top left of the window)
- ❖ Select **Print Batch**
- ❖ Bank Account: Accept **USA Checking**
- ❖ First Check Number: Type **1003**
- ❖ Click **Select All** (right of the window). Click **OK**
- ❖ Check Style: Click **Voucher**
- ❖ Click **Cancel**
- ❖ Click **X** to "Check to Print" windows. Click **X** to close Check window
- ❖ In the check register, because you did not print the batch checks
- ❖ Highlight **To Print** for **US Supplies 34,300.00**
- ❖ Type **1003.** Click **Record.** Click **Yes**
- ❖ Highlight **To Print** for **Telephone America 3,959.00**
- ❖ Type **1004.** Click **Record.** Click **Yes**
- ❖ Highlight **To Print** for **American Auto Service 150**
- ❖ Type **1005.** Click **Record.** Click **Yes**

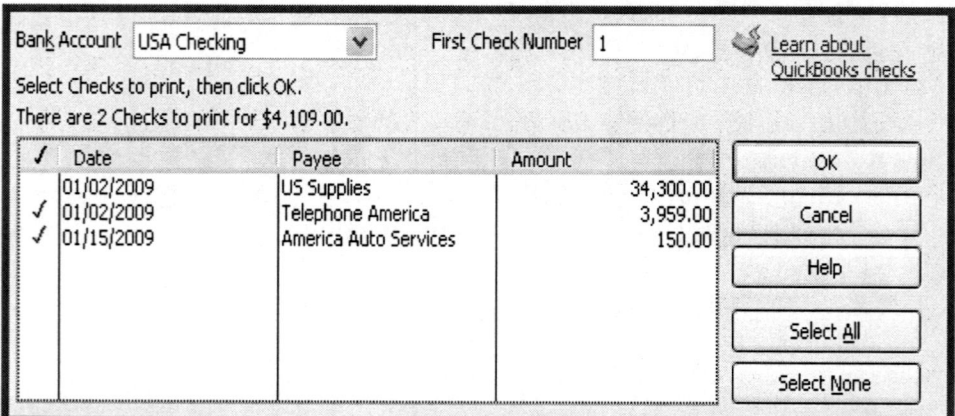

Create Register Report

This is the most used report in the register. It is handy when you want to review a register report for a certain period of time, such as from the beginning to the end of the month. The best aspect of the report is that it will give you the register balance for that time period. To get a correct running balance, you must sort with the dates ascending.

Activities:

- ❖ You're still in USA Checking register window
- ❖ Click **Print** (top left of the window)
- ❖ From: Type **1/1/09**. Press **Tab**
- ❖ Through: Type **12/31/09**
- ❖ Click **OK**
- ❖ Click **Preview** (right of the window)
- ❖ Click **Zoom In**
- ❖ Balance **761,191.00**
- ❖ Click **Close or Print** if printer is ready
- ❖ Click **X** to close Print List window

Quick Payroll 2009

Register: USA Checking

From 01/01/2009 through 12/31/2009

Sorted by: Date, Type, Number/Ref

Date	Number	Payee	Account	Memo	Payment	C	Deposit	Balance
01/01/2009			Opening Balance Equity	Account Openi...		X	800,000.00	800,000.00
01/01/2009	1001	Telephone America	Travel Expense		150.00			799,850.00
01/01/2009	1002	America Auto Services	Automobile Expense:R...		250.00			799,600.00
01/02/2009	1003	US Supplies	-split-	Vend 123456	34,300.00			765,300.00
01/02/2009	1004	Telephone America	Accounts Payable	Vend 123745	3,959.00			761,341.00
01/15/2009	1005	America Auto Services	Automobile Expense:R...		150.00			761,191.00

Edit Register

Nothing is written in stone when it comes to the transactions on your check register. Sometimes, you will discover incorrect or insufficient information on a check. At that point, it is not necessary to void the check, but correct the information on the check. If, for example, the check has not been printed, or released to the vendor or reconciled with the bank statement and the amount is wrong, you can open the check and correct the amount right on the check.

Activities:

- ❖ You're still in USA Checking register window
- ❖ Click **Check # 1002 for 250.00**
- ❖ Click **Edit Transaction** (top left of the window)
- ❖ Bank Account: Accept **USA Checking**
- ❖ No: Accept **1002**. Date: Accept **1/1/09**
- ❖ Click Address box. Type **America Auto Services**. Press **Enter**
- ❖ Type **4000 Austin Lane, Austin, TX 78000**
- ❖ Memo: Type **Repairs and Maintenance**
- ❖ Click **Save & New** (bottom right of the window)
- ❖ Click **Yes** to "You've changed..."
- ❖ Click **Previous** button (top of check register) to **Check #1002**
- ❖ Check **Save & Close**
- ❖ Double click **check 1002** to open check
- ❖ Look! New address is still on the check

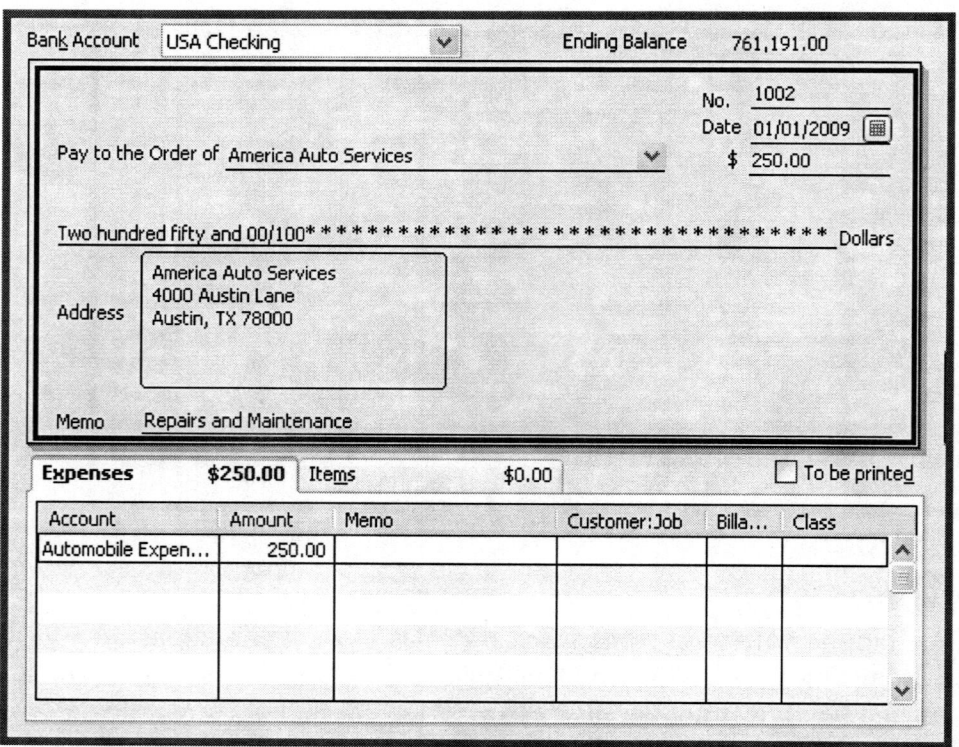

Create Register QuickReport

The second most used report in the check register is the QuickReport. If you want to see all the checks you've written to a vendor or to see what bills from a vendor are still unpaid, open the check register and find the vendor. Click on the vendor and then QuickReport at the top of the register window. All the entries on that vendor are displayed on the screen in a matter of seconds. The best part is you will have the total amount of checks you've written to this vendor.

Activities:

- ❖ You're still in USA Checking register window
- ❖ Click **Telephone America check # 1001 for 150.00**
- ❖ Click **QuickReport**. (top of the window)
- ❖ Date (top left of the window): Select **This Fiscal Year**
- ❖ Click **Print**...(top left of the window)
- ❖ Click **Preview** (right of the window)
- ❖ Click **Zoom In**
- ❖ Click **Close or Print** if printer is ready
- ❖ Click **X** to close Print Report window
- ❖ Click **X** to close Quick Report window

Quick Payroll 2009
Register QuickReport
January through December 2009

Type	Date	Num	Memo	Account	Clr	Split	Amount
Telephone America							
Check	1/1/2009	1001		USA Checking		Travel Expense	-150.00
Bill Pmt -Check	1/2/2009	1004	Vend 123745	USA Checking		Accounts Pay...	-3,959.00
Total Telephone America							-4,109.00
TOTAL							**-4,109.00**

Sort Register

To be able to sort your check register is one of the nicest tools you can ever have, especially for bookkeepers. It would be a good idea to sort your entries by Order Entered that way you don't lose the last entry you made just because the date came much earlier than other checks. The last transaction will always be the last entry you keyed in, so you can make corrections if needed. You can sort by Amount (largest first) for Deposit only and Amount (smallest first) for Payments only.

Activities:

- ❖ You're still in USA Checking register window
- ❖ Sort by (bottom left of the window): Accept **Date, Type, Number**
- ❖ Look! Register is listed by Date ascending order
- ❖ Sort by: Select **Amount (largest first)**
- ❖ Look! Payment column is in ascending order
- ❖ Deposit column should be in descending order
- ❖ Sort by: Select **Amount (Smallest first)**
- ❖ Look! Payment column is in descending order
- ❖ Deposit column should be in ascending order
- ❖ Sort by: Select **Number/Ref**
- ❖ Register is now listed by check number
- ❖ Sort by: **Date, Type, Number**
- ❖ Register lists is returned to original sort condition

Split Entry

You use the Split entry function to separate a bill, when one bill from the same vendor can be posted to different accounts. In this age of superstores and supercenters, it is easy to make purchases that fall into different accounts. For example, if you buy an item for the business automobile, such as a floor mat, and some printer paper for office use. You will have two accounts, and the Split function will help you to categorize the expense into automobile and office expenses.

Activities:

- ❖ You're still in USA Checking register window
- ❖ Click **Check # 1002 for American Auto Services for 250**
- ❖ Click **Splits** (bottom left of the window)
- ❖ In Split window. Click **under Account** (left of the window)
- ❖ Accept **Automobile Expense/Repairs & Maint**. Press **Tab**
- ❖ Amount: Type **200** (Very Important) Press **Tab**
- ❖ Click **under Automobile Expense/Repair**
- ❖ Account. Select **Fuel**. Press **Tab**
- ❖ Amount: Accept **50**. Press **Tab**. Click **Close** (right of the window).
- ❖ Click **Record** (bottom right). Click **Yes** to "You have changed…"
- ❖ Click **X** to close check register

Date	Number	Payee		Payment	✓	Deposit	Balance
	Type	Account	Memo				
01/01/2009					✓	800,000.00	800,000.00
	DEP	Opening Balance E Account Opening B					
01/01/2009	1001	Telephone America		150.00			799,850.00
	CHK	Travel Expense					
01/01/2009	1002	America Auto Services		250.00		Deposit	799,600.00
	CHK	Automobile Expen:	Repairs and Mai...				

Account	Amount	Memo	Customer:Job	Billa...	Class	
Automobile Expense:Repai...	200.00					Close
Automobile Expense:Fuel	50.00					Clear
						Recalc

| 01/02/2009 | 1003 | US Supplies | | 34,300.00 | | | 765,300.00 |
| | BILLPMT | -split- | Vend 123456 | | | | |

Splits

☐ 1-Line

Ending balance   761,191.00

Sort by Date, Type, Number/...

Record   Restore

Make Deposit

After you received a payment from a customer, the amount is sent to the Undeposited Funds account in the Chart of Accounts. You should open the Chart of Accounts and confirm that the amount is in the Undeposited Funds account. Next, go to the Banking menu and open the Make Deposit window. One of the key steps is to make sure you've selected the right checking account where the payment is to be deposited. Once the process is completed, QuickBooks moves the amount from the Undeposited Funds account to the checking account.

Activities:

- ❖ Click **Lists menu**
- ❖ Click **Chart of Accounts**
- ❖ Look for **Undeposited Funds** (toward the top left of the window)
- ❖ The balance is **900,000**
- ❖ Click **Banking menu**
- ❖ Click **Make Deposits**
- ❖ View Payment method type: Accept **All Types**
- ❖ Checkmark **1/15/09 PMT for 900,000**
- ❖ Click **OK**
- ❖ Deposit To: Select **USA Checking**
- ❖ Date: Accept **1/15/09**

❖ Memo: Accept **Deposit**
❖ Click **Print Down arrow** (top of the window)
❖ Select **Deposit Slip**
❖ Click **Preview** (right)
❖ Click **Zoom In**
❖ Click **Close or Print** if printer is ready
❖ Click **X** to close Print Deposit Slip window
❖ Click **Save & Close** (bottom right of the window)
❖ Click **Lists menu**
❖ Click **Chart of Accounts**
❖ Look! **Undeposited Funds balance is 0.00**
❖ Funds are now deposited to USA Checking account

Deposit Summary

Summary of Deposits to USA Checking on 01/15/2009

Chk No.	PmtMethod	Rcd From	Memo	Amount
4005	Check	James Adams		900,000.00
			Deposit Subtotal:	900,000.00
			Less Cash Back:	
			Deposit Total:	900,000.00

Transfer Funds

As you open multiple bank accounts, the easiest way to fund those accounts is to do a Fund Transfer. For example, on a scheduled day of the month, you will be funding your Payroll account from your business checking account. Because the Payroll account does not receive deposits from customers, the only way to fund it, is through the Transfer Funds window. Other accounts, such as Savings or Brokerage, can also be funded in a similar fashion.

Activities:

❖ Click **Lists menu**
❖ Click **Chart of Accounts**
❖ Right click in the window. Click **New**
❖ Click **Bank**. Click **Continue**
❖ Account Name: Type **Petty Cash**

- ❖ Click **Enter Opening Balance**
- ❖ Statement Ending Balance: Type **0.00**
- ❖ Statement Ending Date: Type **1/1/09.** Click **OK**
- ❖ Click **Save & Close**
- ❖ Click **No** to "Set up online…"
- ❖ Click **Banking menu**. Click **Transfer Funds**
- ❖ Date: Type **1/15/09**
- ❖ Transfer Funds From: Select **USA Checking**
- ❖ Transfer Funds To: Select **Petty Cash**
- ❖ Account Balance: Accept **1,661,191.00**
- ❖ Transfer Amount $: Type **100**. Press **Tab**
- ❖ Click **Save & Close**

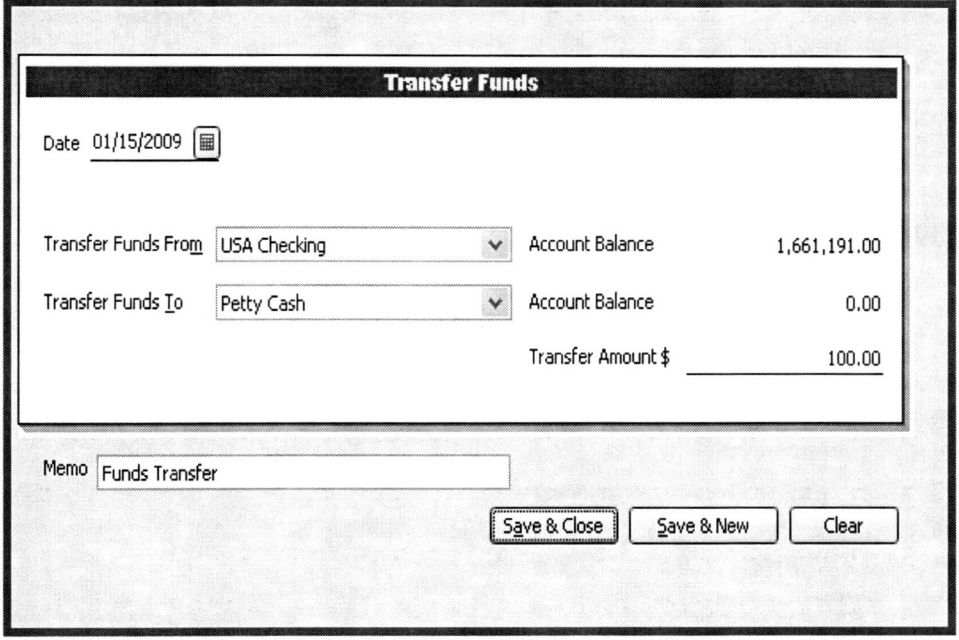

Bank Statement

Bank of United States of America
1234 North Banking Lane
Dallas, TX 75000
1-800-123-9999

Director of Finance
Quick Payroll
123 Adam Lane
Dallas, TX 75000

Customer Activities for the Month Ending 1/31/2009

Beginning Balance   800,000.00

Deposits:
1/15/2009   900,000.00

Total Deposits   900,000.00

Withdrawals:
1/1/2009   CK#1001   100.00
1/1/2009   CK#1002   260.00
1/2/2009   CK#1003   34,300.00
1/2/2009   CK#1004   3,959.00
1/15/2009   CK#1005   150.00
1/15/2009   TFR to X2855   100.00

Total Withdrawals   38,869.00

Ending Balance 1/31/2009   1,661,131.00

Make General Journal Entry

After we received the bank statement, we discovered that the bank underpaid check #1001 by $50; therefore, we increased the amount on the books by $50. Also, the bank overpaid check #1002 by $10 so we decreased the amount on the books by $10. In essence, you are adjusting book balance to match bank balance until you call the bank to correct their mistakes. After they've made the corrections, switch the entries you made to where it was before you started the reconciliation, which makes bank balance match with book balance.

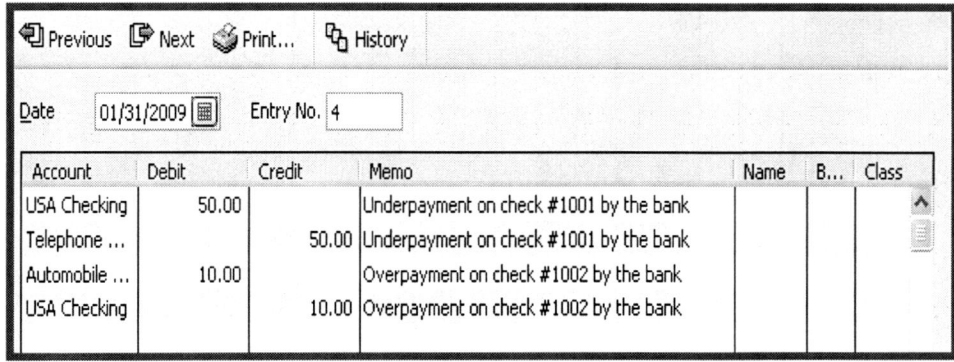

Activities:

- ❖ Click **Company menu**
- ❖ Click **Make General Journal Entries.** Click **OK**
- ❖ Date: Type **1/31/09.** Entry: Accept **4**
- ❖ Click **under Account** (left of the window). Select **USA Checking**
- ❖ Debit: Type **50**
- ❖ Memo: Type **Underpayment on check #1001 by bank**
- ❖ Click **under USA Checking.** Select **Telephone Expense**
- ❖ Credit: Accept **50**
- ❖ Memo: Type **Underpayment on check #1001 by bank**
- ❖ Click **under Telephone Expense**
- ❖ Select **Repairs & Maint under Automobile Expense**
- ❖ Debit: Type **10**
- ❖ Memo: Type **Overpayment on check #1002 by bank**
- ❖ Click **under Repairs & Maint.** Select **USA Checking**
- ❖ Credit: Accept **10**
- ❖ Memo: Type **Overpayment on check #1002 by bank**
- ❖ Click **Save & Close**

> You can highlight memo column right click and use the copy and paste.

Reconcile Bank Statement

As soon as you receive your Statement from the bank, you should look for entries on the statement that are not on the company's check register and entries that are on the check register that are not on the bank statement. Examples are interest income, interest expense, bank fees, deposits and checks that have not been entered either by you or the bank. In the Reconciliation window, you will type the ending balance on the bank statement, in this case **1,661,131.00** which matches your check register balance after you've made the Journal Entries; then click the Mark All button, the Difference (bottom right of the window) must be 0.00.

Activities:

- ❖ Click **Banking Menu**. Click **Reconcile**
- ❖ Account: Select **USA Checking**. Statement Date: Type **1/31/09**
- ❖ Ending Balance: Type **1,661,131.00**. Press **Tab**
- ❖ Click **Continue** (bottom of window)
- ❖ Click **Mark All** (middle left of window)
- ❖ Difference (bottom right of window): **Must be 0.00**
- ❖ Click **Reconcile Now** (bottom right of window). Very Important!
- ❖ Click **Both**. Click **Display**. Click **OK** to "This report display current..."
- ❖ Click **X** to close Summary. **You must have Checkmark all entries**
- ❖ Congratulations! Click **X** to close Reconciliation Detail window

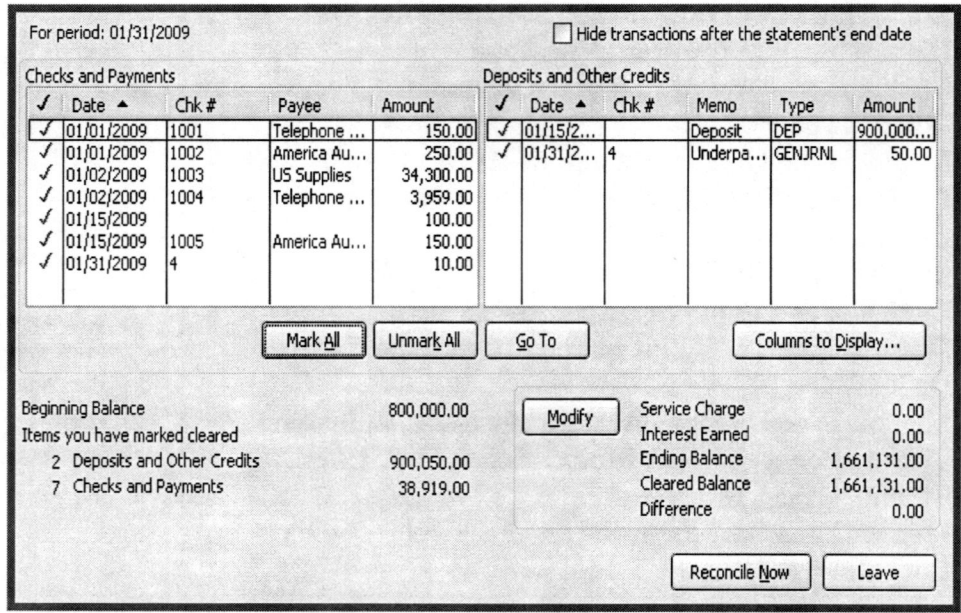

For period: 01/31/2009   ☐ Hide transactions after the statement's end date

Checks and Payments

✓	Date ▲	Chk #	Payee	Amount
✓	01/01/2009	1001	Telephone ...	150.00
✓	01/01/2009	1002	America Au...	250.00
✓	01/02/2009	1003	US Supplies	34,300.00
✓	01/02/2009	1004	Telephone ...	3,959.00
✓	01/15/2009			100.00
✓	01/15/2009	1005	America Au...	150.00
✓	01/31/2009	4		10.00

Deposits and Other Credits

✓	Date ▲	Chk #	Memo	Type	Amount
✓	01/15/2...		Deposit	DEP	900,000...
✓	01/31/2...	4	Underpa...	GENJRNL	50.00

[Mark All]   [Unmark All]   [Go To]   [Columns to Display...]

Beginning Balance	800,000.00	
Items you have marked cleared		
2 Deposits and Other Credits	900,050.00	
7 Checks and Payments	38,919.00	

[Modify]

Service Charge	0.00
Interest Earned	0.00
Ending Balance	1,661,131.00
Cleared Balance	1,661,131.00
Difference	0.00

[Reconcile Now]   [Leave]

Financial: Profit & Loss

In the Banking menu, most of the activities are bank account related. We learned how to write and print both single and batch checks. If you have multiple checks, processing checks in a batch is easier and more efficient. We had three expenses. Two were checks and one was a credit card charge, which all totaled 424. We also had an overpayment and underpayment by the bank for a total of 40. Those activities made the Net Income 1,786,204.73.

Activities:

- ❖ Click **Reports menu**
- ❖ Click **Company & Financial**
- ❖ Click **Profit & Loss Standard**
- ❖ Date: Select **This Fiscal Year**
- ❖ From: Accept **1/1/09**
- ❖ To: Accept **12/31/09**
- ❖ Click **Collapse**
- ❖ Net Income **1,786,204.73**
- ❖ Click **X** to close window

	Quick Payroll 2009
	Profit & Loss
	January through December 2009
	◇ **Jan - Dec 09** ◇
Ordinary Income/Expense	
Income	
Opening Balance Income	▶ 1,905,000.00 ◀
Landscaping Services	75,000.00
Total Income	1,980,000.00
Cost of Goods Sold	
Materials	50,000.00
Discount Received	-700.00
Total COGS	49,300.00
Gross Profit	1,930,700.00
Expense	
Opening Balance Expense	15,000.00
Automobile Expense	434.00
Depreciation Expense	666.67
Payroll Expenses	127,835.60
Telephone Expense	409.00
Travel Expense	150.00
Total Expense	144,495.27
Net Ordinary Income	1,786,204.73
Net Income	**1,786,204.73**

Financial: Balance Sheet

In this chapter, we created and funded a Petty Cash account. We printed the deposit slips and sent the checks to the bank. The Undeposited Funds disappeared from the Balance Sheet report and the balance went into the checking account. If you process all the checks in the Make Deposit window, make sure Undeposited Funds balance is zero in the Chart of Accounts. The checking and savings account balance is 1,863,980.02. Total Assets is now 3,033,353.73.

Activities:

- ❖ Click **Reports menu**
- ❖ Click **Company & Financial**
- ❖ Click **Balance Sheet Standard**
- ❖ Date: Select **This Fiscal Year**
- ❖ As of: Accept **12/31/09**
- ❖ Click **Collapse**
- ❖ Total Assets **3,033,353.73**
- ❖ Click **X** to close window

Quick Payroll 2009
Balance Sheet
As of December 31, 2009

	Dec 31, 09
ASSETS	
Current Assets	
Checking/Savings	
Petty Cash	100.00
Money Market Account	100,000.00
USA Checking	1,661,131.00
USA Payroll	102,749.02
Total Checking/Savings	1,863,980.02
Accounts Receivable	
Accounts Receivable	1,085,625.00
Total Accounts Receivable	1,085,625.00
Other Current Assets	
Payroll Asset	19,415.38
Inventory Asset	25,000.00
Total Other Current Assets	44,415.38
Total Current Assets	2,994,020.40
Fixed Assets	
Truck	39,333.33
Total Fixed Assets	39,333.33
TOTAL ASSETS	**3,033,353.73**

Review Bank Reconciliation Steps

Reconciling your bank statement in QuickBooks is different from reconciling your bank statement in Quicken. With QuickBooks, most of your checks will be written from your bills; that is, if you set up to payment from bills. Therefore, it is important to implement a policy of entering your bills first and then writing checks from bills. In Quicken, if you don't automate your checks, you will first write checks on your checkbooks and then manually key in your checks to the check register. This is where most mistakes are made.

Reconciliation Process:

When you open your bank statement, use the following steps to get started and complete the Reconcile window. In the beginning, you will be running the first trial to see if your bank reconciliation difference is 0.00. If it's not zero, then start the correction and reconciliation process to get you to 0.00, by clicking a checkmark on each entry in the window. This is the summary of the reconciliation process:

- Click Banking menu.
- Click Reconcile
- Account: Select the right account.
- Statement Date: Type statement date from bank statement.
- End Balance: Type the amount from bank statement.
- Service Charge: Type amount and date from statement, select Interest exp.
- Interest Earned: Type amount and date from statement, select Interest Inc.
- Click Continue (bottom of the window) to the Reconcile window.
- Click Mark All button (bottom of the window).
- Difference (bottom right of the window Must be 0.00.
- If it's not 0.00, click Unmark All (bottom right of the window).
- Click Modify (bottom right of the window) to go back to reconcile window.

Major reconciling areas:

Since you are using QuickBooks and entering your bills first before writing checks, you may have a few reconciliation problems, and they may come from these areas:

- You entered wrong amounts from the bank statement to the Reconcile window.
- Your bank made deposits into your account which you don't know about (e.g. Interest earned).
- Your bank made withdrawals which you don't know about (e.g. Service fees)

- You wrote a check to a vendor in a hurry and didn't record it in the check register
- Someone wrote a check to him or herself and didn't record it in the check register
- The bank overpaid or underpaid on a check by mistake.

Minor reconciling areas:

Sometimes the bank will make a mistake in paying a check and the statement will reflect that what they paid is different from what is actually on the check. And sometimes, when you're entering amounts from the statement to the reconciling window or making a journal entry, what you entered might be different from what is actually on the statement. You will be able to find these errors if you use the following steps or look in the following areas:

- Error of Commission: Instead of 23.45, you typed 230.45 or 203.45.
- Error of Omission: Instead of 23.45, you typed 20.00 and left out 3.45 or .45 or 5.
- Error of Transposition: Instead of 23.45, you typed 32.45 or 23.54.
- Error of Multiple Mistakes: Difference is 99.99. You left out .01 and 100.
- Wrong Journal entry: You entered amount as debit when it should be credit
- Duplicate checks: You mistakenly wrote two checks to the same vendor.

Entering amount from bank statement:

When you click Modify, and you're taken back to the Reconcile window, you are now ready to verify and confirm that the amounts you've just entered from the bank statement and the amounts in the Reconcile window are the same. Check the following:

- Account: Verify you are in the right account.
- Beginning Balance: Check that last month's statement ending balance and beginning balance you just entered are the same.
- Ending Balance: Verify you typed the correct Ending Balance.
- Service Charge: Verify you typed the correct total of all Service Charges.
- Interest Earned: Verify you typed the correct total of all Interest Earned.
- Click Continue to go back to the Reconcile window.

Deposits by bank into your account:

Scan through the bank statement and checkmark deposit entries on the Reconcile window. You are checking for outstanding deposit entries without checkmarks.

- Click Report menu, Banking, Deposit Details and Date down arrow. Select Custom. Type beginning and end date on the bank statement.
- Make sure the entry you are looking for is not in the Deposit Details.

- Make a journal entry for that entry. I'll discuss how later in another section.

Withdrawal by bank from your account:
Scan through the bank statement and checkmark checks and withdrawals in the Reconcile window. You are checking for outstanding checks and withdrawals without checkmarks.

- Click Report menu, Banking, Check Details and Date down arrow. Select Custom. Type beginning and end date on the bank statement.
- Make sure the entry you are looking for is not in the Check Details.
- Make a journal entry for that entry. I'll discuss how later in another section.

You wrote checks to vendors not recorded:
After you have checkmarked the deposits and withdrawals in the Reconcile window from the bank statement, you will find a check on the statement that is not a Reconcile window.

- You may have written a COD check and forgotten to record it.
- Click Report menu, Banking, Check Details and Date down arrow. Select Custom. Type beginning and end date on the bank statement.
- Make sure the entry you are looking for is not in the Check Details report.
- Make a journal entry for that entry. I'll discuss how later in another section.

Someone wrote a check to himself/herself:
After you have checkmarked the deposits and withdrawals in the Reconcile window from the bank statement, you will find a check on the statement that is not a Reconcile window.

- This may be a missing check. Someone found the company checkbook and wrote a check to himself/herself and forged the company's signature.
- Find the actual check from the bank statement envelope or request a copy of the check from your bank. Contact your banker immediately for fraud.
- Click Report menu, Banking, Missing Checks, and Date down arrow. Select Custom. Type beginning and end date on the bank statement.
- Make sure the entry you are looking for is not in the Check Details.
- Make a journal entry for that entry. I'll discuss how later in another section.

Bank overpaid or underpaid a check:
After you have checkmarked all the deposits and withdrawals in the Reconcile

window from the bank statement, you will NOT find a check on the statement that is not a reconcile window. That is, you have clicked all the entries and you still have a difference at the bottom right of the Reconcile window.

- Your problem may be an overpayment or underpayment.
- Use the error finding process such as Error of Commission, Error of Omission, Error of Transposition and Error of Multiple Mistakes, which I'll discuss later in another section.

Error of Commission:
If you've clicked all the entries from the bank statement to the Reconcile window and you still have a difference at the bottom right of the window:

- Divide your difference by 2. If you can divide the difference without a remainder, you may have a commission problem at the end of the number. If you can divide the difference by 3 or 9 without a remainder, you may also have a commission problem.
- Look for the amount on the statement that is longer than the one in the Reconcile window. Instead of 20, the bank may have paid 200 ,or instead of 45, bank paid 405.
- When you find it, you will make a journal entry.

Error of Omission:
If you've clicked all the entries from the bank statement to the Reconcile window and you still have a difference at the bottom right of the window:

- Divide your difference by 2. If you can divide the difference without a remainder, you may have an omission problem at end of the number. If you can divide the difference by 3 or 9 without a remainder, you may also have an omission problem.
- Look for the amount on the statement that is shorter than the one in the Reconcile window. Instead of 200, the bank may have paid 20, or instead of 203, the bank paid 23.
- When you find it, make a journal entry.

Error of Transposition:
If you've clicked all the entries from the bank statement to the Reconcile window and you still have a difference at the bottom right of the window:

- Divide your difference by 3 or 9. If you can divide the difference without a remainder, you may a transposition problem.
- Look for the amount on the statement that has the amount switched around. Instead of 245, the bank paid 254.
- After you find it, make a journal entry.

Error of Multiple Mistakes:
If you've clicked all the entries from the bank statement to the Reconcile window and you still have a difference at the bottom right of the window:

- If your difference has few pennies to round to a whole number, for example, 99.99 or any amount closer, you may have a problem of multiple mistakes.
- You first have to look for the amount which makes the difference a whole number, in this case 0.01. Scan through the last digits amount on the bank statement. When you find 0.001, then start looking for the 100.00, which is easy to find, by using the error of commission and omission as explained above.
- When you find it, make a journal entry.

Wrong Journal Entry:
After you have checkmarked the deposits and withdrawals in the Reconcile window from the bank statement, you will find a check or a deposit on the statement that is not a Reconcile window. In other words, if there is an unchecked deposit on the bank statement, look for the same amount in the Reconcile window check column. And if there is an unchecked withdrawal on the bank statement, look for the same amount in the Reconcile window deposit column. You credited deposit instead of debiting it, and you debited withdrawal instead of crediting it.

- Divide your difference by 2. If you can divide the difference without a remainder, you may have a problem of wrong journal entry. You have entered a deposit as a withdrawal or a withdrawal as a deposit.
- Look on the bank statement to see if you can find one half of the amount of the difference. For example, if the difference at the bottom right of the Reconcile window is 200, look for 100 on the bank statement and in the middle of the Reconcile window.

- When you find it, make two journal entries. One is to reverse the mistake you made and another to make the right journal entry.

Duplicate Checks:
For some reason you may have written two checks to the same vendor. Maybe the first as a COD and later, you wrote another check thinking that the vendor had not been paid.

- Click Report menu, Banking, Missing Checks and Date down arrow. Select Custom. Type beginning and end date on the bank statement.
- Look at the check number column to see if you find duplicate check numbers.
- If you discover you wrote two checks and voided one of them, but before you put a stop payment with your bank, the check had already been cashed, you have a duplicate check problem.
- You will need to reverse the voided check to be able to match the bank statement; therefore, you need a journal entry.

Review Bank Reconciliation Journal Entries
We have discussed the potential problems you will encounter while reconciling your bank statement. Now is the time to talk about how to correct them. The goal is to make journal entries for those amounts you found on the bank statement. In other words, you are adding to the Reconcile window any amount the bank added to your bank statement without your knowledge, and you subtract from the Reconcile window any amount the bank subtracted from your bank statement. When you're finished, the Reconcile window should have every amount on your bank statement checkmarked, and the bottom difference must be 0.00.

Earlier, I said there are at least two times you are going to make journal entries. The first one is at the end of the month, when you are making the company-related journal entries. The second is when you receive your bank statements and you are making bank-related journal entries. We talked about company-related journal entries; let's look at the following bank-related journal entries.

Entering amount from bank statement:
You will not need a journal entry. All you have to do is click the Modify button. You will be taken to Begin Reconciliation window, where you can make the corrections needed, if any. Just enter the correct TOTAL of all Services Charge or the TOTAL of all Interest Earned amounts. QuickBooks will make the journal entry for you, in case you need to know what QuickBooks did, if you have to do it yourself next time.

For total Service Charges of 125, QuickBooks would make the following entries:
USA Checking   125.00

Service Charges Expense   125.00

For total interest income of 535, QuickBooks would make the following entries:
USA Checking   535.00
Interest Income   535.00

Deposits by Bank into your account:
If the bank deposited electronic fund transfer (EFT) into your checking from a customer for consulting services you provided in the amount of 150,000, you will increase or debit the checking account (the bank deposited the cash) and increase or credit the services (the customer is paying for). Make the following entries:

USA Checking   150,000
Consulting Income   150,000

Withdrawal by Bank from your account:
What if one of your customers sent you a check for 2,450.50, you deposited the check in USA Checking account, and later the check was returned to the bank because of NSF (Non Sufficient Funds)? The bank will now withdraw that same amount from your account. You will decrease or credit the account the bank withdrew the cash from; decrease or debit the Consulting Income. Make the following entries:

USA Checking   2,450.50
Consulting Income   2,450.50

Or you can move the entries around, like I did below; it's still the same thing. I used the above method to make it easy for you to follow and understand by starting with USA Checking first:

Consulting Income   2,450.50
USA Checking   2,450.50

You wrote checks to vendors not recorded:
You wrote a COD (cash on delivery) check for 3,782.12 in a hurry for office supplies you ordered and later found out you had not recorded it. You will decrease or credit the checking account from which you wrote the COD check; increase or debit the Office Supplies you are paying for. Make the following entries:

USA Checking   3,782.12
Office Supplies   3,782.12

Someone wrote a check to himself/herself:
After you find out someone wrote a 50,000 check to himself/herself, you must make an entry to record the check and balance with the bank statement while you go after the person who wrote the check. You decrease or credit the checking account from which the person wrote the check; and increase or debit Other expenses. You used Other expenses because the account has nothing to do with other accounts in the Chart of Accounts. Make the following entries:

USA Checking   50,000.00
Other Expenses   50,000.00

Bank overpaid or underpaid a check:
When you find out the bank overpaid on a check, if the amount is too small (depending on your company policy), such as less than a dollar, you write if off. However, if the amount is more than a dollar, you make the entry and call the bank for a refund. Whether it is a small or large amount, you must make a journal entry to balance with the bank statement. If the bank overpaid by 50 cents, you decrease or credit the checking account from which the bank overpaid; and increase or debit Other expenses. Make the following entries:

USA Checking   0.50
Other Expenses   0.50

If bank underpaid by 50 cents, you will increase or debit the checking account from which the bank overpaid; and decrease or credit Other expenses. Make the following entries:

USA Checking   0.50
Other Expenses   0.50

Error of Commission:
This is like the overpayment above. For instance the bank paid 200 instead of paying 20. The difference is 180; that is why you can divide the difference by 2, 3 or 9. You will decrease or credit the checking, from which the bank overpaid; and increase or debit Other Expenses. Make the following entries:

USA Checking   180.00
Other Expenses   180.00

Error of Omission:

This mistake is like the underpayment above. For instance: Instead of 900, the bank paid 90. The difference is 810, which is why you should divide the difference by 2, 3 or 9. You will increase or debit the checking account from which the bank overpaid; and decrease or credit Other Expenses. Make the following entries:

USA Checking	810.00	
Other Expenses		810.00

Error of Transposition:

This is a common mistake made by anyone who is new to the accounting or bookkeeping industry. For instance: Instead of 245, the bank paid 254. The difference is 9, that is why you can divide the difference by 3 or 9. This is an overpayment of 9. You will decrease or credit the checking account from which the bank overpaid; and increase or debit Other Expenses. Make the following entries:

USA Checking		9.00
Other Expenses	9.00	

Error of Multiple Mistakes:

In this case the bank made two mistakes in the same month on the same account. It can be tricky to find this mistake, but with practice it is easy to find. If have one round amount you did not click, such as 200, but if the difference is 199.99, then you know you are looking at multiple mistakes. Find the 1 cent and then click the 200 in the Reconcile window—you don't need journal entry. Another example: Instead of 500.20, the bank paid 500.21 (a difference and overpayment of 1 cent), and instead of 5,200 the bank paid 5,000 (a difference and underpayment of 200). If you net the overpayment of 1 cent and the underpayment of 200, you get an underpayment of 199.99. To book the overpayment of 1 cent, you will decrease or credit the checking from which the bank overpaid and increase or debit other expenses. Make the following entries:

USA Checking		0.01
Other Expenses	0.01	

To book the underpayment of 200, you will increase or debit the checking, from which the bank overpaid; and decrease or credit Other Expenses. Make the following entries:

USA Checking   200.00
Other Expenses   200.00

Wrong Journal Entry:
What if, after you have completed any of the above journal entries, you go to the Reconcile window and still you're not in balance? You may have made a mistake by reversing the debit and credit entries:

USA Checking   100.00
Other Expenses   100.00

Instead of booking 100 to debit USA Checking, you booked a credit. You are now faced with double mistake or multiple mistakes. Any time you make a wrong journal entry it will take you two entries to make your entries right. The first one is to correct the mistake you made, and the second one is to make the entry you were going to make in the first place. Your difference will be 200, which is why you should divide the difference by 2 to find the number that is causing the problem. To correct the 100 mistake, you will increase or debit USA Checking; and decrease or credit Other Expenses. Make the following entries:

USA Checking   100.00
Other Expenses   100.00

To book the entry of 100 you were going to make in the first place, you will increase or debit USA Checking and decrease or credit other expenses. Make the following entries:

USA Checking   100.00
Other Expenses   100.00

Duplicate Checks:
What if you find out you wrote another check after you wrote a COD check to the same vendor for 3,782.12 and you immediately void the second check from QuickBooks? And before you can get to the bank, the two checks have been cashed? You have to reverse the check you've just voided. When you write the second check, this is the entry QuickBooks makes for you:

USA Checking   3,782.12
Office Supplies   3,782.12

When you void the second check, this is the entry QuickBooks makes for you:

USA Checking   3,782.12
Office Supplies   3,782.12

When you find out from the bank statement that the vendor cashed the two checks, you have to reverse the check you voided and call the vendor to send you a refund for cashing two checks. You will decrease or credit the checking account from which you wrote the second check; and increase or debit the Office Supplies you are paying for. Make the following entries to reverse the check you voided:

USA Checking   3,782.12
Office Supplies   3,782.12

Chapter Summary

Bank Reconciliation is a major part of your duty at the end of every month. If your bank statement balance is not the same as your checking accounts, the reconciliation window will give the balance difference. If it is a customer deposit that is on statement but not the books, create an invoice, receive the payment, and deposit the check to make your books balance. If it is a vendor check that is not on the books, create a bill and make the payment so the amount is withdrawn from your checking account to make your books balance. With all others, you may create journal entries to make the books and the bank statement balances the same.

What we accomplished:
- Reviewed the Banking submenus
- Wrote checks to vendors
- Recorded credit card charges
- Processed single and multiple checks.
- Ran several register reports
- Practiced the edit, sort and split functions
- Made deposit moving undeposited funds to checking
- Practiced transfer of funds from checking to petty cash
- Created journal entries to balance with bank statement
- Reconciled bank statement with checking account
- Reviewed bank reconciliation steps
- Reviewed bank reconciliation journal entries
- Processed financial statements

Additional Financial activities:
- Paid America Auto Service by check 150
- Paid America Auto Service by credit card 24
- Moved undeposited funds to checking 900,000
- Transfer funds from checking to petty cash 100
- Made journal entry for underpayment 50
- Made journal entry for overpayment 10

Optional Test 9

Questions: True/False

Answer the following questions by placing letter the T or F in the space provided before the question number.

_____ 1. QuickBooks will not allow you to write a check unless the complete vendor's name and address are provided.

_____ 2. Like the Write Check window, the Enter Credit Card Charge window has a Ref No. box where you can identify the number from the charge bill.

_____ 3. In the Loan Manger window, the "What if Scenario" allows you to calculate the monthly payment for the proposed loan.

_____ 4. The Use Register window allows you to select a checking account from where you can write a check but does allow you to select a credit card account.

_____ 5. When transferring funds between accounts, the balance amounts of the respective accounts are not displayed prior the actual transfer.

_____ 6. After you have completed an account reconciliation it is very important to click the Reconcile Now button to tell QuickBooks you're finished.

_____ 7. QuickBooks allows you to transfer funds between the same account and between different accounts.

_____ 8. When you sort a Check Register by amount (largest first) payments are arranged in ascending order while deposits are arranges in descending order.

_____ 9. When writing a check, the check numbers that start with #1 are assigned by QuickBooks it is impossible to start a check number at 1000 or 2000.

_____ 10. After you have completed an account reconciliation, the ending balance and cleared balance must be equal.

Questions: Multiple Choices

Answer the following questions by placing letter A, B, C, or D in the space provided before the question number.

_____ 1. There are many functions in the Loan Manage window, which of these is not an available function?
A. Add a Loan
B. Retire a Loan
C. Edit a Loan
D. Remove a Loan

_____ 2. After you have completed an account reconciliation process, the difference box at the bottom right of the window must be_____?
A. More than zero
B. Less than zero
C. Zero
D. All of the above

_____ 3. When you open the Reconciliation window with entries, you would immediately test if the available entries are enough to complete the reconciliation. Which of these buttons is use for this test?
A. Go To All
B. Mark All
C. Unmark All
D. Cancel All

_____ 4. In the Make Deposit window QuickBooks allows you to perform the following deposit-related activities except...?
A. Print Deposit Slip
B. Print Deposit Summary
C. Order Deposit Slip
D. Print Deposit Bill

_____ 5. When you sort a Check Register by amount (smallest first) which of the following is the best way the window is displayed?
A. Payment in ascending order
B. Payment is descending order
C. All of the above
D. None of the above

____ 6. During the Account Reconciliation process, you create journal entries to balance the statement and the company register except...?
    A. Over and Under payment by bank
    B. Income in Bank statement not in register
    C. Expenses in Bank statement not in register
    D. All of the above, no exception

____ 7. You can use the Split Entry function to separate bills with the following characteristics?
    A. One bill from same vendor
    B. One bill from different vendors
    C. One bill from same vendor with same accounts
    D. One bill from same vendor with different accounts

____ 8. After you have completed the Make Deposit process, you check to make sure that the deposit has been transferred from_____ to _____?
    A. Deposited Funds account to Checking account
    B. Undeposited Funds account to Checking account
    C. Checking account to Deposited Funds account
    D. Checking account to Undeposited Funds account

____ 9. During reconciliation if your difference is divisible by 3 or 9, you know you have an error of_____?
    A. Omission
    B. Commission
    C. Transposition
    D. All of the above

____ 10. When you are performing account reconciliations you would keep you eye on which of the following errors?
    A. Omission
    B. Commission
    C. Transposition
    D. All of the above

Chapter 11

Reports Menu

Objectives: After you've completed this chapter, you will be able to:

- ✓ Explain the Reports submenus and center
- ✓ Company Snapshot and Advanced Reports
- ✓ Memorize reports and Process multiple reports
- ✓ Generate reports under the following submenus:
    - Company & Financial
    - Customer & Receivables
    - Sales
    - Jobs, Time & Mileage
    - Vendors & Payables
    - Purchases
    - Inventory
    - Employees & Payroll
    - Banking
    - Accountant & Taxes
    - Budgets
    - List
    - Customer and Transaction Reports
    - Print and Send Forms
- ✓ Run financial reports and compare results

Review Reports Submenus

Congratulations! You have reached the Promised Land! This is where you are going to see the results of all the entries you've made. The Reports menu has submenus of various reports to help determine if you're going forward or backward financially. One of the activities you may like to do here is to place a report you frequently use on the Icon Bar. Remember to preview a report to see if your results are correct. One way to spot check your report is to look for errors on the Profit & Loss and the Balance Sheet reports, not the Statement of Cash Flows. **Anywhere you see an amount with a minus sign (-) is a sign of error, unless it is a sub-account being subtracted from a main account as in Accumulated Depreciation and Truck account, Discount Received on purchase as a subtraction from Cost of Goods Sold, or Discount Given on sales as a subtraction from Sales Income.** When you find a minus amount, the entry is backward and needs to go from income to expense or vice versa.

- Click **Reports menu**

The following activities are found under the Reports menu:

- **Report Center:** One of the best features of the Report Navigator is that it allows you to see all groups in one window, so you can click a report group and see all the reports in that group, instead of going through the Reports Menu that would only allow you to see one group at a time.

- **Company Snapshot:** This submenu allows you to see the summary of your activities including: income and expenses, account balance, customers who owe money, vendors to pay, and reminders.

- **Advanced Reports:** You have to logon to the internet to use this submenu.

- **Memorized Reports:** The most frequently used report should be customized and memorized, so you don't have to re-customize that report every time you open it. For example, when you open the Profit and Loss Standard, you may customize the report by selecting a date range to see the result of that date, and when you exit the report, you lose all your customization. But if you memorize your report after customization, the settings are saved for future use.

- **Process Multiple Reports:** Normally, you would open a report, review and exit to open another report. Not anymore! QuickBooks has an option that allows you to open all the reports at one time and review them without exiting and coming back. You can also process multiple reports by group instead of opening all the reports individually on your desktop.

- **Company & Financial:** This group has all the reports that are related to the financial status of your business. It includes Profit & Loss: Standard, Detail, YTD Comparison, By Job, By Class and Unclassified; Income & Expenses: Income Customer Summary, Income by Customer Detail, Expense by Vendor Summary, Expense by Vendor Detail and Income & Expense Graph; Balance Sheet & Net Worth: Standard, Detail, Prev Yr Comparison and Net Worth Graph Cash Flow: Statement of Cash Flow and Cash Flow Forecast.

- **Customers & Receivables:** This group contains reports about your customers and their activities. It includes A/R Aging: Summary, Detail, Account Receivable Graph, Open Invoices and Collections: Customer Balance: Summary, Detail, Unbilled Costs by Job and Transaction List by Customer List: Customer Phone List, Customer Contact List and Item Price List.

- **Sales:** If you want to narrow down to Customer sales only, come to this group. It includes Sales by Customer: Summary, Detail, Pending Sales and Sales Graph; Sales by Item: Summary and Detail; Sales by Rep: Summary and Detail.

- **Jobs, Time & Mileage:** This is the best of the best set of reports. If you can learn how to use and interpret these set of reports, the financial life of your business will never be the same—guaranteed! If you want to zero in on costs and profit to find out how much profit you're getting, how much time you are spending on each job, and how much you are spending on each vehicle, you definitely want to come to this set of reports. It includes Job & Profitability: Job Profitability Summary, Job Profitability Detail, Profit & Loss by Job, Item Profitability and Unbilled Cost by Job; Job Estimates: Job Estimates vs. Actual Summary, Job Estimates vs. Actuals, Estimates by Job and Open Purchase order by Job; Time: By Vehicle Summary, By Vehicle Detail, By Job Summary and By Job Detail: Mileage: By Vehicle Summary, By Vehicle Detail, By Job Summary and By Job Detail.

- **Vendors & Payables:** When it comes to finding out how much you paid your vendors and how much you still owe them, this is your destination. It includes A/P Aging: Summary, Detail and Accounts Payable Graph Vendor Balances: Vendor Balances Summary, Vendor Balances Detail, Unpaid Bills Detail and Transaction List by Vendor 1099:Summary and Detail; Sales Tax: Sales Tax Liability and Sales Tax Revenue Summary: List: Vendor Phone List and Vendor Contact List.

- **Purchases:** Because you set up the Purchases Preferences and bought and paid your vendors for inventories, you will have Purchases reports. They include Purchases by Vendor Summary, Purchases by Vendor Detail, Purchases by Item Summary, Purchases by Item Detail, Open Purchase Order and Open Purchase Orders by Job.

- **Inventory:** Inventory valuation is a key task to a business, especially a merchandise business. As you buy and sell inventories, reports are generated by QuickBooks. Inventory reports include Inventory Valuation Summary, Inventory Valuation Detail, Inventory Stock Status by Item, Inventory Stock Status by Vendor, Physical Inventory Worksheet and Pending Builds.

- **Employees & Payroll:** If you decide to use the QuickPayroll, you will have employee and payroll reports. This set of reports includes Payroll: Payroll Summary, Payroll Item Detail, Payroll Detail Review, Payroll Transaction by Payee, Payroll Transaction Detail, Payroll Liability Balances, Payroll Item Listing, Employee Earnings Summary and Employee State Taxes Detail Employee: Employee Contact List, Employee Withholding and Paid Time Off List.

- **Banking:** The Banking set of reports allows you to open, review and print banking reports such as deposits and check reports. This set of reports includes Banking: Deposit Detail, Check Detail, Missing Check, Reconciliation Discrepancy and Previous Reconciliation.

- **Accountant & Taxes:** From time to time, you want to review account balances or transaction activities. This set of reports will give you what you're looking for and then some. It includes Account Activity: Trial Balance, General Ledger, Transaction Detail by Account, Journal, Audit Trial, Voided/Detailed Transactions, Voided/Detailed Transactions History and Transaction Listing by Date; Listing: Account Listing and Fixed Asset Listing Income Tax: Preparation, Summary and Detail.

- **Budgets:** Planning is one of the keys to business success, and budget reports will enable you to see your plans as they relate to your financial goals. It includes Budget—Budget Overview, Budget vs. Actual, Profit & Loss Budget Performance, and Budget vs. Actual Graph.

- **List:** Employee, Customer and Vendor information are always needed in the daily life of a business manager. Since all the required information is provided in the List windows, this is the place you will come for contact information of every person without running from one file to another. It includes Customer: Phone List and Contact List; Vendor: Phone List and Contact List; Employee: Contact List; Other Names: Phone List and Contact List; Listing: Account Listing, Item Price List, Item Listing, Payroll Item Listing, Fixed Asset Listing, Term Listing, To Do Notes and Memorized Transaction Listing.

- **Custom Summary Report:** Most reports you would pull in QuickBooks are preset. If you want to customize your own report, this is the window to use. It allows you to set date ranges, include checks (voided or not) and other choices.

- **Custom Transaction Detail Report:** Not only can you customize a summary report, QuickBooks also allows you to customize transactions. You can add as much detail in your report as you like.

- **QuickReport:** This excellent report allows you to quickly review the activity of every account. It is handy and quick, and can be accessed from every account register. The QuickReport button is located at the top of the register.

- **Transaction History:** If you want to see the history or activities of an account, open that account, click on it, run the Transaction History report, and the history will be displayed for you.

- **Transaction Journal:** To see the debit and credit QuickBooks did on an account, just open the account and run this function. The debit and credit report will be displayed for you.

Memorize Reports

What if you have a series of reports you use frequently? Each time you open these reports, you have to change the Date defaults to see the results of a certain period. Soon, you will get tired of changing the default settings of these reports. The answer is to memorize the reports, by opening and customizing the reports with the dates and defaults settings you would like to see next time you open the reports. You can now use the same report over and over again; you don't have to change the dates.

Activities:

- ❖ Click **Reports menu**
- ❖ Click **Memorized Reports**
- ❖ Click **Memorized Report List**
- ❖ Click **Memorized Report down arrow** (bottom left)
- ❖ Select **New Group**
- ❖ Name: Type **Monthly Reports**. Click **OK**
- ❖ Click **Banking menu**
- ❖ Click **Use Register**
- ❖ Select Account: **USA Checking**. Click **OK**
- ❖ Click on **Check #1001 for Telephone America 150.00**
- ❖ Click **QuickReport** (top of the window)
- ❖ Dates: Select **This Fiscal Year**
- ❖ Click **Memorize**...(top left)
- ❖ Name: Type **Telephone America**
- ❖ Click **Save in Memorized Report…**
- ❖ Select **Monthly Reports**. Click **OK**
- ❖ Click **Reports menu**
- ❖ Click **Memorized Reports**
- ❖ Click **Memorized Report List**
- ❖ Click **Monthly Reports**
- ❖ **Look Telephone America is listed**

Process Multiple Reports

Sometimes, you just want to preview and print one report. All you have to do is go to the Report menu, find the report, open it and print. However, other times you may want to preview and print a set of reports. Now, there is a quicker and easier way to preview and print a set of reports, all at one time. The Process Multiple Reports tool will allow you to choose a group of reports and print them. The groups are Accountant, Banking, Company, Employees, Register Reports and Vendors.

Activities:

- ❖ Click **Reports menu**
- ❖ Click **Process Multiple Reports**
- ❖ Select Memorize Reports From: Select **Employees**
- ❖ **Highlight 1ˢᵗ date under From** (right of the window)
- ❖ Type **1/1/09**. Press **Tab**. Type **12/31/09**
- ❖ **Repeat for next 2 reports**
- ❖ Click **Display**
- ❖ Click **Window menu.**
- ❖ **Click on the 3 reports individually to review**
- ❖ Click **Window menu.**
- ❖ Click **Close All**
- ❖ Click **Company menu**
- ❖ Click **Home Page**

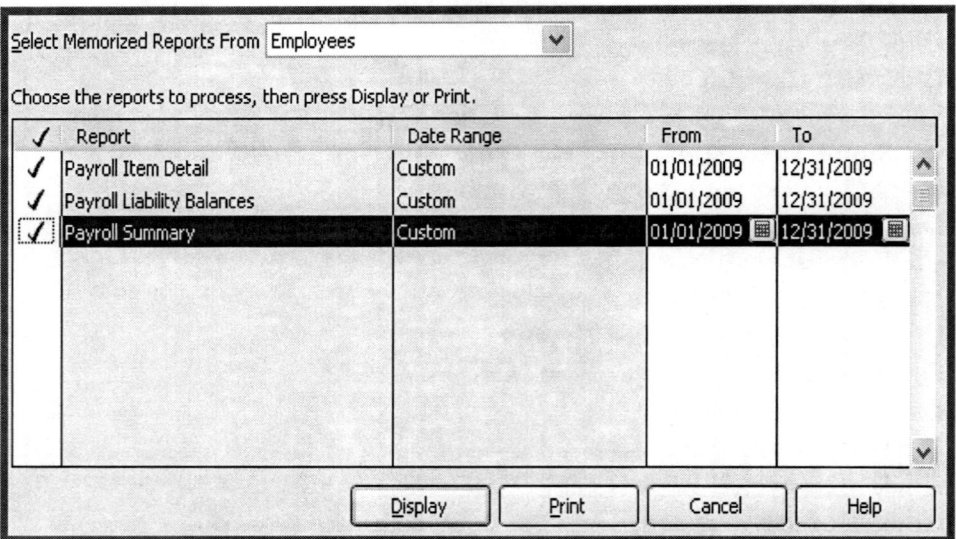

Profit & Loss Standard

QuickBooks has several groups of reports; the first group is Company & Financial, with Profit & Loss statement as a sub report. Often, you want to see how much income is left after you've paid your bills. The Profit & Loss statement will give you the summary of your income and expenses. The balance on this report will determine how much money you have in your bank account. The more net income there is, the more cash is in your bank account. However, not all net income is in your bank account.

Activities:

- ❖ Click **Reports menu**
- ❖ Click **Company & Financial**
- ❖ Click **Profit & Loss Standard**
- ❖ Date: Select **This Fiscal Year**
- ❖ Click **Collapse** (top of the window)
- ❖ Columns (top right): Select **Quarter**
- ❖ You may practice with other reports in that section

Quick Payroll 2009
Profit & Loss
January through December 2009

	Jan - Mar 09	Apr - Jun 09	Jul - Sep 09	Oct - Dec 09	TOTAL
Ordinary Income/Expense					
Income					
Opening Balance Income	▶ 1,905,000.00 ◀	0.00	0.00	0.00	1,905,000.00
Landscaping Services	75,000.00	0.00	0.00	0.00	75,000.00
Total Income	1,980,000.00	0.00	0.00	0.00	1,980,000.00
Cost of Goods Sold					
Materials	50,000.00	0.00	0.00	0.00	50,000.00
Discount Received	-700.00	0.00	0.00	0.00	-700.00
Total COGS	49,300.00	0.00	0.00	0.00	49,300.00
Gross Profit	1,930,700.00	0.00	0.00	0.00	1,930,700.00
Expense					
Opening Balance Expense	15,000.00	0.00	0.00	0.00	15,000.00
Automobile Expense	434.00	0.00	0.00	0.00	434.00
Depreciation Expense	666.67	0.00	0.00	0.00	666.67
Payroll Expenses	127,835.60	0.00	0.00	0.00	127,835.60
Telephone Expense	409.00	0.00	0.00	0.00	409.00
Travel Expense	150.00	0.00	0.00	0.00	150.00
Total Expense	144,495.27	0.00	0.00	0.00	144,495.27
Net Ordinary Income	1,786,204.73	0.00	0.00	0.00	1,786,204.73
Net Income	**1,786,204.73**	**0.00**	**0.00**	**0.00**	**1,786,204.73**

Income & Expense Graph

A picture, they say, is worth a thousand words. This is especially true with the income and expense graphs. QuickBooks has made it interesting and informational by providing a bar graph and a pie chart. The bar graph has two bars: the big one is your income and the small one is your expense. The pie chart is just one, with both income and expenses broken down by percentages. A box to the right further breaks down your expenses with payroll being the largest expense.

Activities:

- ❖ Click **Reports menu**
- ❖ Click **Company & Financial**
- ❖ Click **Income & Expense Graph**
- ❖ Click **Dates…**(top left of the window
- ❖ Graph Date: Select **This Year**. Click **OK**
- ❖ Click **View menu**
- ❖ Click **Add "QuickInsight Income & Expense" to Icon Bar**
- ❖ Label: Type **Inc/Exp Graph**
- ❖ Click **OK** to "Add Window to Icon Bar"
- ❖ Click **2 Forward arrows** (End of toolbar). Look! Graph is listed
- ❖ Click **X** to close Graph window

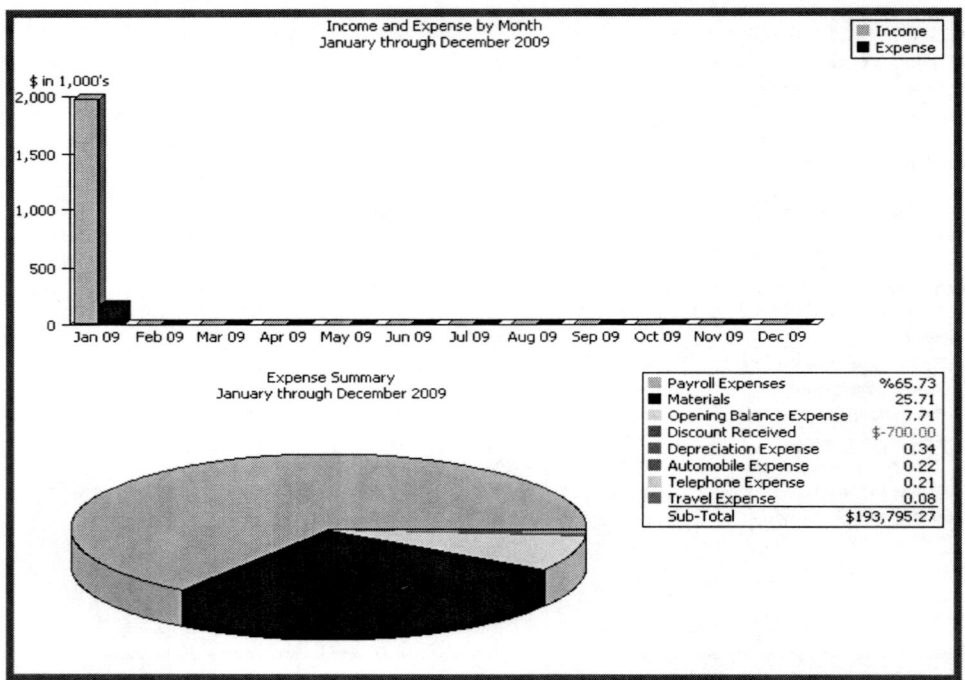

Customer & Receivable Reports

The second group of reports is the Customers & Receivables. The A/R Aging Summary is the first sub-report under this group. The Balance Sheet report will tell you if you have an Account Receivables balance, that is, how much your customers owe you. The next question is, "Who owes you and how long has it been?" The A/R Aging Summary will tell you exactly how long it has been, such as 30, 60, 90 or 120 days. You're a poor collector if you have outstanding A/R of more than 120 days.

Activities:

- ❖ Click **Reports menu**
- ❖ Click **Customers & Receivables**
- ❖ Click **A/R Aging Summary**
- ❖ Date: Select **This Fiscal Year**
- ❖ Interval (days): Type **30**
- ❖ Through (days past due): Type **120**. Press **Tab**
- ❖ You may practice with other reports in that section

Sales Reports

The third group of reports is Sales. The Sales by Customer Summary is the first sub-report under the Sales group of reports. If you have several salespeople who service different customers in different regions, the most effective ways of reporting your results are Sales by Customer and Sales by Rep. You want to use the report to find out who your major customer is, and you want to be able to direct future sales to the competitors of your major customer. This is one way to increase sales.

Activities:

- ❖ Click **Reports menu**
- ❖ Click **Sales**
- ❖ Click **Sales by Customer Summary**
- ❖ Date: Select **This Fiscal Year**
- ❖ Columns (top right): Select **Quarter**
- ❖ You may practice with other reports in that section

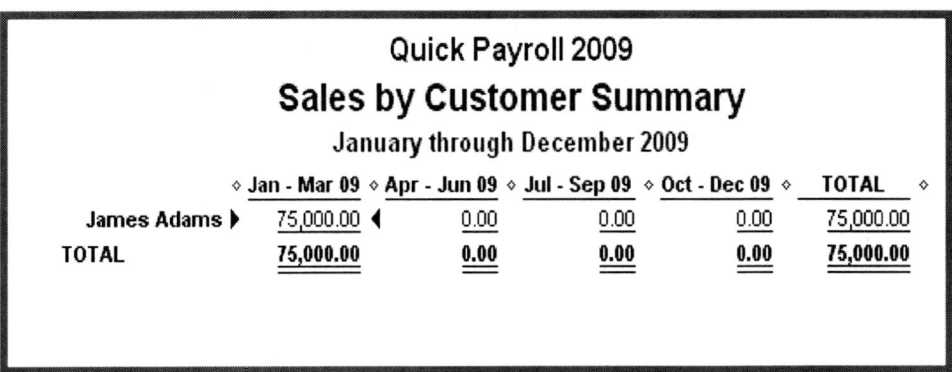

Quick Payroll 2009
Sales by Customer Summary
January through December 2009

	Jan - Mar 09	Apr - Jun 09	Jul - Sep 09	Oct - Dec 09	TOTAL
James Adams ▶	75,000.00 ◀	0.00	0.00	0.00	75,000.00
TOTAL	75,000.00	0.00	0.00	0.00	75,000.00

Job, Time & Mileage Reports

The fourth group of reports is Job, Time & Mileage. The Job Profitability Summary is the first sub-report in this group. You've discovered you're making money, but you want to know which job is making you the most money. Some jobs will require you to spend a lot of money, but make little profit in the process. However, other jobs will require only small investments and with good profit. The Job Profitability Summary report is the key report that shows you the job with the most profit.

Quick Payroll 2009

Job Profitability Summary

January through December 2009

	Act. Cost	Act. Revenue	($) Diff.
James Adams ▶	62,804.19 ◀	75,000.00	12,195.81
TOTAL	**62,804.19**	**75,000.00**	**12,195.81**

Activities:

❖ Click **Reports menu**
❖ Click **Job, Time & Mileage**
❖ Click **Job Profitability Summary**
❖ Date: Select **This Fiscal Year**
❖ You may practice with other reports in that section

Vendors & Payables Reports

The fifth group of reports is the Vendors & Payables. The A/P Aging Summary is the first sub-report under this group. If you look at your Balance Sheet statement, and see Account Payable (A/P) with a balance, you will want to know how long it has been since you forgot to pay your bill. It is a bad business practice to owe your vendors for more than 120 days as it shows that your financial health is in bad shape. It also shows that your vendors are poor collectors with poor collection policies. If you're too busy to run this report, place it on the Icon bar for easy access.

Activities:

- ❖ Click **Reports menu**
- ❖ Click **Vendors & Payables**
- ❖ Click **A/P Aging Summary**
- ❖ Date: Select **This Fiscal Year**
- ❖ Interval (days): Type **30**
- ❖ Through (days past due): Type **120**. Press **Tab**
- ❖ You may practice with other reports in that section

Purchases Reports

The sixth group of reports is Purchases. The Purchases by Vendor Summary is the first sub-report under the Purchases group. From time to time, you will want to run this report to see your purchases by Vendor. You will want to know which Vendor is receiving the most money from you and what they are selling to you. You will want to find out if you're getting any kind of cash discounts for early payments, and if you are using your buying power enough to get price breaks, at least a 10% discount.

Activities:

- ❖ Click **Reports menu**
- ❖ Click **Purchases**
- ❖ Click **Purchases by Vendor Summary**
- ❖ Date: Select **This Fiscal Year**
- ❖ Column: Select **Quarter**
- ❖ You may practice with other reports in that section

Quick Payroll 2009
Purchases by Vendor Summary
January through December 2009

	◇ Jan - Mar 09 ◇	Apr - Jun 09 ◇	Jul - Sep 09 ◇	Oct - Dec 09 ◇	TOTAL ◇
US Supplies ▶	25,000.00 ◀	0.00	0.00	0.00	25,000.00
TOTAL	**25,000.00**	**0.00**	**0.00**	**0.00**	**25,000.00**

Inventory Reports

The seventh group of reports is Inventory. The Inventory Valuation Summary is the first sub-report under the Inventory group. If you sell merchandise to customers, this is one of the most important reports you need to review every month. You will want to know which inventory is stagnant and which is moving fast. From last month to this month, do you still have the same valuation for the same inventory? Valuation should be going down; it is being converted into cash and possibly into profit.

Quick Payroll 2009
Inventory Valuation Summary
As of December 31, 2009

	Item Des...	On Hand	Avg C...	Asset Value	% of Tot...	Sales...	Retail Value	% of Tot...
Inventory								
Flowers	▶ Materials	500	50.00	25,000.00	100.0%	75.00	37,500.00	100.0% ◀
Total Invent...		500		25,000.00	100.0%		37,500.00	100.0%
TOTAL		500		25,000.00	100.0%		37,500.00	100.0%

Activities:

- ❖ Click **Reports menu**
- ❖ Click **Inventory**
- ❖ Click **Inventory Valuation Summary**
- ❖ Date: Select **This Fiscal Year**
- ❖ You may practice with other reports in that section

Employees & Payroll Reports

As a payroll accountant or manager, you want to run as many reports under the Employee and Payroll submenu as possible to get a good handle of what is going on in your department. One of the key reports is the Payroll Summary report, because it adds together all the hours and paycheck amounts you have issued for the period. If you have hourly employees, make sure the hours on this report matches with the total hours you paid to individual employees combined.

Activities:

- ❖ Click **Reports menu**
- ❖ Click **Employees & Payroll**
- ❖ Click **Payroll Summary**
- ❖ Dates: Select **This Calendar Year**
- ❖ Columns: Select **Year**
- ❖ You may practice with other reports in that section

Quick Payroll 2009
Payroll Summary
January through December 2009

	Hours	Rate	Jan - Dec 09
Employee Wages, Taxes and Adjustments			
Gross Pay			
Salary	136	▶	10,384.61 ◀
Salary Sick	12		576.92
Salary Vacation	12		576.92
Hourly	233.5	50.00	11,675.00
Hourly Sick	12	50.00	600.00
Hourly Vacation	12	50.00	600.00
Overtime (x1.5) hourly	5.06667	75.00	380.00
Commission			30,000.00
Bonus			60,000.00
Salary Sick Cashout			480.77
Salary Vacation Cashout			480.77
Total Gross Pay	422.56667		115,754.99

Banking Report

From to time you will want to review the previous month's reconciliation reports. The banking report submenu has previous reconciliation reports you can process to see the details of last month's activities. There are three reports available: summary, detail, and both (summary and detail). You have option to select a report with transactions cleared at the time of reconciliation in pdf or a report with transactions cleared plus any changes made to those transactions since the last reconciliation.

Activities:

- ❖ Click **Reports menu**
- ❖ Click **Banking**
- ❖ Click **Previous Reconciliation**
- ❖ Account: Select **USA Checking**
- ❖ Type of Report: Click **Summary**
- ❖ Click **Display**. Click **X** to close PDF window
- ❖ You may practice with other reports in this section

Quick Payroll 2009
Reconciliation Summary
USA Checking, Period Ending 01/31/2009

	Jan 31, 09
Beginning Balance	800,000.00
Cleared Transactions	
Checks and Payments - 7 items	-38,919.00
Deposits and Credits - 2 items	900,050.00
Total Cleared Transactions	861,131.00
Cleared Balance	**1,661,131.00**
Register Balance as of 01/31/2009	1,661,131.00
Ending Balance	1,661,131.00

Accountant & Taxes Reports

When you run the Balance Sheet report, you will see your assets, liabilities and owner's equity. When you run the Income Statement report, you will see your income, expenses and net income. The Trial Balance report is a "buy one, get two reports." It shows you the balances of both your Balance Sheet and Income Statement. Best of all, it shows your balances in Debit and Credit columns.

Activities:

- ❖ Click **Reports menu**
- ❖ Click **Accountant & Taxes**
- ❖ Click **Trail Balance**
- ❖ Date: Select **This Fiscal Year**
- ❖ Total Debit and Credit are the same **3,228,515.67**
- ❖ You may practice other reports in this section

> On the Trial Balance report the total debits and credits must be equal. Review the accounts though Petty Cash, Money Market Account, and USA Checking are not listed.

Quick Payroll 2009
Trial Balance
As of December 31, 2009

	Dec 31, 09 Debit	Dec 31, 09 Credit
USA Payroll	102,749.02	
Accounts Receivable	1,085,625.00	
Payroll Asset	19,415.38	
Undeposited Funds	0.00	
Inventory Asset	25,000.00	
Truck:Accumulated Depreciation		666.67
Truck:Truck at Cost	40,000.00	
Accounts Payable		1,500.00
Visa Credit Card		524.00
Payroll Liabilities	0.00	
Sales Tax Payable		5,625.00
Office Building Loan		50,000.00
Opening Balance Equity		1,189,500.00
Opening Balance Income		1,905,000.00
Landscaping Services:Materials		75,000.00
Materials	50,000.00	
Discount Received		700.00
Opening Balance Expense	15,000.00	
Automobile Expense:Fuel	74.00	
Automobile Expense:Repairs & Maint	360.00	
Depreciation Expense	666.67	
Payroll Expenses	127,835.60	
Telephone Expense	409.00	
Travel Expense	150.00	
TOTAL	**3,228,515.67**	**3,228,515.67**

Budgets Reports

Without goals, they say, you would not know when one is reached. It's essential to set financial goals; otherwise, you will not have control over your spending habits or work hard enough to reach your income goals. Our goal here is to monitor the payroll budget and during your weekly or monthly meetings, be able to report to the management how the company is doing, whether over budget or under budget for the period under review. It might be you're spending too much on overtime.

Activities:

- ❖ Click **Reports menu**
- ❖ Click **Budgets**
- ❖ Click **Profit & Loss Budget Performance**.
- ❖ Accept **FY 2009—Profit & Loss...** Click **Next**
- ❖ Accept **Account by Month.** Click **Next**
- ❖ Click **Finish**
- ❖ Dates: This **The Fiscal Year**
- ❖ Column: Select **Year**
- ❖ Click **Collapse** (top of the window)
- ❖ You may practice with other reports in this section

Quick Payroll 2009

Profit & Loss Budget Performance

January through December 2009

	Jan - Dec 09	Budget	Jan - Dec 09	YTD Budget	Annual Budget
Ordinary Income/Expense					
Income					
Opening Balance Inco... ▶	1,905,000.00 ◀		1,905,000.00		
Landscaping Services	75,000.00	1,200,000.00	75,000.00	1,200,000.00	1,200,000.00
Total Income	1,980,000.00	1,200,000.00	1,980,000.00	1,200,000.00	1,200,000.00
Cost of Goods Sold					
Materials	50,000.00		50,000.00		
Discount Received	-700.00		-700.00		
Total COGS	49,300.00		49,300.00		
Gross Profit	1,930,700.00	1,200,000.00	1,930,700.00	1,200,000.00	1,200,000.00
Expense					
Opening Balance Expe...	15,000.00		15,000.00		
Automobile Expense	434.00		434.00		
Depreciation Expense	666.67		666.67		
Payroll Expenses	127,835.60	240,000.00	127,835.60	240,000.00	240,000.00
Telephone Expense	409.00		409.00		
Travel Expense	150.00		150.00		
Total Expense	144,495.27	240,000.00	144,495.27	240,000.00	240,000.00
Net Ordinary Income	1,786,204.73	960,000.00	1,786,204.73	960,000.00	960,000.00
Net Income	**1,786,204.73**	**960,000.00**	**1,786,204.73**	**960,000.00**	**960,000.00**

Budget Graph

It's imperative to enter the weekly or monthly meeting with your budget reports; and it's much better to create good graphs to accompany your report. Nobody has time to read 10-page reports and be able to know the major financial results, but with a graph, you will be able to communicate the results precisely and effectively. QuickBooks allows you to present the payroll budget in graphical format.

Activities:
- ❖ Click **Reports menu**
- ❖ Click **Budgets**
- ❖ Click **Budget vs. Actual Graph**
- ❖ Dates…Select **This Year**
- ❖ Click **OK**
- ❖ You may practice with other reports in this section

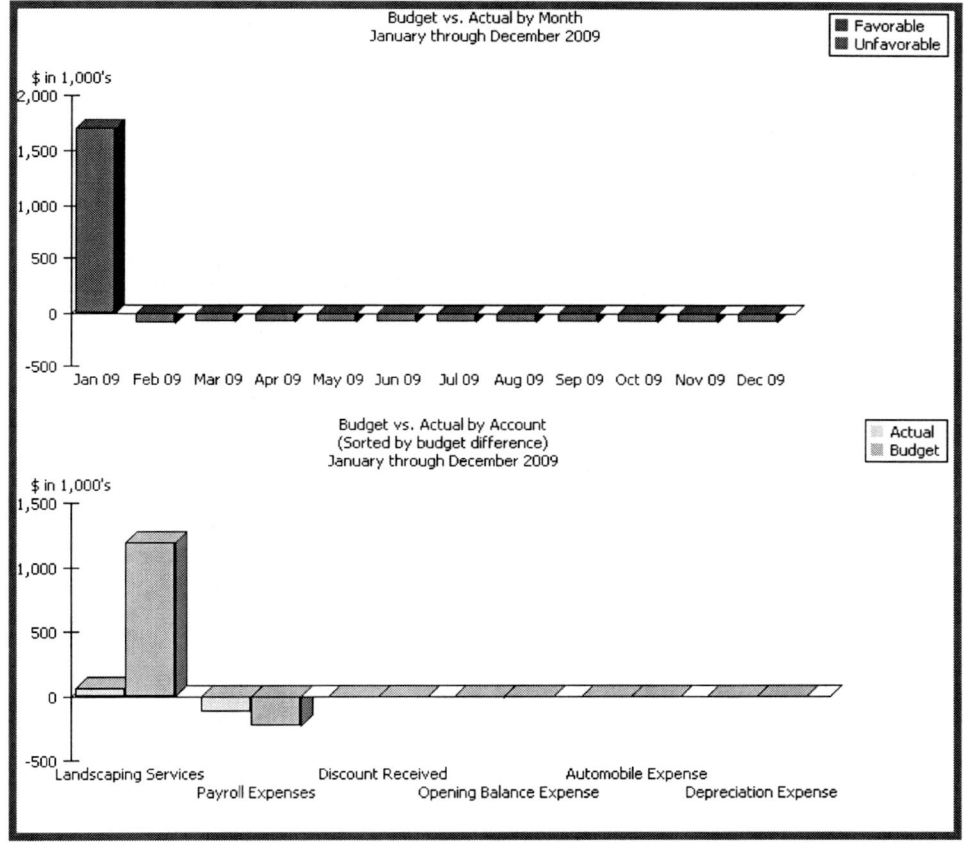

List Reports

Updating your employee database is of utmost importance. That is why from time to time you review the employees contact list to see if there is missing information. You should forward the employee information form to those employees with missing information. The employee contact list should also match the number of employees in the payroll summary report. You want to pay only those you have records on for audit purposes.

Activities:

- ❖ Click **Reports menu**
- ❖ Click **List**
- ❖ Click **Employee Contact List**
- ❖ Sort by: Accept **Default**
- ❖ You may practice with other reports in this section

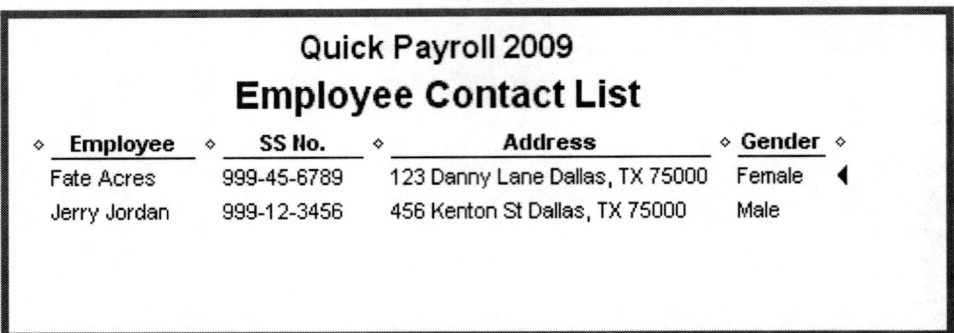

Transaction History

Every transaction has a history, and the history is listed by type, transaction number, date, vendor name, if any, account involved and the paid amount. To see the detail of that transaction, double click on it; you will be taken to the Write Check window, if the transaction involves a check payment. Now you will be able to see the details of the check. Click X to close the check window, preview, and print the report.

Activities:

- ❖ Click **Banking menu**
- ❖ Click **Use Register**
- ❖ Select Account: Select **USA Payroll.** Click **OK**
- ❖ Click **on Fate Acres for 12,212.67**
- ❖ Click **Reports menu**
- ❖ Click **Transaction History**
- ❖ Double click **12,212.67** to see the check window
- ❖ You may practice with other history reports

Quick Payroll 2009
Transaction History
All Transactions

◇ Type ◇	Date ◇	Name ◇	Account ◇	Paid Amount ◇
Paycheck	01/11/2009	Fate Acres	USA Payroll	-12,212.67 ◀

Transaction Journal

If you want to see how QuickBooks made a journal entry on a particular account, this is where to come. Not every account's journal entry is displayed by QuickBooks; some are displayed with just the account balance without showing the debit and credit. Transaction Journal function does not work at the major report level; you have to double click on the account in the main report to open the sub-report and then proceed to the journal entry.

Activities:

- ❖ Click **Reports menu**
- ❖ Click **Company & Financial**
- ❖ Click **Profit & Loss Standard**
- ❖ Dates (top left of the window): Select **This Fiscal Year**
- ❖ Transaction Journal will NOT run in this report
- ❖ Double click **Repair & Maint for 360.00**
- ❖ Transaction Journal will run in this report
- ❖ Click **check number 1002 for 200.00**
- ❖ Click **Reports menu.** Click **Transaction Journal**
- ❖ Look! This is how QuickBooks does the Debit/Credit Journal entries

Quick Payroll 2009
Transaction Journal
All Transactions

Trans #	Type	Date	Num	Name	Memo	Account	Debit	Credit
39	Check	01/01/2009	1002	America Auto Serv...	Repairs and...	USA Checking		250.00
				America Auto Serv...	Repairs and...	Repairs & Maint	200.00	
				America Auto Serv...	Repairs and...	Fuel	50.00	
							250.00	250.00
TOTAL							**250.00**	**250.00**

Print Forms

You might like to know there are more report windows other than from the Reports menu. These little-known windows are located under the File menu. Just click the File menu, and then click Print Forms. You will see a list of forms from which to choose. The Bill Payment Stub is one of them. When you open the window, the default date range is today; if you want a different range of dates, change the Date box and the Thru box with your choice of dates.

Activities:

- ❖ Click **File menu**
- ❖ Click **Print Forms**
- ❖ Click **Bill Payment Stubs**
- ❖ Bank Account: Accept **USA Checking**
- ❖ Dated: Type **1/1/09**. Press **Tab**
- ❖ Thru: Type **12/31/09.** Press **Tab**
- ❖ Accept **Select All** (bottom right of the window)
- ❖ Click **Preview** (right of the window).
- ❖ Click **Zoom In**
- ❖ Click **Next Page** (top left)
- ❖ Click **Close or Print** if printer is ready
- ❖ Click **X** to close Bill Payment window

Bill Payment Stub

	Check Date:	1/2/2009
	Check No.:	1003
	Check Amount:	34,300.00

Quick Payroll 2009
123 Adam Lane
Dallas, TX 75000

Paid To: US Supplies
1234 Downing Rd
Dallas, TX 75000

Date	Type	Reference	Original Amt.	Balance	Discount	Payment
1/1/2009	Bill		10,000.00	10,000.00	-200.00	9,800.00
1/2/2009	Bill	Ussup 200901	25,000.00	25,000.00	-500.00	24,500.00

Send Forms

When you were completing estimates, invoices, purchase orders and bills, you learned how to click "To be e-mailed" at the bottom of the document. If you have chosen to e-mail them, the next step is to go to the Send Forms submenu under the File menu. You have the option to send only one document or send a selected batch of documents. You must subscribe to this service to use it. Remember to edit at least the first e-mail, so you can see if there are errors that need to be corrected on other documents.

Activities:

- ❖ Click **File menu**
- ❖ Click **Send Forms**
- ❖ Accept Checkmark on **Check #1001 for 80,625.00**
- ❖ Click **Edit E-mail** (right of the window)
- ❖ **Check the To: and From: e-mail addresses are correct**
- ❖ In the bottom window. Accept **"Thank you for your services."**
- ❖ Click **Check Spelling** (right of the window)
- ❖ Click **OK** to "Spell check is complete."
- ❖ Click **OK** to close Edit E-mail. Repeat process if you have more e-mails
- ❖ Click **Close** or Send Now if you subscribed to the service

To	kmoore@adamscompany.com
Cc	
Bcc	
From	accountant@quickpayroll.com
Subject	Invoice from Quick Payroll

QuickBooks BILLING SOLUTIONS
Get paid faster!

Let QuickBooks help you get
paid online by credit card.

E-mail Text

Dear Customer :

Your invoice is attached. Please remit payment at your earliest convenience.

Thank you for your business - we appreciate it very much.

Sincerely,

Quick Payroll

Edit Default Text

Check Spelling

Financial: Profit & Loss

There are no financial activities that affect the Profit & Loss statement in this chapter. At this point, you should know the contents of the Profit & Loss statement which include the total income, cost of goods sold, gross profit, operating expenses, which QuickBooks chooses to call just expenses and, finally, the net income which is the bottom line. Also, you need to know that Total Income minus Total Expenses equals Net Income and that amount is now 1,786,204.73.

Activities:

- ❖ Click **Reports menu**
- ❖ Click **Company & Financial**
- ❖ Click **Profit & Loss Standard**
- ❖ Date: Select **This Fiscal Year**
- ❖ From: Accept **1/1/09**. To: Accept **12/31/09**
- ❖ Click **Collapse**
- ❖ Net Income **1,786,204.73**
- ❖ Click **X** to close window

```
                    Quick Payroll 2009
                    Profit & Loss
                January through December 2009
                                          ◇ Jan - Dec 09 ◇
        Ordinary Income/Expense
          Income
            Opening Balance Income   ▶ 1,905,000.00 ◀
            Landscaping Services          75,000.00
          Total Income                 1,980,000.00

          Cost of Goods Sold
            Materials                     50,000.00
            Discount Received               -700.00
          Total COGS                      49,300.00

        Gross Profit                    1,930,700.00

          Expense
            Opening Balance Expense       15,000.00
            Automobile Expense               434.00
            Depreciation Expense             666.67
            Payroll Expenses             127,835.60
            Telephone Expense                409.00
            Travel Expense                   150.00
          Total Expense                   144,495.27

        Net Ordinary Income            1,786,204.73

        Net Income                     1,786,204.73
```

Financial: Balance Sheet

There are no financial activities in this section that have any material effects on the Balance Sheet statement, however it's imperative to know that total assets must equal total liabilities and owner's equity. The net income in the owner's equity section is the same net income from the Profit and Loss statement. Total current assets plus total fixed asset equal total assets. The current assets balance is now 2,994,020.40 and a total asset is 3,033,353.73.

Activities:

- ❖ Click **Reports menu**
- ❖ Click **Company & Financial**
- ❖ Click **Balance Sheet Standard**
- ❖ Date: Select **This Fiscal Year**
- ❖ As of: Accept **12/31/09**
- ❖ Click **Collapse**
- ❖ **Total Assets 3,033,353.73**
- ❖ Click **X** to close window

Quick Payroll 2009
Balance Sheet
As of December 31, 2009

	◇ Dec 31, 09 ◇
ASSETS	
Current Assets	
Checking/Savings	
Petty Cash	▶ 100.00 ◀
Money Market Account	100,000.00
USA Checking	1,661,131.00
USA Payroll	102,749.02
Total Checking/Savings	1,863,980.02
Accounts Receivable	
Accounts Receivable	1,085,625.00
Total Accounts Receivable	1,085,625.00
Other Current Assets	
Payroll Asset	19,415.38
Inventory Asset	25,000.00
Total Other Current Assets	44,415.38
Total Current Assets	2,994,020.40
Fixed Assets	
Truck	39,333.33
Total Fixed Assets	39,333.33
TOTAL ASSETS	**3,033,353.73**

Chapter Summary

Good financial reports are the reward for your hard labor. When you were setting up your preferences, creating accounts and item listing, completing customers' and vendors' information, the ultimate goal was to generate complete and accurate reports. A report is not satisfactory if it does not give you the right information. You were wondering if you have to provide all that information about customers or vendors. No, you don't have to, but if you want a better report, you need to key in some data which are pulled into the report.

What we accomplished:

We ran the following reports, graphs and forms:

- Memorize a report
- Multiple reports
- Profit & Loss
- Income & Expense Graph

- Balance Sheet
- Statement of Cash Flows
- AR Aging Summary
- Sales by Customer Summary
- Job Profitability Summary
- AP Aging Summary
- Purchase by Vendor Summary
- Inventory Valuation Summary
- Payroll Summary
- Deposit Detail
- Trial Balance
- Budget
- Item Listing
- Transaction History
- Transaction Journal
- Print Forms
- Send Forms

Additional Financial activities:
- No financial activities were performed in this chapter

Optional Test 10

Questions: True/False
Answer the following questions by placing letter the T or F in the space provided before the question number.

_____ 1. From time to time you want to preview a group of reports before printing them, QuickBooks can only allow you to process one report at a time not a group of reports at one time.

_____ 2. After running a report it is possible to download the report from the same window into Excel for further calculations, but you must register with QuickBooks for the download service.

_____ 3. Financial statements for a service business is on an accrual basis but you have to set it up in the Preferences submenu under the Edit menu.

_____ 4. The date on a Profit & Loss statement is between two periods, while the date on a Balance Sheet statement is as of one particular date.

_____ 5. In preparing the Balance Sheet statement the total assets must not be equal to the Total Liabilities and Owner's Equity.

_____ 6. QuickReport will always be activated from anywhere including the Home Page but you have to maximize it.

_____ 7. While you are in the Chart of Accounts window, it possible to preview and and print some of the major report than going through the Report menu.

_____ 8. If you want to have an immediate access to a report, it is possible to open the report and place on the Icon Bar.

_____ 9. When preparing a Balance Sheet statement the Net income in the equity section is not the same as the Net Income in the Profit & Loss statement.

_____ 10. When preparing the Cash Flow statement the Net Income under the Operating Activities is the same as the Net Income in Profit & Loss.

Questions: Multiple Choices

Answer the following questions by placing letter A, B, C, or D in the space provided before the question number.

_____ 1. Graphs are very important aspect of reporting especially when you want to see visually the status of a business. All of these reports will display both the Bar Chart and the Pie Chart except...?
A. Income &Expense
B. Accounts Receivable and Accounts Payable
C. Sales
D. Net Worth

_____ 2. If you want to print a report the best action is to look at the submenus under the Report menu. Which of these is not directly under the Report menu?
A. Sales
B. Purchases
C. Inventory
D. Deposit

_____ 3. From time to time you want to see how QuickBooks makes a journal entry behind the scenes, which of the following reports would you run to find out?
A. Custom Summary
B. Transaction History
C. Transaction Journal
D. QuickReport Journal

_____ 4. At the end of the quarter you want to pay the sales tax to a governmental agency, which of these reports would you have to run to determine the amount to pay?
A. Sales Tax Revenue Summary
B. Sales Tax Liability
C. Sales Audit Report
D. Sales Tax Accounts Report

_____ 5. The financial statement that subtracts the Total Expenses from the Total Income to come up with the Net Income is called_____?
A. Balance Sheet
B. Cash Flow
C. Profit & Loss
D. Account Receivable

_____ 6. If a company wants to know the summary of how much it owes other companies separated by months it would have to run which report?
   A. AP Aging Summary
   B. AR Aging Summary
   C. AP Collection Summary
   D. AR Collection Summary

_____ 7. If a company wants to know the summary of how much other companies owe it separated by month it would have to run which report?
   A. AP Aging Summary
   B. AR Aging Summary
   C. AP Collection Summary
   D. AR Collection Summary

_____ 8. At the end of the month a manager wants to see the summary number of who is buying the most of its products, which is the best report to run?
   A. Sales by Job Summary
   B. Sales by Customer Summary
   C. Job by Sales Summary
   D. Job by Customer Summary

_____ 9. A vendor calls and say they have not been paid on a bill, which of the following vendor report would you have to run?
   A. Vendor Tax Summary
   B. Vendor Contact Summary
   C. Vendor Balance Summary
   D. Vendor Receivable Summary

_____ 10. Total Income minus Total Cost of Goods Sold equals to_____?
   A. Gross Cost
   B. Gross Profit
   C. Net Cost
   D. Net Profit

$

Chapter 12

Window & Help Menus

Objectives: After you've completed the chapter, you will be able to:

- ✓ Describe the Window submenus
- ✓ U se the close all function
- ✓ Explain the Help submenus
- ✓ Use the QuickBooks help
- ✓ Use the Year-End guide
- ✓ Run financial reports and compare results

Review Window Submenus

Most users do not remember that they can access any opened windows from the Windows menu. Not only that, but QuickBooks has made it easy by creating the Open Windows box at the left side of the window. Now, you have two options: either to open windows from the Open Windows box or go through the Window menu and click on the window you would like to open.

- Click **Windows menu**

The following activities are found under the Window menu:

- **Close All:** Any time you have too many open windows on your QuickBooks Screen, to remove all these open windows, click the Window menu and Close All. Some windows will not close automatically, especially the Report window if you change the default settings or customize the report, for example, if the Date setting is "Today," and you change the setting to "This Fiscal Year." When Quickbooks gets to the report with changed default setting, it will prompt you with "Would you like to memorize this report?" At this point, you have the option of clicking either Yes or No. Most of the time, you should click No, and this action will release the Close All procedure.

- **Tile Vertically:** This button will allow you to open windows on your desktop vertically. To change the Home page, see the Cascade paragraph below.

- **Tile Horizontally:** This function allows you to open windows on your desktop horizontally. To change the Home page, see the Cascade paragraph below.

- **Cascade:** Cascading your open windows is also available with Quickbooks. **To change the Home page to normal window, click Window menu and click Close All. Click Company and Home page. Drag the right edge to cover the right edge of the computer. Drag the bottom edge to the bottom but leave a small space.**

Close All Windows

The Close All is one of the handy tools you should know how to use. If you have a good working knowledge of Microsoft Office products, you should have a good idea of what Close All can do. You need to try it yourself to know exactly what windows will be closed. The Close All will not close any Modified Reports, especially, if you have changed the settings on that report. The Close All will process your command until it gets to the Modified Report and it will ask if you want to memorize the report.

Activities:

❖ Click **Window menu**
❖ Click **Close All. To remove all open windows**
❖ Click **Company menu**
❖ Click **Home Page**
❖ Click **Window menu**
❖ **Look! You have Tile Vertical, Title Horizontal, and Cascade**
❖ Click **View menu**. Click **One Window**
❖ Click **Window menu**
❖ **Look! Tile Vertical, Title Horizontal, and Cascade are gone**
❖ Click **View menu**. Click **Multiple Window**

Review Help Submenus

In your spare time, you should test drive the Help menu and its submenus. You never know when you will run into a problem and you want QuickBooks to give you directions on how to accomplish a task. It is good practice to use Help to find a simple answer; that way, you have an idea of how to use Help to solve complex problems. The procedure of finding answers in QuickBooks Help is easy; you just have to make up a few keywords on the subject in question. Remember to click the Related Topics at the bottom of every suggested answer; this might give additional information you never thought of before.

- Click **Help menu**

The following activities are found under the Help menu:

- **QuickBooks Help:** The Help menu is one of the most powerful windows on your QuickBooks software. I don't know about you, but I want somewhere I can go, day or night, to get an answer when I need one. QuickBooks Help menu is the one help center that you don't have to dial and wait for all the prompts before getting answers. Get to know how to use the Help submenu windows. You don't know when you would really need it. This book will cover most of the windows; however, occasionally you might want to test a feature and the QuickBooks Help submenu will be there for you 24 hours, 7 days a week.

- **Learning Center Tutorial:** The first of the windows that shows up after you've created a new file is the QuickBooks Learning Center. It is annoying that the learning window keeps popping up every time you open a file. The first task is to disable the window from opening up by clicking the "Show this window at startup" box at the bottom left of the window. Click the box to remove the checkmark already in the box. You can test drive any of the Learning Center windows anytime you want for additional insight on how the software works.

- **Year-End Guide:** At the end of the year, you must visit this window to learn what information is necessary to close the year on sound footing. The checklists in this window are a good start to making sure you are on track to covering the Year-End activities, such as reconciling accounts, accruals, corrections, closing books and adjusting Retained Earnings, etc

Use QuickBooks Help

QuickBooks Help is an invaluable submenu. It's always handy when you run into a problem you don't know how to tackle. Most people don't even remember they have a database of helpful steps that came with their software. It's easy to use; just type the first few letters that relate to your topics, and Help will bring up the closest options for you to select. If you find it, scroll down the left window to see if you can find the main title and continue to look at the subtitle. Click on the word and click Display.

Activities:

- ❖ Click **Help menu**
- ❖ Click **QuickBooks Help**
- ❖ Click **Search tab** (top right of the window)
- ❖ Type **entering ytd**
- ❖ Click **Forward arrow** (right of box)
- ❖ Click **Summarize payroll amounts for this year to date**
- ❖ In the lower window. Scroll down
- ❖ Read the steps on how **"To enter employee year-to-date payroll amounts"**
- ❖ In the lower window

❖ Click **Print Topic**
❖ Click **Cancel or Print** if printer is ready
❖ Click red **X** to close QuickBooks Help window

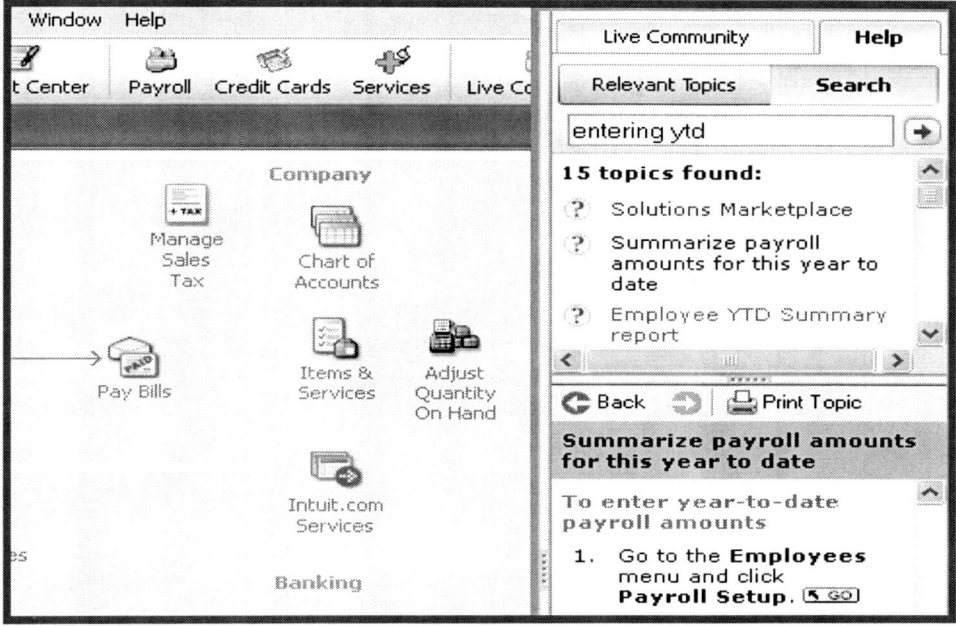

Use Year-End Guide

The end of the year is one of the most key periods of your QuickBooks life. You have various tasks that must be performed at the end of the year. You've heard so many times from accountants, "We are closing end-of-the-year books." To help you go through this period successfully, QuickBooks has assembled the tasks it thinks you need to accomplish. It helps you to make sure no stones are left unturned. As you go through the list, you will check off the ones you've completed.

Activities:

Click **Help menu**
❖ Click **Year-End Guide**
❖ Scroll down. Click on the phrase "**Print and mail Form W-2, W-3, 1099…**"
❖ Read the explanation in the Help window (lower right)
❖ Scroll to the bottom
❖ **Click all the payroll related phrases links**
❖ Read the explanation in the Help window (lower right)

❖ Click **X** to close Year-End window
❖ Click **X** to close QuickBooks Help

Tasks to do if you have employees

If you use the Assisted Payroll Service

☐ <u>Click here for frequently asked questions about year-end tasks</u>

If you are enrolled in QuickBooks Assisted Payroll, the following items are handled by the payroll service for you:

☑
- Pay payroll taxes and other liabilities (Assisted Payroll automatically makes your federal and state payroll tax liability payments)
- Print and distribute W-2s
- Print and distribute W-3s
- Process Form 940
- Process Form 941

If you use QuickBooks Payroll or have no payroll service

☐ A. <u>Confirm you have current payroll tax tables [QuickBooks Payroll only]</u>
☑ B. Clear YTD payroll amounts - QuickBooks does this for you
☐ C. <u>Pay payroll liabilities</u>
☐ D. <u>Review W-2 forms</u>
☐ E. <u>Print & distribute W-2s</u>
☐ F. <u>Print form W-3</u>
☐ G. <u>Process Form 940</u>
☐ H. <u>Process Form 941</u>
☐ I. <u>Verify W4 information</u>

Financial: Profit & Loss

This is your final Profit & Loss report and the purpose of running this report one last time is to make sure you are on the same page with the book; that you are in balance to the penny with the textbook. There are no financial activities since the last chapter, therefore, your gross profit is still the same, 1,930,700 and your net income is still the same 1,786,204.73.

Activities:

❖ Click **Reports menu**
❖ Click **Company & Financial**
❖ Click **Profit & Loss Standard**
❖ Date: Select **This Fiscal Year**
❖ From: Accept **1/1/09.** To: Accept **12/31/09**
❖ Click **Collapse**
❖ Net Income **1,786,204.73**
❖ Click **X** to close window

```
                    Quick Payroll 2009
                    Profit & Loss
                January through December 2009
                                    ◇ Jan - Dec 09 ◇
Ordinary Income/Expense
    Income
        Opening Balance Income  ▶ 1,905,000.00 ◀
        Landscaping Services         75,000.00
    Total Income                  1,980,000.00

    Cost of Goods Sold
        Materials                    50,000.00
        Discount Received              -700.00
    Total COGS                       49,300.00

    Gross Profit                  1,930,700.00

    Expense
        Opening Balance Expense      15,000.00
        Automobile Expense              434.00
        Depreciation Expense            666.67
        Payroll Expenses            127,835.60
        Telephone Expense               409.00
        Travel Expense                  150.00
    Total Expense                   144,495.27

Net Ordinary Income               1,786,204.73

Net Income                        1,786,204.73
```

Financial: Balance Sheet

There are no financial activities in this section since the last chapter. You are running the last Balance Sheet report of the book to confirm your balances with the textbook. The current assets balance is still 2,994,020.40 and the Total Assets balance is still 3,033,353.73.

Activities:

- ❖ Click **Reports menu**
- ❖ Click **Company & Financial**
- ❖ Click **Balance Sheet Standard**
- ❖ Date: Select **This Fiscal Year**
- ❖ As of: Accept **12/31/09**
- ❖ Click **Collapse**
- ❖ **Total Assets 3,033,353.73**
- ❖ Click **X** to close window

Quick Payroll 2009
Balance Sheet
As of December 31, 2009

	Dec 31, 09
ASSETS	
Current Assets	
Checking/Savings	
Petty Cash	100.00
Money Market Account	100,000.00
USA Checking	1,661,131.00
USA Payroll	102,749.02
Total Checking/Savings	1,863,980.02
Accounts Receivable	
Accounts Receivable	1,085,625.00
Total Accounts Receivable	1,085,625.00
Other Current Assets	
Payroll Asset	19,415.38
Inventory Asset	25,000.00
Total Other Current Assets	44,415.38
Total Current Assets	2,994,020.40
Fixed Assets	
Truck	39,333.33
Total Fixed Assets	39,333.33
TOTAL ASSETS	**3,033,353.73**

Chapter Summary

In this section, we worked with two chapters: the Windows and QuickBooks Help menus. There is not much to the Windows menu than to remember that when your QuickBooks window is crowded with open windows, it is time to clear them out with a click of a button, using the Close All function. In the QuickBooks Help chapter, we looked at the Help submenus. It is also important to remember the Learning tutorial is always handy should you need additional information. We also practiced how to use the New Business Checklist and Year-End Guide.

What we accomplished:

In the Window menu, we:

- Reviewed the Window submenus
- Practiced the close all function

In the Help menu, we:

- Reviewed the QuickBooks Help submenus
- Worked with QuickBooks Help to find answers
- Practiced how to use Year-End guide to find information
- Processed financial statements

Additional Financial activities:

- No financial activities were performed in this chapter

Optional Test 11

Questions: True/False
Answer the following questions by placing letter the T or F in the space provided before the question number.

_____ 1. If you want to choose between sole proprietorship, partnership, limited liability company, QuickBooks New Business Checklist is helpful.

_____ 2. You have too many open windows and you want to clear them with a click of a button, the best submenu is the Close All under the Window menu.

_____ 3. You may use QuickBooks Help to find answers but the window does not allow you to print your answers because it takes too long.

_____ 4. It is essential to learn about your privacy, but it is impossible because QuickBooks does not provide such documentation.

_____ 5. You must close your books at the end of the year because it is stipulated in the Close Your Books link within the Year-End Guide Checklist window.

_____ 6. It's essential to print the Trial Balance report the day after the end of the year to make sure all the Income and Expense balances are zero as stipulated in the Print Financial Reports link within the Year-End Guide Checklist window.

Questions: Multiple Choices
Answer the following questions by placing letter A, B, C, or D in the space provided before the question number.

_____ 1. You have your QuickBooks Help window open, what if you want to look for answers by typing few keywords, which of these tabs will you use?
   A. Go To
   B. Find
   C. Search
   D. Look

_____ 2. You forgot that taking physical inventory and reconciling with book inventory is covered in this book, but you remember you can use QuickBooks help, which of the following windows will help you?
A. New Business Finder
B. New Business Checklist
C. Year-End Guide Checklist
D. Year-End Finder

_____ 3. In QuickBooks Help window, after typing a few keywords under the Search tab, what button will you click to display your answers?
A. Backward arrow
B. Forward arrow
C. Top arrow
D. Bottom arrow

_____ 4. You want to find answers by using the QuickBooks learning center, and will have many options, which of the following is not an available link?
A. Inventory
B. Payroll
C. Banking
D. Vendors and Expenses

_____ 5. You want to write a business plan but don't know where to go, and finally you remember you can use the QuickBooks Help, which of these windows will help you to find a business plan template?
A. QuickBooks Finder
B. End Year Template
C. New Business Checklist
D. Business Plan Checklist

Index

V

W

Y

Using QuickBooks with High Speed College Edition

Purchasing this book is one of the wisest investments you'll ever make for your business. If you are looking for an easy to use, step-by-step manual on learning QuickBooks in little or no time, look no further! *Using QuickBooks with High Speed College Edition* by Emmanuel Ike is designed for the college student who wants to be proficient is using QuickBooks and does not have the time to flip through pages of technical books to find out. With this book, you'll learn how to start using your QuickBooks software immediately. The titles are arranged according to the QuickBooks menus. Throughout the book, you will be using real numbers — an excellent way of learning QuickBooks in less time.

SOW Publishing

Please visit our website www.sowpublishing.com and see some of the books we published or in the process of being published. If you want product catalog, price list, or other information, please e-mail us, sales@sowpublishing.com.

Our products include:

1.   Using QuickBooks with High Speed Small Business

2.   Using QuickBooks with High Speed College Edition

3.   Using QuickBooks Payroll with High Speed College Edition

4.   Using Excel with High Speed College Edition

5.   Using Word with High Speed College Edition

6.   Using SQL with High Speed College Edition

7.   How To Repair Your Credit Report

8.   How To Increase Your Credit Score New Edition

LaVergne, TN USA
22 April 2010
180027LV00005B/49/P